'For Them's Sake'

Northchurch Folk Through Two World Wars

Richard North & Ray Smith

Published by New Generation Publishing in 2017

Copyright © Richard North and Ray Smith 2017

First Edition

The author asserts the moral right under the Copyright, Designs and Patents Act 1988 to be identified as the author of this work.

All Rights reserved. No part of this publication may be reproduced, stored in a retrieval system or transmitted, in any form or by any means without the prior consent of the author, nor be otherwise circulated in any form of binding or cover other than that which it is published and without a similar condition being imposed on the subsequent purchaser.

www.newgeneration-publishing.com

New Generation Publishing

Contents

Forward	1
Prologue: Northchurch, Remembrance Sunday 1969	3
Northchurch – August 1914	7
Drummer Walter Frederick DELL	11
Private 6951 Charles TALBOT	17
Captain Arthur Noel LOXLEY	21
Privates 8183 and 9890 Walter and Frederick GEARY	27
Captain Nigel Clement Charles HADDEN	37
Major Hubert Wallace THELWALL	47
Surgeon George H SHORLAND	53
Private 2401 Lionel MORGAN	57
Private 305045 Arthur James FROST	60
Private 25551 Walter HOWLETT	64
Rifleman Charles William ROSS	67
Lance Corporal G7193 Philip Charles FEIST	71
Private 4/6424 Edwin MORGAN	75
Private 18312 Albert ROLFE	79
Private 17760 George BIGNELL	82
Lieutenant Thomas Eric HENDERSON	83
Private 31651 Joseph William ALDRIDGE	87
Private 43247 William James SIBLEY	89
Private 57034 Walter WELLING	92
Private 19159 Walter PURTON	94
Lance Corporal Albert Ernest PICKTHORN	97
Captain Vere Duncombe LOXLEY	105

2nd Lieutenant Royden Spencer Bayspool PORTER	112
Private G13274 Ambrose Alfred BROWN	116
Private 35345 William SEAR	121
Private 41068 Albert John DELL	125
Gunner 110194 Joseph DYER	130
Private 35581 John RANDALL	134
Lance Corporal 45451 William Benjamin Ernest WAITE	138
Private 57034 Arthur WELLING	143
Private 2724 Charlie SUTTON	146
Lieutenant Frank D ALCOCK	149
Private 202817 Alfred Henry DWIGHT	156
Private 76469 George DAVIS	159
Lance Corporal 12930 Richard BEASLEY DCM	161
Lieutenant John Augustus HARMAN	166
Gunner 294266 Alfred CURL	172
Private 48065 Frank Francis (ALLAWAY)	177
Private 235328 Harold Alfred SHRIMPTON	181
Gunner 68745 William HORN	184
Drummer 36316 James Arthur GARMENT	189
Private L/11387 Frank GARNER	192
Private 75902 Charles Thomas MASHFORD	197
Private 23096 Thomas Henry TEAGLE	200
Lance Corporal 4/6982 George CURL	213
Private T/271032 Thomas FANTHAM	217
Private 601505 James DELDERFIELD	225
Private G/89270 Arthur TEAGLE	227
Private G/73574 Charles Henry CARTER	230

Captain Reginald Victor Byron LOXLEY	234
Gunner 101589 George Thomas Keen	240
Lance Corporal James CHANDLER	242
The Return of Peace	247
An Imperfect Peace	259
2nd Lieutenant Charles Arthur BLACKWELL	261
1257744 Sgt Pilot Stephen H Vavasour DURELL, RAFVR	268
5953382 Private Ronald Reginald Frank HUCKLESBEE MM	271
Driver T/175636 Albert James WELCH	279
2nd Lieutenant Geoffrey Albert DELDERFIELD	286
200636 Lieutenant Ronald Charles Boyd-Smith	292
1151718 Sergeant Observer Michael Philip SATOW	298
92188 Sergeant James Reginald BAMFORD	302
39528 Squadron Leader Raymond Thomas HUNN	306
14379260 Private Harold WEEDON	311
5783822 Private Donald Ernest SAUNDERS	320
5961214 Private Edmund Albert BARBER	327
Peter Noel LOXLEY	332
The Coming of Peace?	343
42596 Flight Lieutenant Charles Robert DWIGHT	344
1464909 Leading Aircraftman Donald George BEDFORD	348
3030341 Sergeant Herbert Frederick Wallis OLLIFFE	350
For Them's Sake	355
Appendix 1: First World War Roll of Honour	357
Appendix 2: Second World War Roll of Honour	367
Acknowledgements	370

Forward

The Service of Remembrance, held each year on the second Sunday in November throughout the land, includes the reading out of the names of those from the local community who gave their lives for their country during two world wars. The list of the names normally concludes with four lines from the poem written by Robert Laurence Binyon:

> They shall grow not old, as we that are left grow old:
> Age shall not weary them, nor the years condemn.
> At the going down of the sun and in the morning⊠
> We will remember them.

To which the response is *'We will remember them'*.

But do we? As the generations have grown older, fewer and fewer people remember the servicemen on the list. With the end of the First World War a century ago, it is unlikely that anyone still alive remembers the men who died between 1914 and 1918 and probably this is also true of many of those who died between 1939 and 1945.

This was the starting point for this book. Ray and I began work on this project separately without knowing of the other's interest, and it was only after reading a request for information in the Northchurch Parish Magazine that we finally established contact. After a pint or two in the George and Dragon in Northchurch, we decided that we could work together and combined forces.

It quickly became apparent that the stories of those who died during the First World War effectively give us a history of the war itself. All the major areas of conflict were represented – the Western Front, the war at sea, Gallipoli, Mesopotamia and East Africa and then the influenza epidemic that so tragically killed many of those who had survived the fighting. As we progressed on to the Second World War, the same thread appeared with the retreat from Dunkirk, the campaign in North Africa, the Italian campaign, the war in the air, D Day, and then, post war, the early days of the conflict in the Middle East.

We have tried to put each person and his death in context. Who were they, what was their family background, what did they experience during the war, what were the circumstances leading to their deaths, how did they die?

Our starting point was, of course, the names on the base of the original War Memorial standing in St Mary's churchyard in Northchurch. However, that was only the start. Our research uncovered other names of Northchurch-connected men not recorded on the memorial, some of whom are represented elsewhere. Why their names were not included is now lost in the mist of time, but they have not been forgotten.

We hope that having read the book each reader will be able to say, 'We *have* remembered them'.

Richard North & Ray Smith, March 2017

Prologue

Northchurch, Remembrance Sunday 1969

The Reverend Bernard Hughes, the Rector of St Mary's church in Northchurch, Hertfordshire, stood before a packed congregation on a blowy and overcast Remembrance Sunday. It was fifty years since the signing of the Treaty of Versailles that officially brought the 'War to End War' to a close, and thirty years after the start of the Second World War.

As the Rector led the Service of Remembrance, grey November light illuminated the stained-glass window depicting St George the Martyr, with its dedication to those, *'who gave their lives in the Great War 1914-1919.'* The parishioners of Northchurch had gathered, not only to commemorate those men connected to the village that had fought and died in the two World Wars, but also to rededicate their newly renovated War Memorial Cross.

The previous year, the Northchurch War Memorial lay in pieces, the tall, Celtic-style cross, propped forlornly on its cracked and damaged base. The war memorial was a scaled-up version of the many Celtic cross headstones that stood in many of the churchyards and cemeteries around in the area. When Arthur Martin, a stonemason working for Frederick Martin and Son of Chapel Street, Berkhamsted, originally fashioned the cross and its base from Darley Dale Bluestone nearly 50 years previously, he seemed to have arrived at their proportions by rule of thumb to give the memorial the right overall 'look'. Unfortunately, the base, or die, to give it its proper name, was just too small to support the weight of the ten-foot tall stone cross. That weight took its toll over the years, causing minor cracks to appear in the die. From time to time repairs took place, but by 1968, the cracking had become so severe that people feared the cross would topple over and smash. Until the base was replaced the existing the cross would have to be dismantled.

The Committee for the Restoration of the Northchurch War Memorial was formed at the beginning of 1969, and under the chairmanship of Mr Fred Phillips, the Headmaster of the village school and a Reader at St Mary's church, it set about raising funds for the renovation work. The committee quickly realised that the cost of exactly reproducing the original dedication and roll of honour would be high. The list of 46 men from 1914-1919, their names ordered more or less according to the seniority of their Regiment, Corps or Service, and the 13-alphabetical list of men from 1939-1946, along with the dedication, amounted to 900 individually-cast lead letters. In March 1969, the committee estimated the cost of a stronger replacement base with all the lettering recast to be in the region of £500, about £7,000 in today's terms.

After further consideration, the committee agreed a compromise solution. It commissioned a bigger replacement base, with a simple new engraved dedication, onto which the old cross would stand. The old base, suitably patched up, would remain close by to preserve the names and units of the Fallen. This proposal required the raising of only £320 from the Parish, almost £4,500 in current day terms, although this still represented a substantial amount of money at the time, and fund raising was going slowly. Nevertheless, with contributions of £50 each from the British Legion and Berkhamsted Urban District Council, the restoration work began.

The stonemason commissioned to do the job was Reg Newsam. An experienced stonemason in his late thirties, Reg worked for the company that succeeded Frederick Martin and Son. In fact, as a young stonemason, Reg had worked alongside Arthur Martin. Reg used York Bluestone, which was the nearest match he could find to the original stone, and set to work fashioning the base. Once the new base was complete, a crane moved the broken base and reset it closer to the churchyard wall a few yards from its original position. By the middle of October, Reg had begun to cut the letters of the new dedication and was well on the way to completing work on the memorial in time for Remembrance Sunday.

At the conclusion of the Remembrance Service, the Rector led his congregation out of the church and into the churchyard for the wreath laying. The Northchurch Scouts and Guides, the British Legion and the Armed Forces were among the organisations represented. In their colour parties, the Standard Bearers had to steady themselves against the gusty wind that snatched at their flags as they dipped in salute. At least the rain held off during the placing of the wreaths around the new memorial.

Placed near the churchyard wall, by a large yew tree, was the original base, its cracks now secured with metal ties. The dedication it bore, dating from 1920, was very much of its time *'To the Glory of God and in Memory of Northchurch Men who gave their lives for King and Country 1914-1919'*. Engraved on the new base was a different dedication, also very much of its time, *'In Memory of all those who have given their lives in the service of their country'*. The language of this dedication was from the New English Bible rather than the King James Version Bible, and the sentiment much more general and intended to embrace all those who had given their lives, or who would give their lives in the future, in the service of their country.

At the 11th hour, the people of Northchurch observed two minutes' silence in quiet remembrance and contemplation. Most of the older villagers would have known some of the servicemen who had died between 1939 and 1946 and some would still hold personal memories of those who had lost their lives during the First World War.

So, it was that the parishioners of Northchurch gathered together before their remade War Memorial on Remembrance Sunday 1969, as they have done on every Remembrance Sunday ever since, paying their respects and laying wreaths to the memory of those villagers who had gone to serve in two World Wars, but had not returned.

This is the story of many ordinary Northchurch folk whose lives changed forever during the two terrible conflicts that dominated the 20th Century.

August 1914. Volunteers from Northchurch and Berkhamsted march down Berkhamsted High Street to an uncertain future.
(Source Richard North)

Part 1

1914 - 1921

Northchurch – August 1914

The village of Northchurch in Hertfordshire lies about 28 miles from London in the Bulborne Valley on the old Roman Akeman Street which linked St Albans to Tring, Aylesbury, Bicester and Cirencester. The last census before the First World War, taken in 1911, revealed the population of Northchurch as 1,279, which was not significantly different from the census taken ten years before. The majority of the men in Northchurch earned a hard living from the land working on farms, market gardens, orchards, and cress beds. Even the larger employers in the area, such as East's Timber yard and Coopers & Nephews' chemical works, manufactured products for agriculture and horticulture. Most people left school at the age of 14, or 13 if learning their parent's trade, and manual work was plentiful in agriculture, retail, transport, and domestic service in the local big houses. An ordinary working man typically earned £1 a week, although agricultural labourers only averaged 17 shillings (85p).

The parish church, dedicated to St Mary the Virgin, was the heart of the village. Dating from Saxon times, the building had grown over the years, receiving its tower in the 15th Century and, more recently, a new north aisle in the 1880s. The original Saxon parish had stretched from the borders of Tring almost to Hemel Hempstead, but following the creation of the Parish of Great Berkhamsted in the 13th Century, centred around the new church of St Peter's, the parish became split into two parts. Recent boundary changes had resulted in further land being lost to Berkhamsted. The Rector of St Mary's in 1914 was the Reverend Reginald Henry Pope, who had been the incumbent for five years. Next to the church stood the village school, built in 1864 with an endowment from Mr John Loxley of Norcott Court on land donated by the Lord of the Manor, Lord Brownlow.

Northchurch comprised some 300 dwellings in 1914, with most of the population living in three main areas – the High Street or High Road, which was the former Roman Akeman Street, New Road, leading to Lord Brownlow's estate at Ashridge, and the cottages on the southern side of the High Street clustered around Bell Lane, Alma Road and Orchard End. About a mile to the east of the village centre in the direction of Berkhamsted was Gossoms End, and westwards towards Tring, were the small hamlets of Dudswell and Cow Roast.

The High Street contained a mixture of larger houses and small cottages, many of them half-timbered such as Rosemary Cottage and the Church Almshouses, which dated from Tudor times. Two residents of the Almshouses in 1914 were the elderly sisters, Louisa Payne and Fanny Dell, whose nephew, Walter Dell, was then serving as a drummer with the

Grenadier Guards. There were also some small shops in the High Street including the Post Office and General Stores run by Mr and Miss East, the George and Dragon public house, and the Baptist Chapel, which had replaced a smaller building in nearby Bell Lane in 1900.

Going towards Berkhamsted, before reaching Gossoms End on opposite sides of the road from each other, stood Lagley House and Edgeworth House. At some point in their history both houses were owned by members of the Duncombe family. Further west, on the south side of the High Street, two more large houses stood on opposite sides of Darrs Lane. Northchurch Hall, now long gone, was a large redbrick property owned by Mr Herbert Barnett. At Exhims, the late John Forster Alcock, former Parish Council Chairman and co-founder of the Football Association, had cultivated orchids such as his *Cypripedium, var. Exhims*. His widow, Mrs Augusta Alcock, had recently sold up and moved to a cottage in the village, although she retained an orchard behind the Baptist burial ground. Her elder son, Frank, had recently settled in Rhodesia, while younger son, John, would soon be going up to Cambridge.

Several other large houses were located on the fringes of Northchurch. To the south lay Rossway, owned by General Sir Charles Frederick Hadden, whose son, Nigel, was currently serving with the Royal Artillery in Ireland. To the north-west, adjoining the Ashridge Estate was the Manor of Norcott which included the late Victorian Norcott Court, built by John Loxley, and Norcott Hill.

New Road led north from the High Street past the village school to link Northchurch with Lord Brownlow's large estate at Ashridge. On the west side of the road were a series of small terraced houses. The village policeman, PC Cooling, lived at N°2 and nearby lived John Randall, who cultivated his market garden just behind the church. William and Annie Geary raised their family in another New Road cottage. Their son, Walter, worked for the London & North Western Railway and was an army reservist, having served with the Border Regiment. His younger brother, Frederick, was still with the Border Regiment in Burma. Thomas Feist ran The Compasses public house further up, then after the last cottages, New Road crossed the busy Grand Junction Canal at Northchurch lock. Dating from the 1790s, the canal still conveyed tons of bulky goods between London and the Midlands. Just beyond the bridge, on the right, was the new churchyard extension for St Mary's church. The road then passed over the short London & North Western Railway tunnel and at the top of the hill, was Northchurch Common where New Road met the old Dunstable road from Billet Lane and continued to the Ashridge Estate.

Bell Lane, consisting of a row of small four-room cottages, led to the old Baptist Chapel which stood empty in 1914, although the adjoining burial ground was still in use. The lane then continued uphill across farmland to Shootersway, which boasted several substantial houses.

Among Bell Lane's residents were members of the Brown family. Alma Road, where Albert Sear ran the local dairy and the Bignells lived, led off the west side of Bell Lane. Running behind the cottages in the High Street it joined up with Thorne's Yard, where the Pheasant Public House stood, and then Seymour Road, which continued almost to Darrs Lane. Owing to the orchards beyond, that part of Seymour Road was then known as Orchard End. In 1914, the Curl, Howlett and Welling families were all residents of that area.

Gossoms End, situated between Northchurch and Berkhamsted, contained the local Boys' School, East's Timber Works and the Crooked Billet public house, run by Harry Frost, which had a meadow large enough to host the annual visit of Bronco Bill's Wild West show. Amongst the rows of cottages in Gossoms End lived the Aldridge, Davis, Dwight, Garment, Mashford and Shrimpton families.

Following the redrawing of local government boundaries in 1909, Gossoms End had transferred from Berkhamsted Rural District Council to Berkhamsted Urban District Council, much to the chagrin of Northchurch Parish Council. Apart from the villagers' concerns regarding this encroachment by their larger neighbour, the Parish Council now had to deal with two District Councils. At the same time, Northchurch Parish transferred some of its land to the east of the town to the new Sunnyside Parish.

Five years on, Northchurch Parish still received 72% of the rental income from the cottages in Gossoms End, with Berkhamsted Urban District Council receiving the remainder, but Northchurch was suffering a housing crisis. In July 1914, while diplomatic notes criss-crossed Europe following the assassination of an Austrian Archduke in Sarajevo, Northchurch Parish Council had to borrow £350 to put the Gossoms End cottages in a decent state of repair. Some overcrowded cottages in Orchard End were in an even worse condition and should have been condemned, but there was nowhere for their tenants to go. Working men were willing to pay between a quarter and a third of their weekly wage for a three-bedroomed cottage in Northchurch, but none was available.

Even as the continental empires prepared for mobilization, army reservists like Charles Talbot, whose battalion was based in Ireland, were more concerned that Ulster's opposition to the current Irish Home Rule Bill would lead to civil war there. Meanwhile, on 26th July, James Garment, Lionel Morgan and the other Hertfordshire Regiment Territorials marched to Ashridge for the East Midland Infantry Brigade's annual camp.

In Northchurch, the residents looked forward to the Bank Holiday on 3rd August. None of them could have foreseen that Imperial Germany was preparing to violate Belgian neutrality and attack France and that Great Britain would declare war the day after Bank Holiday Monday.

Over the ensuing 52 months of warfare, more than 220 Northchurch men would fight for their country; some were already serving in the armed forces, some would volunteer, whilst others would be conscripted. Nearly a quarter of them would never return.

Northchurch Village circa 1914
(Source: Richard North)

Drummer Walter Frederick DELL
2nd Battalion, Grenadier Guards

2nd October 1914

Members of the various branches of the Dell family have lived in and about Northchurch for centuries. Walter Frederick Dell was the son of Joseph Dell and his second wife, Ellen. In 1885, Joseph's first wife, Mary Ann, died suddenly aged 37, having already borne four children. Two years later, Joseph married Ellen Howard who would give birth to another four children, their third child, Walter, being born at 39 Gossoms End during the spring of 1894. At that time, Joseph was working at Tring as a platelayer's labourer for the London & North Western Railway. Sadly, Ellen Dell died in 1908 when Walter was just 14, leaving Joseph a widower for a second time.

At the annual prize giving ceremony the following February, 15-year-old Walter Dell left school in Northchurch with the award of a watch for five years' perfect attendance. Three months later, having gained his father's consent, he enlisted at Bedford as a boy soldier for a 12-year term with 2nd Battalion, Grenadier Guards. Walter's Service Record from this time describes him as just 5ft 2½inches tall, weighing 126lbs, with blue eyes and light brown hair.

Boy soldiers enlisted in the British Army as either drummers or tailors; Walter chose to be a drummer. He was one of 3,826 boy soldiers then serving with the British Army, 2,984 of whom were musicians. Drummer Boys continued their education in the Army under the guidance of the Drum Major, who was also responsible for their

Drummer Walter Dell
(Source: Clive Blofield)

welfare and training. This enabled Walter to pass the Army 3rd Class Certificate of Education in June 1909, which tested basic arithmetic, reading aloud, writing dictation passages from an easy narrative, and the composition of a simple letter. Ten months later, Walter demonstrated his ability to deal with interest, fractions, averages and all forms of regimental accounting and take dictation from a more difficult work to pass the 2nd Class Certificate.

In August 1914, 20-year-old Walter was a duty guardsman with 2nd Grenadier Guards at Chelsea barracks in London, while maintaining his skills and appointment as a member of the Corps of Drums (side drum and flute). On 5th August, following the outbreak of war, the incredibly detailed efficient plans and railway timetables compiled in the *War Book*, for assembling the British Expeditionary Force, or BEF, came into effect, and the home battalions prepared to converge on Southampton before crossing to France. On 10th August, the Grenadiers, wearing full campaign kit, and with Walter playing in the Military Band, left their barracks and marched to Buckingham Palace, where King George V, Queen Mary, Queen Alexandra, the Prince of Wales and other members of the Royal Family bade them farewell. A crowd of perhaps 5,000 cheering, flag waving spectators saw the Grenadiers on their way to Nine Elms Railway Station. Many who cheered the departing troops genuinely expected the war to be over by Christmas.

Walter's battalion, now part of 4th (Guards) Brigade, 2nd Division, boarded a requisitioned troopship, SS *Cawdor Castle* at Southampton and sailed at about 20.30. Disembarking at Le Havre the following afternoon, the troops, kept in step by Walter and his fellow drummers, marched about five miles inland to Bléville. Under a hot sun, well-intentioned locals freely gave out strong Normandy cider to help quench the men's thirst. Predictably, many soldiers fell out long before they reached their overnight camp.

The Grenadiers marched back into Le Havre late on 15th August, and boarded a train at about 02.00 to take them eastwards towards the area where 2nd Division, now part of I Corps under General Haig, was assembling. The train terminated at Vaux and the Grenadiers marched in pouring rain to the small village of Grougis, some fifteen miles' northeast of Saint Quentin, where they remained for four days. During this time, all the men received inoculations against typhoid and Walter probably wrote his Will leaving all his possessions to his older brother, Albert.

Germany's war plan to defeat France before Russia fully mobilized its army was originally sketched out by General von Schlieffen in the 1890s. It correctly assumed that the French Army would attempt to seize back Alsace and Lorraine, the *Lost Provinces* annexed to Germany in 1871 after the Franco-Prussian War, whilst relying on Belgian neutrality to shield France's north. Von Schlieffen's plan was to defend Alsace and Lorraine to the west, allowing the French to batter themselves against fortified towns, such as Morhange, and then attack strongly to the north through Belgium, turning south almost alongside the English Channel, to envelop Paris and continue its movement into the rear of the French armies, trapping them against the frontier and forcing France to capitulate.

Two German Armies, von Kluck's First Army and von Bülow's Second Army crossed the Belgian border on 3rd August and swept westwards taking the fortress town of Liège, before turning south towards Mons and the French border. These two Armies, forming the strong right hook, had to march and fight over hundreds of miles on a tight timetable to avoid a war on two fronts.

Despite its send off, the BEF's cavalry division and four infantry divisions had already crossed the channel in such secrecy that just before the battle of Mons, the German Navy was still reporting to Germany's High Command that no British force had landed in France.

On 20th August, the Grenadiers were once again marching under a blazing hot sun to the village of Oisy, which apparently provided good billets, as the BEF advanced alongside General Lanrezac's Fifth Army towards Belgium. The ten-mile march to their next overnight stop at Maroilles was equally hot and on 22nd, they again set off northwards for La Longueville. That afternoon they heard distant gunfire as Lanrezac attacked Bülow's Second Army and, defeated, began to withdraw. Meanwhile, the 320,000-strong tide of field grey of the German First Army under von Kluck was bearing down on Mons and Condé.

Early on the 23rd August, the Grenadiers received orders to cross the Belgian frontier and proceed to Mons. With the enemy close, Walter Dell and the other drummers stowed their instruments on the Grenadiers' transport wagons and adopted their battlefield role of stretcher-bearers and medical orderlies.

The BEF's line centred on Mons was precarious, not least because the British were already nine miles in front of the retreating French. Overnight on 22nd/23rd, General Sir HL Smith-Dorrien's II Corps, facing von Kluck's army, dug in behind the canal running east-west between Condé and Mons and continuing around the north of Mons itself. As it was too small to man this long line continuously, II Corps concentrated on guarding the canal bridges, which remained intact, because Sir John French, the BEF's Commander in Chief, was still planning to advance further north. Haig's I Corps held a roughly north-south salient from the south of Mons to Grand Reng, forming a flank guard facing von Bülow, who was busy pursuing the French.

Von Kluck's men had marched about 140 miles over 11 days by 23rd August, and, expecting no opposition in Mons, approached II Corps' line almost casually in scattered units. Bunching into tight masses as they approached the canal crossings, the Germans were met with accurate, rapid rifle and machine-gun fire that decimated the leading units. However, German artillery soon began to dominate the line and gradually, as they belatedly recognised the strength and skill of their opponents, German assaults became more co-ordinated.

The Grenadiers halted on reaching the southern outskirts of Mons near the junction of I and II Corps as reports warned of German units approaching fast. Ordered to move south, the Grenadiers marched eight miles to Quevy le Petit. With great determination, the Germans were beginning to cross the canal in places. Under great pressure, Smith-Dorrien withdrew from the canal around the north of Mons to his second line about the southern outskirts. The Grenadiers had been at Quevy barely an hour before they were ordered northwards once more, perhaps to link up with II Corps again. The battalion marched seven miles to Harveng, just south of Mons, where it came under German rifle and artillery fire for the first time, but suffered no casualties. In fact, Haig's I Corps had a quiet day at Mons, all of von Kluck's attacks falling on II Corps.

Overnight, Field Marshal French belatedly understood that Lanrezac was now 15 miles behind the BEF and still retreating, so he ordered both Corps to withdraw southwards. I Corps received its orders at 02.00 on 24th and soon 1st Division moved off, followed 45 minutes later by 2nd Division amid some confusion. Fresh orders then came, countermanding the previous ones and sending the Grenadiers north again. Realising that to march north would be absolute folly, the Grenadiers' commander, Colonel Noel Corry, decided to turn his troops around. By this time, the Grenadiers were not only confused, but also extremely tired from the constant marching and the heat. On returning to Harveng, they rested as best they could until, at about 16.30, the Grenadiers received definite orders to withdraw and the 'Retreat from Mons' began.

The Kaiser had allegedly instructed von Kluck to 'sweep aside Sir John French's contemptible little army'. However, that little army of Regulars, ex-Regulars and volunteer Reservists had resisted von Kluck's onslaught and withdrawn intact. From then on, Walter and the other men of the original BEF proudly adopted the nickname of 'Old Contemptibles'.

On 25th August, the BEF reached the Mormal Forest and separated, Walter's Corps going down the eastern side, while II Corps went towards Le Cateau, where General French intended the two Corps to re-unite. Marching southwards, the Grenadiers and the retreating BEF saw few German soldiers, apart from cavalry patrols and the occasional aeroplane. The enemy was equally hot, tired and footsore, but they were not far behind.

That night, 4th (Guards) Brigade took up billets in Landrecies, on the Sambre, where General Haig had established his headquarters. 3rd Coldstream Guards had already erected makeshift barriers to guard the approaches when singing German troops appeared in the twilight, expecting to find an empty village and comfortable billets. Mutual surprise, failing light and fatigue resulted in a confused mêlée. To prevent the Germans from entering the village, additional barricades hastily went up using everything available, including the Grenadier's baggage wagons. The Grenadiers turned out to help the Coldstreamers engage the Germans while General Haig, who was ill at the time, feared the worst. Fortunately, the German battalion was unable to co-ordinate its attack in the dark and eventually withdrew after midnight.

Landrecies had been a minor skirmish, with small losses on either side, but Haig was seriously unnerved and feared his Corps might be overwhelmed. By dawn the next morning, having lost most of their kit, including their drums, in the barricades, the Grenadiers plodded south, away from II Corps, which that day fought at Le Cateau.

On 1st September, seventy-five miles further south, 4th (Guards) Brigade was holding the forest of Villers-Cotterêts as the rearguard for 2nd Division when it was heavily attacked. The German infantry appeared 'doped', either with exhaustion or looted wine, as they blundered through the dense woodland, sometimes firing at one another. However, enemy machine guns dominated the wide, straight tracks that criss-crossed the forest. Several hours of confused fighting in the dense woodland cost the Germans dear, but they surrounded two platoons of Grenadiers, who fought to the last man. By early evening, the fighting had died down and the Guards withdrew towards Betz. The Grenadiers had lost 4 officers and 160 men, but the Guards' gallant defence had allowed their Division to escape intact.

There were four more days of marching south under the blazing hot sun for Walter, without significant contact with the enemy. About 05.00 on 5th September, the Grenadiers reached Fontenay near the River Marne west of Paris and bivouacked, utterly exhausted. The Grenadiers had marched almost two hundred hot, dusty miles since Mons, over hard, uneven cobbled roads with no idea where they were going. On 6th September came welcome new orders, the Germans, having abandoned Schlieffen's big idea of sweeping around the west of Paris, had decided to concentrate on destroying the French Army first. Von Bülow had already changed course and opened a gap with von Kluck, who received orders to close up by turning eastwards. Unwittingly, von Kluck was exposing his flank to the BEF, which received orders to attack.

With the weather becoming more autumnal, the Grenadiers advanced north again and discovered that the Germans had comprehensively looted many of the French properties on their way south. Then, in woods south of the River Marne, fighting erupted on 8th September. The Grenadiers lost one officer killed and eighteen men wounded, but now in heavy, soaking rain their advance continued. During *the Miracle on the Marne,* as it later became known, the French Army, helped by the BEF, successfully blocked the German advance towards Paris. By 12th September, the Battle of the Marne was over and the Allies were advancing again.

The Germans retreated to a ridge beyond the River Aisne known as the Chemin des Dames, after a scenic road made for the daughters of Louis XV, which dominated the Aisne valley from heights of up to 600 feet. The Germans strengthened a series of formidable spurs and gulleys, pointing like fingers from the ridge towards the Aisne, with a complex of trenches backed by artillery emplacements on the rearward slopes.

On 13th September, 4th (Guards) Brigade began the offensive to dislodge the Germans from these new positions, which became known as the Battle of the Aisne. Under heavy fire, the Coldstreamers crossed the River Aisne and managed to consolidate their position. The Grenadiers crossed the river by pontoon bridge the following day, but soon came under heavy fire and suffered considerable casualties. It was apparent that the Allies had insufficient manpower and firepower available to dislodge the Germans from the ridge and so they dug in, creating their own line of trenches. However, the Germans would soon discover that they could not drive the Allies out of their trenches either and the result was stalemate. As heavy shelling continued, the Grenadiers suffered further casualties until, on 17th September, they were relieved and billeted in the town of Soupir. Returning to the front line the following day, the Grenadiers immediately set to work strengthening the newly created trenches.

On 19th and 20th September, the Grenadiers again came under heavy German artillery and rifle fire, killing two men and wounding nine, including Walter Dell, who received a bullet wound to the head. Walter was among the wounded taken by ambulance train to Paris the next day, where motor ambulances transferred them to the Lyceé Buffon, a school in south Paris recently converted into a military hospital. Walter immediately underwent an operation that successfully removed the bullet from his head. Although he was still in great pain, doctors felt sure he stood a good chance of recovery. Unfortunately, Walter's condition worsened as infection set in and on 1st October, he became delirious. Despite strenuous efforts to save him, Walter died the following day.

Walter's burial took place with full military honours at the City of Paris Cemetery, Bagneux, on 6th October 1914. Many of the nursing staff who had looked after him attended his funeral, and some wrote movingly to the Dell family in Northchurch. Walter's family later allowed *The Berkhamsted Gazette* to publish these letters, a common practice at the time that was soon to fade as the Government considered it bad for public morale. When Walter's grave received an Imperial War Graves Commission headstone, his family requested the inscription, 'Truly my home is even in Thee'.

Private 6951 Charles TALBOT
1st Battalion, Bedfordshire Regiment

16th November 1914

Charles Talbot was serving in the Reserves in August 1914 when his mobilisation orders arrived. He was born in the spring of 1879 at his parent's home in Northchurch High Street, the son of John Talbot, a general labourer and his wife, Mary Ann. Charles grew up in the village with older sister Louisa and on leaving school he initially worked as a grocer's porter. In 1899, perhaps seeking adventure in the Boer War, Charles volunteered for the local militia. His application failed, however, as he was only 5ft 2inches tall. Undeterred by this rejection, Charles reapplied in February 1901 and despite his height, this time he was accepted. His enlistment with the 4th Battalion, Bedfordshire Regiment was for twelve years, the first nine years being on active duty and the remainder spent in the Reserves. Two months later, on 29th March, Charles transferred to 1st Battalion, Bedfordshire Regiment.

At the time of Charles's enlistment, 1st Battalion was stationed at Mooltan in India, midway between Delhi and Bombay. It was probably here that he joined the battalion towards the end of 1901. The following year, 1st Battalion moved to the historical city of Jhasi, in the Northern state of Uttar Pradesh, where it spent five years on garrison duties. 1st Battalion left India on 6th December 1907, aboard the troopship *Assaye* and embarked for Aden, arriving there five days later. They remained in Aden on garrison duties for a further 12 months. The battalion finally left for England on 8th December 1908 aboard the troopship *Rohilla*, arriving at Southampton fifteen days later.

Discharged from active duty and transferred to the Reserves, Charles found employment at the grocers and wine merchants, William Cheeld and Co, in Berkhamsted High Street. Here he met and fell in love with Annie Woolley, who originally came from St Lawrence in Jersey. They were married at St Mary's church on 9th November 1910 with John Randall, the Sexton of St Mary's, being one of their witnesses. The newly-weds settled into their marital home at N°4 Unity Cottages in the High Street.

The day after Great Britain declared war on Germany, Charles was mobilised and ordered to report at the Bedfordshire's Regimental Depot at Kempston. Charles and the other local men, including Frederick King from Berkhamsted and Northchurch-born William Tomlin, were given travel warrants and directed to 1st Battalion's home base, which was then at Mullingar in Ireland. Meanwhile, 1st Bedfordshires left Belfast aboard SS

Oronsa and disembarked at Le Havre on 16th August. After a short break at a muddy rest camp nearby, 1st Bedfords set off by train towards Maubeuge, and on 20th August, having joined the 15th Infantry Brigade, 5th Division, II Corps, BEF, under General Sir HL Smith-Dorrien, they marched towards Mons.

Horace Lockwood Smith-Dorrien was born the 11th child of Colonel Robert Smith-Dorrien of Haresfoot House, Berkhamsted in 1858, and followed his father into the army. Educated at Harrow and Sandhurst, and subsequently commissioned into the Sherwood Foresters, Smith-Dorrien was an intelligent and insightful officer who commanded 19th Brigade with distinction during the Boer War. In 1914, Lord Kitchener appointed him to command the BEF's II Corps after Lt. Gen. Sir James Grierson's fatal heart attack in France. Smith-Dorrien's II Corps were to bear the brunt of the German assault at Mons and, apart from evacuating the town itself, held its line until German buglers sounded the *Cease Fire* at midnight. 15th Infantry Brigade had been in Divisional Reserve at Mons, although the Bedfords were shelled by German artillery.

Smith-Dorrien's men had expected to continue fighting on 24th August, but to their surprise, were ordered to retreat and the Bedfords had to disengage under fire. That evening, General French issued unrealistic orders for both Corps to reach Le Cateau by nightfall on the 25th ready to fight a delaying action the following morning, but that meant a 20 to 25-mile march on roads choked with refugees and transport. Smith-Dorrien did reach Le Cateau, but Haig's Corps fell behind and halted around Landrecies. Smith-Dorrien's battalions were still arriving when he received new instructions to continue retreating on 26th. After consulting with his commanders, Smith-Dorrien decided to stand and fight in the open downs west of Le Cateau, alongside the cavalry with the newly arrived 4th Division accepting his command.

The exhausted 1st Bedfords were lucky to be allocated trenches at Le Cateau, which they improved overnight, but later units had little time to dig in. The Battle of Le Cateau on 26th August resembled an old-fashioned battle that Wellington might have recognised, with cavalry and field guns supporting the infantry in sight of the enemy. Despite overwhelming odds, Smith-Dorrien's men held the Germans at bay and by making best use of limited artillery and accurate rifle fire, enabled his Corps to retreat in safety. Having covered the withdrawal of their guns, 1st Bedfords and the remainder of 5th Division, continued south over congested roads. Marching daily, including three night marches and a rearguard fight at Crepy-en-Valois, the battalions' retreat finally ended on 4th September at the village of Gagny, due east of Paris.

Meanwhile, Charles and the other Reservists joined the first reinforcing drafts gathering at Mullingar. Having reported and received their kit, Charles and 90 companions sailed from Dublin to arrive at Le Havre on

30th August. The following day, they rode some of the infamous French railway wagons, marked *40 hommes, 8 chevaux*, to Amiens and from there marched to Le Mans. After two days' rest at Le Mans, they marched to Coulommiers, east of Paris, and on the 5th September, Charles and the reinforcement draft caught up with the main body of 1st Bedfords at Gagny.

Not long after, the Bedfords led the main body of their Division into action against the German *VI Corps* during the Battle of the Marne. On 8th September, 1st Bedfords attacked German lines near the villages of St Cyr and St Ouen, capturing some 200 German soldiers. Some of the prisoners later escaped during indiscriminate British shellfire, but were soon recaptured. Leading the advance across the Marne next day, the Bedfords fought an enemy rearguard, forcing it to abandon several machine guns.

As the Bedfords pressed on, an enemy convoy was captured and many prisoners taken. The Battalion's War Diary entry for 10th September described the countryside as 'strewn with wagons, motors, bicycles, stores, hundreds of great coats, dead & wounded horses', and the retreating Germans as 'demoralised'.

Days of torrential rain began as the Allies pursued the enemy, who actually intended to make a stand on the high ridge beyond the River Aisne. The First Battle of the Aisne opened on the 13th September with a fierce all-day artillery duel. Some large German shells intended for a nearby British gun battery landed among the Bedfords, who prudently drew back. The battalion crossed the Aisne by pontoon and raft to capture the village of Missy, where they remained under heavy shellfire. Elsewhere on the Aisne, the strong German positions along the Chemin des Dames prevented much progress. Late on the 16th, the Bedfords were relieved, marching down a very muddy woodland track and crossing the Aisne to reach billets at Montgard Mill, near Jury, for a few days of rest.

The BEF dug in as best it could in the waterlogged ground, but even those meagre trenches resisted all German counterattacks and the battle settled into stalemate. The Bedfords began a routine of trench duty, which nobody yet realised would become the defining feature of the war.

By now, newly created German and French armies were attempting to out-flank each other northwards, only to collide and entrench, extending the trenches towards the sea. Sir John French, meanwhile, feeling stuck on the Aisne and too far from his Channel Port lifelines, became insistent that the BEF must return to the far left of the French line, nearer to England. Although the French Commander-in-Chief, General Joffre, was transferring whole French armies' northwards across his rear, he gave in and arranged rail transport for the BEF's divisions from Compiegne to a line between Bixschoote, north of Ypres, to La Bassée, near Béthune.

At the beginning of October, 1st Bedfords left the Aisne and travelled northwest by train and French motor bus to Béthune where, on 11th

October, the battalion relieved some French Territorials in trenches at Essars and joined the Battle of La Bassée. When II Corps attacked the following day, the Bedfords advanced without much opposition to occupy Givenchy and a rough, exposed trench beyond. German shellfire increased on the 13th October until, through the smoke and brick dust, the Bedfords were attacked from the front and flank and forced back beyond the village, losing 7 officers and 140 men. However, the German counterattack faded away and two nights later they abandoned Givenchy. When the Battalion re-occupied Givenchy, they found many wounded Bedfords, who had been treated by the Germans.

Attention now fell on the market town of Ypres, just over the Belgian border. Ypres was an important centre of communications, which both sides believed held the key to Flanders, the Channel Ports and victory. Ypres, or 'Wipers', as British soldiers called it, and the adjacent salient lay in a shallow amphitheatre overlooked by German-occupied high ground. Ypres would experience a trilogy of battles, in 1914, 1915 and 1917, like some hellish operatic cycle. The Battle of La Bassée, which the Bedfords had left on 5th November, was the overture for the series of battles that would constitute First Ypres, and they were about to re-join at the climax.

On 6th November, 1st Bedfords were transported to the salient in 'Old Bill' London double-decker buses, requisitioned with their drivers and still wearing red paintwork. They marched through Ypres after dark and relieved 2nd Bedfords south of the Menin Road. The following day German troops breached the trenches on the Menin Road side, but a costly counterattack by the battalion threw them back. Further skirmishes continued over the following days, but on 11th November the Germans again breached the British lines near 1st Bedfords' left and more were wounded. The battalion prepared a new defensive line about 300 yards behind them and on 14th November, they received orders to retreat to it. Before all the men could move however, a surprise German attack led to fierce fighting with several more men being captured, killed or wounded. Among those gravely wounded during the hand-to-hand fighting were Charles Talbot and William Tomlin. William Tomlin died in hospital at Wimereux on 15th November and the following day Charles died, but his grave was lost.

Aside from the Northchurch War Memorial, Charles Talbot's name appears on the Memorial Tablet inside St Peter's Church, Berkhamsted. It also appears on the Menin Gate Memorial at Ypres, which bears the names of more than 54,000 officers and men who died in the area between 1914 and 1918 with unknown graves. William Tomlin's name appears on the Berkhamsted War Memorial.

Captain Arthur Noel LOXLEY
Royal Navy

1st January 1915

The connection between the Loxley family and Northchurch goes back to the early 19th century. On 18th June 1812, John Loxley, a landowner from the village of West Ham, then in Essex, married Elizabeth Smart in St Mary's church. Elizabeth was the only child of William Smart, a wealthy local landowner and owner of Norcott Court, a large manor house located just to the northwest of Northchurch which she would inherit on William Smart's death in March 1838.

John and Elizabeth Loxley had two children, Elizabeth, born in 1814, and John, born the following year. Sadly, Elizabeth died in May 1822 aged only eight. John Loxley (snr) died in 1850, but his widow continued to live at Norcott Court until her death. John junior became a solicitor in the City, practising from 80 Cheapside and married twice. His first marriage, to Emily Augusta Heath, took place at St John's Hackney in 1845. Emily was the daughter of Reverend Robert Heath, Rector of Saddington, Leicestershire, and a niece of Lord Byron. Their marriage was tragically short however as Emily died on 21st May 1846, eight days after giving birth to their son, Arthur Smart Loxley. Seven years later, on 12th July 1853, John Loxley married Anne Pressly, the daughter of an Inland Revenue Commissioner, at St Andrew and St Mark's church in Surbiton. Their only son, Herbert Charles Loxley, was born seven years later.

John Loxley and his family continued to live at Norcott Court with his widowed mother and inherited the estate on Elizabeth Loxley's death in 1887 aged 95. Already a prominent figure in Northchurch, having jointly founded the

Captain Arthur Noel Loxley RN
(Source: Patrick James Coleridge Sumner)

21

village school with Lord Brownlow in 1864, John Loxley served the village as a major benefactor until his death on 6th February 1892.

John's son by his first marriage, Arthur Smart Loxley, was educated at Radley College in Abingdon, Oxfordshire and later graduated from Exeter College Oxford with a Master of Arts. Arthur subsequently followed his maternal grandfather's calling and joined the Anglican clergy. In 1871, aged 24, he was a 'Deacon in Holy Orders, Curate of Northchurch', living at Norcott Court. Two years later, he married Alice Mary Duncombe, the daughter of Reverend William Duncombe whose family owned Edgeworth House.

On 31st October 1874, Alice gave birth to their first child in Lamport, Northamptonshire, where her husband was now Vicar. They named him Arthur Noel Loxley. Three more sons would follow – Vere Duncombe Loxley, born in 1881; Gerald Herbert Loxley, born in 1885; and Reginald Victor Byron Loxley, born in 1887. Their only daughter, Gladys Marjorie Loxley, was born in 1882. All four sons would enter the armed forces and serve during the First World War. Arthur Smart Loxley later became the Vicar of Fairford in Gloucestershire and a minor Canon at Gloucester Cathedral. He died aged 42, on 2nd April 1888, from a heart attack suffered whilst playing the cornet at a local hunt ball.

Arthur Noel Loxley, known as Noel, grew up in Gloucester and was educated at Eton College. In 1888, shortly after his father's death and no doubt seeking adventure, fourteen-year-old Noel Loxley entered the Royal Navy as a cadet. The Royal Navy was essential for protecting commerce within the British Empire and deploying troops across the world in defence of its colonies. With extensive trade routes to defend, Great Britain had the largest fleet in the world, her main challengers in the late nineteenth century being France, Japan, the USA, Russia and, from 1897, Germany.

Loxley began his training at Dartmouth aboard HMS *Britannia*, a converted three-decker battleship permanently moored in the dockyard as a training ship. Cadets spent at least two years learning about the Royal Navy and continuing their education to a good standard. On 15th July 1890, having completed his two years training with good behaviour throughout, sixteen-year-old Loxley left *Britannia* as a Midshipman. The following September, he was assigned to the cruiser HMS *Warspite*, the Flagship of the Royal Navy's Pacific Station at Esquimalt in British Columbia. Loxley was to remain at Esquimalt for the next two and a half years, his service record for this period describing him as 'very zealous and intelligent'.

On the death of his paternal grandfather in February 1892, Noel Loxley inherited Norcott Court, but unable to live there whilst serving in the navy he leased the property out. Two years later on 14th April 1894, Loxley became a Sub-Lieutenant and exactly one year later, a Lieutenant.

November 1895 saw Loxley's next major posting, to HMS *Phoebe*, a Pearl Class cruiser launched in 1890 and based at Cape Hope in South

Africa. Whilst serving aboard *Phoebe* in February 1897, Loxley took part in the controversial Benin Punitive Expedition.

At that time, Benin City was under the Niger Coast Protectorate, now part of Nigeria, and was famous for producing stunning bronze and ivory sculptures. Benin City was the capital of the Edo people whose powerful kings, or *Obas*, had dominated neighbouring tribes for centuries and grown rich trading slaves. Although the abolition of slavery had eroded Benin's power somewhat, the Obas tried to exert influence through their monopoly over the palm oil trade. In 1896, Oba Ovonramwen broke his treaties with Britain by withholding palm oil supplies and since honouring trade agreements was central to the British Empire this was a direct challenge to British authority in the Protectorate.

Acting Consul-General JR Phillips obtained permission to depose Oba Ovonramwen, but a strong enough force could not be assembled for another year so he attempted one last peaceful mission to Benin City with a small, unarmed delegation the following January. Oba Ovonramwen sent a message telling the British to return later, but ignoring the advice of friendly tribal elders, Phillips' delegation approached Benin City on 12th January, where an Edo force ambushed it slaughtering most of the men. This was the sort of atrocity guaranteed to galvanise British opinion and within weeks, an expeditionary force of nine warships was assembled, including *Phoebe,* and the hospital ship *Malacca* carrying 120 marines in addition to her medical staff.

The landing party of marines, sailors and Niger Coast Protectorate troops took Benin City street-by-street before systematically looting the monuments and palaces belonging to Benin's high-ranking chiefs. Fires quickly spread and within three days much of the city was destroyed. By selling most of the plundered treasures in England, the Expedition was able to recover its costs, with many of the Benin bronzes still residing in the British Museum. For services during this campaign, Loxley received the East and West Africa Medal with Benin 1897 clasp.

Loxley returned to Portsmouth for three years in 1897, the same year that Admiral Alfred von Tirpitz became Secretary of State of the Imperial German Naval Office. Within twelve months, the German Reichstag had passed a Navy Act ordering the building of nineteen new battleships. Two years later, this doubled to thirty-eight and the naval race between Britain and Germany began.

In November 1900, Loxley married Gladys Maude Brooke-Hunt at All Saints Church, Ennismore Gardens in Knightsbridge. Gladys was the daughter of Arthur Ernest Brooke-Hunt, a high-ranking civil servant in the Board of Agriculture. Shortly before the wedding, Loxley received news that he was being re-posted to *Warspite* with the Pacific Fleet. There was little time for a proper honeymoon before Loxley and his bride left Liverpool aboard the *Tunisian* for Halifax, Nova Scotia, and then travelled

2,800 miles by train across Canada. During this second posting to the Pacific Fleet, Loxley served aboard both *Warspite* and another cruiser, HMS *Grafton,* returning to Portsmouth in January 1903.

Loxley had an eventful year in 1905 with his elevation to Commander on 1st January, and his elevation to fatherhood on 27th March, when Gladys gave birth to their son, whom they named Peter Noel Loxley. Later that year, Commander Loxley transferred to a newly commissioned armoured cruiser, HMS *Hampshire*, and joined the Channel Fleet. In August 1907, Loxley transferred again to the Royal Navy War College, Portsmouth. This allowed him to meet up with the choir from St Mary's Northchurch, when they visited Portsmouth on their annual outing, and arrange for them to watch the Prince of Wales depart for an official trip to Canada aboard HMS *Indomitable*.

As Britain and Germany's naval race was reaching its height, the battleship HMS *Dreadnought* became the defining warship of the era. Built at Portsmouth Naval Dockyard and launched in February 1906, the 18,110-ton *Dreadnought* entered service the following year. With her improved armour protection and ten 12-inch guns, she surpassed all previous battleships so all battleships after her were known as Dreadnoughts, and all her predecessors, became 'pre-Dreadnoughts'. Although Germany began her own Dreadnought programme in 1907, the Royal Navy maintained its lead.

On leaving the Royal Navy War College in March 1909, Loxley became Flag Captain of the 16,350-ton pre-Dreadnought, HMS *Hibernia*, flagship of Vice Admiral Sir Archibald Berkeley Milne, Commanding the Home Fleet's 2nd Division. A year later, Loxley became Flag Captain to Vice Admiral Sir George Astley Callaghan aboard *Hibernia's* sister ship, HMS *King Edward VII*.

Loxley became a Captain on 22nd June 1911 on the coronation of King George V and moved to The Admiralty in London. In November 1912, he took command of the 24-gun battlecruiser HMS *Inflexible*, based at Malta with the Mediterranean Fleet. A month later Loxley's wife and son followed him to Malta, where they stayed for just over a year. Recalled to Portsmouth on the outbreak of war, Loxley took command of HMS *Formidable* on 2nd September.

Commissioned in October 1904, the 15,805-ton *Formidable* was one of the last pre-Dreadnoughts. Her crew of 780 served four 12-inch guns, twelve 6-inch quick firing guns, sixteen 12-pdr quick firing guns and six 3-pdr quick firing guns, plus four 18-inch torpedo tubes and she could reach a respectable 18 knots.

Formidable was with the Channel Fleet's 5th Battle Squadron when it screened the BEF's transit to France and had helped to transport the Portsmouth Marine Battalion to Ostend on 25th August. Aboard *Formidable*, Loxley had the company of Bruce, an Airedale Terrier given to him by his son.

Just before Christmas 1914, Loxley wrote to his childhood Nurse, Ann Gurney, 'Peter has gone to school, and is just home for his first holidays, which, I expect, he is enjoying as much as I did, but he was much braver going to school than I.' It would be his final letter.

When Admiral Sir Lewis Bayly took command of the 5th Battle Squadron, at Sheerness on 17th December 1914, he sought the Admiralty's permission to conduct the same gunnery exercise off Portland that he had recently completed with his previous Squadron. At 10.00 on 30th December, Bayly's flagship, HMS *Lord Nelson*, leading the battleships *Agamemnon*, *Queen*, *Implacable*, *Prince of Wales*, *Venerable*, *London* and *Formidable*, left Sheerness escorted by the light cruisers *Topaze* and *Diamond*.

With gunnery practice completed on 31st December, Bayly decided to patrol the English Channel and deployed his battleships in line ahead with *Formidable* bringing up the rear, followed by *Topaze* and *Diamond* stationed well astern. Despite reports of U-Boat activity in the area, Bayly judged that the rising wind and rough seas made an enemy submarine attack practically impossible. Leading his two-mile line of battleships at 10 knots, Bayly was unaware that Kapitänleutnant Rudolf Schneider, commanding *U-24*, had been shadowing them all day, hoping for his first kill since leaving Wilhelmshaven just before Christmas.

Having struggled to maintain stability at periscope depth in the rising seas, Schneider decided to surface and attack on the move. At 02.30 on 1st January 1915, undetected in the icy swell 20 miles off Start Point, Schneider closed on the last battleship in the line and ordered a torpedo away. The explosion in *Formidable's* N°1 boiler caused her to lose all steam pressure and develop a twenty-degree list. Believing *Formidable* had struck a mine *Topaze* and *Diamond*, altered course towards her. Nobody observed *U-24* manoeuvring stealthily in the dark around the stricken ship. After fifty minutes, Schneider ran at *Formidable* from the other side, his torpedo exploding near her second funnel. Although Schneider dived immediately, *U-24* scraped beneath *Formidable's* hull, damaging her periscope and conning tower. The rest of the Squadron altered course to get well clear of the danger.

In a rising gale, Loxley, with his second-in-command, Cdr. Ballard, and a signaller, remained at his post, sending flares and rockets off at regular intervals to illuminate the cruisers' rescue effort. The crew waited calmly and without panic for the lowering of the lifeboats. Someone played ragtime on the piano and others sang, while the Chaplain risked his life fetching cigarettes from below. With all the lifeboats successfully launched, (bar one that capsized), the cruisers took off 80 men joined by the Brixham trawler *Provident*. Suddenly at 04.45, over two hours after the first torpedo exploded, *Formidable* began to capsize and within minutes, she sank dragging many swimmers with her. In true naval tradition, Loxley had stayed with his ship, reputedly saying, 'Lads, this is the last, all hands for themselves, and may God bless you and guide you to safety'. Walking to the forebridge, he lit a cigarette and, with Bruce by his side, waited for the end.

The final death toll was 35 officers, including Loxley, and 512 men from *Formidable's* initial complement of 780. Although many men escaped before *Formidable* sank, heavy seas and freezing weather accounted for most of the loss. Loxley's body remains entombed in the wreck with many of his men, but the body of his Airedale washed ashore a few days later. Bruce has a marked grave in Abbotsbury Subtropical Gardens in Dorset.

After weighing the evidence, including Admiral Sir Lewis Bayly's own account, the Sea Lords at the Admiralty ruled on 11th January 1915, that Admiral Bayly was entirely to blame for the sinking. They concluded that, 'the handling of your squadron...was marked by a want of prudence and good seamanship in avoidance of unnecessary risks inexplicable in an officer holding high and responsible command'. Refused a formal Court Martial and relieved of his command on 17th January. Bayly became President of the Royal Naval College, Greenwich the following day.

Arthur Noel Loxley's name appears on the Lamport War Memorial in Northamptonshire, the Chatham Naval Memorial and on a plaque in the south transept of St Mary's Northchurch. HMS *Formidable*'s wreck is now a legally protected War Grave.

Privates 8183 and 9890 Walter and Frederick GEARY
1st Battalion, Border Regiment

2 May 1915 and 29 June 1915

Walter and Frederick Geary's father, William Geary, was a general labourer from Northchurch. Their mother, Annie, came from Derby and it was there that William and Annie were married in the spring of 1877. Over the following years, they raised twelve children in Northchurch. By 1911 most of the children had left home with only William, Annie and their younger offspring living at Bank Cottages in the village.

Walter Geary was born in the village in March 1886, and baptised at St Mary's Church on 4th April. After leaving school in 1900, Walter joined his elder brother, Harry, at Cooper's chemical works in Berkhamsted. On reaching the age of 17, Walter volunteered for the local militia, the 4th Battalion Bedfordshire Regiment, and in 1905, having found a liking for army life, Walter enlisted with 1st Battalion, Border Regiment, for the usual twelve years' service. He received the Regimental number 8137. Walter's enlistment papers described him as being 5ft 3inches tall, with light brown eyes, brown hair and tattoos on both forearms - a dancing girl and a flag.

Walter joined his new regiment at its depot in Carlisle on 8th December 1905, where he received seven weeks' initial training. He then transferred to the Guadeloupe barracks at Bordon Camp in Hampshire where he gained a qualification in mounted infantry. There he remained until August 1906, when 1st Battalion boarded the *SS Soudan* en route for a tour of duty in Gibraltar.

Their two years' garrison duty on Gibraltar was the first overseas posting for 1st Borders since their return from the Boer War some four years earlier. Whilst on Gibraltar, the battalion spent much of its time on individual training and musketry practice as the rocky terrain limited larger scale exercises. Instead, boxing, cricket, football, tug-of-war and other sports were encouraged and a thriving competitive spirit within the Rock's garrison developed. Occasionally, the Spanish authorities even allowed the British troops to enter Spain for picnics.

1st Battalion was next posted to India, docking at Bombay aboard HMT *Plassey* on 22nd October 1908. Three companies were detached for other duties at Bombay, while Battalion headquarters and Walter's company transferred to RIMS *Northbrooke* bound for Madras. Several monsoon storms during the voyage down the west coast of India and Ceylon made the trip to Madras rather unpleasant and the troops were relieved when

Northbrooke finally anchored on 29th October. Madras then had no docks, so the men and all their equipment were ferried ashore in small boats. The final stage of their journey was by train high into the Nilgiri hills, some 6,000 feet above sea level, to Wellington Barracks. The barracks were large two-storey buildings with verandas, built around a large square where football and hockey was played by the troops in their off-duty time. Route marches up and down the steep slopes of the Nilgiri hills were frequent, as were sporting competitions against other regiments in the area.

On 29th September 1910, after almost two years in India, the Battalion moved from Wellington to Rangoon in Burma, arriving there on 7th October. Here, they found the hot and humid climate a complete contrast to the pleasantly cool, eucalyptus-scented air of the Nilgiri Hills. Rangoon's European Barracks, unlike Wellington Barracks, were located in the town, but the ranges and training grounds were a march of some distance away. Sport still played an important part in the battalion's life here, although the humid climate was less favourable for energetic activity. Whilst in Rangoon, Walter became a groom, looking after a battalion officer's horse.

In May 1911, the War Office reduced a soldier's Regular Army service from nine to seven years, after which he completed his twelve-year term with the Reserves. Walter was offered and accepted an earlier discharge the following August, and left Rangoon on 26th January 1912 for the six weeks' voyage back to Gosport. The certificate transferring Walter to the Reserves described his conduct during his time with the Border Regiment as 'exemplary'. It also recorded Walter's interest in taking up any civilian work associated with horses, reflecting his employment as a groom. A few days after arriving in Gosport, Walter returned to Northchurch.

Despite Walter's stated wish to work with horses he subsequently joined the Permanent Way Department of the London and North Western Railway as an Underman, based at Camden in north London. As such, Walter would have worked in the gangs of men who maintained the track and infrastructure of the railway in the Camden area immediately north of Euston Station.

In April 1913, Walter signed up as a 'Section A' reservist at the Militia headquarters in Hertford. Men who had completed their service with the Regular Army automatically transferred to the 'Section B Reserve'. 'Section B' reservists received 3 shillings 6 pence a week in addition to their civilian earnings, with the proviso that they would only rejoin the army in the event of a general mobilisation. By joining the 'Section A Reserve', Walter undertook to rejoin the Army in the event of an emergency not requiring general mobilisation and to attend twelve training days per year. He also agreed not to travel outside Great Britain. In exchange, he doubled his weekly retainer to a generous 7 shillings.

Walter's younger brother, Frederick, was born in Northchurch in spring of 1893 and was christened at St Mary's Church on 4th June. Soon after his eighteenth birthday, Frederick followed Walter into 1st Battalion, Border Regiment. By the time of the 1911 Census, he was a newly enlisted private at the Regimental Headquarters in Carlisle. It is not certain when Frederick was sent to Burma, but as enlisted soldiers were not allowed to serve abroad until they turned 19, he was probably posted there in the early summer of 1912, by which time his brother, Walter, had returned to England.

Soon afterwards, 1st Borders left the heat and humidity of Rangoon and moved to Alexandra Barracks at Maymyo, near Mandalay. Maymyo lies 400 miles inland near the River Irrawaddy, in a high mountain pass, which is why the Government of Burma decamped there every summer to work in the cool of the mountains.

Sport, as ever, occupied much of 1st Battalion's off duty hours, but training was constrained by the dense jungle surrounding the Barracks. In early 1913, 1st Battalion participated in large manoeuvres aimed at showing the British flag in an area of Northern Burma where trouble had been festering for some time. It also provided an opportunity for the troops to undertake more realistic and extensive training than could be provided in Maymyo, including first-hand experience of sanitation and hygiene discipline under field conditions. This would prove invaluable during the coming war.

Frederick and 1st Battalion were still at Maymyo in August 1914, so when Walter and the other Border Regiment reservists were mobilised, they travelled to Wales and reported to 2nd Battalion, Border Regiment at Rosebush Camp near Pembroke Dock. In time, their brothers, Harry and Charles Geary, would also volunteer for army service. On 29th August, 2nd Battalion was ordered to Southampton and departed from Pembroke Dock with 27 officers, 1,068 men and 68 horses. At Southampton, the battalion received word that it was to join the 2nd Battalions of the Yorkshire and Wiltshire Regiments and the Gordon Highlanders in forming 20th Brigade, 7th Division. On 5th September 20th Brigade marched to camp at Lyndhurst in the New Forest, where a further eight battalions were added to the Division's strength.

A month later, 7th Division embarked for Flanders. 2nd Borders, on the troopships *Minneapolis* and *Turkoman*, was the first battalion to arrive, landing at Zeebrugge on 6th October. Orders arrived to assist in the defence of Antwerp, which was then under German attack. The battalion entrained for Bruges, then marched to billets in the village of St André and waited for the rest of the Division to catch up. However, by the time 7th Division had assembled Antwerp was effectively lost and new orders came to hold a number of important bridges and key locations to assist the retreating

Belgian army. Once the Belgian divisions had withdrawn, 7th Division moved westwards to block possible German outflanking manoeuvres and to cover the Channel ports further south.

Initial contact with the Germans came on 15th October, but no casualties resulted. Three days later, the Battalion marched to the village of Kruiseik, southeast of Ypres, and then on to Menin where they came under heavy fire. Retiring to the partially dug trenches on Kruiseik Hill, they received orders to hold it at all costs. Despite overwhelming odds, and an increasing artillery bombardment, the battalion managed to hold on for three days and nights, but at considerable cost. They were eventually relieved on 26th October, their numbers having fallen to just 12 officers and 538 men. Three days later, the battalion returned to Kruiseik Hill in support of the Gordon Highlanders, where a German artillery bombardment inflicted another 55 casualties before they were again relieved.

On the eve of the First Battle of Ypres, the Borders were standing ready in woods northwest of a château near Zonnebecke. Late in the day, orders came for the battalion to move east to the small town of Hooge to support a cavalry advance, and afterwards to Klein Zillebecke where they would dig in. On 2nd November, the Battalion successfully held off a series of fierce German attacks, with both sides suffering substantial losses. The Battalion was relieved later that day and retired to woods near Ypres. After three days' rest, they marched south to the village of Locre and finally, on 17th November, to billets in Sailly, a village to the west of Lille. Overall losses for the battalion since 18th October were 88 officers and men killed, 265 wounded and 258 missing. A draft of officers and men later joined the Battalion to make up the previous weeks' losses.

King George V inspected the troops of 7th Division at Sailly on 1st December during his first trip to the Western Front. The King of the Belgians, the French President, Lord Kitchener, and the Commanders of the French and British Armies accompanied the King.

On 18th December, the Borders took part in an attempt to capture German trenches some 150 yards from their own, but they were repelled costing the Battalion 127 casualties. Two 2nd Borders men later gained the Victoria Cross for their bravery, bringing back wounded soldiers stranded in no-man's-land in broad daylight.

A temporary truce took place on the Borders' front on Christmas Day 1914 allowing both sides to bury their dead who had lain between the trenches since the fighting on 18th December. Unusually, this unofficial truce in the battalion's sector lasted until 8th January. The Battalion remained in the line at Sailly throughout January, suffering casualties on most days from sniper and artillery fire.

Moving to new positions in Fleurbaix, three miles to the west, it was here that on the night of 7th February, a German sniper shot Walter in his right arm. Walter's injury was serious enough for him to return to England for treatment in one of the top floor wards at the French Hospital at 172 Shaftesbury Avenue in London.

News of the war reached Frederick Geary and the rest of 1st Battalion in Maymyo the day it broke out. Speculation was rife among the troops as to which, if any, of the three British battalions in Burma would go to France. 1st Battalion finally left Maymyo on 19th November, with the Band of 1st/10th Gurkhas marching them to the railway station. Here they entrained for Rangoon, arriving there the following morning. At Rangoon, the battalion boarded the P&O Liner *Novara* bound for Calcutta. On 5th December, they entrained again for Bombay, passing 1st/4th Battalion, Border Regiment going the other way to replace them at Maymyo. Three days later, the battalion transferred to the Allen Line liner, SS *Corsican*, for the journey to Port Said in Egypt. The Borders then joined a convoy of ships through the Mediterranean to Avonmouth, where they landed on 9th January 1915, still dressed in their tropical khaki drill uniforms. On the quayside, the battalion was marched through a large shed, emerging from the other end in new winter underclothes and serge uniforms, before entraining for Rugby in Warwickshire where they went into billets.

Training opportunities were limited in the Rugby area, so the battalion spent much of the next few weeks organising and preparing new equipment and supplies. During this time, 1st Battalion joined 87th Brigade, 29th Division, which was assembling in the area. Whilst in Rugby, Frederick wrote his first Will in the form of a letter. On 12th March 1915, King George V took the salute as the whole Division marched past along the Dunchurch to Coventry road watched by vast crowds despite efforts to keep the King's visit secret.

Naturally, Frederick's battalion expected to join 2nd Battalion on the Western Front, but four days after their Royal inspection, 1st Borders entrained for Avonmouth, en route to the Dardanelles in Turkey.

Britain, France and Russia had declared war on Germany's ally, Turkey, in November 1914 after a series of incidents culminating in the closure to allied shipping of the Dardanelle Straights linking the Mediterranean with the Black Sea and blocking the shipment of equipment to Russia as well as threatening the Caucasus oil fields. The Admiralty, believing that naval gunnery alone could reopen the Dardanelles, ordered the Mediterranean Fleet to shell the Turkish forts guarding the Straights. However, no follow-up landings were attempted and despite being damaged the forts remained a threat to shipping. Worse, Turkey was alerted to the poor state of her defences, and began major improvements to the fortifications.

In early 1915, Britain and France made a joint decision to land troops on the Gallipoli Peninsular separating the Dardanelles from the Aegean

Sea and capture the Turkish forts from behind. Success on Gallipoli would materially assist Russian operations against Austria-Hungary in south-eastern Europe and allow troops to attack Istanbul, possibly knocking Turkey out of the war and opening a second front to relieve the increasing stalemate in France.

A naval assault began during the third week of February 1915, in which an advance party of Marines landed at Helles Bay on the tip of the Gallipoli Peninsula. Operations stalled however, when the French pre-dreadnought *Bouvet* hit a Turkish mine and sank with the loss of 639 lives. HMS *Ocean*, HMS *Irresistible* and HMS *Inflexible* also struck mines, the first two sinking as a result. Strong artillery fire from the recently strengthened Turkish fortifications came as another unpleasant surprise to the attacking forces.

A British and Commonwealth invasion force was formed in mid-March, consisting of 29th Division, The Royal Naval Division and the Australian and New Zealand Army Corps (ANZAC). French troops, mainly Senegalese, would also land on the Adriatic side of the Peninsular. On 17th March, 1st Battalion, Border Regiment, minus its transport, boarded SS *Andania* at Avonmouth along with 1st Royal Inniskilling Fusiliers. *Andania*, carrying a total of 70 officers and 1,784 men, made straight for Malta, anchored in Valetta harbour for two days, and then set sail once again.

However, instead of going directly to the Dardanelles as the troops expected, *Andania* sailed to Egypt and dropped anchor in Alexandria harbour, which was full of British, French and Australian troop transport and supply ships. All stores and equipment were unloaded, partly because troops and equipment needed dividing among smaller transports for the landings, and partly because some of the Battalion's equipment had been hurriedly packed in the wrong order. Meanwhile, the Borders marched five miles to a tented camp for a mercifully brief stay in Egypt. Food and water were in short supply, while heat and sand compounded their misery. It was a relief for the Battalion when it conducted a practice landing in the cooler Agami Bay.

On 10th April, 1st Battalion, now divided between *Andania* and two other vessels, set course for Mudros, on the Greek island of Lemnos in the northern Aegean, where the invasion fleet was assembling. Meanwhile, the landing plans were being finalised. Whilst waiting to go ashore Frederick wrote another Will, this time using the standard Army format.

The invasion force left Mudros harbour at dusk on 24th April, and at daybreak the following day having arrived off Gallipoli, the fleet opened fire on the Turkish defences. The battalion transferred on to smaller craft, and then Frederick, in 16 Platoon, 'D' Company, headed for the designated landing beach. 1st Borders were supposed to be in reserve, but although they landed successfully at about 09.00, there was confusion among neighbouring regiments allowing the Turkish troops to mount a strong counterattack. It almost succeeded, but 1st Battalion and other troops charged the advancing Turks, driving them back. The Allies' line was stabilised, but the battalion had already lost half its strength.

The surviving troops quickly dug in and prepared for the Turks to launch a night attack. When the Turks did attack, HMS *Implacable*, lying offshore, opened fire and they withdrew. The following day was much quieter, enabling 1st Battalion to improve their positions, but conditions on the beaches were atrocious. The invasion plan had assumed the enemy would retreat, but stiffening Turkish resistance kept the beachhead small and cramped. Wounded men attended by over-stretched medics with insufficient means to transfer them to the ships, remained exposed to enemy fire on the crowded beach. The front-line troops fared little better. Short of food, water and sleep and under constant artillery and sniper fire, the majority soon suffered mental and physical exhaustion. However, 1st Battalion appreciated their European winter serge uniforms during the cold April nights on Gallipoli. The following evening, 1st Battalion received orders to dig new forward trenches to complete a straight east-west line across the entire peninsula.

At 08.00 on 28th April, 'A' and 'B' Companies, supported by 'C' Company and Frederick's 'D' Company, attacked the Turkish lines with the intention of seizing a nearby ridge called Gully Spur. The battalion advanced with surprisingly few casualties even as the men, in full battle order, scrambled down into Zighin Dere, later renamed Gully Ravine, and up the other side. Then, at about 13.20, the Turks launched a fierce counterattack, driving the Borders back. Fortunately, observers aboard HMS *Queen Elizabeth*, grasping the situation, turned her guns on the Turkish troops with devastating effect and the advance resumed. Eventually, a new line was established with the help of reinforcements. The success of the advance was a remarkable achievement considering that the men had not slept for several days, were running short of food and water and had neither decent maps, nor information regarding the enemy's strength. That night, new trenches were prepared linking Gully Ravine with the cliff side. Mercifully the next two days were relatively quiet.

1st Battalion was relieved on 1st May, going into reserve in Gully Ravine, where the men could wash and bathe for the first time since they landed on the Peninsula. Unfortunately, Turkish troops launched an unexpected night attack and 1st Battalion was ordered to reinforce the Royal Inniskilling Fusiliers. 'A' Company went into the trenches first at midnight, followed by the remainder of the battalion at 02.30. To reach these trenches, the troops had to cross some 500 yards of open ground and there were some casualties. At 04.30, the order came for a counterattack at dawn although ammunition was still in short supply. The battalion and French troops launched further counterattacks the following day to force the Turks back to their trenches and during one of these engagements Private Frederick Geary, aged 21, was killed. Along with many others who died at Gallipoli, his body remained unidentified. In the Will Frederick made at Mudros Harbour all his personal belongings were bequeathed to his Mother.

With his bullet wound healed, Walter Geary was discharged from hospital in London on 13th March 1915, and sent to 3rd Battalion, Border Regiment which was used to hold soldiers recovering from wounds, together with other reinforcements waiting for overseas postings. After two months retraining with the battalion at Shoeburyness in Essex, Walter was posted to 1st Battalion. In early May, Walter was part of a draft of 300 men and 10 officers sent to Alexandria where they boarded the *Orsyra* for Gallipoli. Whilst on board on 25th May Walter took the opportunity to write a fresh Will. Landing the next day, the new draft immediately joined their unit in the reserve trenches. Their arrival was greeted by a Turkish artillery bombardment and although the shelling did little harm, it was a bad omen. Since mid-May, sinkings by U-boats and enemy torpedo boats had driven the Royal Navy away from Gallipoli's coast depriving the Allies of Naval gunnery, while their lack of land based artillery was becoming a serious problem.

In the weeks between 1st Battalion's landing in late April, and Walter's arrival with the first reinforcements, the Peninsula had turned into a lethal labyrinth. Rugged terrain and constant fighting had created tangled defences crowded so closely together that the opposing sides often shared the same trench with only a barricade between them. Lack of timber and the thin sandy soil over rock, made the construction of deep trenches practically impossible and most had high sandbag walls. Turkish snipers were particularly adept at exploiting any weak spots in the Allied trenches. Movement was hazardous, grave digging difficult and recovering bodies from no-man's-land suicidal. As May turned to June, temperatures rose and everywhere the stench from the corpses and animals decomposing in the open, or lying in shallow graves, significantly increased. Then there were the swarms of flies.

Every morning, extra training was organised for the new men, most of whom were inexperienced and undertrained, to acclimatise them to conditions on the Peninsular and integrate them into the battalion. Apart from the regular rifle and kit inspections, these extra sessions would have included the importance of good hygiene, which considering the disgusting conditions at Gallipoli was just as important.

Walter first entered the firing line in a night relief on 5th June when the battalion moved from reserve positions into Turkish trenches captured the previous day. In places, no-man's-land was merely a sand bag wall and many of the communication trenches needed clearing of enemy dead, even as the Turks were trying to bomb the British out. Attempts to dispose of the many flyblown corpses surrounding their new position proved almost impossible unless they were close to the trench parapets when grapnels and ropes could be used and the bodies buried as best as possible.

A successful surprise night attack by the battalion on 10th June captured Turkey Trench after a fierce bomb and bayonet fight, but a supporting attack against Boomerang Redoubt by the South Wales Borderers failed with heavy loss to both sides. The Turks eventually recovered most of Turkey Trench the next day however, after several counterattacks. By now, 1st Battalion totalled some 700 officers and men, but of those men only about 300 had landed alongside Frederick Geary on 25th April.

Meanwhile, the next big assault was being planned for 28th June, and intended to clear the head of Gulley Ravine and push about half a mile up the coast to Fusiliers Bluff, to prepare the way for the capture of Krithia village. 1st Borders were to spearhead 29th Division's assault by attacking Boomerang Redoubt and Turkey Trench on the east of the Ravine fifteen minutes before the main artillery barrage lifted.

The Battalion left Gully Beach at 16.30 on 27th June to reach the forward trenches from which they would launch their attack. It was the hottest day of the campaign so far and before long, the troops, still wearing woollen serge uniforms and carrying full combat gear, were sweating profusely. Halfway up the gully, the Borders took a short break while their Chaplain conducted an impromptu service concluding with the hymn *'Abide with Me'*.

A two-hour artillery bombardment, supplemented by a French trench mortar, began at 09.00 on 28th June, concentrating on Boomerang Redoubt. As the last shells fell, the Borders' assault parties from 'A' and 'B' Companies dashed forward through the dust and overwhelmed the stunned defenders in Boomerang before Turkish artillery could react. With relatively light casualties, the Borders were able to make hasty repairs to the badly battered trenches. Although the initial assault troops were now relatively sheltered, the men coming over to reinforce them across open ground suffered badly from exploding Turkish shrapnel shells. Moving on to Turkey Trench, the troops were shocked to find that the Turks had filled in a large section following the earlier raid, and replaced it with a new trench. Without cover, all the assaulting party were killed or wounded by fire from the new trench; the support troops fared little better. When reinforcements arrived however, they linked up with the Borders in Boomerang and the Turkish garrison surrendered.

Meanwhile, at 11.00, the main barrage lifted on to the Turkish reserve lines and the rest of 87th Brigade attacked with 156th Brigade alongside. Then 86th Brigade leapfrogged 87th to attack Turkish trenches higher up the Ravine and 1st Battalion advanced up Gully Ravine to convert the captured Turkish reserve trenches into fire trenches and link up with the battalions either side, repeatedly having to beat off fierce Turkish counterattacks throughout the afternoon and into the night. 1st Battalion remained astride Gully Ravine working on the captured trenches short of Fusilier Bluff in reserve, before returning to the firing line on 1st July.

Overall casualties for 1st Battalion during the battle were 2 officers killed, 7 officers wounded and 153 men killed or wounded. One of those wounded was Walter Geary, who suffered gunshot wounds to his chest and neck. Walter's Service Record initially shows him as '*Missing in Action*', so it is likely that medical orderlies found him after the battle. Initially passed to the medical staff of 87th Field Ambulance, Walter was taken to the tented Advanced Dressing Station in Gully Ravine. A horse ambulance later transported Walter to the Casualty Clearing Station, (CCS), on Gully Beach.

What happened next was commonplace in the confusion of battle, especially during the Gallipoli Campaign. It seems that the Gully Beach CCS transferred Walter to the Hospital Ship *Somali*, anchored off Helles Bay, which transported wounded soldiers from Gallipoli to hospitals on Malta. Walter's name appeared in *The Times* of 6th August, among the list of those recently wounded in action at Gallipoli, probably based on information sent from the CCS. This came as a shock to his family, who had received no communication from the War Office as to his fate. As a result, both Walter's mother and brother, Charles, who was serving as an Army Service Corps as a Driver, contacted the War Office asking for confirmation whether he had survived, and if so, where he was. Walter's former employer, the London and North Western Railway, wrote a similar letter to the War Office, but Walter's Service Record contains no replies to any of these letters. According to the document formalising his Will, dated June 1916, Walter died of his wounds aboard the *Somali* on 29th June 1915, and his body was buried at sea. Like his brother Frederick, Walter left all his personal possessions to his mother.

Both Frederick and Walter's names now appear on the Helles Memorial on the Gallipoli Peninsula.

Captain Nigel Clement Charles HADDEN
14th Battery, Royal Field Artillery

9th April 1916

The Haddens were an old Aberdeen family of hosiery manufacturers with a long tradition of voluntary service, both civic and military. Nigel Hadden's father and grandfather both came from Nottingham, the base of the family's hosiery business. In addition, the family also had a strong connection with India. Charles Stanton Hadden, Nigel's paternal grandfather, travelled with a cousin to the highlands of Ceylon in 1840, where they joined the British rush to clear the jungle and plant coffee. By 1870, the Haddens, and men like them, helped to turn Ceylon into the world's largest coffee producer.

The Hadden family's association with Northchurch began in the mid-1860s when Charles Stanton Hadden purchased the 17th century estate of Rossway to the south of the village. He had most of the old house demolished and commissioned the Italianate style Victorian country house that still stands today. Construction of the new house ended in 1867, but the Haddens had been in residence for less than ten years when they faced financial ruin.

In about 1875, the coffee rust fungus, *Hemileia vastatrix*, reached Ceylon and spread rapidly across the plantations, wiping out 95% of the island's coffee production in under two decades. Plantation owners had no choice but to plant another crop and most of them chose to grow tea. Reconstructing their plantations took considerable time and money, so as a temporary measure the Hadden family decided to leave Northchurch and rent out Rossway. It was not until 1903, with their financial problems resolved, that the Hadden family returned to their Northchurch home.

Nigel Clement Charles Hadden was born at 69 Onslow Gardens in Kensington on 26th February 1893. The same year his father, Lieutenant Colonel Charles Frederick Hadden, became Chief Inspector at the Royal Arsenal at Woolwich. Lieutenant Colonel Hadden had received his Commission in the Royal Artillery twenty years earlier and quickly moved up through the ranks, becoming the assistant to the Superintendent, Royal Laboratory in 1885 and Inspector of Laboratory Stores three years later. By 1901, he was a member of the influential Ordnance Committee, undertaking a thorough review of the artillery requirements for the British Army and later became the Commandant of the Ordnance College at Woolwich. Lieutenant Colonel Charles Hadden subsequently served as Director of Artillery at Woolwich from 1904 to 1907, and was a member of a special committee set up by Prime Minister, Herbert Asquith, to explore the new concept of using aircraft to spot enemy positions for the artillery. He was later Master General of the Ordnance and a Member of Army Council and in the 1908 King's Birthday Honours, he received a KCB. Between 1913 and 1915, Hadden was President of the Ordnance Board and Royal Artillery Committee with the rank of Major General. Outside of army life, between 1915 and 1922 Major General Sir Charles Frederick Hadden KCB was the Chairman of Northchurch Parish Council and in 1919, he became the High Sheriff of Hertfordshire.

His son, Nigel, attended Winchester College, Hampshire between 1906 and 1910 where, not surprisingly, he became a Corporal in the school's Officer Training Corps. In 1910, he embarked on his own military career in the Royal Artillery and entered the Royal Military College at Woolwich as a Gentleman Cadet. Hadden received his commission in July 1912 and the following month Second Lieutenant Hadden was posted to 43rd Battery Royal Field Artillery, XII Brigade, 1st Division, based at Deep Cut Barracks, Farnborough, Surrey.

Hadden's new Battery was equipped with the 4.5-inch howitzer, which was probably the best artillery field piece of its day. It had entered service with the British Army in 1909 to replace the old 5-inch BL howitzer. Served by a detachment of six men, the 4.5-inch howitzer was simple, reliable and, when elevated to 45°, could lob its 35.1-pound high explosive shell as far as 4.6 miles, outranging all other guns of its calibre.

One of Hadden's first tasks at Deep Cut, in September 1912, was to lead his new unit through the Command and Army Manoeuvres around the Newmarket and Cambridge area. 43rd Battery remained at Deep Cut until October 1913 when it moved to Victoria Barracks in Clonmel, the county town of South Tipperary in Ireland. Hadden was still in Clonmel when war broke out the following August.

Upon mobilisation, Hadden transferred to 14th Battery, 4th Brigade RFA coming under the

Captain Nigel Clement Charles Haddon
(Source: British Library)

command of the 7th (Meerut) Division of the Indian Army. The Battery embarked for France on 9th September 1914, but had to wait for the arrival of the Meerut Division, whose departure from India had been delayed by the German raiders *Emden* and *Konigsberg* operating in the Indian Ocean. The Indian troops finally landed at Marseilles in mid-October, but further delays ensued while they received modern rifles. The division eventually saw action as a complete formation during October and November 1914 at the Battle of La Basseé during the defence of the nearby villages of Festubert and Givenchy-lès-la-Bassée. Not surprisingly the Indian troops, being used to somewhat different conditions, found the European late autumn and winter conditions particularly harsh.

The German Army decided to stand on the defensive on the Western Front over the winter of 1914/15, while concentrating on the Eastern Front, where fewer German divisions had been having a bigger success against the Russian Army. Another major victory there would bolster Austria-Hungary and might discourage Romania and Italy from joining the Allies.

The BEF also badly needed this respite to rebuild its strength as its overall expertise was falling as Territorials and raw Dominion troops replaced the old Regulars lost in 1914. In particular, the shortage of experienced junior leaders, lieutenants, sergeants and corporals, was a serious problem. The Indian Army divisions were used to internal security and mountain warfare in small formations and although their artillery benefitted from well-trained professionals such as Nigel Hadden, their different units were unused to fighting as a full division. Meanwhile, the Kitchener volunteer battalions, formed from the men who had enlisted when war broke out, were still under training in Britain and would not be ready for some time.

The French priority was straightforward, they would retake as much occupied territory as possible, not merely for sentimental reasons, but because it contained important resources that French industry needed back. That winter, Joffre chose to cut out the German salient between Reims and Arras, which bulged towards Paris, by attacking east from Artois and north from Champagne. Like the BEF, the French Army was also desperately short of heavy artillery, even mounting old fortress guns on improvised field carriages. The French only had enough big guns to attack one area of the front at a time, which allowed the Germans to concentrate their reserves and stifle each attack. Moreover, French tactics were costly, the Champagne offensive alone cost France some 250,000 casualties.

Joffre needed fresh troops when he again attacked at Artois and Champagne in the spring of 1915. He also needed the BEF, small as it was, to attack elsewhere along the front to divert German reserves. Politically the BEF itself also needed to show it could do more to help France, as soon as the Regular 29th Division arrived, it took over trenches from the French IX Corps, to free it for operations in Artois.

A plan for the first offensive by British Empire troops on the Western Front was approved in mid-February. General Haig's First Army was to eliminate the German salient around Neuve-Chapelle, midway between Béthune and Lille, on a 2,000-yard front using the Indian Corps and IV Corps. Their attacks were to converge on Neuve-Chapelle, before moving on to secure the high ground of Aubers Ridge thus threatening German communications to Lille. At the same time, the French would attack in Artois. Aerial reconnaissance provided accurate trench maps allowing the attacking battalions to rehearse their initial assault in detail.

The British artillery planned to adopt the new method developed by the French over the previous months. A sudden, swift, massed artillery bombardment was to smash the enemy's wire and trenches until the moment the infantry attacked, when the guns switched to laying down a barrier of shells (*barrage* in French), to stop German reinforcements reaching the battle. The BEF allocated 100,000 rounds, one-sixth of its total stock of artillery shells, for the whole battle. For the first time ever, aircraft guided the artillery onto their specific objectives, something that Hadden's father had pioneered during his time as Director of Artillery at Woolwich. Ominously, 29th Division was diverted to the Dardanelles forcing the French to cancel IX Corps' supporting attack in Artois.

At 07.30 on 10th March, almost 500 guns, including Hadden's battery, opened fire. Hadden's 4.5-inch howitzers, and the heavier artillery with half the 18-pdr field guns, concentrated on the trenches, while the remaining 18-pdrs fired on the wire using shrapnel shells. After 35 minutes of bombardment, the guns lifted from the trenches and began firing a barrage behind the lines to isolate the battlefield. Five of the eight assault battalions took their objectives, including Neuve-Chapelle itself, but delays on the flanks and poor communication between the two Corps caused the attack to lose impetus.

The British barrage at Neuve-Chapelle was the heaviest concentration per yard of enemy line that fired until 1917, with the bombardment penetrating the German lines up to a depth of some 1,200 yards over a two-mile front. Despite a counterattack by 16,000 Germans, Neuve-Chapelle remained in British hands. It had not, however, been possible to prevent the Germans bringing up reserves to stabilise their lines and the second objective of capturing Aubers Ridge, and then breaking out, had failed. When Haig suspended the battle on 12th March, First Army had suffered over 11,600 casualties. The BEF had shown it could mount a substantial offensive alone and, understanding that artillery had been pivotal, realised that it needed more guns and much, much more ammunition. The Germans also took note and strengthened their defences.

The Germans had their own ammunition difficulties when they returned to the offensive at Ypres on 22nd April. To compensate for their lack of high explosive shell, the German High Command authorised the first use of a lethal chemical weapon, chlorine gas, which was to have far-reaching consequences.

Meerut Division was again in action with First Army the following month in a renewed attempt to take Aubers Ridge. This time their assault was in support of a major French attack against the German lines on Vimy Ridge to the south. Once again, a heavy bombardment preceded the assault, but there were no extra guns available and only enough shells to sustain a 45-minute bombardment.

At 05.30 on 9th May, the artillery opened fire on the trenches and barbed wire defences that the Germans had worked hard to strengthen in the past weeks. When the bombardment ceased and the assault troops entered no-man's-land, they found to their horror that the bombardment had had a very limited effect. Shelling resumed at 06.15 to suppress intense machine gun fire from undamaged German positions, although it was unclear whether any British troops were now in the target area. At 07.45 Hadden's battery and others of the Meerut Division, received orders to lay down another barrage, but this only provoked retaliatory fire from the German guns. By 08.30 the infantry attack had come to a standstill, with isolated pockets of troops spread across the battlefield. Preparations for a fresh assault at 13.30 ended after a German artillery bombardment inflicted many casualties in the assembly areas. By evening, the British attack had ended and any troops that had managed to get close to the German lines gradually filtered back to their own trenches overnight. With reserves of artillery shells discovered to be extremely low the British ended the battle the next day. The assault on 9th May resulted in over 11,000 British casualties, most of them within yards of their own front line.

On 13th May, a final attempt to take Aubers Ridge began with a preliminary bombardment by 433 artillery pieces along a 5,000-yard front. The larger 6-inch howitzers concentrated on the German trenches to create gaps for the attacking infantry to pass through, while the 4.5-inch howitzers and some of the field guns disrupted the German support lines. Most of the 18-pdr field guns fired shrapnel shells at the wire defences - although they had previously proved to be unsuitable for wire cutting, the shortage of high explosive shells made their use unavoidable.

At 22.00 on 15th May, the infantry was in position and 90 minutes later they attacked. This was the first night assault that the BEF attempted, and the first wave of attackers, exploiting the element of surprise, managed to break through the German lines in places. The Indian infantry however, suffered badly from machine gun fire. At 01.45, the artillery launched another barrage to coincide with the next attack but over the coming hours, the battle turned into a repeat of the earlier attempts to take Aubers Ridge. First Army's casualties increased by a further 16,000, and once again it highlighted the need for far more artillery and suitable ammunition to be in place before it was possible to make a tangible mark on the German defences.

Throughout the summer of 1915, the shortage of big guns with sufficient and suitable ammunition and the diversion of experienced formations to the Dardanelles continued to hamper the BEF on the Western Front. Fresh divisions of Kitchener's New Army began to arrive however, and French pressure on the BEF to support their next major push in Artois was becoming hard to resist. As result, during late September 1915 the British agreed to mount a subsidiary attack in the mining district around the village of Loos in support of a renewed French effort to take Vimy Ridge.

Haig objected that his troops would be attacking over flat ground which could easily be swept by machine gun fire, but Joffre insisted the British must attack Loos and Haig was overruled. For the reserves, Sir John French chose two Kitchener divisions, 21st and 24th, which had only arrived during September and had never seen the trenches or been under fire. French also insisted that he keep these reserves well back and under his personal command, not Haig's. There was still too little heavy artillery for intense shelling, so a long, continuous bombardment to wear down the German troops and grind down their trench works was proposed. Just before the assault, the first British use of chlorine gas would augment the shellfire. By employing a cloud of poison gas with smoke hiding his flanks, Haig could suppress German machine guns over a wider front, but only if the wind was right for the use of gas. Haig had to attack when the French did so. If the weather was unsuitable for gas on the day, he would attack on a much narrower front.

At first light on 21st September 1915, Hadden's battery was among the 110 heavy guns and 84 guns and howitzers that began a steady, day and night bombardment of the German trenches. Four days later, at 05.48, a mine exploded under the German lines, about 200 yards left of the Meerut Division's Bareilly Brigade. Two minutes later, men of the Special Brigade, Royal Engineers opened almost 5,000 chlorine gas cylinders and a sickly yellow cloud, formed over no-man's-land, but the failing breeze only moved it slowly towards the German positions. At 06.00, British troops, including New Army divisions of Kitchener volunteers, left their trenches wearing anti-gas hoods while the artillery barrage lifted onto the German second line. The chlorine gas cloud had mixed results. German troops of *13th Regiment*, opposite the Meerut Division, reported that, 'Protected by these clouds the English managed to get to our trenches', but men of the Bareilly Brigade could not see in the yellow fog and lost their way.

Overall, the first day went well. British troops overran the village of Hulluch and Loos fell, presenting a genuine opportunity to break through the German's second line, but it had to be captured quickly. Unfortunately, thanks to poor planning, the inexperienced reserves arrived too late, tired and disorganised to exploit the initial success. German reinforcements were quicker, and although 21st and 24th Divisions made some progress, several counterattacks threw them back, almost routing them.

Loos proved once again that it was possible to overwhelm strongly fortified German lines, albeit at considerable cost, but that to breakthrough required a swift and strong follow up. The Battle of Loos cost the British over 61,000 casualties including some 7,800 killed and cost Sir John French his job as Commander in Chief of the BEF. By December 1915, having lost the support of the Government, he resigned and was replaced by Sir Douglas Haig. The Battle of Loos was also the last battle that Lieutenant Nigel Hadden was to fight on European soil.

Following the Allied declaration of war against Turkey, units of the Indian Army, known as 'Force D', had landed at Fao in Mesopotamia to safeguard the Anglo-Persian oilfields and the pipeline that ran to the oil refinery at Abadan on the Shatt al Arab River. On 25th November, British troops occupied Basra and by the end of 1914, after the Battle of Qurna, they had consolidated their position, securing the nearby oilfields.

The Turks knew to wait for the better weather in April before mounting their first serious attack against the British base at Shaiba. Their attack was successfully repulsed, however, with the Turks incurring heavy losses. This easy success encouraged 'Force D', under Lieutenant General Sir John Nixon of the Indian Army, to contemplate an offensive rather than a defensive stance. He gained permission for an advance to the town of Kut al Amara, although Nixon's eyes were actually fixed on Baghdad further north. Without usable roads or railways, the only way to supply a large force was by the two long, meandering rivers that gave Mesopotamia its name. General Nixon sent his main force up the Euphrates and 6th Division under Major General Charles Townshend up the Tigris. Both columns were supplied by river steamers, towed barges and a motley collection of smaller craft. The Euphrates advance soon stalled against vigorous Turkish resistance, whereas Townshend, driving his division through the exceptional summer of 1915, reached Kut, which the Turks abandoned on 27th September after a finely balanced two-day battle.

Meanwhile, Austen Chamberlain, the Secretary of State for India, was worried that the morale of Indian troops on the Western Front was adversely affected by their recent heavy casualties. The Viceroy of India had similar concerns, but was also worried that setbacks in Flanders and the deadlock on Gallipoli threatened British prestige and could strengthen the burgeoning home rule movement in India. On a practical level, Flanders was simply too distant for Indian reinforcements to reach easily, while the British Army Service Corps struggled to cater for the various dietary requirements of Hindu, Muslim, Parsee and other Indian battalions. It was therefore proposed that 3rd (Lahore) and 7th (Meerut) Divisions should be withdrawn from France as soon as possible and sent to Mesopotamia where they might be supplied and reinforced directly from India. Orders for the transfer of the Indian Corps to the Mesopotamian Expeditionary Force arrived in late October 1915 and 14th Battery, RFA, with newly promoted Captain Nigel Hadden, prepared to move to a new battleground.

At Kut, General Nixon was keen to continue the 120 miles to Baghdad. Townshend objected that his division was too weak and his supply lines, currently almost 400 miles long, too stretched, but Nixon held sway and the advance continued. Weary and already short of rations, 6th Division reached the extensive Turkish defence works at Ctesiphon, only 22 miles from Baghdad, and attacked at dawn on 22nd November. The Battle of Ctesiphon was badly coordinated and only part of the first line was captured. Although held for 36 hours against fierce counterattacks, the second line remained intact and its Turkish defenders, under German Field Marshal, Baron von der Goltz, showed no signs of giving up. By the 24th, with half of his force killed or wounded, Townshend could get no further and, with Nixon's agreement, he retreated the hundred miles back to Kut al Amara.

On 4th December, the hungry and exhausted Anglo-Indian force arrived at Kut and dug in. Four days later, some 12,000 Turkish troops arrived and laid siege to the town. With the Tigris at its lowest ebb, Townshend could only eke out what he had and wait for the river to rise bringing the arrival of relief or fresh supplies. On Christmas Eve 1915, the Turks made their only concerted effort to capture Kut by assault, after which they left just enough troops to contain the garrison and sent the rest down the Tigris to create a series of positions to block any relief force.

The two Indian Divisions were due at Basra on 1st December, but fear of submarine attack in the Mediterranean delayed their departure from Marseilles. The Indian divisions, stopped in Egypt to receive fresh equipment, before continuing separately to Basra. Delays caused by inadequate port facilities and overcrowding at Basra had forced 7th Division's units to make their way up the Tigris one by one as they obtained transport. Sappers of the Meerut Division had already built a road from the Shatt al Arab, but it still took a two-week march to reach Ali Gharbi, where the 11,500-strong relief force under Lt. General Sir Fenton Aylmer was assembling. By the time the ships containing Haddon and the rest of 14th Battery dropped anchor at Basra in February 1916, infantry of the Meerut Division had already been in action three times on the Tigris.

Heavy rain throughout February had filled the marshes and put a halt to operations. At the beginning of March, the Relief Force resumed its advance along the muddy, narrow strip of land between the Tigris and the Suwaikiyeh Marsh to the next obstacle, the Dujaila Redoubt on the south bank. By now, the Kut garrison was subsisting on mules and horses, which the Indian troops would not eat and they had to resort to shooting wild birds for food.

The plan of attack on Dujaila required a surprise bombardment at dawn before the assault. The infantry made a successful night approach, but their artillery could not keep up. At first light on 8th March, the infantry found the Turkish trenches lightly manned and the redoubt apparently undefended, but they were told to stick to the plan and wait, in full view of the enemy, for the bombardment. The first guns to arrive came into action at 07.00, since surprise was already lost, but by the time all the batteries had assembled, registered and completed their fire plan it was 10.00 and the Turks had reinforced their defences before the infantry attacked, with predictable results.

After failing at Dujaila, Aylmer decided to advance along the north bank instead. On 5th April, his Anglo-Indian force attacked the Turkish garrison at Hanna, which immediately withdrew three and a half miles to their next position at Fallaliyeh. Two Indian Brigades attacked Fallaliyeh that night and again the defenders withdrew, but the day's fighting had cost another 2,000 casualties. In an effort to prevent the Turks re-organising, the Meerut Division passed through and advanced four miles to the next Turkish line at Sannaiyat while its artillery struggled to follow in the mud. The Division was supposed to attack the Sannaiyat position in the early hours of 7th April, but at daybreak the infantry were still 800 yards away from the trenches. The Turks unleashed a murderous fire, halting the attack and bringing down 1,200 men. Then, as the British and Indian troops tried to dig in, strong winds caused the marshes to overflow, drowning some of the wounded. Artillery positions were also threatened and Hadden's gunners hurriedly threw up earthen banks around them to keep the water out.

As the food shortage in Kut al Amara became critical, 7th Division received orders to advance as far as possible without committing itself to an engagement with Turkish forces. On 8th April, the troops only advanced another three hundred yards before coming under fire, forcing them to dig in, a thousand yards from the Turkish trenches. After dark, a five-minute bombardment of the Turkish defences, followed by the firing of British rockets, fooled the Turkish troops into sending up flares and revealing their positions. This allowed a more accurate bombardment, providing an opportunity for infantry of 13th Division to approach within 300 yards of the Turkish trenches.

At 03.00 on the 9th April, 13th Division executed a carefully planned assault stretching six hundred yards with 7th Meerut Division in reserve. The assault troops gained the first line of trenches, but the Turks counterattacked with hand grenades driving the British out again.

Hadden was in a dugout near the Abu Romans Mound observing for his battery, when at 08.00 they were heavily shelled by Turkish artillery. An hour later the shelling stopped, and Hadden moved to a trench about two hundred yards from his own battery. While he was there, the Turks resumed their shelling and Hadden set off back to his observation post to direct his Battery, crossing open ground in the process. Shells were coming slowly at intervals and one exploded close by, but he walked calmly on. He was only a few yards from the Battery's dugout when another shell seemed to burst right on him. Horrified witnesses expected to see him blown to pieces, however Hadden struggled across the last remaining yards and fell wounded into the dugout.

It was an hour before a field ambulance could take Hadden to a dressing station. He seemed quite conscious and without pain, and it appeared that he had only received a shrapnel injury to his thigh. Later, when at the dressing station however, medical troops discovered that a piece of shrapnel had passed through Hadden's abdomen, and he died ten minutes later, two hours after being hit.

On Wednesday 12th April 1916 a telegram, addressed to Major General Sir Charles Hadden, arrived at Rossway; it said simply 'Deeply regret to inform you that Captain N.C.C. Hadden R.F.A. died of wounds April 9th Tigris Line. Lord Kitchener expresses his sympathy.'

Exactly two weeks later, a large congregation of parishioners and friends from neighbouring parishes gathered at St Mary's Church to hear Rev. R.H. Pope conduct a memorial service for Captain Nigel Hadden, RFA. The Choir led the congregation in two hymns, *Peace, Perfect Peace* and *On the Resurrection Morning*, and Canon Wood read the lesson.

All further attempts to relieve Kut al Amara failed and the besieged garrison surrendered on 29th April. Turkish treatment of the other ranks was appalling; of the 10,061 combatants who surrendered, about 4,000 were to die in captivity. The Relief Force's casualties between 5th and 23rd April were just under 10,000 men, more than a quarter of the force. In the four months between January and April, during the efforts to relieve Kut al Amara, they had lost some 23,000 in battle casualties alone, plus all the uncounted numbers of sick men.

Nigel Clement Charles Hadden's body was buried about three quarters of a mile from the Tigris River on the right bank, equidistant between Abu Roman and Mason's Mounds. His father later received a hand-drawn map showing the location of the grave, although the actual grave was later lost. Nigel Hadden's name is one of 40,682 soldiers who died during the operations in Mesopotamia from the autumn of 1914 to the end of August 1921 and recorded on the Basra Memorial in modern day Iraq. His name also appears in Winchester College's War Cloister and on a brass plaque on the south wall of the nave at St Mary's Church, Northchurch.

Major Hubert Wallace THELWALL
1st Battalion, West India Regiment, attached 15th Battalion, Nottinghamshire & Derbyshire Regiment

23rd April 1916

The Thelwalls originated from the town of Thelwall in Cheshire and migrated to the Vale of Clwyd, now part of Denbighshire, during the thirteenth century. Later the family settled in the area around Plas-y-ward, near the parishes of Ruthin and Llanrhydd and for several centuries this became the seat of the family's main branch. By the mid-Tudor period, the Thelwalls had become one of the county's leading families with one member, Simon Thelwall, sitting in the House of Commons as the Member of Parliament for Denbighshire. That same Simon Thelwall later became a notorious persecutor of Catholics, sentencing at least one man to death by hanging, drawing and quartering in his capacity of Deputy Judge of the Court of the Marches. Another Simon Thelwall also represented Denbighshire during the reign of Charles I and fought for Cromwell alongside several other family members during the English Civil War. Another 17th Century ancestor of Hubert Thelwall, a Welsh lawyer named Eubule Thelwall, became Principal of Jesus College, Oxford.

Hubert Wallace Thelwall, known in the family as Bertie, was born at Branston Lodge, Southsea, Hampshire on 11th February 1876. His father, Lieutenant Colonel Eubule Daysh Thelwall, had recently retired from the Royal Marine Artillery. Eubule Thelwall had begun as a naval cadet aged 12 in 1840 and was first commission into the Royal Marine Artillery in 1848, becoming 1st Lieutenant three years later. He served aboard HMS *Leopard* between 1853 and 1856 during the Crimean War against Russia and was present at the siege of Sebastopol. Rising through the ranks, Eubule Thelwall became a Captain in 1859 and two years later was transferred to the British North America and West Indies station in Bermuda. In 1865, he married Mary Elizabeth Dorothea Williams, the daughter of a local clergyman, at Aber in Denbighshire. Promoted again to Major in 1872, Eubule Thelwall retired at Portsmouth three years later at his own request, and was promoted to the Honorary rank of Lieutenant Colonel.

Two years later, the Thelwall family consisting of Eubule and his wife, Mary, their sons Bevis, Eubule, John, Hubert and Ernest and daughters Mary, Gertrude, Hephizibah, Rosabel and Gwynedd, moved to Ballasalla House, a large, eight-bedroomed mansion, complete with private trout stream, in the Parish of Malew on the Isle of Man. Not long afterwards, Eubule Thelwall became a Manx Justice of the Peace.

After six years on the island, the Thelwalls decided to auction off most of the contents of Ballasalla House and move to Berkhamsted. Here they settled at 205 Charles Street and later moved to Oak Vale in Shrublands Road, becoming regular worshipers at St Mary's, Northchurch. In 1885 Hubert started as a 'Day Boy' at Berkhamsted School.

Eubule Thelwall had played cricket for his native Denbighshire in his youth, and Hubert, sharing his father's love of the sport, became a regular player for various local junior cricket teams, with his exploits frequently being reported in *The Bucks Herald*. Tragedy struck the family in May 1889, when Hubert's older brother, Eubule Howard Thelwall, died suddenly aged only 18. Eubule Howard had suffered with heart disease for a number of years, something that would afflict the other brothers in later life.

With his family's strong military background, it is not surprising that Hubert decided to follow a career in the army. On 3rd October 1893, he enlisted for twelve years with 1st Battalion, Nottinghamshire & Derbyshire Regiment, The Sherwood Foresters. Aged 18, Hubert stood just over 5 feet 8 inches tall, and had grey eyes and fair hair. Within five months, Hubert was appointed lance corporal and eleven months later, became a corporal. Hubert's rise through the ranks continued with acting sergeant in February 1896 and sergeant two years later, but just twelve days after that promotion, on 21st March 1898, Hubert left the army due to family circumstances.

At that time, Article 1142 of the Army Code allowed trained men to buy themselves out early upon a simple payment of £18. Hubert had served with the Sherwood Foresters for just four years and 170 days. He immediately travelled to Dooars, in the foothills of the eastern Himalayas, to take over his elder brother's tea plantation. Bevis Thelwall, who had bought Hubert out of the army, had been seriously ill for some time and he died at Dooars shortly after Hubert's arrival.

Hubert's time at Dooars was however expectantly brief. On 11th October 1899, the Second Boer War broke out between the British Government of South Africa and the Afrikaner settlers living in the Orange Free State and the Transvaal, who wanted full independence. During the ensuing war against the Boers, volunteer contingents from across the British Empire fought alongside the British Army. One of these volunteer groups called 'Lumsden's Horse' was formed in Calcutta by Lt. Col. Dugald Mactavish Lumsden of the Assam Valley Light Horse. Lumsden's Horse recruited tea planters, railway engineers and other British expatriates around a core of volunteers from Indian Army regiments, including Lumsden's own. Hubert and his younger brother, Ernest, employed by the Lungla Tea Company of Sylhet, were among the tea planters who enrolled in 'B' Company, N°1 Section of Lumsden's Horse.

'A' Company of Lumsden's Horse left Calcutta on 26th February 1900, bound for Cape Town. 'B' Company, which included Hubert and Ernest Thelwall, sailed a week later and landed at East London on the Eastern Cape. Both companies joined the army of Lord Roberts, the British Commander in Chief, at Bloemfontein the following month. On the 21st April, Lumsden's Horse left their camp to join General Tucker's Division, which had been holding some hills captured a month earlier following the Battle of Karee Siding. Lumsden's Horse saw its first action on 30th April, suffering twelve casualties. During that engagement, while 'B' Company was leading a column intended to flush the Boers out of a line of small hills, Hubert became separated from the rest of the company during heavy fire. Fortunately, a lull in the fighting allowed Hubert to retrieve his horse and rejoin his Company.

For a time, Hubert worked in the remount department at Johannesburg until the depot closed. Lumsden's Horse later participated in the advance against Pretoria, the Boer capital, which fell in June 1900. Hubert fell ill the following month and spent a short period in hospital before the doctors decided to send him to England to recover. At the end of 1900, a victorious Lumsden's Horse returned to India to great acclaim. For his service during the Boer War Hubert later received the Queen's medal with three clasps, (Johannesburg, Cape Colony and Orange Free State).

Hubert had regained his liking for army life and never resumed the life of a tea planter. On 6th October 1900, he was commissioned 2nd Lieutenant with the West India Regiment based in Jamaica. Eight months later, he became a 1st Lieutenant. The carefree life of the Regiment's subalterns was described at the time as: 'In the daytime the young West Indian Army officer gets through his early morning work as quickly as possible and then scrambles, schoolboy fashion, into the playing fields... After dinner, he becomes the social animal, and the mess-room and barrack-yard know him no more till midnight.'

Fifteen months later, in January 1902, Hubert was seconded for eight months to the Colonial Office in London. His role was to help establish a new West African Frontier Force covering Northern and Southern Nigeria, The Gambia, The Gold Coast and Sierra Leone.

Back in England, Hubert's mother, Mary, died suddenly on 31st January 1903, aged just 59. Her funeral took place at St Mary's, Northchurch the following month, with her coffin being buried in the churchyard in a plot set aside for the Thelwall family.

Not long after returning to Jamaica, Hubert heard that another secondment awaited him. This time it was to the West African Regiment, based in Freetown, Sierra Leone, doubtless as a result of his earlier experience establishing the West African Frontier Force. Hubert arrived at Bristol aboard the *Port Maria* on 3rd September and spent some time with his ageing father in Berkhamsted before leaving Liverpool aboard the *Bututu,* bound for Freetown,

Although the West African Regiment had once been instrumental in consolidating Britain's position as the leading colonial power in West Africa, by 1903 its only responsibility was the defence of Sierra Leone alongside a battalion of the West African Frontier Force. On 1st March 1908, Thelwall received a local promotion to Captain and with it came responsibility for liaison with the West African Frontier Force in Sierra Leone and in Nigeria.

While Hubert flourished in Africa, tragedy struck again at his family home at Oakdene in Shrublands Road. On 24th June 1908, another of his brothers, 33-year-old John Humphrey Thelwall, died from heart disease. John Humphrey had also been a tea planter in India, but ill health had forced his return to England. The following February, Hubert's last surviving brother and old comrade with Lumsden's Horse, Ernest Adair Thelwall, died in India aged only 32.

There was cause for some celebration in the Thelwall household later that year however, with the marriage at St Mary's, Northchurch of Hubert's sister, Gynnedd, to Hugh Ralph Satow, a son of Samuel Augustus Mason Satow, a Master in the Chancery Division of the High Court in London who lived in Berkhamsted.

Ending his secondment to the West African Regiment in May 1909, Hubert departed Lagos aboard the *Landana* for England. He remained at home for six months before returning to Jamaica in his substantive rank of Lieutenant. On 1st December 1910, Hubert married Angel May Holland Hastings, the eldest daughter of Commander WCH Hastings, RN, at St Andrew's Church, Half Way Tree, in Jamaica. Angel had been born in Jamaica in 1885 where her father had remained after he retired from the Royal Navy.

Following his honeymoon, Hubert returned to the West India Regiment's establishment and was appointed Regimental Adjutant nine months later. Regimental life continued as before, with Hubert's prowess at tennis faithfully being chronicled by the local newspaper, *The Gleener.* In 1912 Hubert returned to Sierra Leone where one battalion of the West India Regiment was based with his wife and whilst there their first son,

Major Hubert Wallace Thelwall (Source: Simon Thelwall)

Bevis, was born. Sadly, he died 5 weeks later. On 12th November 1913, Hubert was promoted to Captain.

In August 1914, Hubert was again visiting Sierra Leone, having left his pregnant wife in England. He hurriedly returned home, possibly arriving in time to see his ailing father. Lieutenant Colonel Eubule Thelwall had been in declining health since his wife's death, and had been cared for by his three daughters. He died at Oakdene on 23rd September, aged 86. Eubule's funeral was held at St Mary's, Northchurch on 26th September 1914 and he was buried in the churchyard alongside his wife. A few weeks later, Hubert became a father for a second time when Angel Thelwall gave birth to a son, Gerald Eubule Hastings Thelwall, in London.

On his return to England, Hubert applied to rejoin his old Regiment, but instead received an attachment to an unusual unit, 15th (Service) Battalion, (Nottingham Bantams), The Sherwood Foresters. Overwhelmed by the flood of volunteers responding to Lord Kitchener's call in 1914, the Army initially stuck to its pre-war standards and rejected men under 5ft 3inches tall. Alfred Biglan, Member of Parliament for Birkenhead, subsequently suggested that able-bodied men below the regulation height should be allowed to join special battalions. A sceptical War Office offered no objection to Biglan raising such a battalion at his own expense and the call went out for 'small and pugnacious' men between the height of five foot and five foot two, with an expanded chest measurement of 33 inches, to volunteer for a new 'Bantam' battalion. Biglan attracted enough recruits to form two battalions and the idea caught on among other County Regiments.

Consequently, in February 1915, the Nottingham Bantams became the Sherwood Foresters' newest battalion and that June, it left Nottingham for Masham in Yorkshire to join 105th Brigade, 35th (Bantam) Division. Officially taken onto the strength of the Army on 27th August 1915, 15th Battalion moved to Bulford Camp at Tidworth on Salisbury Plain. The following month, Hubert Thelwall, now a Major, became the Battalion's Second in Command.

The Nottingham Bantams spent the autumn and early winter months of 1915 training, route marching and digging endless practice trenches in and around Bulford Camp. Initially put on notice to sail for Mesopotamia in December and issued with oversized tropical uniforms, new orders came on 28th January 1916 for the Division to embark instead for France. At 09.00 the following day, the Battalion's Transport, led by Hubert, 2 fellow officers, 102 men, 21 vehicles and 9 bicycles entrained for Southampton. The departure of the Battalion's main body, 29 officers and 892 men, was delayed until 1st February when they crossed by the Folkestone - Boulogne route. Next day they entrained for St Omer and marched from there to Renescure, where Hubert and the Battalion Transport had spent a few days waiting their arrival.

The Battalion spent the following month training in the area southeast of St Omer as the British Army introduced new divisions as its contribution to the proposed Franco-British Summer Offensive. Meanwhile, on 21st February, at Verdun, 130,000 German troops backed by 1,000 guns began the battle intended to 'Bleed France White'; that battle would have an enormous impact on subsequent British battle plans.

On 7th March, the Nottingham men marched to Le Touret, just north of Béthune, for attachment to 10th South Wales Borderers who would give them practical instruction in the front-line trenches. Of note was that Bantams always carried the additional weight of two filled sandbags for placing on the trench fire-steps to stand on so that they could shoot over normal-height trench parapets. The Battalion settled into a routine of two weeks in billets followed by four days in the trenches.

Two weeks later, on 23rd April 1916, the Nottinghamshire Bantams were in the trenches east of Béthune, in the Ferme du Bois sector, which their War Diary for the day described as 'very quiet, enemy particularly inactive'. The Diary continues however: '... 1 casualty – Major H W Thelwall – killed'. How Hubert came to die is uncertain, but a German sniper probably picked him out as an officer by his height among the diminutive Bantams.

Major Hubert Wallace Thelwall's body now rests in the impressive Le Touret Military Cemetery just outside Béthune. Towards the end of 1916, members of the Thelwall family arranged for the placing of a brass plaque commemorating Hubert and his two brothers Bevis and Ernest on the south wall in St Mary's, Northchurch. Hubert's name does not appear on the Northchurch War Memorial, but is shown on the Berkhamsted memorial.

Hubert's wife, Angel and son, Gerald, returned to Jamaica in November 1916, where they remained for several years.

Surgeon George H SHORLAND
Royal Navy

31st May 1916

George Shorland came from a long line of Wiltshire and Somerset medical practitioners. Born in Westbury on 18th March 1876, George was educated at All Saints School in Bloxham, Oxfordshire and then, between 1891 and 1893, at Lancing College. In 1894, George entered Guy's Hospital, London to study medicine, graduating in 1901 and becoming a Bachelor of Medicine, Bachelor of Surgery or MBChB. He worked at the Cambridge Infirmary for a time before moving to the City Hospital in Whitechapel High Street. George also did occasional locum work for St Pancras Station, where he was Medical Officer and also at the Clearing House in Seymour Street, near Euston Square. He continued his railway links as an honorary surgeon to the Railway Benevolent Institution.

In 1904, George married Gertrude Harriet Mawson in Wetherby, and their only son, John, (known as Jack), was born in 1906. In 1911, the family were living in Harpenden but later moved to Hillside, Flower Lane in Mill Hill, North London where George conducted his surgery. Regarded as indispensable at the outbreak of the war, George was refused permission to sign-up. Instead, George became a Special Constable, training the First Aid contingent of the 'Mill Hill Specials', whilst providing the majority of their medical supplies at his own expense.

During 1915, George and his family moved to The Anchorage in Northchurch High Street, opposite the Church Cottages, and soon obtained permission to serve as a surgeon in the Royal Navy. On 3rd November that year, he joined the officers of the battlecruiser, HMS *Invincible*, 3rd Battlecruiser Squadron, alongside Surgeon Cyril OH Jones, under the

Surgeon George Shorland
(Source: Lancing College Archives)

direction of Fleet Surgeon Walter J Bearblock.

Invincible was the first Battlecruiser built anywhere in the world. Completed in October 1908 at Armstrong-Whitworth's Elswick Works on Tyneside, and commissioned on 20th March the following year, *Invincible* was 567 feet long and displaced 20,135 tons. Parsons Turbines produced 41,000 shaft horsepower driving four screws to give her a top speed of around 26 knots. With eight 12-inch BL guns, sixteen 4-inch QF guns and carrying fourteen 18-inch torpedoes, *Invincible* had formidable firepower. She had already seen action at the first major encounter between British and German warships of the war, the Battle of Heligoland Bight, and in December 1914, *Invincible* and her sister ship, *Inflexible*, destroyed Admiral von Spee's Cruiser Squadron, including SMS *Scharnhorst* and SMS *Gneisenau,* off the Falkland Islands. Initial repairs to the damage *Invincible* incurred took place at Port Stanley with further repairs made at Gibraltar. After a full refit during April and May 1915, *Invincible* became the flagship of Rear Admiral HLA Hood, who had assumed command of 3rd Battlecruiser Squadron on 27th May. *Invincible* underwent a further refit at the beginning of May 1916 before sailing to Scapa Flow for gunnery exercises with the Squadron.

The German High Seas Fleet had entered the war significantly smaller than the Royal Navy despite an intensive shipbuilding programme. By May 1916, the British Grand Fleet totalled some 150 ships including 28 dreadnoughts, 9 battlecruisers, 26 light cruisers and 77 destroyers, whilst the High Seas Fleet numbered only 99 ships including 16 dreadnoughts, 6 pre-dreadnoughts, 5 battlecruisers and 61 destroyers.

The initial strategy adopted by Admiral Reinhard Scheer, the Commander of the High Seas Fleet, had been to bombard England's east coast towns, such as Scarborough and Hartlepool, to lure British warships from their bases into screens of U-boats, waiting to torpedo them. Having alienated opinion in neutral countries by killing innocent civilians during these bombardments without sinking a single warship, Scheer adopted the riskier strategy of using his battlecruisers as bait. Thus, Admiral Franz Hipper's battlecruisers started to attack British merchant shipping in the area between Norway and Denmark known to Germans as the Skagerrak and to the British as Jutland. As well as deploying screens of U-boats to sink British warships leaving port, Scheer positioned the bulk of the High Seas Fleet ready to pounce on the remaining warships.

Early on 30th May 1916, the Admiralty's Room 40, which secretly possessed copies of the German naval codes, deciphered a signal indicating that the High Seas Fleet would shortly put to sea. Admiral of the Fleet, Sir John Jellicoe, immediately ordered the Grand Fleet to leave its moorings at Rosyth and Scapa Flow as soon as it was dark enough to evade any U-boats in the area and intercept the German Fleet.

By midnight, several hours before the ships of the High Seas Fleet had left their base at Wilhelmshaven, the British Squadrons were at sea. Aboard *Invincible,* Fleet Surgeon Bearblock supervised the conversion of the mess deck into a hospital, ready to receive stretcher cases. George Shorland and Cyril Jones organised the two well-stocked distributing stations, one forward and one aft, the stretcher parties and well-trained first-aid parties of supernumerary workers, writers, cooks, stewards, and canteen hands.

Having evaded the incomplete U-boat screen, the Grand Fleet divided into two groups - the main battle fleet under Admiral Jellicoe, and the battlecruiser fleet commanded by Admiral Sir David Beatty - and steered eastwards across the North Sea. Meanwhile, the German High Seas Fleet steamed northwards from Wilhelmshaven in a similar formation, with Hipper's faster battlecruisers ahead, screening the main battle fleet under Sheer. By early morning on 31st May, the two fleets were unknowingly heading straight for each other, the Admiralty having mistakenly informed Jellicoe and Beatty earlier that the German Fleet had yet to leave port. Beatty's battlecruisers made visual contact with the German battlecruisers at 15.30 and Hipper, attempting to draw Beatty towards the main German Fleet, turned south. Minutes later, both sides opened fire. The battlecruiser *Indefatigable* was hit by two shells and began sinking by the stern. Thirty seconds later, she blew up with the loss of all but two of her 900 crew. Shortly afterwards HMS *Queen Mary* was hit and sank with the loss of another 1,880 men. At around this time Jellicoe apparently uttered the infamous words 'something appears to be wrong with our bloody ships today.' The moment Beatty sighted the main German fleet steaming towards him, he turned his ships north, away from the impending trap and towards Jellicoe's fast approaching main force.

Meanwhile, Admiral Hood's 3rd Battlecruiser Squadron, consisting of *Invincible*, with her sisters *Inflexible* and *Indomitable,* was ahead of the Grand Fleet's main body. The light cruiser HMS *Chester*, a Squadron escort, signalled *Invincible* that she had observed distant gun flashes and was investigating. At 17.30, *Chester* suddenly confronted four light cruisers of the German 2nd Scouting Group looming out of the haze. *Chester* opened fire, but incoming gunfire quickly killed or wounded the crews of her partially shielded 5.5-inch guns. It was not long before *Chester* had only one main gun left in action, but Rear-Admiral Hood came to *Chester's* aid. *Invincible* opened fire on SMS *Wiesbaden* and, as her sisters joined in, the Germans attempted to escape into the mist. As they turned, *Inflexible* hit SMS *Pillau* and *Invincible* destroyed *Wiesbaden's* engine room, stopping her dead, but then both sides' destroyer escorts intervened, effectively stopping the action while the big ships dodged torpedoes.

Hood's Squadron reformed after the mêlée and steered westward, towards Beatty. At 18.15, Jellicoe turned the Grand Fleet to port, putting

Beatty's battlecruisers between him and the approaching German Fleet to conceal his battleships until Scheer was committed to battle with Beatty's squadrons. When Hood re-joined Beatty, his Squadron found itself in the lead and the first to come into range. At 9,000 yards' range, the three battlecruisers opened fire on Hipper's Flagship, the battlecruiser SMS *Lutzow,* and her sister, SMS *Derfflinger. Indomitable* hit *Derfflinger* three times while *Inflexible* and *Lion* scored direct hits on *Lutzow,* but it was *Invincible's* two hits below her forward waterline that eventually sealed *Lutzow's* fate and led to her being scuttled after the battle.

In the confusion, *Invincible* suddenly presented a clear target to *Lutzow* and *Derfflinger,* which both fired three rapid salvoes. At 18.33, one of *Derfflinger's* shells pierced the thinner roof armour of *Invincible's* 'Q' turret and detonated in the gun house, blowing off the roof. Because the blast doors in the turret's shell hoist had been propped open for action, the flash from the explosion travelled down the shaft, igniting stacks of cordite as it went and tore into 'Q' turret's magazine. This initiated a chain of explosions and in less than fifteen seconds, *Invincible's* central ammunition stores erupted in a huge fireball that sent debris four hundred feet into the air and split her in two. Surgeon George Shorland and Rear-Admiral Hood died alongside 60 other officers, 965 sailors and 5 civilians. HMS *Badger* rescued the six sole survivors. Witnesses later recalled a deathly silence immediately after the explosion, and the terrible, unforgettable eight hundred feet high pall of smoke that hung over the scene. The defining photograph of the Battle of Jutland shows *Invincible* with her bow and stern sections pointing skyward, shortly before she disappeared under the waves.

Sensing defeat however, the German battleships retreated to Wilhelmshaven under cover of their light cruisers. The battle cost Germany 1 battlecruiser, 1 pre-dreadnought, 4 light cruisers and 5 destroyers. The Royal Navy had lost 3 battlecruisers, 4 armoured cruisers, and 8 destroyers, but Jellicoe had 24 battleships ready for action next day, whereas several of the surviving German ships required months of repairs. Although not the decisive victory like the Battle of Trafalgar 110 years earlier, Jutland effectively neutralised the German High Seas Fleet as a serious threat for the remainder of the war. It was the largest battleship action in history and the last major naval battle fought by surface ships alone, with neither submarines nor aircraft taking part.

Today the wreck of *Invincible* is a designated War Grave. George Shorland's name appears on the Northchurch War Memorial, as well as on War Memorials at Portsmouth, Guys Hospital, Lancing College, Bloxham School and Mill Hill.

Private 2401 Lionel MORGAN
1st Hertfordshire Regiment

12th June 1916

Lionel Morgan was born on 16th November 1895, in the hamlet of Pimlico near Abbots Langley and christened at Holy Trinity Church, Leverstock Green the following January. Lionel was the third son of Amos Morgan, a gardener from Totternhoe in Bedfordshire and Ruth Morgan from nearby Eaton Bray. Amos Morgan later moved his family to Northchurch and began work as a farm labourer and shepherd at Norcott Hill Farm. After leaving school, Lionel joined his father there working as a shepherd's assistant. Lionel was popular for his bright disposition and had many friends in the village. When he reached 18, Lionel enlisted with 1st Battalion, Hertfordshire Regiment (Territorial Force), commonly known as the 'Hertshires', and trained with the local section of 'F' Company.

Lionel was enjoying his first Annual Camp in Ashridge when war broke out and the Territorial Force was embodied. The Hertshires then moved from their headquarters in Hertford to join the East Anglian Division assembling at Bury St Edmunds for home defence. At this time, Territorial battalions could not be compelled to serve overseas, but individuals could volunteer to go and if more than 80% of a battalion's men volunteered, and they proved their proficiency, they could go as a unit. Those who stayed behind then became the core of a new, 'second line' battalion.

On 1st November, the majority of the battalion having volunteered to fight overseas, the Hertshires received orders to prepare to leave. Two days later they received modern Short Magazine Lee Enfields to replace their old-fashioned, Territorial issue rifles. On 5th November, the Hertshires arrived at Folkestone on two trains and crossed the Channel aboard the *City of Chester*. They landed at Le Havre about midday the following day and marched to N°2 Rest Camp just outside the town. Here they were allocated to 4th (Guards) Brigade, 2nd Division, the only Territorials among these elite Guards battalions, and acquired a new nickname 'The Herts Guards'.

The Battalion then moved to billets near St Omer where, on 10th November, General Sir John French spent a few minutes to inspect one of the Herts Regiment's Companies, perhaps to see the Hertshires efficiency for himself. The following day the Battalion was rushed to Ypres in former London buses. Marching through the centre of Ypres, the Hertshires experienced German shrapnel shellfire for the first time. They spent the final stages of the First Battle of Ypres holding some of the trenches on the Menin Road and at Nonne-Bosschen without seeing a single German, but suffered several casualties from German shells.

On 20th November, with the fighting at Ypres effectively over, the Hertshires left the front line and marched to Meteren, a village midway between Lille and Dunkirk, which the Germans had recently lost. At Meteren, they joined the other battalions of 4th (Guards) Brigade to spend four weeks refitting and training.

The Hertshires returned to the front line on 23rd December near Béthune. Christmas Day was relatively quiet, but there was no unofficial Christmas Truce for them and two men were killed by German rifle fire. January 1915 began routinely with the Hertshires rotating between the front-line trenches and resting in billets. The Hertshires' eight companies merged to conform with the Regular Army's four-company organisation, but the Battalion made such an impression that these new companies received numbers; a privilege normally reserved for Guards battalions. 'F' Company merged with 'B' Company to form N°2 Company, although Northchurch people still referred to 'our' company as 'F' Company for some time afterwards. At the end of January, a replacement draft of 2 officers and 195 men joined the Battalion.

Apart from a minor engagement in early February, when an officer and two men became casualties, the battalion's sector remained relatively quiet, with each side probing each other's defences. However, the arrival of spring the following month brought ever greater German artillery fire and sniping that inflicted increasing casualties. One Hertshire gained a Distinguished Conduct Medal during this time for rescuing a wounded soldier of 1st Battalion Kings Royal Rifle Corps, who had been stranded in no-man's-land for two days.

In April, Lionel was stricken with synovitis, a painful inflammation of the joints, which was serious enough for him to return to England. After treatment, he was able to spend some convalescent leave in Northchurch before he returned to France.

In mid-May, the Hertshires took part on the Battle of Festubert, another attempt to gain the high ground at Aubers Ridge, in co-operation with French troops attacking further south at Vimy Ridge. Although in a support role, the Hertshires still suffered substantial casualties with five officers wounded, 17 men killed and another 91 wounded. Regrouping took most of the next three months, with new recruits and returning wounded arriving to make up the Battalion's losses. As the BEF grew, it was re-organised to create a new, Guards only, division. On 19th August 1915, the Hertshires transferred to 6th Brigade, (still within 2nd Division), and 1st Coy, the Herts Guards marched into Béthune to bid their Guards comrades farewell.

In early September, the Hertshires moved to another section of the front line, further south near the German held mining town of Loos. On 25th September, during the Battle of Loos, the British used chlorine gas for the first time. It was a disaster for the Hertshires and the rest of 2nd Division who were located on the extreme left of the attack. A change in the wind caused the gas, codenamed *Accessory*, to blow back and overwhelm the Division, causing several casualties. A further gas attack two day later fared little better. The remainder of 1915 passed with little fighting as both sides settled in for another cold, harsh winter facing each other yards apart in the trenches.

As January 1916 opened, further drafts of men joined the Battalion and the normal routine of occupying the front-line trenches, interspersed with periods in billets around Béthune continued. Kitchener divisions were now arriving in France, although some were far from ready. The battalions of a brigade in 39th Division were so behind in their training that they had to remain in England forcing the Hertshires and three other experienced Territorial battalions to transfer to 39th Division as 118th Brigade to replace them.

After spending March settling into their new brigade, the Hertshires resumed routine trench life through April. On 1st May, the Battalion took over trenches near Givenchy, just north of the place they had attacked during the Battle of Loos. Nine days later, an exploding mine provoked the opposing German troops to launch a short artillery attack on the Hertshires' trenches, injuring two men. In an act of heroism, Sergeant George Gregory carried the two men to safety and later received the Military Medal for his actions.

Although the Battalion's War Diary records several spells of duty in the front line for early June, no details are given. On 6th June, the Hertshires relieved 17th Sherwood Foresters in the line at Gorre and three days later, Lionel Morgan was admitted to N°33 Casualty Clearing Station at Béthune with very serious wounds. The cause is unknown. Early on 12th, Lionel received Holy Communion from the Hospital Chaplain and passed away peacefully at about 10.00. Lionel's burial took place at the Béthune Town Cemetery the following day. Seven weeks later Lionel's elder brother, Edwin, who was in France with 2nd Battalion, Bedfordshire Regiment, was to die during the Battle of the Somme.

Private 305045 Arthur James FROST
1/8th Territorial Battalion, Royal Warwickshire Regiment

1st July 1916

Arthur James Frost was a Londoner, born the seventh child of Harry and Mary Frost in 1882. Harry Frost was a coachman who lived with his family at 4 North Row, Hereford Mews, near St George's Church in Hanover Square. By 1890 Harry Frost had left London and moved his family to Hertfordshire, becoming the licensee of the Crooked Billet public house in Gossoms End, where he remained until his death in 1915.

The 1901 Census shows Arthur Frost working as a drapery assistant at Shepherd & Manning's store in The Drapery, Northampton. Ten years later, the Census records him working at another draper's shop and living in Woolwich, south London. By 1914, Arthur had moved again and was living and working in Birmingham. Here he enlisted with the local Territorial Battalion, 1/8th Royal Warwickshire Regiment, which had been embodied at Aston Cross that August.

Towards the end of February 1916, Arthur's future comrades found themselves on the Somme, where the French and British armies met and the great Franco-British offensive planned for the summer would take place. The Warwicks's trenches around Foncquevillers, to the north of Albert, were in a particularly sorry state after the winter and were very basic. Corrugated metal roofs and waterproof sheets provided the only shelter against the elements and offered scant protection against whichever explosive the Germans chose to lob at them, like the light *Minenwerfers* or 'Minnies', as the Tommies called them. These were short-range trench mortar bombs that caused havoc when they dropped into trenches and exploded. Tit-for-tat exchanges of mortar and artillery rounds of various calibres soon became a daily occurrence and it was in this dangerous environment over the next few months that the Warwicks set about improving their trench systems.

Having completed his training, Arthur joined the Warwicks in France during the spring of 1916. By then, the German Army had launched its powerful offensive at Verdun and the French Army, large as it was, was struggling to hold on. As a result, more and more French divisions intended for the Somme moved to Verdun, requiring British divisions to replace them.

With the coming of fine, spring weather, both sides sent up aircraft to observe what the other side was doing. Improvements in technology had recently enabled detailed maps of the German lines to be prepared from aerial photographs and this would become an important strategic asset for allied planners. Naturally, both sides tried to limit their enemy's use of the air, and at the end of March, the Battalion's War Diary records the loss of a British reconnaissance aircraft shot down by a Fokker monoplane. During March, the battalion also saw its first *Stahlhelm*, the new German steel helmet that was replacing the spiked *Pickelhaubes* for front-line troops. The sinister and iconic *Stahlhelm* had already familiar to the French at Verdun. British troops began to receive new dish-shaped Brodie steel helmets, the following month.

On 18th April, the Battalion began a week of training in preparation for the summer offensive. Then it was back to the front line and the daily routine of artillery exchanges for the remainder of the month. Arthur and his mates soon became attuned to the distinctive sounds made by approaching German shells and other projectiles, becoming expert at quickly identifying their type, calibre and likely point of impact and then decide whether they posed an immediate danger or not.

Leaving the front line on 8th May, the Battalion marched north to Sailly-au-Bois where they billeted for two nights. Three days later, the Warwicks reached Gézaincourt for two weeks of intensive battle training. Further tactical exercises at Brigade level and lengthy route marches, intended to get the Battalion's troops as fit as possible, followed. On 1st June, the Battalion returned to Sailly-au-Bois, providing working parties to improve the trench system. On 13th June 1/8th Battalion, together with its sister 1/6th Battalion, were temporarily attached to 11th Brigade, of the Regular 4th Division, for the forthcoming offensive. The Warwickshire battalions then spent two weeks training at Beauval with the Regulars. By the end of the month, Arthur and his comrades were in the front line at Mailly-Maillet ready for the start of what was to become the Battle of the Somme.

The Germans had first clashed with the French Army on the Somme in September 1914. Unable to make further progress, they began an intensive programme of construction on their first and second line in February 1915, exploiting high ground and other features to the full. They continued to pour concrete, barbed wire, timber, and labour into these defences for almost eighteen months. German front-line trenches included large dugouts sunk deep into the chalk that provided secure, comfortable shelter for the defenders against the heaviest bombardments. Concealed machine gun positions, observation points and strongly wired redoubts were located throughout the trench system. Villages along the German front line were also fortified and merged into their defences.

British Commanders were aware that the Germans had done much work on their defences, but were confident that the 1,010 field guns and 427 heavy guns brought up during the previous few weeks, together with significant help from French artillery, would be enough to destroy them. Furthermore, with the end of the Gallipoli Campaign and increased production back home, there was no longer a shortage of artillery shells. In fact, about two million shells of all calibres were available for the Somme Offensive alone.

24th June was a very dull day, with low cloud and heavy rain following the previous day's thunderstorms. At 06.00, the assembled British artillery commenced firing a bombardment planned to last four days. Reconnaissance flights began later that day to monitor the bombardment's progress and patrols went out each night to assess the condition of the German wire.

Two days later, the British 4th and 29th Divisions in the Beaumont-Hamel sector, released poison gas, which slowly drifted towards the German lines directly in front of the battalion's position. Many guns were firing up to 500 shells each day at the bombardment's peak, and aircraft reported significant damage to the German barbed wire defences. However, on 27th June, thick mist and heavy rain shrouded the Somme, halting aerial reconnaissance and making artillery observation impossible. Consequently, orders came to delay the start of the offensive by two days; it would now begin on 1st July.

Continued raiding confirmed that the German front line remained strongly manned and brought mixed news regarding the state of the German wire. Shellfire had destroyed it in places, but elsewhere the wire entanglements remained intact or had only opened narrow gaps. This was due in part by the type and quality of the British artillery shells. Most had been shrapnel rounds, which were inefficient wire cutters. High explosive shells generally tangled wire without cutting it, but they did at least destroy dugouts and emplacements. Many shells fired at the German lines had also failed to explode. Although the weight of the bombardment was impressive, the concentration on the forward trenches had suffered by including areas that were not objectives for the first day. In addition, there were never enough heavy guns available to destroy all the German gun batteries.

Arthur's battalion had orders to attack an old German strongpoint on the Redan Ridge called the *Heidenkopf* Redoubt, (or the Quadrilateral to the British), which jutted out from the German front line between the villages of Beaumont-Hamel and Serre. Their objective was to capture the first four lines of German trenches, a depth of approximately 750 yards. 1/6th Warwickshires were to follow 1/8th across no-man's-land and push on beyond them. The officers assured their men that any Germans who survived the artillery bombardment would be too stunned to resist the attack.

By 02.00 on 1st July, Arthur's battalion had formed up in the assembly trenches as the British artillery continued to pound the German trenches. Eight mines, enormous explosive charges placed by engineers at the ends of long tunnels under enemy strongpoints, detonated shortly before Zero Hour. Then more than eighteen tonnes of Ammonal detonated beneath the 'Hawthorne Ridge Redoubt' in Arthur's sector. The explosion, which was filmed by an Army cameraman, has become one of the most famous images of the battle.

Immediately the barrage lifted from the first line of trenches onto the second line, the German defenders knew that British infantry were about to attack and they scrambled up from their deep dugouts, grabbed their machine guns, and manned their firing positions. Further back their artillery began to shell no-man's-land.

When the whistles blew at 07.30, Arthur, loaded with rifle, bayonet, 170 rounds of ammunition, two grenades, water bottle, gas mask, a pick or a shovel, two empty sandbags, a ground sheet, a haversack with a cardigan and two day's rations, clambered into no-man's-land and deployed with his comrades in lines 100 yards apart. The High Command, concerned by the patchy standard of training amongst New Army Divisions, had decreed that the attacking infantry should walk across no-man's-land in rigid, parallel lines to maintain cohesion.

The nearest German trench to Arthur's Battalion was 800 yards away. Along most of the 14-mile front of attack, men got no further than a few yards before German machine gunners began to cut them down. Arthur's battalion was lucky. The Germans had already decided that the Quadrilateral was indefensible, so only a token force with a single machine gun manned it. German engineers had set a substantial mine beneath the redoubt, which they intended to explode after British troops had occupied it. Instead, the redoubt's machine gun jammed almost immediately and the German mine was detonated prematurely, killing *Heidenkopf's* garrison. The Warwickshires then swarmed over the Quadrilateral and neighbouring trenches before the shock of the explosion had subsided. They pushed on further, but although a party reached the German fourth line, defensive fire from the third and fourth line trenches was taking its toll. The divisions on either flank failed to make any progress, allowing German machine guns to enfilade Arthur's battalion, particularly from Serre, while determined German bombing counterattacks drove them back. Heavy shelling in no-man's-land then effectively cut them off. Of the 1/6th Warwickshires following up, only 25 men reached Arthur's battalion. By mid-afternoon, most of the remaining British troops were concentrated around the Quadrilateral under German machine gun and rifle fire, which slowly reduced their numbers. Finding themselves in an untenable position, the survivors eventually withdrew to the British trenches.

About 800 men from 1/8th Territorial Battalion, Royal Warwickshire Regiment, went into battle on 1st July; of those, 563 became casualties. Among those posted as missing that day was Private Arthur James Frost, aged 34. There was no news for several months, but confirmation eventually came that he had been killed on 1st July. Arthur's body now lies in the Serre Road Nº2 Cemetery, which today stands adjacent to the land once occupied by the Quadrilateral.

Private 25551 Walter HOWLETT
7th Battalion, Bedfordshire Regiment

1st July 1916

Walter Howlett was born in early 1897 into a family with a long-established Oxfordshire, Buckinghamshire and Hertfordshire surname with numerous branches of the Howlett family living in all three counties. Walter's father, William, came from near Chinnor. William's early life was not particularly easy as, following the death of his father Emanuel, the family fell on hard times. The 1871 Census records William, aged 15, living as a pauper in the workhouse in nearby Thame. Six years later William's life had picked up, for on 26th December 1877 he married Lucy Lay in St Mary's, Northchurch - his occupation being described as a labourer. Four years on, William was living in Orchard End, with Lucy looking after a two-year-old daughter. Nine more Howlett children followed, including Walter. Sadly, by April 1911, five of them had died.

When William completed his 1911 Census form at Orchard End, he listed his wife Lucy, sons Thomas, William and Walter, and daughters Alice and Ethel. Both Williams were working in one of the many local garden nurseries, Thomas was a bricklayer's labourer, while fourteen-year-old Walter was about to leave school.

Sometime in 1915, perhaps as soon as he was old enough, Walter enlisted at Bedford in the 7th (Service) Battalion, Bedfordshire Regiment, otherwise known as the 'Shiny Seventh', in which Walter Purton, another Northchurch man, was already serving. When conscription loomed later that year, Walter's older brother, William, enlisted with the Royal Welsh Fusiliers.

Walter was probably with the draft of 70 men and 5 officers that joined the 'Shiny Seventh' at Bray-sur-Somme on 6th May 1916. A further 49 men arrived five weeks later. 7th Bedfords had been in France since July 1915, serving with 54th Brigade, 18th (Eastern) Division, and had spent much of its time holding trenches in the Somme sector. General Ivor Maxse, 18th Division's commander, was a tactical innovator and firm believer in meticulous training.

Walter joined 'C' Company and with the Somme Offensive scheduled for the end of June, he took part in the preparations for the attack. Each day the men spent many hours training, laying telephone cables and digging new assembly and communications trenches and then yet more training. On 12th June, the 'Shiny Seventh' marched 35 miles to billets at Picquigny for intensive battle training with the whole of 54th Brigade. Each man there learned every detail of the Brigade's objective for the first day, the Pommiers Redoubt, a strong, fortress-like position designed for all round defence dominating the Montauban-Mametz road. The 'Shiny Seventh' and 11th Royal Fusiliers were to be the assault battalions, with the 6th Northamptonshire Regiment following in support and 'mopping up'. Every man learned what had to be done and how, so that they could achieve their objectives without orders.

Thoroughly prepared, the 'Shiny Seventh' entered front line trenches at Carnoy on 24th June just as the massed artillery began its four-day bombardment of the German lines, but then bad weather delayed the attack until 1st July. The battalion, meanwhile, was relieved on 28th June and spent one last night in billets, resting as best they could and cleaning their equipment.

'C' Company's first objective was Emden Trench on the opposite side of a small valley, then to advance through the support and second line trenches towards their final goal, Pommiers Redoubt, a total of about 2,000 yards. Apart from this redoubt and a strong German machine-gun position called *Kasino* Point, the German trenches here had been badly smashed and it was likely that German troops would set up their machine-guns in no-man's-land once the bombardment lifted. To counter this, a creeping barrage of shrapnel shells was to sweep the ground ahead of the infantry as they advanced. Each platoon carried two red and yellow flags to signal their progress to artillery observers.

At about midnight on the 30th June, the assault battalions of 54th Brigade stood ready in the Carnoy trenches. The artillery bombardment continued through the night, increasing in intensity until 'Zero hour' at 07.30, when it was due to 'lift' from the forward trenches onto the second line. At 07.28, the eight large mines excavated by British sappers detonated. A two tonne mine obliterated *Kasino* Point on Walter's front, and even though 'C' and 'B' Companies were being showered with debris, they immediately climbed from their trenches to get a head start across no-man's-land before the barrage lifted.

'C' Coy passed quickly through the gaps in their wire, doubled down the slope and formed up in the valley below. Reaching Emden Trench, the Company came under the German artillery barrage, but ran through it and suffered few casualties among the men. The Company pushed on, but they had no officers after Emden Trench and heavy fire eventually forced the men to take cover. Relief came as 'B' Company advanced on their right and silenced the machine guns that pinned them down. Within an hour, the first Bedfords had reached Pommiers Redoubt and a mixed force of Bedfords and neighbours from 6th Royal Berkshires slowly fought their way through.

How far Walter Howlett got is unknown. By the day's end, the 'Shiny Seventh' had achieved all of its objectives, but at the cost of 79 dead and

242 wounded. Among the 24 dead from 'C' Company was nineteen-year-old Walter Howlett whose body lay unidentified somewhere in no-man's-land. With no known grave, Walter's name is now one of 72,000 names engraved on the brooding War Memorial at Thiepval, representing the British and South African soldiers without graves who died during the Battles in the Somme area between 1915 and 1918.

Rifleman Charles William ROSS
1st /16th (County of London) Battalion, (Queens Westminster Rifles)

1st July 1916

Charles William Ross had an exotic upbringing, far removed from pastoral Northchurch. He was born in 1889 in Suva, the capital of Fiji, where his father, John Kenneth Murray Ross, was a Colonial Civil Servant. Charles' mother, Christian Ross, was the daughter of another colonial official, Thomas Stenhouse, of Bombay. John Ross was later to become Controller of Customs for Fiji, and in June 1910 he was awarded the Imperial Service Order. The following year John Ross became a member of the Legislative Council for Fiji and returned to the UK about three years later, becoming a barrister.

The town of Suva had only become the new capital of Fiji in 1891, so the area around the commercial and government centres for the colonial civil servants where Charles grew up was relatively new. Senior colonial officials in Fiji like John Ross and his family led a privileged, but very insular life, socialising exclusively among themselves in the local clubs and hotels such as The Grand Pacific. Native Fijians remained in their villages, while indentured Indians and Kanaks, the Melanesian inhabitants of the nearby island of New Caledonia, performed most of the manual labour, especially on the sugar cane plantations spread across Fiji's many islands.

Charles and his brothers were probably educated together at home, or with small groups of other European boys, until they were old enough for formal education. As no established senior schools existed in Fiji, Charles and his older brother, John Stenhouse Ross, went to be educated in England. They lived with their grandmother, Mary Jane Stenhouse, two maiden aunts and a couple of servants at 3 Wedderburn Road, Hampstead.

By 1911, Charles was living with his 17-year-old brother, Kenneth, and their maiden aunts, Amy and Helen Stenhouse at Whitelea, a house set in two acres of grounds off Shootersway in Northchurch. The Census describes Charles's occupation as 'of private means' with brother, Kenneth, who was also Fijian born, being 'at school'. When war broke out three years later, Kenneth was a medical student at the London Hospital in Whitechapel. Joining up as a Surgeon probationer in the Royal Army Medical Corps Kenneth's military service ended after just four months when he left to resume his studies.

Charles enlisted in October 1915 at Westminster as a Rifleman with 1st/16th (County of London) Battalion (Queens Westminster Rifles), The London Regiment. Having left Northchurch, he was then living with his parents in Forest Hill, South London. After mobilising at Buckingham Gate in London, the Queens Westminster Rifles (or QWR) moved to billets in Leverstock Green, near Hemel Hempstead, before crossing to France in November 1914. The battalion spent six months in the Armentières sector before moving up to Ypres at the end of May 1915. In February 1916, they transferred to the newly reformed 169th Brigade, 56th (1st London) Division, which was concentrated in the Hallencourt area, just south of the River Somme.

Through early 1916 and up to the start of the Somme Offensive, the QWR absorbed a substantial number of new recruits almost on a daily basis, some 354 being added during May alone, bringing the total up to 29 officers and 938 men. When precisely Charles Ross joined his Regiment in France is unknown, but it is probable that he was one of those arriving with one of the May drafts.

During June, the QWR were in the Halloy area, to the north of Amiens, where they were employed digging new assembly and shelter trenches to accommodate the assault battalions ready for the planned offensive. To mislead the enemy, the troops dug new trenches at night, removing the tell-tale chalk spoil before morning, while work on existing trenches took place during the day. Although particularly bad weather at the beginning of June hampered progress, work on the trenches was complete by the third week of June and on 24th, the battalion began three days of practice attacks on dummy trenches in preparation for the real thing. On 30th June, the QWR moved to the trenches at Hebuterne and took up their positions opposite the German trenches at Gommecourt, about eight miles north of Albert. The battalion's War Diary records their strength on that day as 44 officers and 922 men.

Of the divisions attacking on 1st July, 46th (North Midland) Division and 56th Division (including the QWR) were the furthest north. Their assault on Gommecourt was intended to protect the left flank and draw German reserves and artillery away from the main offensive stretching south to the River Somme. A secondary objective was to remove the symbolic German salient around Gommecourt Wood, which represented the westernmost point in France that German troops had reached. The London Rifle Brigade and Queen Victoria's Rifles (QVRs) would be the assault battalions for 169th Brigade, supported by engineers and light mortar batteries. Three companies of QWRs would follow behind with instructions to overtake the QVRs and attack the Quadrilateral Redoubt at the same time as men of the 46th Division. A smokescreen would protect all the attacking troops.

At 07.30, their officers waved 169th Brigade over the parapet and the men disappeared into the smokescreen. The QVRs immediately encountered uncut wire and as they struggled to make gaps, German machine guns firing into the smoke hit their company officers. Soon the Queen's Westminsters ran into them and the combined battalions swept over two lines of enemy trenches. However, coming under fire from the right, they took shelter in the sunken Gommecourt to Puiseux road, a few yards in front of the German third line.

The Queen's Westminsters, now led by only five inexperienced platoon commanders, attacked up the main communication trench into the third line. They bombed their way along the trenches towards Gommecourt Cemetery and the Quadrilateral, joined on the way by officers and men of the 1/5th Cheshires. An hour after Zero, a small party of QWRs, led by a Cheshires officer, reached the Quadrilateral but a stronger German bombing party forced them back. Attempts by their reserve companies to reinforce the dwindling force of QWRs, QVRs and Cheshires collapsed under fierce German artillery fire. Facing strong counterattacks by the German 170th Regiment, and with no sign of 46th Division, they were forced steadily back into the German first line, where they held on, bombarded by trench mortars and grenades.

At about 20.20, the 30 or so able bodied men of various battalions holding the trench were told to make a break for it through the intense rifle and machine gun fire. The last standing QWRs officer was shot and killed as he reached the British trenches. Of the 750 QWR officers and riflemen who went over the top, four out of five were either killed, wounded or missing and the battalion ceased to exist as a fighting unit.

Charles William Ross, aged 27, was one of those killed during the day's fighting. With no known grave, Charles' name appears on the Thiepval Memorial. His parents later arranged the placing of a commemorative stone plaque in his memory on the South Wall of St Mary's Church.

Charles's brother, Kenneth, qualified as a doctor in 1917 and remained in England throughout the war. On 29th September 1920, he married Edith Russen at St Mary's Church, but

Rifleman Charles Ross Memorial Tablet, St Marys Northchurch
(Source: Richard North)

died suddenly, aged only 27, on 4th February the following year of diphtheria and meningitis. His body now lies in St Mary's churchyard. John Ross, and his wife Christian, continued to live in Forest Hill, South London before moving during the 1930s to Glendair in Doctor's Commons Road, Berkhamsted. They celebrated their golden wedding anniversary there in 1936. John Ross died three years later and Christian Ross, aged 89, died in 1949.

Lance Corporal G7193 Philip Charles FEIST
4th Battalion, Duke of Cambridge's Own (Middlesex Regiment)

2nd July 1916

Philip Charles Feist was born in Cuckfield, Sussex in 1888, the son of Thomas and Elizabeth Feist. Thomas Feist was a gardener, who by 1911 had become Head Gardener at Woodhill House, a small country house just outside Hatfield. Sometime between 1911 and 1914, Thomas Feist decided to change career, bring his family to Northchurch and become the licensee of The Compasses public house in New Road.

In 1911, Philip, who had followed his father's former profession, worked as a gardener in the gardens of Luton Hoo, Bedfordshire. He lodged in 'The Bothy', a substantial house, built to accommodate the unmarried gardeners, which was attached to Luton Hoo's Home Farm.

Soon after the outbreak of the war, Philip enlisted with 4th Battalion, Duke of Cambridge's Own (Middlesex Regiment) at Mill Hill. In August 1914, 4th Middlesex was based at Devonport with 8th Brigade, 3rd Division. Landing with the BEF that month, it was one of the first battalions to engage the enemy at the Battle of Mons during which, fighting alongside the Royal Fusiliers, they held up eight attacking German battalions until overwhelmed by artillery fire and manpower. As a result, the decimated 4th Middlesex had to be withdrawn from the front line to be rebuilt.

Philip Feist arrived in France on 7th April 1915 as part of a draft of 107 men and reached 4th Middlesex four days later near Westoutre, about 8 miles southwest of Ypres. They went straight to the front line and spent the next seven days adjusting to life in the trenches. Over the following weeks, during the Second Battle of Ypres, German artillery regularly bombarded the battalion's lines inflicting a number of casualties each day. On 17th June, 4th Middlesex moved to what remained of Vauban's old town ramparts of Ypres, which artillery fire from both sides had gradually reduced to rubble.

The Battalion executed its first major attack on 19th July, following the explosion of a huge mine under the German lines at Hooge. The Battalion's War Diary describes the events – 'The ground heaved and rocked for some seconds and then clouds of earth, bricks, wood and German [sic] began to fall. Forty seconds after the first shock the heads of the columns ascended the parapet and made their way through a dense cloud of dust to their objectives....'. The resulting crater was some 200 feet wide and 50 feet deep. The fighting lasted two days and was a deemed a success, although the Battalion's advance into German-held territory was less than hoped and had cost the Middlesex some 300 casualties.

The Battalion's move to a training camp at the beginning of September coincided with the arrival of heavy rain and because of a shortage of tarpaulins only about half of the battalion and their equipment could be sheltered. The War Diary describes the ground itself as a swamp, and the number of soldiers reporting sick increased dramatically. By mid-September, the weather had improved enabling 4th Middlesex to restart training. When not training, they spent most of their time in working parties rebuilding defensive positions in Sanctuary Wood, southeast of Ypres, were they were close enough to the lines to suffer the frequent depredations of German shell and sniper fire.

On 19th/20th September, a hidden German sniper, using a captured British rifle, shot eight of the Battalion's men, killing three. The Middlesex mounted an urgent search until the sniper was finally located 30 feet up, concealed among the branches of a tree. Although practically invisible from the ground, he was sniped by British marksmen the following day. A series of minor attacks mounted by both sides meant that by the end of September, when 4th Middlesex completed their tour of trench duty, 6 officers and 32 of their men had been killed with 8 officers and 119 men wounded, and a further 117 posted as missing. Steady losses continued well into October and 4th Middlesex was suffering the strain of three months' fighting. The Battalion moved to a rest camp at Steenvoorde, where its men were among the cheering troops inspected by King George V and the Prince of Wales, on 27th October.

In mid-November, the Battalion was transferred to 21st Division, joining 63rd Brigade at Armentières a few days later. Winter was setting in and frost hardened the mud, making trench maintenance somewhat easier. Unfortunately, the month's end brought incessant rain which washed away much of the earlier repair work. Returning to billets at Armentières on 1st December, Philip and his mud-encrusted comrades were pleased to have good bathing facilities and excellent ironing rooms for their clothes.

After just two days' rest, 4th Middlesex returned to trench duty. Their final trench raid of the year took place on 16th December. Following the usual artillery barrage to stun and isolate the enemy trenches, the raiding party encountered minimal resistance and seized a number of documents providing useful intelligence.

Christmas Day 1915 saw British and German artillery exchanging shells in place of goodwill gifts. The 4th Middlesex ate Christmas Lunch on 28th December, once the men were safely back in their billets at Armentières, with, according to their War Diary, sufficient Christmas puddings to supply every man with a liberal helping. A concert followed that evening.

The Battalion saw in the New Year back in the trenches. At 23.00, (midnight Berlin time), the Germans greeted 1916 with bursts of machine gun fire and shouting and a few hours later, an artillery exchange caused a considerable amount of damage to the Battalion's trenches. Clear blue skies that month saw aerial activity increase on both sides and the Middlesex witnessed the destruction of a British plane by anti-aircraft fire. Later, heavy rain once again reduced the trenches to quagmires and running streams of water, whilst frequent shelling continued to weaken the parapets.

An intelligence gathering raid to capture documents and prisoners on 25th January, found the Germans well prepared and the 4th Middlesex raiding party, mostly former cyclists, lost an officer and three men killed, with a further seven wounded. The retaliatory German bombardment killed another three men and wounded two more. The next day, a direct hit on a Battalion dugout killed four more men and severely injured eight. Philip and a weary 4th Middlesex returned to billets on 28th January.

February and March 1916 followed the same routine. When the weather was favourable, aircraft from both sides patrolled the skies, trying to spot targets for their artillery to smash. Occasionally, Philip would have viewed 'dog fights' between opposing machines.

On 20th March, 4th Middlesex withdrew from the front line to Strazeele, 14 miles west of Armentières. Over the previous seventeen weeks, it had suffered 180 casualties, including 33 men killed. Constant rain and sleet marked the first few days of the Battalion's ten days at Strazeele, preventing many of the activities it had planned. Only at the end of the month, two days before they were due to leave, did the weather improve sufficiently for the troops to venture outdoors for a route march and field training.

The Middlesex left Strazeele by train on 31st March heading towards Allonville, seven miles outside Amiens and about twelve miles from the front line. Here, the Battalion spent a few days training and playing as much football as possible, but before long, 4th Middlesex was occupying trenches at Ville-sur-Ancre, which was the Battalion's first introduction to the Somme sector. Unlike northern France, the terrain here was hilly with chalk not far beneath the surface. Although harder to dig, chalk trenches usually drained well and were more or less self-supporting, even during heavy rain.

Daily exchanges of fire with the Germans continued and casualties began to rise again. On average, the Battalion fired around 250 rifle-grenades at the German trenches every day. Artillery took over in the evenings, and shelling continued throughout the night, making sleep impossible for men not on duty.

The Battalion entered new trenches near Fricourt sector in mid-May, and the fine weather brought fresh problems. Aerial activity was increasing considerably and chalk spoil from newly dug trenches was clearly visible to reconnaissance aircraft. Although the Middlesex men were grateful for the better protection offered by chalk trenches, wherever they looked the glare of sunlight reflecting off the newly-dug white trench walls hurt their eyes.

Nine days before the Somme Offensive, officers received instructions to rest their men as much as possible during the day. Sporting tournaments were organised, football matches being extremely popular, and concerts took place in the evenings. As June closed, the men were 'looking very fit', according to the 4th Battalion's diarist, and 'quite eager to get to grips with the Enemy'. By now, Philip had been appointed a Lance Corporal.

4th Middlesex moved into assembly trenches in the Fricourt sector on the night of 27th June ready to attack, but, as elsewhere, they were stood down to wait two days in full battle gear for the new Zero hour. 21st Division's objective was the strongly fortified village of Fricourt, which 4th Middlesex was to outflank and attack from behind. To the right, 7th Division would be attacking the village of Mametz.

At 07.25 on 1st July, the leading platoons of 4th Middlesex's 'A' and 'B' companies clambered into no-man's-land to form up, but were immediately raked by German machine gun fire and forced back into their trenches. They regrouped to try again and once more suffered the brunt of machine gun fire from Fricourt, but the remaining platoons of 'A' and 'B' Companies advanced, while 'C' and 'D' Companies followed. All but one of their officers and most of their NCOs lay dead or wounded before the Battalion reached the German first line trench. The Middlesex pressed on in small groups, with perhaps forty reaching a sunken road, but the Germans put up a strong defence. Forty-five minutes after the start of the attack, it became apparent that further progress was impossible until fresh troops from other battalions arrived. 4th Middlesex consolidated their limited gains, then, at 11.00, new orders came to protect the right flank where other troops of 63rd Brigade would be advancing. By nightfall, Fricourt was still in enemy hands, although some men from 7th Division penetrated the village during the night.

Of the 100,000 British troops who went into action on the Somme on 1st July, some 60,000 were lost, including 20,000 dead. There were no specific orders for the second day of the battle, so Corps commanders tried to complete their first-day objectives where possible.

On 2nd July, 21st Division re-organised and attacked Fricourt again, taking it with help from men of 4th Middlesex. Survivors of the Battalion advanced to Lozenge Alley, where they encountered heavy enemy resistance which checked their advance and led to more casualties. 4th Middlesex was held in reserve until it was eventually withdrawn. Over the course of four days, it had lost 146 officers and men killed, 341 men wounded, with 15 missing, believed killed, and 38 missing.

Among those killed during the fighting for Fricourt on 2nd July was Lance Corporal Philip Feist, aged 28. His body remained unidentified on the battlefield and his name now appears on the Thiepval Memorial.

Private 4/6424 Edwin MORGAN
2nd Battalion, Bedfordshire Regiment

1st August 1916

Edwin Morgan, the second son of Amos and Ruth Morgan, was born in Bovingdon, Hertfordshire in February 1891, and christened there on 7th June. Ten years on, the family had moved to High Barnes, Nash Mills, Abbots Langley, where Amos Morgan worked as a domestic gardener. The Morgans later moved to Northchurch with Amos working as a shepherd at Norcott Hill Farm.

After leaving school Edwin decided to sign up as an Army Reservist, and by April 1911 he was training at Hertford with the 4th (Extra Reserve) Battalion, Bedfordshire Regiment. Men enlisted in the Special Reserves for six years and were liable for call-up in the event of a general mobilisation. Special Reservists had six months of full-time initial training, on the same pay as a regular soldier, and afterwards committed themselves to undertake three to four weeks of refresher training every year. When not training, Edwin spent his time working at Dudswell Farm and at Ley Hill.

In August 1914, Edwin was mobilised at Berkhamsted and reported to the Regimental Depot. On 19th September, he was sent to 2nd Battalion, Bedfordshire Regiment, which had recently returned to England from South Africa to join 7th Division. Having refitted for European warfare, 7th Division left Southampton two weeks later and, after briefly stopping at Dover to take on additional supplies, landed at Zeebrugge on the 7th October. Eleven days later, just before the First Battle of Ypres, the Division briefly skirmished with German troops for the first time on the Ypres to Menin Road.

Edwin landed in France on 2nd November, probably with the 20-man draft that joined the battalion five days later. The mobile war was ending and both sides now faced each other in hastily dug trenches. On 17th November 1914, Edwin's battalion relieved 2nd Border Regiment, in which Walter Geary was then serving, in the trenches southwest of Fleurbaix, Pas de Calais. The Bedfords would rotate in and out of these trenches for the next four months.

The snow was quite thick when the Bedfords returned to the Fleurbaix trenches on Christmas Eve. That evening, at about 20.00, lights appeared along the German parapets, hanging from Christmas trees, and German soldiers started singing in their trenches; *'Stille Nacht'* – 'Silent Night', followed by *'O Tannenbaum'*. The Bedfords apparently responded with a rendition of a recently popular ditty, sung to the tune of *'The Church's*

One Foundation':
> 'We are Fred Karno's army, the ragtime infantry,
> We cannot fight, we cannot shoot, what bleeding use are we?'

Not long after, a German officer called from his trenches in English, 'I want to arrange to bury the dead - will someone come out and meet me?' Cautiously, an officer of the Bedfords went out, accompanied by three men. They met five Westphalians of the 15th Regiment, whose leader apparently spoke excellent English, having lived in Brighton and Canada. They wished to bury about twenty-four of their dead, but would not do so at night fearing British artillery fire. Uncertain what to do next, both sides returned to their trenches.

At 10.00 on Christmas Day, with the thick snow still crusted by overnight frost, a German officer and two unarmed men left their trenches holding a white flag and spoke to a Captain of the Bedfordshires. The German officer formally requested to bury their dead and both sides agreed an informal cease-fire until 11.30 to complete the task. The Battalion's War Diary described the large garrison of soldiers lining the German parapets as, 'a young lot from 19-25 years well turned out & clean'. The Bedfords' CO gave strict instructions that no enlisted men should approach enemy lines without definite orders and only men on duty were to show themselves. Additionally, no Germans were to come near the Bedfords' trenches, but British officers could inspect the German wire. Having buried their dead, the German and British troops returned to their trenches. This was the legendary 'Christmas Truce' which has since gone down in history. Two days later, the Bedfords returned to their billets for three day's rest before re-entering the front line on 30th December.

The Battalion began the Battle of Neuve Chapelle in reserve on 10th March 1915. Two days later, the Germans counterattacked and although the Bedfords suffered many casualties, they recaptured much ground and took 50 German prisoners in one action. The Bedfords were again heavily engaged in the second attempt to take Aubers Ridge, during the Battle of Festubert on 16th May, suffering over 121 casualties. A month later, another attack in the Givenchy area fared little better, with the Battalion losing another five officers and men killed and 74 wounded.

The Bedfords' final battle of 1915 was at Loos. The Battalion's objectives were the villages of Vermelles and Cit-St-Elie, but the preliminary bombardment proved ineffective and the Bedfords suffered a high number of casualties from heavy rifle fire. Despite some initial success, the battalion's position became untenable and they were forced to retire to their trenches. The Battle of Loos ended in failure on 28th September. Edwin and his colleagues spent the remainder of 1915 conducting minor sorties and alternating between trench duties and rest periods in billets.

On 19th December, the Bedfords transferred to 30th Division and began 1916 holding trenches near Maricourt. The year began quietly enough; apart from occasional casualties caused by random shells and sniper fire, the principal enemy at that time was the weather. On 19th January, Edwin wrote a Will in his pay book, which may have been a replacement for one he had lost. By the end of February, with mud everywhere and repairs impossible, conditions in the trenches had become so intolerable that the men were being relieved every 48 hours.

At the end of March, the Bedfords moved to Grovetown Camp near Bray-Sur-Somme ready to begin training for the Somme Offensive. On the opening day of the battle, 30th Division, of which the Bedfords' formed part, were on the far-right flank of the British line alongside the French Army. Their orders were to take Montauban where British and French artillery had overwhelmed the defences and cut most of the German wire. 2nd Bedfords, following close behind the assault battalions, cleared the enemy's dugouts and trenches and captured 300 Germans and 4 machine guns in the process. 30th Division took all its first objectives in an hour and was in Montauban by 10.00.

Consolidation of the Division's gains was completed on 2nd July, despite four German counterattacks. During this time, Edwin helped to dig and wire a completely new trench under heavy shellfire which the Battalion named 'Bedford Trench'. That day, the German High Command ordered 15 heavy artillery batteries from Verdun to reinforce the Montauban sector. The weary Bedfords were relieved by South African infantry the following day.

Planning for a major British attack against the German second trench system, which ran along the Bazentin Ridge through Longueval to Guillemont, now began. Lying between Montauban and Guillemont was Trones Wood. Neglected and choked with undergrowth, it needed capturing before the main assault could take place. For three days, 30th Division attacked the wood and each time the Germans responded with counterattacks blocking progress. As a result, the Bedfords were called out of reserve and entered the fighting.

At 02.40 on 11th July, the fiercest British bombardment to date fell on Trones Wood. Within an hour, 'A' and 'B' Companies were leading the Bedfords, alongside 20th King's (Liverpool) Regiment through shelling and machine-gun fire into the southern edge. Once inside the wood, darkness and thick undergrowth restricted visibility and the Bedfords were soon stumbling onto strongly held German trenches. After much fighting the Battalion finally established footholds in the southeast and southwest sides of the Wood. The Battalion patrolled aggressively and held on against repeated enemy attacks until it was relieved at 01.00 on 13th, having suffered 244 casualties.

On 30th July, the battalion successfully attacked the German second line at Maltz Horn Farm, which the Bedfords captured in support of the Liverpool battalions' advance. 2nd Bedfords made contact with French troops on their right and dug in along Maltz Horn Ridge under heavy shellfire. That day's action cost the Bedfords a further 192 casualties including Edwin, who was seriously wounded in his thigh and arm. Edwin was transported the eleven miles to N°5 Casualty Clearing Station at La Neuville, near Corbie, where he died at 16.00 on 1st August aged 25. Edwin now lies in Corbie Communal Cemetery Extension, just north of the town, beneath a headstone inscribed, 'Until the day break and the shadows fade away'.

In his Will, Edwin left all his personal possessions to his mother, who had moved to New Road, Northchurch with Amos. All four of their sons had gone off to fight for their country; Lionel and Edwin were now dead, but their eldest, Harry, was still serving in France with the Royal Field Artillery, while their youngest son, Shirley, was by then a conscript in the Hertfordshire Regiment's Reserve Battalion.

Private 18312 Albert ROLFE
1st Battalion, Bedfordshire Regiment

1st August 1916

Albert Rolfe was born at West End Farm Cottages, Cheddington, Bucks, on 18th October 1892, to George and Mary Rolfe. George, who came from New Mill, Tring, worked as a straw and hay binder on West End Farm, whilst Mary came from Gossoms End. Albert's parents were married in 1882 and they had ten children in total, although four of them had died by 1911. Albert spent his formative years at West End Cottages, attending the Countess of Rosebery's Infant's School from 1897 and Cheddington's National Mixed School from 1899.

In time, George and Mary moved to a three-room dwelling in Cow Roast, and Albert began his association with the Baptist Chapel in Northchurch. By the age of 18, Albert was working as a farm labourer in the Northchurch district, but later trained to be an electrician. He was still living in Northchurch when he became engaged to Jennie Burrows who came from St Saviours Parish near St Albans. They married at St Mary's, Northchurch on 27th December 1913 and later moved to 33 Russell Rise, Luton.

Shortly after the war began, Albert enlisted with 1st Battalion, Bedfordshire Regiment at Bedford. Having completed his initial training, Albert landed in France on 27th July 1915 in the same draft as fellow Northchurch man George Bignell, qualifying them both for the 1914/15 Star.

The new draft of men joined the rest of the battalion at Abeele, near Baillieu. 1st Bedfords had already seen considerable action during the battles of Mons, Le Cateau, the Marne, the Aisne, La Bassée and the First and Second Battles of Ypres. During the Second Battle of Ypres in April and May 1915, the battalion fought at Hill 60 and incurred heavy losses from artillery fire and poison gas. By the end of August 1915, drafts of reinforcements, including Albert Rolfe and George Bignell, had made up for the earlier losses and the battalion's strength stood at 23 officers and 952 men.

At the beginning of August, 1st Bedfords moved to the Somme Valley where they were to spend the next few months. The Battalion's War Diary for 17th September 1915 described the trenches in their sector as being in, 'a very indifferent repair', and that a great deal of work was necessary to make them defendable. To make things worse, the opposing trenches were only about 160 yards away, close enough for either side to easily lob trench mortar bombs and other short-range missiles at each other. Consequently, the men in the fire trenches felt very exposed.

Ration parties carried food, water and stores on foot to the firing line along poorly maintained communication trenches for up to a mile always under constant threat of attack. At night, the Battalion sent out patrols to monitor the German trenches and cut their barbed wire whenever possible. Gradually, the trenches were improved, but the autumn rains soon undermined much of their work. The Bedfords ended 1915 resting in billets at Bray-sur-Somme.

On 2nd January 1916, the Battalion returned to trenches in the Arras area. It was cold and wet and the troops did what they could to keep warm and safe from the ever-vigilant German snipers. February brought high winds that blew snow showers in all directions. Despite this, the Battalion began a heavy programme of training, including the use of the recently introduced Lewis machine guns, bomb throwing practice and frequent route marches.

A thaw towards the end of March slowly turned the trenches into walkways of mud. In places, they were too shallow to offer much protection and required a considerable amount of repair work. Trench mortars were a particular problem through April and May and the battalion had to endure heavy bombardments associated with enemy raids on neighbouring battalions.

When the Battle of the Somme began on 1st July, 1st Bedfords were on fatigues near Arras, but they were suddenly ordered to move to Ginvenchy-le-Noble. After a week of training in bayonet fighting, the Battalion marched by stages to the Somme. At Ville-sur-Ancre they began preparing for battle, starting on 17th July with a full check of tools and equipment, before moving up to positions east of Mametz where they were held in reserve.

Britain's second major attack on the Somme began before dawn on 14th July, when British troops tore a three-mile gap in the German second line behind a surprise five-minute bombardment. Scottish soldiers attacked Longueval and South African troops, also of 9th (Scottish) Division, partially occupied the neighbouring Delville Wood; it was the beginning of a long and costly struggle to clear it of German troops. British soldiers also reached High Wood, but failed to secure it before fresh German reinforcements flooded in. Thus, began a dogged struggle between the British, determined to widen their three-mile salient, and the Germans, who were equally determined to squeeze it shut.

On 23rd July, 1st Bedfords took over positions between High Wood and Delville Wood and began to push the line forward by constructing seven small, fortified Lewis gun posts. The plan was to link up the posts the following night, but instead the Battalion was unexpectedly relieved and reached bivouacs at Pommiers Redoubt early on 25th July. Over those two days alone, constant shellfire cost the Bedfords 6 wounded and 24 killed.

On the morning of 27th July, 1st Bedfords were supporting 1st Norfolk Regiment in an operation at Longueval. Heavy shellfire and machine-gun fire from a German redoubt on the Delville Wood side of the village stalled the Norfolks until the Bedfords reinforced them and attacked a nearby fortified house. The redoubt and the fortified house subsequently fell and 132 German soldiers were captured. Norfolk Regiment bombers in turn silenced a German machine gun post that was stopping another company of Bedfords at the central crossroads, whilst the Bedfords Lewis Guns and rifles fired on an enemy counterattack inflicting 50 casualties. By mid-morning however, shellfire and more enemy machine-gun fire prevented further progress and the battalion was forced to partially withdraw. It was relieved the following morning, having lost 9 officers and 303 men, 64 of them killed.

Longueval came under attack again on 30th July, in support of a major operation against Guillemont to the south. The Bedfords were sent into the ruins of the village to relieve 2nd Kings Own Scottish Borderers. Coming under relentless shellfire, Albert's battalion was unable to reach the Scottish Borderers' positions and spent the 31st pinned down by machine guns and artillery. By the time men from 1st Norfolks arrived to relieve both the Scottish Borderers' and the Bedfords' forward companies, Albert had been seriously wounded and taken to Nº13 Field Ambulance. There Albert died of his wounds on 1st August 1916, aged 23. His body now rests in the Dernancourt Communal Cemetery.

Albert's parents were living at Bottom House, Wigginton, when he died. His widow, Jennie, living at 32 Havelock Road, Luton, requested the words, "To Memory Ever Dear", for his headstone. Albert's name does not appear on the Northchurch War Memorial, but appears on the Memorial Tablet in the porch of Northchurch Baptist Church and also on the Luton Roll of Honour.

Private 17760 George BIGNELL
1st Battalion, Bedfordshire Regiment

4th August 1916

George Bignell was born in 1891, one of eight children of George and Elizabeth Bignell from New Mill, Tring. Not long after the arrival of their first son, Herbert, the Bignells moved to New Road, Northchurch, where their remaining children were born. George senior worked as a labourer at Cooper's chemical works in Berkhamsted, as did his son Herbert. With their family increasing, by 1901 the Bignells had moved to a larger property in Orchard End. Ten years later the family were living at 6 Alma Road, Northchurch, with George now working at Cooper's, as a machine driver. By then, his brother, Herbert, had left to become an attendant at an asylum near Kings Langley.

Shortly after the war began, George enlisted with 1st Battalion, Bedfordshire Regiment at Bedford and landed in France on 27th July 1915, in the same draft as Albert Rolfe. Albert and George probably became close friends during their years' service with 1st Bedfords. Apart from their Northchurch backgrounds, both George Bignell's parents and Albert's father came from New Mill, Tring.

George was alongside Albert Rolfe when the Battalion arrived on the Somme during mid-July and was seriously wounded during the Bedfords' attempt to capture Longueval on 27th July 1916. Having been taken to 36 Casualty Clearing Station, located close to the railway at Heilly, George succumbed to his wounds there on 4th August, three days after the death of his mate Albert. In all, their 30 hours of fighting in Longueval cost the Bedfords 22 killed and over 200 wounded. George's body now lies in the Heilly Station Cemetery, Mericourt-l'Abbe, just south of the River Ancre.

Lieutenant Thomas Eric HENDERSON
1st Battalion, South Staffordshire Regiment

31st August 1916

Thomas Eric Henderson was born in Islington in 1876, the third son of John Thomas Henderson, a wealthy silk merchant and publishing director of Scottish descent, and his wife Theresa. In 1891, the Hendersons were living in a large, detached Italianate-style villa in the exclusive area of Aberdeen Park in Highbury, north London, where they employed four servants. Later the family moved to a large house in Darrs Lane, Northchurch, which they named Fordell after the Henderson Clan's ancestral home near Dalgety in Fife.

Henderson was educated at University College School, passing the London Matric with First Class Honours in June 1893. Seven years later, he was working as a China and General Merchant's Clerk, but still living at his parent's home in Aberdeen Park. In May 1910, Henderson entered Guy's Hospital as a dental student, where he qualified three years later. At Guy's he won the First Year's Dental Prize in 1911 and the Second Year's Prize the following year. Henderson became an Assistant House Surgeon between January and March 1912 and an Assistant Demonstrator in Dental Metallurgy the following June.

In September 1914, The Public Schools Battalion, a 'Pals' battalion exclusively for public school men to serve together, came into being. Membership was by application only and having been accepted, Henderson left his dental practice to be one of the first to join as a Private. That December, the Battalion moved from its original base at Kempton Park racecourse to Warlingham in Surrey. Officially known as 16th (Service) Battalion (Public Schools), Middlesex Regiment, the Army viewed its ranks as a pool of officer candidates for other regiments and Private Henderson, Thomas Eric, was one of those selected for promotion. On 14th July 1915, Henderson was commissioned into the South Staffordshire Regiment as a Second Lieutenant, initially gaining experience with 4th Battalion, before joining 1st Battalion, which had already seen considerable action on the Western Front.

1st South Staffs had returned to England from garrison duty in Pietermaritzburg, South Africa in September 1914. After joining 22nd Brigade, 7th Division in the New Forest, it was sent to assist the Belgian Army in defending Antwerp. Arriving too late to prevent the fall of the city, 7th Division took up defensive positions to cover the Belgian Army's retreat. Men of the 7th Division were the first British troops to entrench in front of Ypres, and suffered extremely heavy losses during the first battle for the town. By February 1915, the Division had returned to fighting strength and saw action at the Battles of Neuve Chapelle, Aubers Ridge, Festubert and the Second Action of Givenchy.

Henderson and two fellow 4th Battalion officers joined their new battalion at Bray-sur-Somme on 28th May 1916. In the trenches, 1st South Staffs was enduring increasingly heavy artillery and rifle grenade fire from the opposing front line, the battalion's War Diary estimating that some 700 German shells struck its positions on the evening of 31st May alone. Two weeks later the battalion moved to billets at Mericourt and spent seven days preparing for the Somme Offensive.

The South Staffs was one of 7th Division's assault battalions attacking alongside Philip Feist's 4th Middlesex Battalion in 3rd Division on 1st July. Mametz village was the Division's objective, but first Henderson's platoon had to pass a strongpoint named Bulgar Point. At two minutes to Zero hour a substantial mine detonated beneath the strongpoint, obliterating its machine gun nests and allowing 1st South Staffs to reach the first German trench with very little loss. Machine guns firing from further back inflicted many casualties however, but Mametz fell in the late evening. The South Staffs consolidated their gains over the following days while the rest of 7th Division captured the nearby village of Fricourt. On 5th July, the exhausted Staffordshires were relieved and entered billets at Buire-sur-Ancre, about seven miles from the new front line.

After eight days' recuperation, the South Staffs moved north to the valley behind Bazentin-le-Petit ready for the next set-piece British attack scheduled for 14th July. The battalion, supported by two British aircraft strafing German positions, helped open a three-mile gap in the German second line from Longueval up to Pozières. However, the battalion halted before High Wood, which dominated its surroundings from a low ridge, but, unknown to them, the defending Germans had retreated. When orders finally arrived in mid-afternoon to take the Wood, the Germans had recovered and re-occupied it. Fighting stretched into the night until the enemy forced the South Staffs to halt about halfway into High Wood, where they dug in as best they could. A co-ordinated attack with other battalions next day failed to unseat the Germans from the remainder of the Wood and the South Staffs withdrew to Mametz.

Following their ordeal, the South Staffs moved to billets near Vaux-en-Amiénois, just north of Amiens. Departing on 12th August, the battalion relocated to a camp near Albert, where they enjoyed two weeks' rest before 7th Division returned to the Front. On 29th August, the battalion left its camp near Fricourt to relieve the Royal Welch Fusiliers from the eastern edge of Delville Wood. Nestling into Longueval, Delville Wood had seen some of the bitterest fighting in the war so far. Whoever held the wood controlled Longueval and the approaches to Givenchy. The 3,150-

strong South African Brigade attacked Delville Wood at dawn on 15th July, but being outnumbered they could only secure the southern edge. Days of vicious close quarter fighting followed. When the South Africans were relieved on 19th July, 766 of their troops lay dead. In over six weeks of attack and counterattack, Delville Wood became a mass of black, splintered tree trunks, tangled wire and unburied bodies, earning it the nickname, *Devil's Wood*. By the end of August however, only the eastern edge of the wood remained in enemy hands. It would remain that way until troops could sever its connection to Ale Alley and the other German trenches with brewery-related names. Early on the 27th July, the Fusiliers began bombing their way along Ale Alley, up Beer Trench and along Vat Alley, slowly clearing the Germans away from the Wood. It was their gains that 1st South Staffords was ordered to hold against counterattack.

Through heavy rain, Henderson, as second in command, guided 'A' Company along roads rendered almost impassable by mud, but by midnight, 18 Officers and 700 men of the South Staffords were holding about 550 yards of linked shell holes, waist deep in mud and water, in what passed for trenches. While 'C' Company settled behind in support with 'D' Company in reserve, 'B' Company took over the Battalion's front from the east of Devil's Wood, held by the North Staffords. Henderson's company, occupied the recently captured 'brewery trenches', snaking from Delville Wood towards Ginchy. Two Lewis guns covered a 50-yard gap between 'A' Company and 21st Manchesters to their right.

Rain fell heavily throughout the next day, as did German artillery and gas shells, particularly on the Battalion's rear areas and Delville Wood itself. Rifle ammunition and 50 boxes of Mills Bombs, the standard British hand grenade, were carried up and work was started to strengthen the battalion's front. Messengers and ration parties were forced to cross open ground to reach the forward positions, so a 200-yard communication trench was dug overnight in 'A' Company's sector

Thomas Henderson's Grave at the Delville Wood Cemetery (Source: Richard North)

to provide a safer route.

Steady German shelling overnight turned into a heavy barrage at 10.00 on the 31st, cutting off 'A' and 'B' Companies, while preventing 'D' Company from moving forward. Three hours later, fresh German storm troops in steel helmets, unencumbered by equipment, but carrying plenty of hand grenades, attacked up Ale Alley and Bitter trench. Although 'B' Company's Mills bombers and riflemen, reinforced by 'C' Coy, drove the enemy off, barely a few replacement boxes of Mills bombs reached them through the barrage. As casualties mounted, Henderson took over command of his company, but the German troops made no gains until a lull at 16.10.

At 16.30, five German aircraft marked the South Staffs' positions with lights and an intense bombardment began, reducing the companies to below half strength. Soon the Battalion's trench mortars were out of action. At 19.00, the bombardment lifted and German assault troops attacked again with grenades up Ale Alley and Bitter Trench. Battalion headquarters received a message from Henderson reporting that 'A' Company was holding fast in Ale Alley, but had no more bombs and that German troops were pressing hard. An enemy rush then split the Battalion. The remains of 'B' and 'C' Companies, about 40 men, fell back to a shallow trench just inside Delville Wood, from which they kept the enemy back. Henderson led the survivors of 'A' Company back to the North Staffords trenches, where they constructed a temporary barricade and stopped the attack with rifle fire.

Enemy shelling and sniping continued through that night, but counter-fire held the Germans in the brewery trenches. The German counterattack cost the South Staffords 1 officer and 36 men killed, 7 officers, and 84 men wounded and 2 officers, including Thomas Henderson together with 146 men 'Missing in Action'. The Battalion's War Diary commented, '2/Lieut HENDERSON behaved very gallantly but was helpless owing to shortage of bombs. This Officer has been missing since the attack'.

By 3rd September, British soldiers had secured the area and later discovered Thomas Henderson's body. He was buried in Delville Wood Cemetery, at the southern end of Delville Wood. His headstone bears the text, 'Greater love hath no man than this'. Apart from the Northchurch War Memorial, Thomas's name appears on the Guy's Hospital Memorial in London. Delville Wood has since regrown, but much of it is still inaccessible due to unexploded ordinance.

Private 31651 Joseph William ALDRIDGE
11th Battalion, Northumberland Fusiliers

24th September 1916

Joseph William Aldridge was born in Orchard End, Northchurch in 1887, the son of Joseph, a blacksmith's labourer and his wife Annie. Census returns show that the Aldridge family had lived in the Northchurch area since at least 1851, while his mother's family came from nearby Hawridge. Annie Bryant was a domestic servant for a Northchurch solicitor when she met Joseph's father and they married around 1885. Joseph had two younger sisters, Ethel and Edith, both born at 40 Gossoms End. After leaving school Joseph worked as a labourer, first for a coachsmith and later with a bricklayer. By 1911, the Aldridge family had moved to 55 Gossoms End.

Joseph was a keen and accomplished footballer, playing for Northchurch's team, the 'Black and Ambers'. He was a defender in the Northchurch squad that reached two Cup Finals in the 1908-1909 Season. In April 1909, his team played Croxley in the West Herts Minor Cup Final at Hemel Hempstead Football Club's Gadebridge ground. The match went into extra time, but after 140 minutes' play the score remained 2-2 so a replay was agreed for the following Saturday. Northchurch fielded the same team for the replay to beat Croxley 1-0 and lift the West Herts Minor Cup, their first ever trophy. However, when the two teams met again the following Monday for the Apsley Charity Cup Final, the 'Black and Ambers' were spent and lost to Croxley 4-0.

Joseph's military service records no longer exist, but other records show that he enlisted with the Bedfordshire Regiment at Berkhamsted in 1915, receiving the regimental number 26808. In 1916, Joseph transferred to 11th Battalion Northumberland Fusiliers with a reinforcing draft containing at least 44 ex-Bedfordshire Regiment men allocated a block of regimental numbers from 31651 to 31694. 11th Northumberland Fusiliers had landed at Boulogne with 68th Brigade, 23rd Division in August 1915. Soon afterwards, the battalion marched to the Belgian border, remaining midway between Hazebrouck and Armentières until it relocated to the area south of Loos in March 1916. That June, 11th Northumberland Fusiliers began intensive training for the Somme Offensive, although they stayed in reserve on the opening days of the battle.

By 4th July, 23rd Division had relieved 34th Division in the line before la Boisselle and in the early hours of 7th, the battalion led the Division's attack on Bailiff Wood and the struggle for Contalmaison which, over five days, cost the Fusiliers 292 casualties.

Shellfire inflicted more losses, with 15 casualties being incurred on 19th

July alone. Between 20th and 22nd July, drafts totalling 546 replacements joined the Fusiliers at Franvillers, bringing the battalion's overall strength to 31 officers and 1,166 men. It is likely that Joseph Aldridge and the other Bedfords were part of this reinforcing draft.

Returning to the battle on 26th July, the Fusiliers resupplied Mills bombs to the firing line through German barrages that inflicted 14 casualties, 5 of them shellshock cases. On 7th August, 'A' Company attacked the German Intermediate Line in the Mametz area, but fell back under heavy trench mortar, rifle and machine gun fire. A few days later, the Fusiliers left the Somme sector and moved north to Ypres, where they spent four weeks providing working parties for the Royal Engineers. Joseph and his mates were able to use the Divisional baths on 22nd. The sheer pleasure of a clean shirt and underwear against clean skin after weeks of wearing the same clothes in the filth of the trenches can only be imagined.

Re-entering the trenches on 25th August, the Northumberland Fusiliers found the front line somewhat quieter than when they left. However, on 31st August, the British released gas along the Division's front and the Battalion shattered the quiet with an unsuccessful platoon-strength raid. In retaliation, German artillery bombarded the Fusiliers' positions the next day until long-range counter-battery fire from British heavy guns put a stop to it.

A few days later, the Fusiliers withdrew to billets just outside St Omer and returned to the Somme sector on 10th September. Eight days later, the Battalion entered the support line behind Martinpuich, which had been captured a few days earlier during the battle that first introduced tanks to warfare. The Battalion occupied the abandoned German trenches leading from Martinpuich called Starfish and Prue on 22nd September and began a series of minor actions to capture nearby enemy outposts, keeping the Germans off balance to prevent them establishing a new, strong defensive line.

Bombing operations continued on 24th September and 68th Brigade attacked a communication trench named 'Twenty Sixth Avenue', while German medium artillery shelled the Battalion's area. The Battalion's War Diary entry for that day records losses of 29 wounded, 8 killed and 6 missing, including Joseph Aldridge. Joseph's final resting place is unknown, and consequently his name appears on the Thiepval Memorial alongside thirteen comrades from 11th Northumberland Fusiliers who also died that day.

Private 43247 William James SIBLEY
6th Battalion, Northamptonshire Regiment

26th September 1916

On 7th December 1884, Sarah Ann Sibley, the unmarried daughter of Samuel and Elizabeth Sibley, gave birth to a boy in Roestock, near Colney Heath, Hertfordshire. The following month the Vicar at St Mary's, North Mymms, christened the baby William James Sibley.

William grew up with his mother at his grandparent's home in Roestock. Grandmother Elizabeth died in 1893 and three years later William's mother married Robert Pateman. In 1901 William, then aged 16, was working as a domestic gardener and living with his mother, stepfather, young half-brother and Grandfather Samuel in the same house in Roestock. Ten years on William worked as an under gardener at Roestock Hall, a large redbrick house owned by retired Admiral Sir John Fellowes KCB.

Sometime over the next three years, William came to the Northchurch area, probably finding a gardener's job at one of the local large houses. On 11th December 1915, William Sibley and two friends, or workmates, of similar age from Potten End, George Bedford and William Chapman, enlisted at Berkhamsted with the Bedfordshire Regiment. The three received consecutive regimental numbers.

On 22nd June 1916, William, now a soldier and based at Felixstowe, married a 27-year-old clerk called Nora Abigail Moore at St Mary's Church, Northchurch. Nora's father, James Moore, was a gardener like William. Less than a month later, on 7th July 1916, William and his two Potten End mates embarked for France. Soon after landing, all three men were transferred from the Bedfordshire Regiment to join the 6th Battalion, Northamptonshire Regiment. They reached their new regiment at the small Somme village of Bois de Tailles, near Etinehem, as part of a draft of 300 men.

6th Northants was brigaded with 7th Bedfords in 18th Division, under that meticulous trainer, General Ivor Maxse. Although the Northants supported the assault battalions on 1st July, it lost some 201 men killed or wounded over the first three days of the Somme Offensive. The battalion captured Trones Wood two weeks later, but at the cost of another 303 officers and men.

Shortly after receiving their Northamptonshire cap badges and new regimental numbers, William and his comrades moved north to Wallon-Cappel, 13 miles west of St Omer, where the newcomers became 6th

Northants men. On 28th July, the Battalion marched twelve miles in particularly hot weather to Bailleul for further training. Unfortunately, an outbreak of diarrhoea combined with the heat forced many soldiers, especially the newcomers, to fall out on the march. However, by 16th August, the Battalion was fit enough to spend five days in the front line at Armentières, while intensifying its training when out of the line.

6th Battalion returned to Bailleul on 25th August for another two weeks' training, before moving south to a new training site at Arquèves, midway between Arras and Amiens, where the Battalion prepared for the capture the village of Thiepval.

The Germans attached great importance to Thiepval. Since their arrival in September 1914, they had heavily fortified the village and nearby ridge, building complexes of concrete gun emplacements, trenches and tunnels such as *Schwaben, Stuff, Zollern and Chateau* Redoubts. The ruined chateau was all that could be seen of the village, but from their redoubts, German soldiers could survey the Ancre valley and the area around Albert. Thiepval had resisted frontal assault on 1st July, but British advances between then and the Battle of Flers-Coucelette now allowed 18th Division to attack northwards into Thiepval's southern flank.

Four Anglo-Canadian divisions were to the attack Thiepval Ridge on 26th September. Made to appear routine, the preparatory shelling continued until Zero Hour which, to maintain surprise, was at the unusual time of 12.30. At 09.15, 'B' Company, including William, left their dugouts and by 11.35, 6th Northants was ready in the support trench. In front, 12th Middlesex waited in the assault trench and some 500 yards beyond them lay the Chateau Redoubt. The Brigade's final objective was the *Schwaben* Redoubt, over a mile distant. As the first shell of the hurricane bombardment exploded on the dot of Zero, the Middlesex, and 11th Royal Fusiliers on the left, dashed forward into the stunned defence. Also at Zero, one of two Mark I tanks advanced from Thiepval Wood, reaching the chateau at the same time as the Middlesex and suppressing the machine guns there.

German artillery belatedly shelled the assault trenches, but did not prevent 'C' Company leading the Northants forward. By 13.40 'B' Company had reached the German trench south of Thiepval Chateau and was consolidating. Unfortunately, their tanks became ditched at the chateau, so when 12th Middlesex became pinned down by machine guns and snipers hiding in shell holes it was the Northant's 'B' Company that came to help them out. By 17.00, the three 54th Brigade battalions had taken almost all of Thiepval village, but the Germans counterattacked with showers of bombs. 'B' Company, which had no officers left, dug-in, with men of the other battalions resisting German bombing grenade attacks until almost midnight. Only the northwest corner of Thiepval remained to be captured before the *Schwaben* Redoubt could be attacked; 7th Bedfords would have to tackle that the next day.

The capture of Thiepval cost 6th Battalion 28 officers and men killed, 114 wounded and another 22 either missing in action, or shell-shocked. Initially listed as missing, and later confirmed as killed, William Sibley's body remained unidentified on the battlefield. William's name now appears on the Thiepval Memorial, close to where he died. His widow, Nora, remarried in the autumn of 1922.

As to the two men who enlisted with William in 1915, William Chapman outlived his friend by only three days, while George Bedford died of wounds on 17th February 1917. Both George Bedford and William Chapman's names now appear on the Potten End War Memorial. All three friends were 31 years old.

Private 57034 Walter WELLING
6th Battalion, Princess Charlotte of Wales's (Royal Berkshire Regiment)

29th September 1916

Walter Welling was born in the Spring of 1891, to Frederick and Alice Welling of Orchard End, Northchurch and christened at St Mary's on 6th May. Walter had four sisters and a younger brother, Arthur. His father, Frederick, worked as a cressman on one of the local watercress beds. In 1906, Frederick died suddenly aged only 44, leaving his family to fend for themselves as best they could. Alice Welling, her sons Walter and Arthur and her youngest daughter, Ethel, remained in the family home in Orchard End. Walter and Arthur worked as labourers while Alice took in laundry to make ends meet.

Walter did not join the initial rush to volunteer in 1914, but his regimental number, 5779, indicates that he attested with 1st Battalion, Hertfordshire Regiment between late October and early November 1915.

On 17th January 1916, Walter, who was still undergoing military training, married Kate Keen at Berkhamsted Register Office. Their daughter, Doris Kate Welling, was born six weeks later, on 27th February.

Walter remained in England until the beginning of July 1916, when he was despatched to France ready to join the Hertshires. After the heavy losses incurred at the beginning of the Somme Offensive however, many battalions were in urgent need of replacement troops. Among them was 6th Battalion, Princess Charlotte of Wales's (Royal Berkshire Regiment). On 5th September, 399 soldiers from the Hertfordshire and Cambridgeshire Regiments, including Walter Welling and fellow Northchurch man, Arthur Garment, were transferred to 6th Royal Berkshires, in 18th Division. Six days later, the newly reinforced Berkshires arrived at Léalvillers, in the Somme sector, for detailed battle training, including realistic mock attacks on a specially constructed replica of Thiepval village.

On 26th September, 18th Division attacked Thiepval Ridge, but as 6th Berkshires consisted mainly of new recruits, it remained in Brigade Reserve at Crucifix Corner. Although not called on to fight, the battalion provided parties to carry forward water, food and ammunition throughout the night. 18th Division had full ownership of Thiepval 24 hours later, but the village would not be fully secure while the *Schwaben* Redoubt, the highest point on Thiepval ridge, remained in German hands.

The Berkshires' Brigade, with 7th Bedfords, attacked the *Schwaben*

Redoubt on 28th September and the Berkshires took over trenches captured by their assault battalions to wait in case of counterattacks. Having spent all the previous day and night without shelter in Authille Wood Valley, the Berkshires were suffering badly from lack of sleep. They remained waiting in *Bulgar, Nameless* and *Schwaben* trenches throughout the following day as the Germans struggled to retake the *Schwaben* Redoubt.

Over those two days sporadic shelling wounded 56 Berkshires and killed 6. Walter Welling was probably among those severely wounded during this time and he died on 29th September, aged 25. Walter's short funeral took place in an Extension to the Communal Cemetery at Warloy-Baillon, due west of Albert, which was used by the Field Ambulances based there.

Private 19159 Walter PURTON
7th Battalion, Bedfordshire Regiment

24th October 1916

At St Mary's, Northchurch on 4th January 1891, George Purton, an agricultural labourer, and his wife Elizabeth saw their eighth child, three-month-old Walter, christened. Walter grew up with two brothers and six sisters in Northchurch High Street. Elizabeth Purton was from Berkhamsted, while George came from nearby Little Gaddesden. All of their nine children were born in Northchurch and in 1911, the Purtons were living in Orchard End, with Walter's elder brother, William, working on a farm. Two of Walter's sisters were paper machinists. Walter himself was by then a chemical worker at Cooper's factory in Berkhamsted.

In September 1914, Walter enlisted at Bedford and joined 7th Battalion, Bedfordshire Regiment, 'The Shiny Seventh', which was training at Codford, Wiltshire. On 25th July 1915, the 31 officers and 820 men of The Shiny Seventh, boarded a train to Folkestone and crossed the Channel aboard the SS *Onward,* landing at Boulogne the following morning. Through August 1915, the Shiny Seventh stayed near the village of Talmas, north of Amiens, where they were kept occupied on route marches, digging trenches and training. At the beginning of September, they entered front line trenches for the first time near the village of Bécordel-Bécourt, opposite the German-held village of Fricourt. The Bedfords spent the next twenty-two days in the trenches monitoring the build-up of German forces in that sector.

The Battalion remained in the same area for the next five months as the war on the Western Front settled once more into a wintry stalemate. At the beginning of March 1916, the Shiny Seventh was ordered south to a sector near the village of Corbie, after which it moved to Bray-sur-Somme, remaining there until the start of the Somme Offensive. The Battalion's War Diary uses the phrase 'nothing to report' 25 times during the period between March and the end of April 1916 while preparations were underway for the offensive.

New, reinforcing drafts arrived at the beginning of May, including fellow Northchurch man, Walter Howlett. From then, until the 21st June, the men of 7th Battalion followed a detailed, daily training regime of practice attacks, bayonet fighting, bombing, sniping, use of the Lewis machine gun, signalling and message running all in preparation for the offensive. On 24th June, the Battalion moved to Carnoy as the massive artillery bombardment preceding the main attack began, and before it had finished on 1st July, the Shiny Seventh crossed no-man's-land.

7th Bedfords, attacking alongside 11th Royal Fusiliers, took the fortress-like Pommiers Redoubt on schedule, even though they had lost almost all of their officers and NCOs beforehand. The Battalion consolidated Pommiers Redoubt against counterattack and held it through to 2nd July. In all 306 other ranks became casualties; among the dead were Walter Howlett and 87 fellow soldiers.

After resting behind the lines for a few days, the Bedfords were in reserve for 54th Brigade during the Battle of Bazentin. Following some uncertainty over where they would go next, the Battalion moved north to Flanders and arrived at the steam mill on the west side of Bailleul near the Belgian border. Here the Bedfords rested for eight days before moving to front line trenches at Erquinghem, southwest of Lille, arriving there on 5th August.

The next five weeks were spent training at three locations - Bois des Vaches, an area used by the Allies for field exercises including fighting in dense woods, La Thieuloye, northwest of Arras, and finally back at the Somme in the area around Raincheval. On 23rd September, the Shiny Seventh moved to Varennes, seven miles northwest of Albert ready for the assault on Thiepval Ridge.

Held in reserve on 26th September, the Bedfords watched from Thiepval Wood as their brigade's two assault battalions, closely supported by 6th Northants, took most of Thiepval Village. Having relieved the exhausted Brigade overnight, the Bedfords bayonet charged enemy-held trenches in the northwest corner of Thiepval Village the next day, killing about 100 Germans and taking another 36 prisoners, thus completing its capture.

The formidable *Schwaben* Redoubt remained untaken however, so at 13.00 on 28th, the Shiny Seventh advanced northwards along the original German front line on the left flank of 53rd Brigade's assault on the redoubt itself. Although a captured German map enabled supporting artillery to target most of the enemy machine-gun posts, the Bedfords initially suffered badly from their fire. Nevertheless, after an hour the Battalion reached its objective on the redoubt's west face. It then faced many hours of hand-to-hand combat and grenade fighting to stay there. By the evening, the redoubt was still only partly in British hands and it took until the following day for 55th Brigade to capture it. The Germans knew that whoever occupied the *Schwaben* Redoubt could see well into their rear so they were not giving it up lightly. Their infantry counter-attacked with everything they had including grenades, trench mortars and even flame throwers, and fought 18th Division to a standstill until 39th Division relieved it on 5th October. It would be another nine days before the Germans finally gave up hope of retaking the redoubt.

On 30th September, the Shiny Seventh arrived at billets, 'badly battered, but with their tails up', having lost 5 officers and 58 men killed and 10 officers and 147 men wounded in several days of continuous fighting. Training began immediately and the Battalion was given time to rebuild. On the same day, 158 fresh recruits arrived from England and General Sir Douglas Haig paid an informal visit.

On Saturday 21st October, in heavy rain, the Suffolks and Essex battalions of 53rd Brigade successfully captured Regina Trench, near Courcelette which was about three miles northwest of Thiepval, during a four-division attack to take more of Thiepval Ridge. The Bedfords held a Voluntary Church Service next day and took over the defence of Regina Trench that night. The Trench was badly battered and knee deep in mud, but on Tuesday 24th, the Germans made an attempt to retake it, killing Walter Purton in the process. Aged only 25, Walter Purton now rests in the Regina Trench Cemetery, near Courcelette village. His headstone simply reads, 'Rest in Peace'.

After his death, the Army found Walter's Will to be missing and made enquiries of his father. Walter's sister, Amy Purton, later certified that she had once seen his Will written in a small, brown Army book, bequeathing his personal possessions equally between his mother and father. The Army accepted Amy's statement and they divided Walter's possessions as he wished.

Lance Corporal Albert Ernest PICKTHORN
'B' Company, 28th Battalion, Australian Infantry

3rd November 1916

About a mile to the west of Northchurch, along the Grand Junction Canal, is Cow Roast Lock. It was here, at the Lock House, where Thomas Pickthorn was lock keeper, that his wife, Sarah Miriam Pickthorn, gave birth to a son, Albert Ernest, in May 1888. Thomas and Sarah later arranged for Albert's christening at St Mary's, Northchurch and, as with their previous three children, the Baptismal Register records his surname as Pickthorne.

On 2nd April 1911, the night of the Census, Albert was living with his parents at Cow Roast Lock, and working as a gardener. Eleven days later, however, Albert left Liverpool docks aboard the 5,041-ton *Pakeha*, en route to Fremantle in Western Australia ready to start a new life. He did not plan to return.

Three years later, on 30th July, with the European crisis deepening by the day, the British Government cabled a secret message to the Government of Australia warning that war could be imminent. Australia immediately ordered a partial mobilisation of its citizen forces and militia, partly as a precaution for home defence and partly with an eye to raising an expeditionary force to support Great Britain.

Following their experiences during the Second Boer War, both governments had reformed their military preparations. The Australian Defence Act established a 'citizen army' for home defence supplementing its Militia forces. Australia also formed a permanent military Staff and, in co-operation with New Zealand, established a joint academy to train their own officers. Germany's growing naval strength, plus the fact that Thursday Island, located off the coast of Queensland, lay only 200 miles from the German Protectorate of New Guinea, prompted Australia to create her own navy. In 1909, service with the citizen army at home became compulsory, although service outside the Commonwealth of Australia would remain voluntary.

Australia agreed to submit her armed forces to the authority of the Imperial General Staff should she declare war alongside Britain. To allow the seamless integration of their forces Australian military organisation, training, uniforms, weapons and equipment were as close to the current British Army models as possible. Australian military regulations broadly conformed to King's Regulations in wartime with two important exceptions: apart from capital crimes such as murder, Australian troops would not suffer the death penalty and Australian pay scales were five times higher than their British equivalents. Both matters would later cause resentment amongst British soldiers.

As an autonomous Dominion, Australia had the right to decide whether to declare war alongside Great Britain or not, but on 3rd August, the Commonwealth of Australia offered her navy and 20,000 troops for service anywhere under British direction. London gladly accepted. The following day, Britain declared war on Germany and steps began immediately to create the Australian Imperial Force (AIF) for overseas service with the Citizen Force training camps preparing to receive their first AIF recruits.

On 15th August, voluntary enlistment for overseas service with the AIF officially opened to all subjects, whether born in Australia or Britain. Before they could attest, AIF volunteers faced a tougher medical examination than their British counterparts. Potential AIF recruits, aged between 19 and 38, had to meet the same standards as the Australian Militia, which meant being physically fit, standing at least 5ft 6inches tall and having a minimum chest measurement of 34inches.

The first AIF contingent had been organised into battalions, equipped and partly trained by mid-September, but raiding by the German light cruiser SMS *Emden* in the Indian Ocean delayed its departure for France. The German East Asia Squadron's threat to Australia ended in November when an Anglo-Japanese force captured its home port of Tsingtao and the Australian cruiser HMAS *Sydney* sank *Emden.* Citizen Force units previously mobilised for coastal defence stood down, leaving the home defence organisation to concentrate on raising and training further contingents for the AIF.

At this time, Albert was working as a contractor in Woodanilling, a small town 158 miles south of Perth, Western Australia. On 2nd March 1915, Albert presented himself for enlistment, giving his age as 26 years and 9 months. His medical examination followed at nearby Kattaning, where he was vaccinated against smallpox and enteric fever. Albert's enlistment papers record he was 5ft 9inches tall and weighed 125lbs, with a fair complexion, fair hair, grey eyes with a good level of fitness and a 33½-inch chest.

The Army took Albert's oath on 4th March at Black Boy Hill Camp, Western Australia, and posted him to 24th Battalion for three months' basic training. That April, Albert's company, and another company from 24th Battalion, became the nucleus of a new battalion at Black Boy Hill. As 28th Battalion, it would join the newly created 7th Brigade of 2nd Australian Division. On 2nd June, Albert transferred to 'B' Company shortly before the 28th moved to Fremantle for transfer overseas.

A week later, the Battalion boarded HMAT A11 *Ascanius*, for the four-week voyage to Egypt. The last man, horse and item of equipment were aboard by 16.30, and later that evening *Ascanius* slipped her moorings and steamed out of Fremantle. Despite seasickness, and about fifty minor cases of measles and influenza, morale was high and discipline, particularly concerning hygiene and sanitation, was good. The whole Battalion was inoculated against smallpox and typhus whilst aboard and a routine of lectures and military training was introduced to occupy the men and make up for the short period of training at Black Boy Camp. The only grousing was over food, especially the War Office scale of rations, which was, said a battalion history, 'inadequate to satisfy the appetites of a meat-eating race like the Australians.'

Although a 'Pommie', Albert was not alone aboard *Ascanius*, around half of the original 28th Battalion men were British born. Overall, about a quarter of the men who served with the AIF had been born outside Australia, most of them in Great Britain.

On 24th June, Albert and his mates sighted the east coast of Africa and on 26th, *Ascanius* entered the Red Sea, reaching the Port of Suez eight days later. Having disembarked, the Battalion proceeded in four trains to Abbasia, just outside Cairo, where the hot Egyptian climate dictated camp routine. Albert and his mates woke at 04.30, and attended parades between 06.00 and 09.00 before the heat built up. Instruction and lectures took place in huts between 10.30 and 13.00, and further parades between 16.30 and 19.00. Route marches and field exercises took place during the cool of the night.

In Egypt's hot, dry, climate and poor sanitary conditions, dysentery became common among the Australians. The 'well manured' local soil quickly turned to a fine dust that coated everything. Almost 10,000 horses held nearby at a remount depot contributed to the swarms of flies and foul dust. Although measles also returned, the men were not downhearted, as they expected to be getting to grips with the Germans in France soon.

Once the Battalion was considered free of measles, a quarter of the men were allowed to leave camp after evening parade on weekdays, midday on Saturdays and 08.00 on Sundays. Albert and his mates relished the opportunity to indulge in a little sightseeing in Cairo and haggle for souvenirs.

During a night exercise on 16th August, the Battalion returned to camp with orders to take over garrison duties in the Cairo Citadel the following day. This old Crusader fortress held the entire stock of ordnance and reserve ammunition for the British Army of Occupation in Egypt, but the Battalion also found the storerooms filled with rats. Fortunately, 28th Battalion stayed there less than a fortnight before marching along the desert road, by way of the Tombs of the Khalifs, to Aerodrome Camp at Heliopolis where they prepared for action at a place they had never heard of, called Gallipoli.

The Battalion entrained at Qubba Station on 3rd September, and the following day, exactly six months after Albert enlisted in the AIF, 28th Battalion boarded the Hired Transport *Ivernia* at Alexandria bound for Mudros. Arriving at Mudros Bay on 10th September, the battalion transhipped to a small packet ship, SS *Sarnia*, and immediately steamed for Gallipoli.

By September 1915, British, French and ANZAC troops had been on the Gallipoli Peninsula for almost five months. Recent offensives at Sari Bair heights, Scimitar Hill and Hill 60 had failed and the Mediterranean Commander-in-Chief, Sir Ian Hamilton, saw no prospect of breaking through without 95,000 reinforcements. Sober analysis in London however, was leading to the conclusion that Gallipoli was diverting men and materiel from the Western Front to no good effect and that it was time to pull out. When Hamilton heard of the possible evacuation, he angrily predicted it would cost fifty percent in casualties. Hamilton's intemperate outburst earned him the sack, but he had a point. Attempting to break contact and slip away in full view of an active enemy is the most difficult of all military operations. Lord Kitchener therefore offered 25,000 reinforcements, including 28th Battalion AIF, to relieve the exhausted troops and stabilise the front before an organised withdrawal could take place.

Albert and his battalion landed at William's Pier, in ANZAC Cove, where they spent the night. The sight and overpowering smell that met them defied belief. The bodies of many former combatants still lay unburied on the rocky terrain, and hordes of corpse-fed rats and flies spread deadly epidemics. The Allied toehold along the coast was long and narrow and no point was truly out of the firing line. Clean, fresh water was always scarce and despite the closeness of the sea, washing was a rare luxury. At dawn on 11th September, Albert and his mates were rudely awakened when a destroyer, close to the shore, opened fire on Turkish positions; it was a fitting introduction to war on the Gallipoli Peninsular.

Albert's battalion soon relieved the New Zealand Otago Battalion on the Apex, an important salient and key to the ANZAC's line. The opposing trenches ran along high ground between 100 and 250 yards apart, either side of two gullies. A Turkish blockhouse dominated the highest point, called The Pinnacle, and as it was only fifty yards from the Australians' trench it could fire into their right-hand positions. Should the Turks take the Apex, all the ground captured the previous August at great cost to the Australians would be lost.

The Battalion occupied four posts on the Apex; 'A' and 'D' Companies took turns in the two left-hand posts, while Albert's Company took turns with 'C' Company manning the two posts on the right. Every six or seven days, the companies alternated between the front-line posts and reserve positions 300 yards behind, near the head of the Chailak Dere.

These trenches were up to six feet deep and offered good protection from bullets and shell splinters. Dug recently in a firm conglomerate that needed no extra support, they quickly wore out men and tools alike. The men in support still had to dig the communication and support trenches. Consequently, when Albert was not guarding trenches, he was spending long, weary hours digging them. The Battalion faced the daily hazards of trench mortars, grenades, artillery shellfire and especially snipers. The Turks produced some expert snipers, forcing the Australians to adapt their tactics quickly.

After twenty-four days in the confines of the Apex, 28th Battalion moved to a quieter sector called Cheshire Ridge. Albert's Company was relieved first, moving to the lower portion of the Cheshire Ridge on 4th October, with the main body following the next day.

If the Apex Salient had the characteristics of hill fighting, life at Lower Cheshire Ridge, a razor-edged feature facing the steep northwest slope of Sari Bair, was more akin to mountain warfare. From 27th Battalion on their right, 'B' Company's line ran through a hilltop to a section that had no trench, just ledges and footholds cut into the rock face and towards their left, firing bays were reached by tunnels excavated from the Australian side. The battalion's northern boundary rested on Aghyl Dere, which flowed diagonally across the trench line and contained a breastwork, or defensive wall, manned by 54th Division, that spanned the Dere with a gap below for the stream.

Nowhere were the Turks nearer than 600 yards - too far for grenades and trench mortars - but the sector was characterised by daily bursts of Turkish shrapnel fire and the occasional large calibre high-explosive shell fired into Chailak Dere and the beach behind. The battalion's tenure of Cheshire Ridge began in drenching rain, then after two weeks, temperatures plunged, especially at night. Five days later, on 27th October, a wind and dust storm tormented Albert and his mates for several hours. Fortunately, the Turks were having an equally tough time and hostile activity noticeably diminished.

While the Battalion was crowded into the Apex, its average weekly losses were four men killed, three men dying of wounds, fifteen men wounded and twelve men evacuated sick. Whilst on Cheshire Ridge, however, its weekly losses were only one man killed, one man dying of wounds, seven men wounded, but thirty-four men being evacuated through sickness.

After nearly seven weeks in the firing line, the Battalion was finally relieved at the beginning of November, and moved into Divisional Reserve at Taylor's Hollow. 'B' Company was again the first to leave, followed over the next couple of days by the rest of the Battalion. While nominally 'at rest', 28th Battalion spent the next five weeks at Taylor's Hollow, either labouring on general works for the Royal Engineers or shifting tons of supplies for the Beach Commandant. Albert suffered a serious injury on one of these working parties and was put aboard a hospital ship to Gibraltar. Admitted to the General Hospital there on 9th November, doctors treated him for *Haemothorax*, or internal bleeding in the lung cavity.

It is not recorded whether Albert returned to Gallipoli before the troop evacuation the following month, but he was certainly with his battalion when it boarded the *Ansonia* at Mudros and landed with his mates at Alexandria on 10th January 1916. They joined the Suez Canal defences with orders to defend the crossing at Ferry Post, but the Australians also helped to unload the ferries and other vessels landing there. Whilst at Ferry Post Albert began to suffer from sciatica, probably from a slipped disc, and on 24th February, he went to 7th Field Ambulance at Ismalia for a week's treatment.

Shortly after Albert re-joined his mates, they heard that at last 2nd Australian Division would be leaving for the Western Front. On 16th March, Albert's battalion embarked at Alexandria for the five-day voyage across the Mediterranean to France. HMT *Themistocles* turned out to be the most comfortable troopship that the 28th had encountered and by the time they landed at Marseilles, the men were in good spirits, apart from Albert.

Albert was now suffering severe pain and a high fever from a serious inner ear infection named *otitis medea*. In those pre-antibiotic days, *otitis medea* was difficult to treat and often caused permanent deafness. On 23rd May, Albert entered N°2 Australian General Hospital at Marseilles where he was to stay for two weeks. After treatment Albert went to the ANZAC's Base, but four days later, a relapse forced him back into hospital. After a further three weeks' treatment, Albert spent three days in a convalescent hospital before being sent to 2nd Australian Division's new depot at Étaples.

Finally confirmed fit for active duty on 31st July, Albert re-joined his unit and immediately entered 28th Battalion's first major battle on the Somme. On 27th July, Australian 2nd Division had relieved 1st Division after the capture of Pozières and on 4th August, Albert's Brigade attacked trenches north of Pozières between the Bapaume Road and the track to Courcelette. After some initial confusion, the Australians got into their stride, taking their first objective with relative ease, and continuing towards their second. The Germans counterattacked strongly through the night, with 7th Brigade beating off a particularly large attack at 04.00 the next morning. The Battalion then pushed forward alongside 27th Battalion to the second objective where they dug in. During ten days of attack and enemy counterattack, whole brigades lost so many men that single battalions were relieving them. For its part, Albert's battalion came out of the line with only 130 men deemed fit for duty, including Albert, who was appointed Lance Corporal in VII Platoon on 13th August.

As the Somme Offensive continued, the Australians went north along

Pozières Ridge to capture Mouquet Farm, generally known as 'Mucky Farm'. Australian 2nd Division returned to the fighting towards the end of August suffering further loss for little progress. Relieved by Canadian troops at the month's end, the Australians moved to the relative quiet of the Ypres Salient on 5th September, to recuperate.

Autumn brought increasingly wet weather to the Somme, and the ubiquitous, deep, cloying mud became its defining feature. Originally planned for 21st October, a major assault to capture the Ancre Heights, a southern extension of Thiepval Ridge, had been delayed by bad weather. The French had launched a counter-offensive at Verdun however, so to keep the Germans off-balance the British continued attacks with limited objectives against enemy salients and strongpoints.

Albert's battalion returned to the Somme sector at the end of October, entering the line around Gueudecourt and Flers, just south of Bapaume. Australian 7th Brigade was attached to the Australian 1st Division for an attack against the Gueudecourt salient, as a prelude to the Battle for the Ancre Heights. In pouring rain, the Brigade attacked the German salient, with Albert's battalion placed on the far-left flank. Albert went over the top alongside his platoon sergeant, Sergeant Cunningham, and Privates Cook, Bonsey, Johnson, Dawkins and Kelly as RFA 18-pounder field guns fired shrapnel overhead to keep the enemy down.

The moment the Aussies climbed their parapet they came under a withering fire from German machine guns and artillery forcing the men to take refuge in shell holes well before they could reach their objective. Their slightest movement then attracted sniper and machine gun fire. After a time, reinforcements arrived and the battalion again tried to advance, but hostile fire remained too strong and again they went to ground. At last dusk fell and the survivors made their way back to Australian lines, leaving their dead on the battlefield.

The first battalion roll call for three days took place late the following day. Albert and at least twenty-two other men from 28th, Battalion, including Privates Bonsey and Kelly, remained unaccounted for. A week later, they were reported 'Missing in Action sometime between 3th and 6th November'.

Two months later, Albert's sister, Florence, wrote to the Red Cross at Carlton House Terrace, London, asking whether they could obtain news of her brother. Mrs Selby Smith of Dudswell and a Colonel Reid from St Leonard's-On-Sea also contacted the Australian Red Cross Society in London regarding Albert. The Red Cross made inquiries with the German authorities and interviewed eyewitnesses in hospitals and rest camps on both sides of the Channel. In the meantime, the Australian Army returned Albert's personal effects to his father at Cow Roast Lock. They included photographs, letters, a belt, a clasp knife and a whistle on a chain.

Any hopes Albert's family still held ended in June 1917, when Florence and Mrs Selby Smith received letters from the Red Cross quoting eyewitness testimony, 'which leads us to believe, that he was killed in action on Nov. 5th 1916.' Red Cross Officials interviewed Sergeant Cunningham and Privates Cook and Johnson at the 3rd Australian Auxiliary Hospital at Dartford in Kent, and Private Dawkins at a Rest Camp in Boulogne. They all testified that they saw Albert fall half way across no-man's-land when a shrapnel shell burst, instantly cutting down six or seven men. Private Cook said, 'He was hit through the chest with shrapnel and lived only a few minutes. I knew him well, he being the only man of that name in the Company'. Private Dawkins believed it was, 'one of our 18-pounder shells', which, 'fell short and killed seven of our men. Pickthorn was one of the seven, and I myself saw him fall.' The Australian Red Cross Society forwarded these 'unofficial' eye witness testimonies to Albert's sister and Mrs Selby Smith so that, distressing as it was, Albert's family knew as much as possible about the circumstances of his death.

On 26th July 1917, a court of inquiry ruled that Albert had died in action sometime between 3th November and 6th November 1916. Albert's name is among those now inscribed on the Australian Memorial at Villers-Bretonneux.

Captain Vere Duncombe LOXLEY
Royal Marine Light Infantry

13th November 1916

Vere Duncombe Loxley was the second son of Reverend Arthur Smart Loxley and his wife Alice. He was born in Fairford, Gloucestershire on 7th September 1881, where, three years earlier his father had become Vicar of the impressive church of St Mary. Vere spent his early years at the vicarage in Fairford, being looked after by Ann Gurney, the same nanny who had moved with the family from their earlier home in Lamport.

Vere Loxley was educated at Horris Hill Preparatory School in Berkshire and later at Radley College. Choosing to follow his elder brother, Arthur Noel Loxley, into a military career, Loxley entered the Royal Naval College to train as an officer in the Royal Marine Light Infantry. Loxley's first report from there stated that he 'promises well.' The next report was however, not quite as favourable - 'inattentive, appears capable and fairly quick in learning...' Loxley received his commission on 2nd September 1900, and became a Lieutenant, Royal Marines on 1st July the following year.

Since the mid-19th century, there had been two distinct branches within the Royal Marines, the Royal Marine Artillery (RMA) and the Royal Marine Light Infantry (RMLI). The Royal Marines were the spearhead of landing parties, performing the traditional light infantry role of striking fast and hard to capture key objectives and provide a secure beachhead for the main body of naval ratings and blue-jacketed RMA. The RMLI fought in this role during the Crimean War and numerous Victorian colonial

Captain Vere Duncombe Loxley
(Source: Patrick James Coleridge Sumner)

expeditions, such as the destruction of Benin City, in which Loxley's elder brother, Arthur, had taken part.

However, despite being the experts in military matters aboard ship, the advice of RMLI officers was sometimes ignored and they were considered the social inferiors of their Naval equivalents. Consequently, the Admiralty took steps to improve the standing and promotion prospects of RMLI officers. The RMA already manned the rearmost main turrets on big warships and any secondary guns that they might take ashore. From 1901, the RMLI served a number of the 4-inch and 6-inch guns aboard naval vessels and from 1902, RMLI officers were encouraged to assist the Gunnery Lieutenant RN with small arms, physical drills and gymnastics, work parties and wireless telegraphy.

In November 1902, Loxley joined the newly commissioned London class battleship HMS *Venerable*, which sailed from Malta with the Mediterranean Fleet. During his time on Malta, Loxley spent his free time organising the football team and boat racing crews, whilst also becoming fluent in German. He returned to Portsmouth at the end of July 1905 with a note on his Service Record describing him as a 'zealous officer'.

In April 1906, Loxley transferred to HMS *Dido*, an *Eclipse* class, 11-gun, cruiser launched in 1896, which sailed with the Channel Fleet and later with the Home Fleet. In early 1908, Loxley transferred to a *Challenger* class cruiser, HMS *Encounter*, of the Royal Navy's Australian Squadron, protecting Britain's South Pacific possessions from its base at Sydney. During his stay in Australia, Loxley added French to his linguistic repertoire.

Recalled to the Marines' Portsmouth Division at Eastney Barracks in May 1910, Loxley became a Captain RM and began learning Spanish. Two years later, he spent seven months aboard the gunnery training ship, HMS *Magnificent*, a former battleship docked at Dartmouth, his conduct there being summarised as 'zealous, good judgement'. After two months at HMS *Exmouth* Loxley's final sea posting was to HMS *St George*, a former cruiser converted to a depot ship for Destroyers, which joined the Humber Patrol following the outbreak of war.

In September 1915, Loxley transferred to the Royal Marine Brigade and embarked for Gallipoli. Two RMLI battalions had sailed with the original Anglo-French taskforce the previous February that had attempted to force the opening of the Dardanelles by Naval power alone. After that operation failed, the RMLI returned to Gallipoli with the military invasion force on 29th April, under the command of 1st Australian Division. By the time of Loxley's arrived on Gallipoli in mid-October, the RMLI had already suffered heavy losses from combat and disease following six months of heavy fighting. Work to improve their trenches and dugouts was now underway in anticipation of a harsh winter ahead and Loxley spent his first week getting the feel of the environment in the RMLI trenches, whilst the weather was becoming very wet and cold.

Writing to a cousin on 6th November 1915, Loxley put a brave face on the trying conditions, describing the trenches as, '... certainly a great deal more cosy than ever I expected them to be. The sound of shells, bullets etc., when you are perfectly certain they cannot hit you, get quite soothing after a bit and help to send one to sleep at night, this is not swank but a solid fact. One quite misses the bang – ping – whiz – when one gets back to the rest camp.'

Loxley, who had since been appointed Second in Command of 1st Royal Marine Battalion, continued, '... The officers out here are quite nice and the Colonel is a dear and as for the men they are perfectly topping...' though Loxley was in no doubt that the men watched new officers closely for signs of nervousness.

Looking across the rest camp towards the setting sun, and the field hospital atop a low ridge, Loxley wrote, 'The whole space in between is thick with men, washing, smoking, playing football, some in their dugouts singing songs to a concertina accompaniment or writing letters home – they write a lot – two bands are playing one a Scotch one with its bagpipes which can be heard for miles and everywhere are troops returning home to their bivouacs with picks and shovels over their shoulders and rifles slung...'

Seven days later, Loxley assumed command of the Battalion for one week when the Colonel fell ill. Heavy rain flooded the trenches while the Marines struggled to repair their crumbling sides. When it stopped raining, high winds threw up sandstorms, making life even more intolerable. Then, towards the end of November, it began to snow.

The best Loxley could hope to do was maintain morale, as neither his men, nor any of the Allied forces on the Peninsula, were fit for offensive action with their sick lists swollen by frostbite and exposure cases. Meanwhile, the War Cabinets in London and Paris debated the merits of beating Germany on the Western Front, against seeking shortcuts to victory on secondary fronts such as Gallipoli. Finally, on 8th December, the British and French Governments decided on a stealthy withdrawal from the Gallipoli Peninsula.

The scheme to evacuate 80,000 allied troops, not to mention the disposal of stores and equipment, was a masterpiece of deception and was restricted to the highest level. Every night for ten days, front line troops gradually withdrew to positions near the beaches ready for picking up by Royal Navy boats on the final night. About a quarter of the total force, including most of the Marines, remained in the trenches as a rear guard while destroying the remaining stores. Although rumours were rife, the troops did not learn of the evacuation until 13th December, even though the rearward move had already begun.

To deceive the Turks and lend some sense of normality, activity continued around the hospital tents, although the wounded were the first to be evacuated. Empty ration carts clattered as noisily as possible up to the front lines, then stole away loaded with excess stores on muffled wheels, while small parties of soldiers rushed up and down the line firing rifles and machine guns to imitate well-garrisoned trenches. British artillery introduced lengthening ceasefires at night, accustoming the Turks to quiet periods lasting up to four hours, so the guns might withdraw unmolested. Meanwhile, the Turks continued their daily routine of shelling Allied positions, unaware that anything was amiss.

The evacuation of Gallipoli commenced overnight on 19th/20th December 1915, while Loxley and his fellow Marines worked hard into January to appear to be a large force. They fixed rifles in empty trenches, rigged to fire when a container filled by dripping water was heavy enough to pull the trigger. Some Marines even wore French uniforms to occupy French positions. The first RMLI officers and men departed on New Year's Eve and by 7th January, the strength on the Peninsula was about 13 officers and 800 men. The following night, 208 officers and men remained and the night after that, they had all gone. For his 'gallant and distinguished service' at Gallipoli, Loxley was Mentioned in Despatches.

The withdrawal of such a large a force in contact with an undefeated enemy offered a small glimmer of success in a campaign that had otherwise been a costly fiasco. While their future was discussed in London, the Marine battalions recovered from their Gallipoli ordeal with four months of light duties on the island of Lemnos. Just as the hot Mediterranean summer was about to start, the Marines were ordered to the Western Front, 2nd Battalion, leaving first on 8th May 1916. A week later, Loxley, with 24 fellow officers and 1,021 men of 1st Battalion, left Mudros aboard HMT *Aragon* en route to Marseilles. Landing there on 19th May, they boarded a troop train to Pont Remy then marched to billets at Longpré, in the Somme sector, where Loxley discovered that he had become an Acting Major and that his Battalion had joined 63rd (Royal Naval) Division.

Winston Churchill had formed the Royal Naval Division, (RND), from surplus reservist sailors under Admiralty command in 1914. The RND fought on Gallipoli as an independent division, but it eventually became an Army Division, having absorbed 1st and 2nd RMLI and one Army Brigade. However, the Division obstinately retained its nautical traditions and consisted of battalions named after famous Admirals such as Hawke, Howe, Hood, Nelson and Drake.

After ten days spent re-equipping and training, 1st RMLI went north to Hersin, some 12 miles west of Lens. They arrived there on 2nd June for six weeks training and familiarisation with Western Front conditions, including the Marines' initiation into gas warfare. The gas masks of that time, called gas helmets, were simply cloth bags, impregnated with neutralising chemicals, worn over the head and tucked into the uniform collar. The Marines, peering through the two circular windows of the gas helmets, were taught to breathe in through the nose, drawing air through the damp cloth, and exhale through the outlet valve clamped between their teeth. Gas drills followed, which involved walking through a chamber filled with gas, to give the men confidence that the damp, uncomfortable gas helmets really did work.

The Marines entered front line trenches at Angres on 14th July, two weeks into the Somme Offensive, and immediately an exploding shell wounded Loxley in his left thigh. Surgeons safely removed the shrapnel at hospital at Étaples, and Loxley returned to England to recover, possibly convalescing at his mother's home in Little Cloisters, Gloucester.

Loxley returned to France on 2nd September and re-joined his battalion at Angres five days later. The Battalion's routine of trench duty and training had continued mostly unchanged during his absence, although the Marines had received Lewis guns to replace their old Naval Maxims. The Battalion underwent intensive assault training at Dieval between 20th September and 4th October, and then marched south to Mailly-Maillet for a further three days' training while Loxley and five other officers familiarised themselves with the local trenches. By 18th October, the Marines had moved to Hédauville where a group of officers, including Loxley, reconnoitred the trenches between the village of Hamel and the north bank of the River Ancre from which they would be attacking. What the officers found horrified them.

The assault against Beaumont Hamel, north of the Ancre, had failed on 1st July, so the offensive's main effort had shifted from the Ancre sector to exploit successes further south. German artillery, bad weather and neglect had left the support trenches filled with mud, water and lumps of chalk, the remaining dugouts offered virtually no shelter and the communication trenches, which ran across a nearby ridge, were clearly visible from the Germans lines. The Marines duly entered the trenches at Hamel on 23rd October, and began work to make them serviceable for the battalions that would support the forthcoming attack. Meanwhile, the artillery preparation began. For ten days before dawn every morning, British guns pounded the German front with a hurricane bombardment, but no attack followed. British planners hoped that German troops would tire of these false alarms, thus dulling their reactions when the real assault arrived. Finally, at 21.00 on 12th November, the exhausted Marines moved to their assembly areas, ready to move up to the German wire in no-man's-land.

The RND were to attack along the north side of the Ancre valley on a four-battalion front extending 1,200 yards in total. Hood Battalion was on the right of the first wave, against the River Ancre, then Hawke and Howe Battalions with 1st RMLI on the left, next to 51st (Highland) Division, which would attack Beaumont Hamel itself. The remaining battalions of each brigade deployed directly behind the first row as a second wave, 2nd RMLI supporting 1st RMLI. The RND's four army battalions, including 4th Bedfords, were spread across the rear in reserve. Several hours before Zero, the assaulting battalions crept through the rain into no-man's-land and lay waiting in the open, 200 yards from the German trenches. This would give them a head start when the attack began.

Their initial objective was the three lines of German trenches rising before them, the nearest being some 200 yards from the Marines, and the farthest lying about 800 yards away. Beyond, was a valley containing a road known as Station Road running from Beaumont-Hamel to Beaucourt Station and parallel to that was Station Trench, the second objective. The road from Beaumont Hamel to the village of Beaucourt-sur-l'Ancre and the trench alongside it formed the third objective, while the final objective was the capture of the aptly named Muck Trench. The RND's battalions were to attack leapfrog fashion, one moving onto the next objective while the other consolidated what it had just taken. Loxley's 1st Battalion was to capture the first and third objectives, while 2nd RMLI was to capture the second and fourth objectives. Unfortunately, unknown to the RND there was a large strongpoint in the middle of the German front line held by about 600 men.

At 05.45 on Monday 13th November, the whistles sounded and Loxley's Marines rose up amidst the darkness, thick fog and artillery bombardment. Although lulled by the daily spoof bombardments, German artillery quickly began to react and enemy machine-gunners were ready to defend their positions. As the Royal Marines struggled through the cloying mud, heavy German shellfire killed Loxley and his fellow company commanders. Half of the Battalion's casualties for the whole battle took place in those terrible first few minutes. The brigade on their right had some success however, and 51st Division captured Beaumont Hamel. When the battle ended two days later the RND had achieved all its objectives, but 1st RMLI had suffered 362 casualties amongst the 490 Marines who had attacked. Of those, 88 men and 10 officers, including 35-year-old Loxley, had died. The Knightsbridge Cemetery, situated in the middle of a field just outside the village of Mesnil now contains Loxley's grave along with those of many of his fellow Marines who died during the attack.

Writing Loxley's obituary, Lt. Col. Lywood, RMLI, described him as, '... one of the best types of a British officer and English gentleman; he was simply loved by his men ... Always devoted to his company or detachment he was always ready to lead them in fighting or in manly games....'

A Memorial Service for Major Vere Duncombe Loxley, led by the Bishop of Gloucester, was held in Gloucester Cathedral's Lady Chapel at noon on 28th November 1916. Most members of the closely-linked Loxley and Duncombe families and many family friends attended.

The Battle of the Ancre was the final phase of the Battle of the Somme. It was successful in that both Beaumont Hamel and Beaucourt were captured, but Serre and the northern part of the German front line remained in enemy hands. The Ancre salient was to prove to be a very dangerous area to be posted during the following winter.

2nd Lieutenant Royden Spencer Bayspool PORTER
2nd Battalion, Infantry (Territorial Force), Honourable Artillery Company

6th February 1917

Royden Spencer Bayspool Porter was born in July 1890, at Streatham, Surrey, the son of George Joseph Bayspool Porter and Mrs Ada Porter. He was baptised on 8th September 1890 at St James the Apostle in Lambeth. Royden's father, was a partner in a busy firm of London solicitors, Farrar, Porter & Co, which had offices at 2 Wardrobe Place, Doctors Common, close to St Paul's Cathedral. The Porter's family home was at Tower Lodge, 44 Crystal Palace Park Road, Sydenham, where they employed three servants. Perhaps unsurprisingly, when Royden completed his education he joined his father's firm as an articled clerk and in 1912 he was admitted as a solicitor.

In 1914 Royden Porter was living in Thames Ditton, Surrey. On 6th October, he enlisted with the Honourable Artillery Company (HAC) as Private 2449, and joined 'A' (Reserve) Battery based at Armoury House in City Road, just outside the City of London boundary. Founded to defend London by well-to-do City gentlemen in the reign of Henry VIII, the HAC is possibly the oldest regiment in the British Army. During the Boer War, the HAC joined the City Imperial Volunteers for its first service overseas and in 1908 it transferred to the newly created Territorial Force after a special Act of Parliament had been passed to safeguard its property and privileges. Although the HAC was primarily a field artillery unit, in 1914 it also possessed a half-battalion of infantry, which was quickly made up to full strength and sent to France on 18th September. A 2nd Infantry Battalion was then raised to replace it.

As the Territorial Force was only the third line of Britain's home defences, after the Royal Navy and the Regular Army, it received older, cast off equipment. In August 1914, the HAC still had obsolete 15-pounder field guns of Boer War vintage which were insufficient to train the flood of new recruits. Fortunately, members of the HAC lacked neither funds nor influence. Vickers, the armaments firm, loaned additional 15-pdrs and HAC members made good shortfalls of equipment through private purchases. Armoury House, being so close to the City, only offered limited training facilities for riding, driving and horsemanship, so the HAC hired horses, stables, and a field some miles away at Greenford.

Private RSB Porter quickly progressed up the ranks; appointed Lance Corporal on Boxing Day 1914; Acting Corporal a few days later and promoted to Acting Sergeant the following March. In April 1915, his Battery joined the Essex Battery, Royal Horse Artillery, in the small Suffolk village of Great Bealings, east of Ipswich, for training exercises. These proved most unsatisfactory, because both batteries were expected to share the same equipment.

On 5th October 1915, Porter was one of six HAC NCOs commissioned into 2nd Battalion, Infantry, HAC as Second Lieutenants. He joined 'B' Company, which was camped in Richmond Park, before moving into winter billets around Wimbledon that November. In January 1916, the Battalion was sent to help dig new defences for London at Rayleigh and Thundersley in Essex, the men being billeted across the Thames in a disused brewery at Green Street Green, Orpington. After six months' digging, 2nd Battalion had a brief stay near Epson Downs racecourse, before moving to the Tower of London at the end of August, where they prepared for service in France.

At 06.00 on 1st October 1916, 2nd Battalion marched out of the Tower of London to entrain for Southampton. Leaving the Battalion transport at Southampton Docks to follow later, the Battalion boarded *La Marguerite*, an old paddle steamer that once took holidaymakers to Margate from London Bridge. Early the following day, the Battalion landed at Le Havre and marched to a rest camp for the night.

On 3rd October, the Battalion boarded a train for an unknown destination, although the men were eventually told that they would be joining 7th Division, currently holding the line near Ploegsteerte Wood, south of Ypres. The Battalion detrained at Steenwerck and marched northeast to the Front, where half the Battalion immediately entered the trenches for familiarisation training. The rest were issued with gas masks and given training on how to survive gas attacks. The Battalion's first trenches had been well maintained and duck-boarded, but the high local water table meant they were not very deep. Two newly laid light railway lines brought ammunition and rations forward and could send wounded men rearwards in relative comfort.

Shortly after the Battalion's arrival, its positions were shelled by heavy German railway guns many miles to the rear. Although the railway guns were out of range of British artillery they tried to make their use unpopular by shelling the German soldiers opposite whenever they fired. The railway guns were to prove a constant menace over the coming months.

Its first four days and nights in the trenches cost the Battalion three men killed and thirteen wounded. Once relieved, they marched to an extremely muddy, hutted camp with duckboard tracks at nearby Papot for four days' rest. After another four-day spell in the trenches, the Battalion went into support in even less salubrious dugouts before returning to Papot on 31st

October. Here, well-earned baths and clean underclothing awaited the men, along with the news that they would shortly be participating in the final offensive on the Somme.

Two days later, the Battalion marched to new billets in barns and farm buildings at Steenwerck, alongside the River Lys. Although the Lys was swollen by recent rains and threatening to flood, Brigade HQ refused the Battalion's request to move to higher ground. The rising waters soon cut off 'D' Company altogether along with the Battalion Transport. A first attempt to move the transport resulted in a cart and two horses falling into a deep, unseen ditch; fortunately, the horses survived. Finally, the Battalion's CO encountered 7th Division's Deputy Assistant Adjutant General and persuaded him to authorise an evacuation of the billets and Royal Engineers were called in to construct temporary bridges to get the Transport clear.

At 08.30 next morning, having been issued dry socks in fresh billets, the Battalion marched east to Moulle, near St Omer, for two weeks' extensive training, but the morning after arriving, the Battalion was instructed to leave for Beaumont-Hamel the next day. The Battalion began its 82-mile march south on 13th November, but before reaching their next billets at Ligny, the men began showing signs of strain caused by their earlier soaking in the Lys. Many men fell out on the march as flood-damaged boots began to disintegrate, while others went down with colds and chills. Reaching Raincheval on 22nd November, the Battalion found itself in an area so congested with troops and transport that it took over two hours to cover the final two miles to its billets, some 13 miles northwest of Albert.

On 29th November, the Battalion's 'A' and 'C' Companies took over positions at Beaumont-Hamel with 'B' and 'D' Companies placed in support. After many weeks of shelling, fighting and movement, there had been no possibility of building an elaborate trench system. The front line was improvised from a badly damaged, captured German trench, with shell holes for outposts, with mud about a foot deep in places. By the time that they were relieved on 2nd December, the Battalion had lost six men to German snipers, and several others injured. The Battalion then moved to an enormous, captured deep dugout constructed in a hillside to shelter German reserves from British artillery. It was about two hundred yards long, with galleries accessible by chalk steps leading up to the front-line trenches. There were bunks for over 300 men, mobile generators providing electric lighting and the Officers Mess even came complete with tables and chairs. Small wonder Beaumont-Hamel had resisted capture for so long.

Three days later, the Battalion returned to the front line. By now, the weather had deteriorated and movement between trenches and outposts was almost impossible. Frequently, the only way to avoid a soaking was to use the corpses of unburied soldiers as stepping-stones. Men occupying the forward outposts only had waterproof capes over their uniforms, which did little to keep out the biting cold, let alone the rain.

Each period of garrison duty lasted 24 hours without hot food, which was usually too dangerous to deliver, or cold on arrival. Four straight days spent in freezing, wet, outposts, under constant threat from artillery and rifle fire, with just 24 hours to recover before returning, reduced the men to utter exhaustion. Worse, many began to suffer from trench foot. Trench foot is caused when waterlogged feet, swelling in tight boots, combines with reduced circulation of blood to the extremities owing to cold conditions. Initially the feet turn blue or red and become very numb, but if immersion in cold water continues, the cells in the feet are starved of oxygen and begin to die. Blisters and sores break out, allowing bacteria and fungi to invade the dead tissue. In the years before antibiotics, gangrene would develop, by which stage only amputation could save the man's life.

On 11th December, with the Somme Offensive finally over, the Battalion left the Front and moved into huts at Bertrancourt for six days. Here the men bathed and two companies were issued with new boots and clothing. When 2nd HAC returned to Beaumont-Hamel for another ten-day tour of front line duty, it was in a new trench system some three-quarters of a mile long. With the serious fighting over for the winter, the Battalion was fortunate to incur only three casualties during the next ten days. The Battalion entered the reserve trenches on 5th January 1917, but an artillery barrage inflicted several casualties four days later, and during the evening of 13th January, a German shell burst in the cookhouse killing seven men, wounding fourteen and destroying all the Battalion's stores, rations and utensils.

The Battalion withdrew from the front line the following week, and moved to the village of Rubempré for training. By now, Porter was displaying symptoms of typhoid: high fever, sweating and diarrhoea. Known also as nervous fever, enteric and gastric fever, typhoid thrives in unsanitary conditions and throughout history it has killed more soldiers on campaign than their enemies ever did. Although all British soldiers were routinely inoculated against *salmonella typhi*, which causes typhoid fever, the vaccine could not guarantee full immunity.

Royden Porter was transferred to 24th General Hospital in Étaples where he died on 6th February, aged 26. The text on his headstone in the Étaples Military Cemetery was chosen by his parents who had recently moved to Fendley House in Cow Roast. It reads 'For ever with the Lord'.

Private G13274 Ambrose Alfred BROWN
2nd Battalion, Queen's (Royal West Surrey Regiment)

2nd April 1917

Ambrose Alfred Brown, recorded on the Northchurch War Memorial as J Ambrose Brown, was born in Melbourne, Australia in 1898, the eldest son of Ambrose and Susie Brown. Ambrose's father, was brought up in Northchurch, but originally came from Deanshanger, Buckinghamshire. He had emigrated to Melbourne aboard the *Blairgowrie* eight years before and worked as a boundary rider and fencer on a wool station, while seeking employment as a fitter. In Australia he met his Susie, and they were married at Wagga-Wagga on 11th November 1896. Two years later Ambrose, his wife and their infant son, left Australia for England aboard the *Darmstadt*.

In 1901, the family was living in Bell Lane, Northchurch where Ambrose senior worked as a general labourer at East's Timber merchants in Gossoms End. Ambrose and Susie Brown would have to two more boys – William Richard, born in 1903, and the appropriately named Sydney Melbourne, born in 1908. By 1911, Ambrose had become an engineer's labourer and had moved his family to larger premises in Alma Row, Northchurch. In 1912, Ambrose junior left school and started work at the West End Brush Works in Berkhamsted. In his free time, he took a keen interest in the Northchurch Village Club in New Road.

With the coming of war, Ambrose senior went to work at Coventry Ordnance, and later at Singer Motors, moving his family to 44 Northfield Road, Stoke. In early 1916, Ambrose junior, now aged 18, was called up under the Military Service Act and sent to 9th (Reserve) Battalion, Queen's (Royal West Surrey) Regiment, for basic training. Having been issued with his Field Service Pay Book, Ambrose wrote a short Will on page 13, dated 1st September 1916, giving his unit as 9th Queens RWS and leaving everything to his mother.

Ambrose subsequently joined 2nd Battalion, Queen's Regiment, which had been in France with 7th Division since October 1914. The Battalion had participated in all the major battles on the Western Front, most recently during the Battle of the Somme at Delville Wood. Ambrose, wearing a small cross attached to the cord of his identity tags, probably joined 2nd Battalion with a draft of 267 men at Huppy on 13th September.

Soon afterwards, the Battalion moved to the Ypres Sector, where, on 19th September, Ambrose began his first spell in the front-line trenches. Fortunately, it was a quiet week, mostly spent in trench repair and maintenance. The Battalion had a month of training and manual labour, both in and out of the trenches, before their next tour in the front line began on 23rd October. The Battalion then had to endure several days of hostile attention from field and medium artillery, machine guns and snipers, before being relieved by 22nd Manchesters on 29th October. Through November, the Queen's marched with their brigade by stages towards the Somme, entering the front line at Beaumont Hamel before the month's end.

Ambrose found that five months of fighting in the area had dramatically changed the character of front line defence works. Instead of occupying continuous trenches and dugouts with most of the Battalion, the Queen's now occupied individual posts, spaced 20 to 30 yards apart, with an NCO and six men in each. Including Lewis gun, bombing and sniping posts, only one company held the line at a time, while the others sheltered in dugouts or billets further back. By mid-December, it was becoming so cold in the exposed posts that companies had to be replaced every 18 hours.

Christmas Day 1916 was spent out of the line. After Battalion Church Parade, the companies had their Christmas dinner at 13.00: 'Roast Goose - Roast Beef - plum pudding - oranges - apples - nuts - cigarettes and beer. All seemed pleased' the War Diarist noted. It is possible that Ambrose helped prepare the officers' dinner, because at some point he became an Officer's Servant, or Batman, and derived great pleasure in cooking small tarts and other dainties for them.

At the beginning of 1917, the Battalion was in the front line close to Beaumont-Hamel enduring the harsh cold and a problematic sniper in 'Hope Post'. On 5th January, 9th Devons captured Hope Post but had not managed to consolidated it when they handed it over to a small party from 'D' Coy, the Queen's. A German counterattack subsequently drove the Queen's out after their Lewis gun jammed with mud and the post had to be retaken by the Battalion's bombers. This minor action cost the Queen's 13 casualties.

In mid-January, the routine of working parties and training out of the line at Mailly-Maillett was disrupted by heavy snow. Soldiers spent long periods huddling around improvised fires to keep warm, although the War Diary recorded on 17th, 'Snow fight between H.Q. Section and A & B Coys - easy win for H.Q.' The Battalion left the front line towards the end of January and marched sixteen miles west to billets at Puchevillers for intensive training.

In late 1916, British aerial reconnaissance confirmed indications of a new network of defensive works under construction behind the German front line. Fighting on the Somme, and at Verdun, was stretching the German Army's manpower almost to breaking point, even as British artillery strength was growing. The German High Command recognised that it could not hold the Somme against a renewed Allied offensive in the

Spring, so it ordered a stronger, modern line to be built across the base of the Somme salient, before evacuating the salient, leaving nothing behind. The new line, named the *Siegfried* position, or *Stellung*, ran about 90 miles between Arras and the Aisne opposite Soissons. Being much shorter than the existing Somme front, the *Siegfried Stellung* required 14 fewer divisions to hold it. Central to the *Siegfried Stellung* were successive lines of well-hidden fire trenches, dugouts, pillboxes and strong points up to two miles deep, protected by thick belts of barbed wire and sited on reverse slopes. Assaulting infantry would first have to fight through a screen of scattered outposts, about 1,000 yards deep, on forward slopes, which would fragment their advance. The attackers would then be exposed to crossfire on the skyline, before even reaching the main defences. Meanwhile, German reserves stood by in concrete shelters to counterattack and throw the survivors back to their own lines.

Similar positions were created behind the existing lines to the north and south of the *Siegfreid Stellung*, all named after characters from Wagner's Ring Cycle. Collectively, these *Stellungen* became known to the British as the Hindenburg Line, after the German Army's titular chief, Field Marshal Paul von Hindenburg.

On 9th February 1917, the Germans began the systematic devastation of the Somme salient, before gradually withdrawing to the *Siegfried Stellung* between 15th and 18th March in an operation codenamed *Alberich Bewegung* or Alberich Manoeuvre.

Unaware of *Alberich* and the *Siegfreid Stellung's* full significance, Allied preparation for the 1917 Spring Offensive on the Somme continued. Ambrose's battalion completed its training on 20th February, and then spent several weeks moving between various military camps, and working on roads and tramways, finally arriving at Bolton Camp, west of Beaumont-Hamel, for tactical exercises using live grenades.

The Battalion returned to the front line at Puisieux, opposite Bucquoy, on 12th March. By then the Army Command had realised that the Hindenburg Line was unfinished and, hoping to disrupt German plans for an orderly retreat, ordered 7th Division to capture Bucquoy. Aerial reconnaissance reports said the village appeared empty, but the next day patrols from the Queen's found Germans still entrenched behind three belts of wire, with only one gap, together with many machine gun posts. Objections from 7th Division HQ were over-ruled from above, so that night 2nd Queen's attacked Bucquoy, alongside 22nd Manchesters. Small parties of Queen's, braving hostile machine guns and artillery, penetrated two belts of the German wire, but were stopped by the third. Ordered to withdraw, the Queen's managed to re-occupy their front-line posts before dawn on 14th, but 113 men had been lost. Two days later, the German Army evacuated Bucquoy.

As British troops followed the Germans, they found lethal booby traps, delayed action mines, old and sick civilians and desolation. During *Alberich*, the retreating Germans took thousands of French civilians into forced labour, destroyed their villages and roads, removed or spoiled all sources of food and polluted the water supplies.

On 18th March, the Battalion went into billets at Mailly-Mallet. Their dead from the action on 13th/14th were buried the following day. Ambrose and his comrades spent the next week repairing damage to the road between Serre and Puisieux inflicted during *Alberich*. Meanwhile, 7th Division was ordered to drive the German rearguard out of the fortified village of Croisilles, eight miles southeast of Arras, with all haste.

On 27th March, the Battalion's working parties were cancelled and Ambrose and his comrades were sent north to support an attack by the 22nd Manchesters and 1st South Staffordshires. The attack went in at 05.15 the next day, but both assault battalions were stopped by a thick belt of uncut wire. The Queen's returned to billets while artillery was brought up to cut the wire and pound Croisilles' defences.

A larger, co-ordinated attack, by 21st and 7th Divisions and I Anzac Corps along a ten-mile front, was organised to capture Croisilles and Ecoust-Longatte. 7th Division was instructed to capture Croisilles and establish a line of outposts on the slopes below the Hindenburg Line. Three battalions, 2nd Queen's, 21st Manchesters, and 1st South Staffordshires, were to form up overnight for a dawn attack at 05.15 on 2nd April. The Queen's were to capture the Factory Road and establish a forward line of posts to cover the north of the village, while 'D' Coy took a German strongpoint. One platoon from 'A' Company, under 2nd Lieutenant Gardner, was to be held in reserve.

The night was frosty and brightly moonlit, which helped Ambrose's battalion marching down a valley to their start positions, but it also enabled German outposts to direct an artillery barrage down the valley. There was further delay when part of the friendly barrage fell short, but the Battalion managed to start soon after Zero hour. The Queen's immediately came under machine gun fire from a flanking railway embankment, but it was suppressed by the Lewis Gun sections and by 07.30 the battalion had secured the Factory Road. At 07.55, the reserve platoon came forward to the railway and drove a party of the enemy out of their position on a flank. 'D' Company advanced under a Stokes Mortar barrage and by 10.30 it had taken the strongpoint after it had been re-bombarded. By the end of the day, 7th Division had achieved all of its objectives and Croisilles had fallen, but 2nd Queen's had lost 42 wounded and 25 men killed during the attack, including Ambrose Brown.

A few days after his death, Ambrose's parents received letters from his Company Commander, his Platoon Officer and the Regimental Chaplain. His officers both testified to his popularity in the Battalion. 2nd Lieutenant Gardner also wrote that Ambrose '... was one of a party who bravely attacked a German machine-gun.' Captain Secretan said he was shot through the head by a bullet and had died instantly, which the Chaplain confirmed. They said he was buried with a church service, under a cross by the roadside, south of the village of Croisilles.

Several of his comrades were buried alongside Ambrose in what later became the Croisilles British Cemetery. On the standard headstone, which replaced Ambrose's original cross, is the text chosen by his family, 'That whether we wake or sleep, we should live together with Him'.

Private 35345 William SEAR
12th (Transport Workers) Battalion, Bedfordshire Regiment

8th April 1917

By the spring of 1915, Britain had been at war for almost two years and the number of volunteers was falling. The Government quickly needed to identify men of fighting age who could make up for the rising losses, whilst protecting vital industries. Consequently, in July 1915, Parliament passed the National Registration Act, which called for the compulsory registration of all men and women between the ages of 15 and 65, resident in England, Scotland and Wales. Each individual had to provide their details such as their name, address; marital status and dependents, if any; occupation and any specialist skills.

The results became available in September 1915 and identified just over five million males of military age who had not signed up, of which over two-thirds were not in key positions in terms of skill or employment. The following month, Lord Derby became Director-General of Recruiting and within a week, he created a deferred enlistment scheme, which, unsurprisingly, people called the 'Derby Scheme'. Under the Scheme, men aged between the ages of 18 and 40 voluntarily attested to join the Army Reserve, but remained at home to await their call-up. Married men were promised that single men would be called before them. The War Office then announced that voluntary enlistment would end on 15th December 1915 and that compulsory service would follow.

The Military Service Act, that introduced conscription, came into effect in March 1916. Men between the ages of 18 and 41 on 2nd November 1915 were now liable to be called-up for service unless they were married or widowed with dependent children, or else worked in one of the reserved professions. The following May, the differentiation between married and unmarried men was removed, and the upper age limit was soon raised to 45. Military Service Tribunals were constituted by local councils to hear appeals for exemption from military service made by individuals or employers on their behalf. These Local Tribunals were usually chaired by the Mayor or a magistrate and included members who understood local employment needs as well as a military representative. Grounds for appeal included personal hardship for the man and his dependents, infirmity and ill health, work in the national interest and conscientious objection to military service. Applicants dissatisfied with the Local Tribunal could appeal to County Appeal Tribunals, which either upheld the Local Tribunal's decision or sent the case back for reconsideration.

William Sear, a married man of 39, received his call up papers under the Military Service Act in the late summer of 1916. He belonged to the extended Sear family of Orchard End, Northchurch, with his grandparents, aunt and uncles all living close by. William was born in 1877, the second son of Walter and Emily Sear. His brother, James, was two years older and there were also two younger brothers and a sister.

Emily Sear died in the summer of 1890, aged only 36, leaving Walter to bring up his young family, so his sister moved in to help as a housekeeper. After a time, Walter found a new wife, Annie, who came from Berkhamsted and the family moved to 1 Clarence Road, on the corner of King's Road. Here Walter and Annie started their own family and by 1901, William had two stepbrothers and two stepsisters.

The Sears were a family of skilled tradesmen; William's grandfather James and his uncle Arthur were both carpenters and his younger brother, Frederick, became a plumber. William's father, Walter, elder brother, James, and William himself were all bricklayers, with his brother, Albert, also learning the trade. In later years Uncle Arthur diversified by keeping an orchard, one and a half acres of watercress beds, a dairy supplied by his own cows and a flock of poultry. Arthur, who also acted as Northchurch's undertaker, still took on small, local building contracts and he came to employ William as a bricklayer and general handyman.

William later met and courted Kate Mary Jones from Kempston in Bedfordshire where they enjoyed a summer wedding in 1907. The newlyweds made Orchard End their home and attended the Baptist Chapel in Northchurch, where William's grandfather was one of the leaders.

By 1914, Arthur Sear's business had expanded, and, apart from William, he employed eight other people. The war was soon to bring changes as, one by one, the men left for military service. William became increasingly important to the daily running of Arthur's business as he took on more jobs, including the management of the milk round.

In the late summer of 1916, married men such as William were being called up for the Army. Arthur, as William's employer, immediately appealed to keep him and on 28th October, they both appeared before the Berkhamsted Rural Tribunal. Although Arthur told the Tribunal that William was his last remaining employee of the nine working for him before the war, the appeal failed. A month later Arthur and William took their case to the County Appeal Tribunal at Hertford, but they received a most unsympathetic hearing.

With his appeal for exemption rejected, William was ordered to report to the Watford Recruiting Office on 15th January 1917. Following his medical examination, William was classified as 'B1', meaning that he was fit for service in a support capacity and able to march five miles, see to shoot with glasses, and could hear well.

William was sent to the 12th (Transport Workers) Battalion,

Bedfordshire Regiment, which was based at Croydon and belonged to the Home Defence Army. Transport Workers battalions were authorised to provide parties of men to supplement civilian labour in docks, canals and railways where there was a manpower shortage. They mostly handled munitions cargo, but they often prevented ports from becoming blocked ensuring that the BEF's supply lines flowed freely. Most men in the Transport Workers battalions had been transferred from other units because of ill health or wounds that made them unfit for active duty. Others, like William, were conscripts whose medical grade disqualified them from front line service. William and his comrades wore army uniform, were subject to Army discipline, were taught how to march and how to salute, but did not carry weapons. Working harmoniously alongside civilians, they earned civilian wages, but were expected to pay for their own food and billets.

12th Bedfords was responsible for providing support in the ports of Folkestone, Rochester, Chatham, Sittingbourne, Weymouth and Newhaven. William joined a detachment working at the port of Newhaven on 6th February 1917 and was billeted with a Mrs Annie King in a small terraced house in Evelyn Avenue.

From his arrival in Newhaven, William appeared very nervous and seemed depressed. He frequently complained of pains in his head and that he had been ill before being conscripted. On the evening of Tuesday 3rd April, eight weeks after arriving in Newhaven, William confided to a comrade that he was feeling ill and suffering from memory loss. On his comrade's advice, William reported sick to the Battalion's Captain the next day and was advised to visit Newhaven's military hospital. Here a doctor diagnosed William as suffering from neurasthenia and prescribed medication. William returned to Evelyn Avenue at 11.00 and later went out telling Mrs King that he was going for a stroll and would be back by 15.00; no one saw him alive again.

When William failed to report for duty next morning, enquiries were made of Mrs King who stated that she had not seen him since he left the previous afternoon. The following Sunday morning, a man from Newhaven was passing a workshop in the hamlet of Piddinghoe, about a mile north of Evelyn Avenue, when he noticed that a board had been removed from one of the workshop's doors. Thinking it unusual, he looked inside and saw the body of a soldier hanging from a beam. He immediately informed the police, but by the time a constable arrived at the scene, others had cut the body down. It was William Sear.

A formal inquest convened at Newhaven on 10th April 1917, heard statements from seven witnesses, including Mrs King, members of William's battalion and William's wife Kate, who had not seen her husband since his conscription. Having considered the witnesses' statements, the Coroner's Jury agreed that William had committed suicide by hanging himself whilst insane at the time.

With hindsight, it was probable that William had found it increasingly difficult to cope with the strain of the extra workload put on him whilst in Northchurch. William's conscription into the army, the Tribunal process, and finally the enforced move from Northchurch to Newhaven were too much for him.

Returned to Northchurch, William's body now lies in the old Baptist Chapel's burial ground in Bell Lane beneath a Commonwealth War Graves Commission headstone.

Private 41068 Albert John DELL
19th Battalion, Manchester Regiment

23rd April 1917

Another member of the Dell family's Northchurch branch who went off to war was Albert Dell. Born in 1892, Albert was the eldest son of Joseph and his second wife, Ellen. The years between 1908 and 1911 had seen considerable changes in the Dell family; Ellen Dell died in 1908 and the following year Albert's brother, Walter, enlisted as a boy soldier with the Grenadier Guards. Joseph Dell died in 1910 and the following year, Albert's sister Florence married and moved to Wigginton taking her 12-year-old younger brother, Edwin, with her. Albert, meanwhile, had started work as a printer's compositor and seems to have developed a love of books.

In 1911, Albert was lodging with a Mrs Ruth Engledow and her family at 38 Gossoms End, next door to where he grew up. Sometime before 1914, he left Gossoms End for Hinckley, Leicestershire. Here he started to court Hilda Mackey, who lived at 48, Queens Road, a small 'two up two down' terraced house, not far from Hinckley town centre. It is possible that they later became engaged to be married.

In the summer of 1915, Albert enlisted with the Leicestershire Regiment at Hinckley and spent the following November training with 3/5th Battalion at Belton Park near Grantham, Lincolnshire. Whilst at

Private Albert Dell
(Source: Clive Blofield)

Belton Park, Albert wrote to his stepsister, Alice Eglesfield, telling her, 'We are being worked pretty hard just at the present but it is doing us all the good in the world, and I am sure that my health has greatly improved since I joined up'. In February the following year, Albert was still in England, at Bulwell Park, north of Nottingham. Although Albert's military service records no longer survive, it is likely that he was with a reinforcing draft that joined 1/5th Battalion, Leicestershire Regiment near Arras in March 1916.

The 1/5th Battalion, had originally gone to France in February 1915, joining 138th Brigade, 46th (North Midland) Division the following month. At Hooge, in July 1915, it was among the first British battalions to encounter German flame-throwers, and the following October, the Battalion participated in the attack on the Hollenzollern Redoubt during the Battle of Loos. In December 1915, 46th Division was sent to Egypt. Half the Division reached Egypt on 13th January 1916, while 1/5th Leicesters waited with the remainder at Marseilles for suitable transport. However, when at last the Battalion had boarded HMT *Andania*, they were ordered to disembark and return to the Western Front, where the rest of the Division would join them, because, following the successful evacuation of the Gallipoli Peninsular, the Division was no longer required in the Mediterranean.

By March 1916, 1/5th Leicesters found themselves a few miles north of Arras at Vimy, where the hard chalk was ideal for underground warfare. French, British and German engineers were all busy tunnelling deep beneath no-man's-land to lay explosive charges large enough to obliterate entire lengths of enemy trenches.

Albert's battalion was one of several providing shifts of working parties to assist the tunnellers. They passed sandbags of excavated material up the tunnels and stacked them inside the entrance, ready to be used for night-time trench repairs, thus hiding the chalky earth in plain sight. Work in the airless, claustrophobic tunnels was hard and dangerous. Tunnellers, using small tools in as near silence as possible, stopped periodically to listen for the sounds of German digging. Both sides tried to collapse enemy tunnels by setting off small explosive charges next to them called *camouflets*. On one occasion four men of Alberts's Battalion were working alongside French miners when a German *camouflet* blew in their tunnel. Two Leicesters, half-naked, bruised and choking, managed to crawl from the ruined shaft, but the others were never seen again.

It was a great relief for the Leicesters to be withdrawn and sent to Lucheux, south of Arras, during May, but they were also there to train for the great Somme Offensive. Perhaps fearing the worst, Albert wrote his Will on 18th June.

When 1/5th Leicesters were in reserve for 46th Division's unsuccessful diversionary attack on Gommecourt Salient on 1st July, Albert was among those fortunate to survive the attack and the Battalion returned to billets at Bienvillers to recover. On 12th July, the Battalion moved to Bailleulmont where the men could have baths and spent their time generally refitting. Refreshed, they returned to the front two days later, this time further north at Monchy-au-Bois. Here, they found the trenches ruined by rain and heavy shelling and worse, they were full of gas cylinders left after a successful cloud attack on 14th July, some of which were still hazardous with residual chemical. German prisoners later admitted that the gas had caused serious casualties in their companies.

The troops set to work clearing the trenches and re-installing pipes and cylinders for another gas attack employing 'White Star', which consisted of a mix of chlorine and phosgene and '2-red Star', a flammable, but deadly hydrogen sulphide, or H_2S. At the time the gas valves were opened on 17th July, Albert was delivering supplies with a ration party. At 22.00, a heavy, thick cloud of 'White Star' and H_2S crossed the lines and German rifle fire diminished, but the enemy's artillery retaliated immediately. Writing later to his Aunts, Fanny Dell and Louisa Payne, who were living in the Northchurch Almshouses, Arthur recounted, '... Heavies, shrapnel, whizzbangs, trench mortars, rifle grenades, bullets and old Harry himself came by, and to cap the lot it started to rain. We took what shelter we could and arrived at the dugout about an hour later than we should have done. In spite of all the gifts our friends over the way had showered on us, not a man was hurt, unless I say an officer who was injured slightly in the heel owing to one of his men displaying excessive haste in going up a trench with his bayonet fixed, but then some people always are in such a hurry'.

On 18th July, the battalion returned to Bienvillers where Albert had a comfy billet in a barn. Unfortunately, Bienvillers was well within the range of German heavy guns and two days later they opened fire, dropping some 100 rounds into the village at 08.00. Two hours later they fired another salvo. Albert Dell was sitting in his billet, having just finished cleaning his equipment, when a shell exploded directly above the barn spraying shrapnel bullets through the damaged roof. Albert and his mates rushed into the barn's cellar where he discovered that he had suffered a head wound.

Albert was bandaged at the Regimental Aid Post, before going to a local dressing station for a more thorough examination. That afternoon, Albert was transferred to a Casualty Clearing Station and examined under general aesthetic in case he had more shrapnel inside his body. Fortunately, the surgeon found none, and Albert went to N°7 Canadian General Hospital at Étaples to recover. Albert wrote a letter from there to reassure his Aunts, which he ended by urging them, 'not to be anxious over me for I shall soon be all right, as I always was rather lucky'.

Following his discharge from hospital, Albert probably remained at

Étaples before being posted to a different battalion, 19th Manchester Regiment. Since the start of 1916, as the BEF grew larger and its units saw rising casualties, the Army had struggled to ensure that there were enough experienced soldiers in the battalions that had suffered heavy losses. Consequently, so that depleted battalions could be rebuilt, men who had recovered from wounds were no longer automatically returned to their old regiments, but instead were sent where they were most needed.

Albert was most likely with the draft of 78 men that joined 19th Manchesters at Bailleulval, about seven miles southwest of Arras, in mid-December 1916. After a few days of training, Albert and the new draft were inspected by the Battalion's Commanding Officer. Three days later, the Battalion entered the front line to spend the Christmas period maintaining their trenches as best they could in appallingly cold and wet weather.

The weather was hardening when the battalion left the front line on 6th January 1917. On arrival at Bouquemaison, the men's feet were inspected for trench foot, a serious hazard for soldiers spending lengthy period in cold, wet trenches. After a short stay at Bouquemaison, the Battalion marched five miles to Pommera, where their training for the next planned offensive began in earnest.

The Battalion returned to front line duties on 6th February at Achicourt, just south of Arras, finding it very quiet, as both sides were preparing their next moves. The Manchesters were then employed repairing bridges, pipelines and even a local cinema behind the lines in the Beaumetz area. Later, the Battalion was ordered to march south to the Madeleine Redoubt, just west of the village of Mercatel. For four days, the Battalion came under heavy German artillery fire, and suffered a number of casualties. However, the Madeleine Redoubt proved a good base for the Manchesters to mount reconnaissance raids to establish German strength and, when possible, take some German prisoners.

Once the German withdrawal to the Hindenburg Line had started, Albert's battalion followed them closely across the ruined territory they had vacated. Close enough that on 2nd April, 19th Manchesters lost nearly 40 men killed whilst attacking Hénin-sur-Cojeul, directly in front of the new German defences.

A week later, on Easter Monday, the Battalion supported 2nd Wiltshires as they attacked out of a blinding snowstorm to open the First Battle of the Scarpe. Two of 19th Manchesters' Companies lost men helping the Wiltshires to dig in along a sunken road. The Canadians also assaulted Vimy Ridge, followed by further Anglo-Australian and French attacks.

On 23rd April, the Second Battle of the Scarpe began with the Manchesters in reserve on the west side of the Cojeul River. At 09.15, they received orders to cross the river and proceed to the slope before the village of Héninel. By 11.30, they were in position and as the Manchesters advanced to their first objective, the old British front line trench, heavy artillery and machine gun fire broke up their advance and the Companies became intermingled. Having reached the trench, the Battalion had to re-organise, but then at 17.00, new orders arrived. The Battalion, supported by 18th Kings (Liverpool), was to attack an 800-yard long German trench overlooking Cherisy within the hour. Major CL MacDonald, who kept the Battalion's War Diary, expressed deep concerns that the objective was too wide, the time for briefing company commanders and men too short, and that the Germans would be alert for another attack.

MacDonald's misgivings were proved correct. The Manchesters attacked promptly at 18.00 but the advancing troops were too spread out to maintain effective contact and British shells dropped short of the enemy trenches inflicting casualties among the men. Albert's comrades managed to penetrate the German trench in a few places, but found it heavily defended, while the expected support from 18th Kings arrived late. Having consolidated the sections of trench they had captured, the Manchesters were relieved the next day.

Among the many casualties on 23rd April was Private Albert Dell. Albert's body was never formally identified after the attack and his name is now preserved on the Arras Memorial. Albert left his £5 War Loan Bond, books and possessions in Northchurch to his sister, Alice Eglesfield. He bequeathed the rest of his money to his girlfriend in Hinckley, Hilda Mackey, along with his remaining collection of books.

Gunner 110194 Joseph DYER
'D' Battery, 50th Brigade, Royal Field Artillery

14th June 1917

Joseph Dyer came from a family closely associated with the Grand Junction Canal that passed through Northchurch and Berkhamsted. He was born in February 1891, the second child of a barge family whose members were briefly living in the hamlet of Walton, near Aylesbury. Joseph's father, William John Dyer, was a canal boatman from Fenny Stratford, and his mother came from Berkhamsted. They were married around 1879 and Joseph's elder brother, Arthur William, was born in Berkhamsted about a year later.

When Joseph was only a few years old, his parents returned to Berkhamsted, settling in George Street, which was then part of the eastern side of Northchurch Parish, close by the canal. Four more children, Walter, Alice, Sarah and Fred, were born there between 1894 and 1903. Joseph grew up in George Street, initially at N°100, and then N°2 and finally at N°3.

Joseph's father captained his own barge at the turn of the century, but by 1911 William had left the boats and was working as a general labourer alongside his eldest son Arthur. Later however, the family moved to the Lock House in nearby Raven's Lane, so it appears William did not give up his canal life entirely. Joseph, having left school, worked as a domestic gardener, whilst younger brother, Walter, was a labourer at one of Berkhamsted's breweries.

Walter was the first of the Dyer brothers to enlist and on 22nd August 1914, he joined 3rd Norfolk Regiment. Joseph and elder brother, Arthur, enlisted later, Arthur joining as an infantryman with 11th Essex Regiment and Joseph as a Gunner with the Royal Field Artillery (RFA). After completing his training, Joseph went to France at the start of 1916, at which time he made his Will.

Joseph served in 'D' Battery, 50th Brigade RFA, 9th (Scottish) Division, which was the first New Army Division to be formed and sent to France. The 9th was at the Battle of Loos and later, in April 1916, absorbed the South African Brigade, so that 'Jocks' and 'Springboks' fought alongside each other during the Battle of the Somme. An artillery brigade of the Royal Field Artillery contained four batteries of six guns each. Three batteries, 'A', 'B' and 'C', had 18-pdr field guns and the fourth, 'D' battery, had 4.5-inch howitzers. Howitzers lobbed their shells high into the air, (unlike 18-pdr shells with their 'flat' trajectory), so they could drop down into trenches or reach targets sheltering close behind hills.

During 1916, Joseph saw a great deal of action, being wounded twice and also gassed. On each occasion, Joseph's injuries were serious enough for him to receive treatment and convalesce in England. Joseph returned home for a fourth time in January 1917, following news that both his brothers Arthur and Walter had died in action a few months before.

Joseph's elder brother, Arthur Dyer, had married Caroline Piper in 1911 and they had returned to Berkhamsted to live with Arthur working as a baker for a Mr Barnes in Chapel Street. In 1915 Arthur joined 11th Battalion, Essex Regiment and was killed on 23rd September the following year during the Battle of Flers–Courcelette which formed part of the Somme Offensive. Joseph's younger brother, Walter had enlisted in Berkhamsted a few days after the war had started and was sent to France with 1st Battalion, Norfolk Regiment as a drummer. Having survived the Somme Offensive, Walter's battalion had moved to the quieter sector near to Festubert, east of Béthune, where he was severely wounded by an exploding German trench mortar round and died at an Advance Dressing Station of 13th Field Ambulance on 1st December 1916.

After consoling his grieving parents, Joseph re-joined his battery in France as the Germans were withdrawing to the Hindenburg Line. Meanwhile, 9th Division, under XVII Corps, was preparing for the Battle of Arras which was intended to draw the Germans away from the French offensive on the Chemin-des-Dames. The larger guns began the systematic destruction of German batteries three weeks before Zero-day, a process helped by the German practice of grouping gun batteries together. The main British bombardment began on Thursday 5th April, reducing the German front line to 'nests of men scattered about' according to a Bavarian Regimental history. The 4.5-inch howitzer batteries had the task of destroying barbed wire using shrapnel shells with the new instantaneous fuse. They were also given targets to be shelled with gas at ten hours before Zero. Meanwhile, the infantry sheltered in the labyrinth of chalk tunnels dug beneath Arras.

Squalls of snow and sleet blew into the German defender's faces as they stared towards Arras on Easter Monday, 9th April. Suddenly, at 05.30, British 18-pdrs created a moving curtain of high explosive shells, which, the Division's artillery commander believed would give better protection than shrapnel in a creeping barrage, and behind which all three brigades of 9th Division advanced. At that moment, Joseph's 4.5-inch howitzer battery also joined in a continuous bombardment of the German support line to cut off reinforcements. 9th Division stormed Athies and successfully took their third objective, the Point-du-Jour Ridge. Meanwhile their artillery brigades began to move forward, but hauling heavy ordnance across broken country was still a slow process in 1917.

To 9th Division's left, the rest of XVII Corps also did well, and further to its left the Canadian Corps captured Vimy Ridge, forcing many German batteries to move. German artillery had been silenced during the first days and infantry reserves had been held too far back to intervene, but by 14th April, German guns in new, unidentified positions, began to take their toll and the arrival of reinforcements enabled the Germans to mount vigorous counterattacks. The British offensive lost momentum and both sides consolidated their positions. Two days later, the French attacked on the Aisne and at Chemin-des-Dames. The infamous 'Nivelle Offensive' named after the French Commander-in-Chief, failed to break through the German defences and had a traumatic effect on the morale of the French Army, with many divisions mutinying.

On May Day, 'B', 'C' and 'D' Batteries were redeployed for their second attack, the Third Battle of the Scarpe. At 03.45 on 3rd May, 'B' and 'C' batteries opened fire on the German lines from a range of about 4,400 yards while Joseph's 'D' battery, positioned 200 yards' eastwards from the other two batteries, fired two rounds per minute. The attack was a disaster. The infantry, largely inexperienced reinforcements, lost contact with their barrage and poor counter-battery fire exposed them to fierce German bombardments. Unfavourable winds had also prevented 'D' Battery from completing its bombardment of nearby railway lines.

On 11th May, all four Batteries came under the orders of 4th Division for the successful bombardment of a German held chemical works at Roeux. 'D' Battery, shooting from 4,400 yards' range, initially fired their guns at a rate of three rounds per minute, slowing to one round every two minutes just before the three-hour barrage ended. By 16th May, the infantry had captured the chemical works as well as several nearby German trenches, but the British battles, collectively known as the Battle of Arras, officially ended the next day.

On 18th May, Joseph and his fellow Gunners were withdrawn from the front line for a seven-day rest. When the Brigade returned to action, it was to harass the German rear with 'D' Battery targeting a German headquarters in a nearby wood. During the month of May 'D' Battery alone fired a grand total of 7,820 high explosive shells, but only 282 shrapnel and other miscellaneous shells.

As June opened, and mutiny was spreading through the French Army, the BEF did all it could to keep the German Army occupied. The Batteries participated in a series of attacks spread over four days, including decoy attacks, during which British infantry raised dummy figures above their trenches to confuse the Germans and wear them down. During a heavier barrage to support fresh infantry advances on 5th June, 'D' Battery fired gas shells at the German headquarters, provoking German artillery to retaliate in kind by firing gas shells at the British positions.

Four days later, one member of 'D' Battery sustained wounds during another German bombardment. Shelling the following day inflicted no further casualties and only caused minimal damage, but on 14th June, a German shell exploded close to 'D' Battery's position killing Joseph Dyer and another Gunner, Albert Gardiner, from Swindon. The bodies of both 26-year-old men now lie in the Point-du-Jour Military Cemetery, near the village of Athies.

It is not known why, of the three Dyer brothers who were killed during the war, only Joseph's name appears on the Northchurch Memorial. However, all three brothers' names, appear together on the Berkhamsted Memorial.

Private 35581 John RANDALL
11th Battalion, Essex Regiment

2nd July 1917

The Randall family represented one of the cornerstones of Northchurch life. John Randall's father, William, was a well-known market gardener and a founder member and former President of the Berkhamsted Co-operative Society. William Randall also founded and ran the men's recreation room in the village from his family home in New Road. He was also the Sexton at St Mary's church, performing the roles of verger, gravedigger and caretaker, just as his father, James Randall, had done for many years. Overall, the Randalls contributed some 40 years of service to the church. A plaque and stained glass window, at the north-west corner of St Mary's, now commemorates their service as Sextons.

John Randall was born on 10th November 1885 and christened at St Mary's the following January. John's mother, Rosetta, was the daughter of a lock keeper named Richard Talbot. Rosetta and William Randall had seven children altogether, but only five were still living by 1911. For many years, William cultivated a two-acre walled garden leased from the Diocese of St Albans behind Northchurch School, which contained three large greenhouses as well as flower and vegetable beds. Meanwhile his mother acted as caretaker for the Church Reading Room. John grew up in the family home at 6 New Road, and after leaving school, not surprisingly, he started to help his father with his market garden and greengrocer business.

A year later in April 1901, John, aged 16, signed up as a Boy 2nd class in the Royal Navy. He was then 5ft 1½inches tall, with light brown hair and grey eyes. John went to the Devonport training base, HMS *Impregnable*, with the intention of signing up for the standard 12 years' service in the Royal Navy when he reached the age of eighteen. His Naval service was brief however, as a few weeks after signing up, he, or more likely his father, purchased his discharge for the sum of £10, equivalent to just over £1,000 in today's terms.

John returned to Northchurch and resumed his life working for his father. In 1910, he married Beatrice Lane in St Mary's Church in Wavendon, Buckinghamshire, and they settled into their new home next door to his parents in New Road. By then, with William Randall reaching the age of 60 and in declining health, John was effectively running his father's business. William Randall died on 30th August 1912, leaving his estate, valued at £419, to his wife Rosetta. John maintained his father's links with the Berkhamsted Co-operative Society, sitting as a member on its Governing Committee. He also took over his father's sexton duties at St Mary's where he was already a keen bellringer. John's combined salary for the duties of church cleaner and sexton was set at £26 a year.

At the outbreak of war, John, who was responsible for running his market garden, maintaining another six acres of grassland, working in the Co-operative Society and fulfilling numerous church commitments, was already helping the war effort at home. In addition, by the end of 1915 John and Beatrice had three children to raise, Mary, William and Beatrice.

John Randall, wife and children (Source: Kay Weedon)

However, in May 1916 following the extension of the Military Service Act to married men, John received his call-up papers.

John applied to the Berkhamsted Rural Tribunal on 20th May for exemption from military service, stating that he had nobody to look after his business. He was successful and granted an exemption until 1st September. John went before the Tribunal again on 14th October and heard that his exemption would be extended to 1st January 1917, but no longer.

In November 1916, John appealed to the County Tribunal, but it upheld the Local Tribunal's view that, 'the agricultural interest was not sufficient to warrant total exemption'. It seems neither Tribunals viewed John as a big enough food producer to keep him out of the army. With his appeal rejected, John returned to the Berkhamsted Rural Tribunal, to learn that he would have no further exemptions, although he was granted a little more time to put his affairs in order.

On 6th January 1917, John dug his last grave in Northchurch, and a few days later travelled to Watford and reported to the Recruiting Officer. After completing his fourteen weeks of basic infantry training, John joined 'C' Company, 11th Battalion, Essex Regiment.

Formed in September 1914, 11th Essex had served in France since August 1915 and took part in the Battle of the Somme the following year during which Joseph Dyer's elder brother, Arthur, who was serving in the

Battalion, was killed. During the spring of 1917, the battalion moved to the Loos sector, where it was responsible for trenches known as '14 bis Right'. John and a fresh draft of 50 men, joined the battalion on 9th May, while it was resting in billets at Les Brebis, a small hamlet between Béthune and Lens.

Over the next couple of months, the Battalion settled into a routine of a few days' rest at Les Brebis, followed by up to seven days spent in the '14 bis' trenches. It was a period of constant raiding by both sides, with 11th Essex frequently involved, either taking part in the raids themselves, or suffering from the inevitable German shelling in retaliation for raids mounted by neighbouring units. The Battalion came under particularly heavy bombardment by *Granatenwerfer* rounds in early June, suffering 56 casualties in three days.

Granatenwerfers, small grenades fired from launchers, were not the only problem the Essex faced. By mid-June, temperatures in northern France were soaring and large numbers of exhausted men began to fall out on the march from the trenches back to their billets. Their next spell in the trenches coincided with a sharp increase in German activity and on the night of 24th June, the Battalion successfully fought off enemy raids against two of its outposts.

On 28th June, John's 'C' Company carried out a large, combined raid against a fortified redoubt on Hill 70, east of Loos, alongside a company from 2nd Durham Light Infantry. Apart from the usual aims of taking prisoners and documents to obtain identifications, wrecking machine-guns and dug-outs and causing general mayhem, the raiders also had the job of escorting three parties from 3rd Australian Tunnelling Company who were to examine and demolish the German mine system in that sector.

The Essex and Durham companies successfully captured a section of the German front line and held it for an hour before they withdrew. During that hour, the raiding party fought off constant German counterattacks. It was fierce hand-to-hand fighting and the raiders inflicted serious loss on the enemy, but there were grievous British losses too, mainly inflicted by *Granatenwerfer* and other trench mortar bombs, as well as from snipers firing from behind shields. The British raiders destroyed several dugouts when their occupants refused to surrender, while the Australian troops successfully located and demolished three German mine shafts.

Having achieved their objectives, the raiders withdrew, but after a roll call, John was reported 'Missing in Action'. In fact, John had been badly wounded and captured, but because the Germans were unable to establish his identify, they could not inform the Red Cross of his fate. It took eight months before confirmation came that John had died of his wounds sometime between 28th June and 2nd July 1917, whilst a prisoner. The Germans had buried his body, but his grave was subsequently lost.

On 24th February 1918, a memorial service led by the Rector, Reverend RH Pope, was held at St Mary's, Northchurch in memory of four Northchurch soldiers who had died during the previous few months - Privates John Randall, Alfred Curl, Arthur Frost and Gunner William Horn. Mourners laid spring flowers on the temporary War Shrine that stood in the church. Because John Randall had been a bellringer, his old colleagues rang a 'dumb peal' in his honour following the service. John Randall's name now appears on the Loos Memorial, which commemorates over 20,000 officers and men with no known grave, who died in the Loos sector.

Lance Corporal 45451 William Benjamin Ernest WAITE
Machine Gun Corps (Infantry)

11th July 1917

William Benjamin Ernest Waite was born in Stonesfield, Oxfordshire on 23rd September 1884, the first son of Benjamin and Harriet Waite. Benjamin, an agricultural labourer, was Oxfordshire born, while Harriet came from Peckham Rye in south London. Benjamin and his family later moved to Hertfordshire and settled in a cottage on Berkhamsted Common. Their next move was to Thorne's Yard, in the centre of Northchurch with Benjamin working as a cowman on one of the local farms. On leaving school William started work as an under gardener.

On 16th September 1905, William married Rose Maria Maple from nearby Chartridge, in St Mary's, Northchurch and their first son, William Benjamin Waite, was born in the village two years later. In 1911, when their first daughter, Eva Harriet, was born, William and his family left Northchurch and moved to Long Stratton, Norfolk where he worked as a domestic gardener.

At the outbreak of the War, William, now aged 30, had moved again and was working as a domestic gardener in Dunmow, Essex. With his wife Rose, daughter Eva and sons William Benjamin and Horace Leslie to support, William did not volunteer for military service in the early days of the war. However, on 8th December 1915, just before the introduction of compulsory conscription, Walter decided to attest under the Derby Scheme. William had a medical examination at Dunmow, his papers showing that he was 5ft 6inches tall and weighed 143 pounds. He was provisionally allocated to the Middlesex Regiment and put on the Army Reserve list to await his call-up.

With the formalities over and a day's Army pay in his pocket, William returned to work as a domestic gardener wearing a red crown on a grey armband as a public sign of his new military status. It would be five months before William received his call-up papers, by which time Rose was expecting their fourth child. On 3rd June 1916, William was posted to 5th Battalion Middlesex Regiment, but on 27th July, he was transferred to the Machine Gun Corps.

Sir Hiram Maxim invented the first self-powered, water-cooled machine gun in 1885 and, with the support of Vickers, developed it into a highly effective weapon. Accepted for use by the British Army in 1891, it was first used in the 1893 Matabele Wars, then in India in 1895, and very usefully during Kitchener's re-conquest of the Sudan in 1896. That year Vickers bought out Maxim's patents and began to develop a lightened, more modern version, which became the highly successful Vickers Machine Gun. After the Boer War, when Maxims were used by both sides, the British Army requested more Maxims per battalion, but the Exchequer would only pay for two per battalion. The British Army officially adopted the Vickers Gun in November 1912, but owing to their cost in 1914 the BEF went to France equipped with Maxims. Accusations of war profiteering later forced Vickers to slash the price of both guns.

Meanwhile the German Army adopted an all-steel Maxim in 1908 and began large-scale production at Spandau in Berlin, also allocating two guns per battalion. By August 1914, the German Army had some 12,000 MG08 Maxims, many more than the British Army, mainly because the Germans had many more battalions. Realising that defensive machine gun fire works best when it is co-ordinated, the Germans organised them into dedicated companies under specialist officers with six guns for each of their three-battalion regiments.

The British Army adopted the much lighter, air-cooled Lewis Gun in October 1915, which replaced the Vickers Gun and increased the offensive firepower of infantry platoons. In turn, the Vickers Gun was re-classified as a Heavy Machine Gun and organised into specialist companies, one per Brigade, similar to the German model. However, the British Army went one stage further by creating a Machine Gun Corps to administer these companies and train dedicated officers and men. The new Corps' depot and training centre was established at Belton Park near Grantham, Lincolnshire. This was the family seat of Lord Brownlow, who also owned the vast Ashridge Estate to the north of Northchurch. The Machine Gun Corps also established a base depot and training school at Camiers, near Étaples in France.

The .303 inch, (7.69mm), Vickers Machine Gun alone weighed 28.5lbs plus 10lbs of cooling water contained in a jacket around the barrel. It was normally mounted on a tripod, weighing a further 20lbs, and fed by canvas webbing belts holding 250 rounds of bullets. When firing continuously, the Vickers shot one bullet every tenth of a second, giving a 'cyclic' rate of 600 rounds per minute, but as it took several seconds to load a fresh belt, the maximum practical rate of fire was actually 500 rpm.

Each Infantry Machine Gun Company had 16 Vickers Guns organised into four Sections of two Subsections. A Subsection had two machine guns served by a six-man detachment each. The gun was normally fired by N°1, who led his detachment and carried and placed the tripod; N°2 guided the canvas ammunition belt into the feed block and carried the gun; N°3 kept N°2 supplied with fresh ammunition belts, while the remaining three men were reserves who re-filled the belts and carried the ammunition and spare parts. Every man was trained to operate the gun and could replace any other member of the team if they became casualties. Horse drawn limbers carried the guns, tripods, spare parts and ammunition. A General Service Wagon carried water, the cooks, and all personal kit, all under the Company's Transport Sergeant.

While William was training at Belton Park on 3rd January 1917, he was appointed an unpaid Lance Corporal. He left Folkestone for France three months later, and spent a week at the Corps 'B' Depot at Camiers before, on 18th April, joining 97th Machine Gun Company in the Somme valley. 97th Company MGC provided fire support for 97th Brigade, 32nd Division, which had been earmarked for an ambitious assault on the Flanders Coast, codenamed Operation HUSH, which would support the planned British summer offensive at Ypres.

In late May, William was sent to the Machine Gun School at Camiers, for the standard Vickers machine gun course. It covered the assembling and disassembling of the gun, repairs and maintenance, gun placement, roles and responsibilities within the team, target practice, trench and limber drill and fire direction. Part 1 was entirely instructional with no time limit, Part 2 involved timed tests on the use of the gun with points awarded for each test. A soldier scoring over 50 points became a '1st Class gunner', and 25 points were required to become a 'Qualified gunner'. Anything less meant failure and immediate transfer from the Corps.

On 10th June, having passed successfully, Walter returned to 97th Machine Gun Company. Ten days later, 97th Brigade crossed the border into Belgium with XV Corps to relieve French troops holding a bridgehead on the German side of the Yser Canal, opposite Nieuport on the north Belgian coast, which German troops had occupied the since the middle of October 1914. To protect their gains, in November 1914 the Germans had formed the *MarinesKorps Flandern* to guard the coast and develop Ostend, Zeebrugge and Bruges as bases for German submarines and surface raiders to attack Britain's sea-lanes.

Minelayers and the Royal Navy's Dover Patrol could only contain the danger posed from these bases, not eradicate them entirely, so early in 1917, Admiral Sir Reginald Bacon proposed an ambitious amphibious landing on the Belgian coast, supported by a northward attack from the Yser. The small town of Middelkerke, within striking distance of Nieuport, was chosen for the landings. It had fewer defences because it had a recently-built sea wall, and, unbeknown to the Germans, its Belgian architect had escaped to France and taken all his drawings with him which the British now had. While submarines and aircraft built up a picture of the shore, specialised landing equipment was designed and a full-size section of sea wall was built for practical tests and training.

The plan was to land a sizeable force of infantry with cyclists, artillery, trench mortar batteries and motor machine guns from three large pontoons, each about 170 yards long and 10 yards wide. The Dover Patrol would provide three pairs of shallow draught coastal gunboats to manoeuvre the pontoons inshore under cover of a huge smoke screen generated by 80 vessels. When the invasion force landed, British Divisions, including William's, were to break out of the Yser bridgehead and advance north to join it and recapture the ports of Ostend and Zeebrugge.

The most imaginative aspect of Operation HUSH however, was the intention to support the attacking infantry with tanks. The British were the first to use tanks in warfare the previous September and now proposed to land three Mark IV tanks from each pontoon. Each tank had additional grips fitted to their tracks and carried a specially designed ramp for scaling the sea wall.

HUSH was soon incorporated into the overall plan for the capture of Flanders, and became a bold flank attack to be launched once the German lines around Ypres had been broken. The target date was set for late July/early August. So, with the pontoons built and training for HUSH well under way, 32nd Division, including William's 97th Machine Gun Company, took over the Nieuport and the Yser bridgehead from French troops on 20th June 1917.

Next day, *MarineKorps* patrols captured 11 men from 32nd Division and their commanding Admiral realised that the British were planning something. He immediately planned a spoiling attack along the coastal sand dunes, aptly codenamed *STRANDFEST*, or Beach Party, to be launched on 9th July. Meanwhile, more British Divisions moved into the area and the first of 200 heavy guns and aircraft of the Royal Flying Corps and the Royal Naval Air Service began to arrive.

On 6th July, the German Marines began a steady bombardment of the bridgehead, while their assault troops massed undetected because British aircraft were grounded by fog and low cloud. The bad weather also forced the Germans to delay *STRANDFEST*, but on 10th July, 58 artillery batteries and three 24cm naval guns firing from shore batteries began a crushing barrage on the British bridgehead, destroying all but one of the bridges over the Yser. The Germans included gas shells filled with either lethal diphosgene or a new agent called Blue Cross, that induced intense nausea causing men to pull off their gasmasks. 97th Brigade was on the right of the bridgehead, facing German occupied Lombartzyde, but 2nd Brigade, to its left among the coastal sand dunes, suffered the worst of the barrage. At 20.00, *MarineKorps* storm troops, backed by flamethrowers, attacked down the coast, supported by strafing aircraft.

Trapped and blinded by sand, gas and smoke, 2nd Brigade was practically wiped out, but the Germans deliberately limited their attack on 97th Brigade to the first two lines of breastworks as they feared the land behind could easily be flooded. William's Brigade counterattacked that night and restored all but 500 yards of its front near Geleide Brook. During the counterattack and shelling on 11th July, 32-year-old William Waite was killed. His body remained unidentified and his name is now recorded on the Nieuport Memorial in Belgium.

STRANDFEST destroyed any hope of a surprise British attack along the Belgian coast. The offensive at Ypres went ahead on 31st July 1917; today the Third Battle of Ypres is well known as 'Passchendaele', but Operation HUSH would eventually be forgotten.

Soon after William's death, his widow, Rose, and their four children moved from Marks Hill, Dunmow to stay with a Mrs Dell in Fox Road, Wigginton, before moving to Orchard End, Northchurch the following September.

Private 57034 Arthur WELLING
74th Company Machine Gun Corps (Infantry)

8th August 1917

Arthur Welling was born in Northchurch towards the end of 1896, the younger son of Alice and Frederick Welling. He was christened at St Mary's Church and grew up in Orchard End with his parents, his brother, Walter, and four sisters. After Frederick Welling's death in 1906, the children rallied around to support their mother and by the age of 14, Arthur was bringing money home as a labourer, along with his elder brother Walter.

In August 1914, Arthur was too young to serve overseas and, perhaps out of consideration for his mother, he did not join up straight away. He later enlisted at Berkhamsted and went to the Northamptonshire Regiment.

Sometime after his three months' basic infantry training, Arthur transferred to the Machine Gun Corps and commenced another three months of specialist training at their base at Belton Park. Here he received a new regimental number, 57034, and a new cap badge of a pair of crossed Vickers machine guns surmounted by a crown. Once he was proficient in the care, maintenance and employment of the Vickers machine gun, Arthur embarked for France and more training at the Corps depot and school at Camiers, near Étaples. Following this course Arthur transferred to 74th Company MGC, which provided the heavy machine gun support for 74th Infantry Brigade of 25th Division.

The 25th Division had arrived in France at the end of September 1915 and helped defend Vimy Ridge from the German's spring attack in 1916. On 3rd July, Albert's Brigade was attached to 12th Division, which had unsuccessfully attacked the small Somme village of Ovillers-la-Boisselle, three miles northwest of Albert, with great loss of life. The next day it relieved the remnants of 32nd Division, which had also suffered enormous losses.

74th Brigade's first major action was to spearhead a renewed assault on Ovillers-la-Boisselle on 7th July. The Brigade attacked from the south at 08.00, and an hour later, 36th Brigade, 12th Division, attacked from the west. Two battalions of 74th Brigade had advanced across the head of Mash Valley towards the village, but heavy German machine gun fire prevented further progress. Despite heavy losses from an artillery barrage, 36th Brigade managed to take the first three German trench lines.

The Brigades consolidated their foothold in the German line and overnight linked up with a battalion from 75th Brigade. In the early hours of 8th July, 36th Brigade advanced again. Although hampered by mud, the battalions were able to penetrate some 200 yards into the ruined village. Meanwhile, two battalions of 74th Brigade advanced with a battalion of 75th Brigade on its left from the southeast and successfully gained the German trench that ran up to the village church. That evening, 74th Brigade renewed its attack in conjunction with 11th Lancashire Fusiliers. Although one Fusilier Company was caught in the British artillery barrage after advancing too far, the Fusiliers held on and a company of Royal Irish Rifles went up to help consolidate their gains. 12th Division was relieved overnight on 8th/9th and 74th Brigade returned to 25th Division.

Eight days later, Arthur's Vickers Guns supported another 74th Brigade attack on Ovillers-la-Boisselle, this time from the east, between three battalions from 48th Division attacking from the northeast, and the south. Fighting lasted until the evening of the 16th July, when the village finally fell into British hands, and that night 25th Division was withdrawn to recuperate.

Amid heavy overnight thunderstorms on Wednesday 27th September, 74th Brigade relieved 146th Brigade, 18th Division, in front of the *Schwaben* Redoubt. Arthur's Machine Gun Company and 74th Brigade were in support on Thursday afternoon when 18th Division attacked the Redoubt, securing its southern and western faces by the evening. Overnight patrols from 74th Brigade gained footholds in the German front line and linked up with units of 18th Division. The process of relieving the tired troops holding the Redoubt's western face began on Friday 29th, but was interrupted by a fierce bombing fight. 74th Brigade waited in the wind and rain until the grenade fight eased, allowing their relief at 03.00 next morning.

The first three months of 1917 were spent in the relative quiet of the Ploegsteert sector, due south of Ypres, although raids and minor operations were commonplace. The 25th Division was one of those chosen to make the assault on the natural stronghold of Messines Ridge and moved between the Wulveringhem-Messines and the Wulveringhem-Wytschaete roads. Occupied by the Germans since 1914, Messines Ridge dominated the ground southeast of Ypres and its capture was essential to reduce casualties in British attacks in the area. A preliminary bombardment by some 2,300 guns and 300 heavy mortars began on 21st May, but news of the mutiny within the French Army, following the failure of the 'Nivelle Offensive', gave the operation added importance.

At 02.50 on 7th June the barrage stopped. Sensing an imminent attack, the German defenders left their underground shelters ready to repel the advance by the allied troops. For the next twenty minutes, with machine guns loaded and aimed at the allied lines, the German troops waited. Suddenly, the ground beneath them shuddered and then erupted into numerous balls of fire. Over the previous months, Allied engineers had constructed twenty-two mineshafts and associated tunnels beneath Messines Ridge and placed some 600 tons of high explosive ready for zero hour. As General Herbert Plumer, Second Army's Commander, remarked to his Staff prior to the attack, 'Gentlemen, we may not make history tomorrow, but we shall certainly change the geography.'

At 03.10 on 7th June, 19 out of the 22 mines were detonated under the German trenches in the greatest man-made explosion to date. The awful roar was heard as far away as Dublin as some 10,000 German soldiers were killed. Two of the mines exploded on 25th Division's front, one either side. 74th Brigade attacked on the right near one of the craters, with Arthur's machine guns in support, and 7th Brigade attacked on its left. The attack was a total success and a week later, the Division made a further attack, successfully pushing the front line forward another 800 yards. Overnight on 22nd/23rd June, 25th Division was relieved to rest and recuperate in the area of Bomy, near St Omer. Two weeks later, 25th Division moved to the Ypres sector and began preparations for the next big British offensive.

On 31st July 1917, the opening day of the Third Battle of Ypres, 25th Division was in Army Corps Reserve positions at 'Belgian Chateau'. The following day, the Division relieved the tired units of 8th Division and took over its positions facing Westhoek and Bellewaarde Ridge, to the east of Ypres. 25th Division was to prepare for a renewed attempt to take Westhoek planned for 10th August. Although there was no major action in this sector for nine days, it was by no means quiet; the artillery of both sides was active in counter-battery fire and seeking to destroy each other's machine gun positions.

The Brigade had been active in the line for a week when, on 8th August, Arthur and two of his comrades from 74th Company were killed, quite likely by shellfire. The grave of one of those killed, David Willis Ratcliffe, is located in the Huts Cemetery in Flanders, which was used by field ambulances during the Battle. The bodies of Arthur and the man killed with him, William Charles Hazelden, remained unidentified on the battlefield. Arthur's and Private Hazelden's names are now among those preserved on the Menin Gate Memorial at Ypres.

Private 2724 Charlie SUTTON
51st Battalion, Australian Infantry Force

26th August 1917

In September 1883, John Sutton, an unemployed bootmaker from Hackney, East London, enlisted for 12 years' service in the Scottish Rifles. Employment in the boot and shoe industry varied considerably from year to year and bootmakers often joined the army seeking a more reliable living. John would later spend three months in prison for theft and desertion, before the Scottish Rifles went to India in March 1885, for six years on garrison duties.

In April 1891, John returned to England and transferred to the Reserves. That summer he met and married Sarah Ann Brooks, known as Annie, in Portsea, Hampshire and resumed his career as a bootmaker. Annie Brooks originally came from Northchurch and was one of nine children of William Brooks, a local cressman, and his wife, Lucy. John and Annie's first child, Lily, was born in Hampshire in 1893 and clearly, the family travelled around in search of work as their next child, William, was born the following year at Wickham in Essex.

Their youngest child, Charles, commonly known as Charlie, was born in 1895 at his parents' home in Northchurch High Street and christened at St Mary's Church. That same year, having completed five years in the Reserves, John Sutton left the army, but life as a bootmaker was still precarious. In April 1900, he re-enlisted for a one-year term, leaving his wife and three children in Northchurch, where Annie Sutton made ends meet as best she could by selling boots. Soon after leaving the Army again, John Sutton moved his family to the Court Estate in Rushden, Northamptonshire, a major boot and shoe producing area. However, by this time John was no longer a bootmaker, and described himself as a market gardener. Charlie and his older brother Willie were then employed as farm labourers and Lily had left home.

In October 1913, having reached the age of eighteen, Charlie boarded *SS Armadale*, of the Australian Steam Shipping Company, and sailed from the Port of London to start a new life in Western Australia. Charlie landed at Freemantle on 7th December, and spent the next two years working as a farm labourer.

His father's army career may have discouraged Charlie from volunteering in 1914, so what prompted him to enlist on 18th April 1916 is uncertain, but the Gallipoli Campaign, although deemed a failure, had prompted a fresh surge of volunteers in Australia. When Charlie enlisted in

51st Battalion (Western Australia), Australian Imperial Force, (AIF), he stood 5ft 9ins tall and weighed exactly 154lbs. He had fair hair, blue eyes and a scar on his lower right leg.

In February 1916, it was decided to double the size of the AIF by splitting existing battalions in half. 51st Battalion was formed in Egypt during March 1916, with a cadre of Gallipoli veterans from 11th Battalion. Both battalions were then brought up to strength with new recruits like Charlie. After basic training, Charlie with the sixth reinforcement draft left Freemantle on 10th October 1916 aboard the troopship A23 *Suffolk* for the eight-week voyage to Plymouth. Charlie spent two months training on Salisbury Plain, minus a short spell in hospital with laryngitis, before crossing the Channel aboard SS *Victoria* to arrive at Étaples on 3rd February 1917.

51st Battalion had been in France with 13th Infantry Brigade since June 1916. It had taken part in the heavy fighting around Pozières and Mouquet Farm during the late summer, incurring over 650 casualties. The Battalion then moved to a quieter sector near Steenvoorde, by the Belgian border, where the major battle was not with German soldiers but with rain and mud. However, the Battalion soon returned to the Somme where the 'Aussies' spent the cold winter months working hard to improve their trenches. Charlie joined the Battalion at Flers on 10th February 1917, but two weeks later, it moved to Buire-sur-l'Ancre for a period of intensive training.

In March, 51st Battalion, now at full strength and well trained, re-entered the line at Vraucourt, northeast of Bapaume ready to participate in a major assault on Noreuil, two miles away, as part of the larger Battle of Arras. Noreuil was one of the fortified villages designed to hold up Allied troops as the Germans withdrew to the Hindenburg Line. The 51st and 50th Battalions attacked north of the village on the morning of 2nd April, with 49th and 52nd Battalions in support. 51st Battalion advanced quickly at first, but discovered a previously unknown trench blocking the way to its objective. Heavy fire from Noreuil delayed the Battalion's advance further until the two reserve battalions threw their weight into the battle and its objective, a sunken road east of the village, could be taken. During this attack, and the subsequent defence of the village over the next two weeks, Charlie's battalion suffered 239 casualties. Relieved on 19th April, the Battalion returned to Buire-sur-l'Ancre to recover.

Whilst at Buire-sur-l'Ancre on 25th April, the battalion celebrated the second ANZAC Day. This marked the anniversary of the Australian and New Zealand Army Corps' first major battle at Gallipoli with anniversary dinners for all ranks being held. After a month at Buire-sur-l'Ancre, the 51st Battalion marched to Albert and entrained for Caëstre, close to the Belgian border, arriving on 16th May.

On 7th June, 51st Battalion participated in the attack on the Messines

Ridge, helping to capture the village of Wytschaete. Five days later, the battalion was relieved from the front line and moved to Wardrecques, southeast of St Omer, for further training. During this time, Charlie wrote his Will. Overall, considering the heavy fighting, the Battalion's casualties for the month of June were relatively light, with only 24 officers and men killed, and 81 wounded.

On 30th June, Charlie's battalion moved to a camp near the village of De Seule by the Franco-Belgian border to spend two weeks building up its strength for the next major offensive around Ypres. On 14th July, 51st Battalion returned to the front line and participated in two raids on the German lines, which consolidated the gains made some days earlier. However, a German retaliatory raid captured three Australian Lewis guns on the night of 19th July, and a chastened Battalion returned to camp the following day.

At the beginning of August, 51st Battalion moved close to the village of Kemmel, due south of Ypres. On 8th August, the battalion stood ready to support an attack conducted by 57th Division, although, in the event, its men were not required to fight and were put on fatigue duties instead. Shortly afterwards on 26th August 1917, while the battalion provided working parties near the village of Wulvergen Charlie Sutton was killed.

The circumstances of Charlie's death are unclear, his Service Record merely notes that he 'died in action'. Charlie's body now lies in the cemetery at La Plus Douve Farm nearby. Charlie has no memorial in Great Britain; his name however appears on the Australian War Memorial in Australia's Federal Capital, Canberra.

Lieutenant Frank D ALCOCK
3rd/2nd Battalion, 2nd King's African Rifles

3rd September 1917

Frank Alcock was born in Hampstead, London on 1st November 1885, the eldest son of John Forster Alcock and his third wife, Augusta Lackland Alcock. John Forster Alcock came from Sunderland and was the son of a successful shipping broker. He and his younger brother, Charles, were educated at Harrow School where they both developed a passion for football. After leaving Harrow, John entered his father's shipping business and in May 1862, aged 21, he joined the Honourable Artillery Company, a Volunteer unit based just north of the City of London.

Wishing to continue playing football after leaving Harrow, the Alcock brothers formed the Forest Football Club at Chingford in 1859, named after Epping Forest, and John Forster became the club's first captain. Their ground was already a popular venue for local football matches, but at that time organising fixtures involved more than just agreeing dates; they also had to agree the rules of play. Each public school played its own version of football; some mostly kicked, but Harrow mostly dribbled and Rugby School mostly carried. Pitch, team and goal size also varied, as did the scoring.

Consequently, representatives of leading public schools and football clubs, with the Alcock brothers representing Forest FC, had a series of meetings at a London pub to form an association with unified rules. At John Forster's suggestion, the rules used at Trinity College Cambridge were adopted as their starting point and he successfully defeated a move to allow 'hacking', the deliberate kicking of a player's legs, by a narrow majority. Eventually, on 26th October 1863, the Football Association formally came into being and its first match, a fourteen-a-side affair between the FA President's XIV and the FA Secretary's XIV, was played in London's Battersea Park. The Alcock brothers were on opposing sides, Charles scoring the only goals to give the President's XIV a two-nil win over JF Alcock's team.

Gradually, John Forster Alcock devoted more time to his growing shipbroker and ice merchant business, trading as John F Alcock and Co., from its offices at 98 Bishopsgate, London and later at nearby 21 Great St Helens. The firm's ice came from a man-made lake owned by the Alcocks near the town of Kragerø in Norway. John Forster thus withdrew from the Football Association and football in general. Frank's uncle Charles, however, went on to run both the Football Association and Surrey County

Cricket Club. Charles Alcock established the Football Association Challenge Cup in 1871 and led The Wanderers, Forest FC's new name, to win the first FA Cup Final at the Oval the following year. His team also defeated Scotland in the first ever soccer international. Later he organised the first cricket Test match against Australia and arranged All England's international cricket tours until his death in 1907.

Soon after Frank was born, John Forster Alcock moved his family from Hampstead to a house close by St Peter's Church in Berkhamsted High Street, where Frank's sister, Augusta Theodora, was born in 1888. With a growing family to house, in July 1890 John Forster Alcock purchased Exhims, a large house on the junction between Darrs Lane and the High Street in Northchurch for £1,500. Frank's younger brother, John Forster (junior), was born at Exhims on 14th March 1896.

Aside from his shipbroking interests, John Forster Alcock became involved in the Northchurch community. He was the Chairman of the Parish Council for several years and represented Northchurch alongside fellow Parish Councillor, Sir Charles Hadden, in opposing the expansion of Berkhamsted Urban District Council's boundary in 1909. He also unsuccessfully contested a seat on Hertfordshire County Council. John Forster Alcock was a Trustee of the Berkhamsted and Northchurch Conservative Club, a sidesman at St Mary's Church, a member of the Church of England Missionary Society and helped to organise social events, such as whist drives, for the Northchurch Working Men's Club. He also belonged to the Royal Horticultural Society, breeding prizewinning temperate orchids in the large conservatory at Exhims. His own orchid varieties featured regularly in *The Orchid Review*, including one dating from 1909 named in his honour - Cymbidium *Forster Alcock*.

Frank Alcock was educated at Temple Grove Preparatory School in East Sheen and then at Kelly College, Tavistock, where he became a monitor, or prefect, and later Head of School House. Unsurprisingly, sport featured prominently in Frank's life at Kelly College. He tried athletics, gymnastics and swimming, but it was as a rugby forward that he fared best, being described in the *Kelly Chronicle* as, 'A good forward with plenty of strength and weight. Led the pack well and kept going the whole time'.

After his first summer vacation, Frank enrolled in the Kelly College Cadet Force and did well from the start, taking 2nd place in the Recruit's Class, Winter Term, 1900. By the 1901 Summer Term, Frank was a member of the school rifle squad shooting for the Challenge Shield at Honiton, Devon, that June. Frank was a Cadet Lance Corporal by the 1902 Easter Term, and was becoming an experienced rifle shot. Appointed Corporal the following year, he became a Colour Sergeant just before he left the College. The *Kelly Chronicle* of February 1904 reported his departure: 'At the end of the term we lost Col.Sergt. Alcock, who for the last two years has been Captain of the Eight. In addition to being an excellent shot himself, he possessed a knowledge of rifle shooting and a zeal for his duties which made him invaluable as a right-hand man. May we be so fortunate as to find a successor like him!'.

Whilst at Kelly College, Frank was also an active member of the Debating Society, which usually met in the School House dining hall. The *Kelly Chronicle* commented that Frank 'demonstrated a combative and direct debating style.' At a debate in February 1901, Frank spoke in support of a motion condemning the Government's handling of the Boer War. Two months later, speaking against the motion, 'That this House deplores the fact that the ancient custom of duelling has been abolished,' Frank said he 'felt very seriously that such hon. gentlemen as were at large on the other side of the House should be either put in chains or lunatic asylums,' adding amid cheers that, 'For his part, he was very glad the table of the House was between them'.

After leaving Kelly College in 1903, Frank joined his father's shipbroking business at 21 Great St Helens. Wishing to maintain his martial skills, Frank followed his father into the Honourable Artillery Company (HAC), enrolling on 7th October 1907. Frank shot for the HAC and belonged to the rifle team that competed for the *Daily Telegraph* Cup at Bisley in 1908. The winning team, from the London Scottish (TF), included the future discoverer of penicillin, Alexander Fleming.

By now, Frank was living in London at Ingram House Residential Club in Stockwell Road, Lambeth. Ingram House, opened in 1905, was a red brick, cross-shaped building, which enabled every room to have a view. It boasted 208 bedrooms, clubrooms, a dining room, lounge, library and smoking room, together with recreational facilities, including a gymnasium, billiard room, tennis courts and, of particular interest to Frank, a miniature rifle range.

John Forster Alcock died on 13th March 1910, leaving his entire estate to his widow, Augusta. The shipbroking business was wound up and Frank decided to leave the City for a new life overseas. He resigned from the HAC on 30th October 1911, having served for 4 years, and left England for Africa.

During the late 19th century, the discovery of quinine had allowed Europeans to venture from their coastal trading posts to explore 'Darkest Africa' and discover enormous resources. The established colonial powers, Britain, France, Portugal and Spain, were joined by brand new European nations; Belgium, Italy and especially Germany, in the so-called 'Scramble for Africa', which carved up African territory. The Congress of Berlin of 1885 brought some order by formalising existing spheres of influence. Great Britain's territory included Egypt and British East Africa in the north and Cape Colony, Transvaal, Orange Free State, Bechuanaland and Rhodesia in the south. Between them, breaking a continuous line of red down the map of Africa, lay the territory of German East Africa, comprising what are today the countries of Rwanda, Burundi and Tanzania. On the west coast of Africa, to the north of the Cape Colony, Germany also acquired German West Africa.

Frank was farming in Rhodesia in 1914 when Britain declared war. The next day he volunteered for active service and was accepted, but instructed to continue farming until he was required. Frank had to wait until February 1916 before finally enlisting as a Private in 2nd Rhodesia Regiment.

With the coming of war, British and German colonists were keen to take part in the fighting, although the Governors of both German East Africa and British East Africa were not. However, Rhodesia's first contingent of 500 infantrymen was raised in October 1914 and placed at the disposal of the Imperial Government in London. Like Great Britain, Rhodesia had no shortage of volunteers, so enlistment with a 2nd Rhodesia Regiment opened on 24th November 1914 and training began immediately.

The Allies moved quickly to dispossess Germany of all her overseas territories and deny the Kaiser's navy safe harbours and secure telegraphic lines outside Europe. In November 1914, British Empire troops made an amphibious attack on the town of Tanga in German East Africa, only to be routed by the local protection force, the *Schutztruppe*, under its experienced commander, Colonel Paul von Lettow Vorbeck. Lettow Vorbeck realised that it would only be a matter of time before his East African *Schutztruppe* would face overwhelming British Empire forces and be defeated. He therefore adopted guerrilla-style tactics; raiding communications, ambushing supply columns and patrols, avoiding pitched battles and only fighting when he had the stronger force. In so doing, he hoped to tie down a considerable number of Empire troops who might otherwise fight on the Western Front.

Lettow Vorbeck took his native *Askari* soldiers to the dense bush around Mount Kilimanjaro in the northeast, from where he could reach numerous white settlements. More importantly, he could strike at the terminus of the regionally important Usambara Railway and at the equally strategic railway line connecting the British port of Mombasa with the economic heartland of British East Africa. His small, but effective, force was fighting on home territory, living off the land, and travelling light, easily out-manoeuvring the larger forces. In this central belt of Africa, tsetse fly reigned supreme, crippling any force relying on pack animals.

In March 1915, 2nd Rhodesia Regiment entrained for the coast of Portuguese East Africa, present day Mozambique, where they boarded SS *Umzumbi* to take them up the coast to Mombassa, whence they travelled inland by train. There followed a series of inconclusive skirmishes, there being too few Empire troops to trap the *Schutztruppen* into fighting. By October however, South African forces had seized German West Africa, today's Namibia, freeing 20,000 reinforcements to allow a full-scale sweep of German East Africa from the north. A strong pincer movement around the base of Mount Kilimanjaro during February and March 1916 forced von Lettow Vorbeck's withdrawal south into the bush. Heavy rains, and the loss of horses and mules to sleeping sickness from tsetse fly bites, impeded the South African-led pursuit. Hundreds of men fell ill and went to hospital. By 25th March, when 2nd Rhodesian Regiment was ordered to return to Nairobi to rest, the Battalion had been reduced to just 389 men, half its original strength.

Frank Alcock enlisted at Salisbury, Rhodesia, on 14th March 1916 and spent the next four months in training. He was one of 35 new recruits that caught up with 2nd Rhodesia Regiment in early July at Msiha, close to the Lukigura River in German territory. Within hours, the regiment's camp came under precisely timed shellfire intended to cause the maximum disruption and deny the men of their sleep. The Germans fired ten shells at lunchtime, four at 14.00 when the men were resting from the heat, fifty between 16.00 and 18.00 when the men fed and watered the animals, ten at midnight and finally about twenty-five during the night. The *Schutztruppen* maintained this routine for a month. Meanwhile, as conditions in the regiment's camp deteriorated, fever and dysentery became a regular scourge. Added to this was the ongoing problem of lice, while the animals continued to die of sleeping sickness.

A medical inspection on 6th August classified 86 out of 300 Rhodesians as unfit for service, with many more described as doubtful. Relief only came after a fresh offensive forced von Lettow Vorbeck's troops to retreat further south towards Kissaki, destroying bridges and anything else that would impede the advancing British Empire units. Another medical review of the Regiment found that of the 53 men on duty on 26th October, only 30 were truly fit to do so; a further 120 men were expected back following hospital treatment.

The British Empire forces, including the depleted 2nd Rhodesia Regiment, continued to chase von Lettow Vorbeck southwards under appalling conditions. The unrelenting tsetse flies killed thousands of transport animals, their bloated bodies abandoned either side of the tracks, rotting in the heat and covered in maggots. Millions of blue redheaded blowflies compounded the misery by constantly buzzing around the advancing troops and laying their eggs whenever they could and quickly producing more maggots. Lack of fresh water and unrelenting dysentery, malaria, festering sores and fever continued to wear down the troops.

By 21st December, the Regiment had so few fit men that it was no longer an effective fighting force. Consequently, at 07.00 on 11th January 1917, a small body of gaunt men styled 2nd Rhodesia Regiment, turned from the Rufigi River towards Morogoro, some 120 miles from the coast. Only 91 of the original 800 men stepped off the train at Morogoro, where, at the end of March, they learned that their regiment would be returning to

Rhodesia. Incredibly, only 32 of 2nd Rhodesians died from wounds or disease, although on average, every man reported sick ten times and went to hospital twice during the regiment's time in East Africa.

It was evidently clear that Europeans, and even South Africans, struggled to cope in East African conditions. A major recruiting drive among British East African peoples began in January 1917 to expand the native Kings African Rifles (KAR), but there was a shortage of European officers to lead them. Some of the fitter 2nd Rhodesia Regiment men, including Frank Alcock, opted to remain in East Africa, and were awarded local Commissions.

With his experience of the East African bush and proven marksmanship, Frank joined 3rd battalion of the expanded 2nd Battalion KAR, which recruited from the region he used to farm, and was put in charge of the machine guns. The new Battalion's training ended in early summer 1917 with the opening of a fresh offensive. By then von Lettow Vorbeck's dwindling force was being pressed further south against the Portuguese East Africa border.

At the end of May, 3/2nd KAR, comprising 29 British officers, 215 men, 130 machine gun carriers, 130 stretcher bearers and 1,170 porters, left Nairobi with Lindi Force. They were en route to the small port of Lindi, in the south of German East Africa, which British forces had captured the previous September. Their orders were to prevent the *Schutztruppen* from crossing into Portuguese territory.

On 10th June, Lindi Force advanced from Lindi in two columns, the smaller contingent proceeded via Naitiwi and Mayani, while the main column, including Frank's machine guns, operated to the east of Mandawa from Mkwaya Creek, where the Royal Navy had made a successful landing. The operation was complete by 13th June having forced von Lettow Vorbeck's forces to abandon the area. Troops spent some weeks consolidating their gains and sending out patrols to track the retreating *Schutztruppen*. The KAR received several air-cooled Lewis machine guns in mid-July, to replace their heavy, water-cooled Maxims, and training with the new, lighter guns started immediately.

Lindi Force advanced again on 2nd August, and attacked von Lettow Vorbeck's troops for 48 hours, driving them further into the bush. By mid-August, heavy rain had begun and Lindi Force found itself in an area of impenetrable, German-owned sisal and rubber plantations, close by swampland. On 15th August, an attempt to dislodge von Lettow Vorbeck from a nearby ridge failed after a torrential rainstorm. The Battalion's War Diary said of the following hours 'Everybody was very wet cold and miserable this night as we had nothing to change into or sleep in, a fitting night to bring out fever in the officers and pneumonia in the men'.

By now, Frank Alcock was very ill and was one of six officers sent back to Lindi during August. Frank was admitted to 1st General Hospital,

Lindi, where the Matron remembered him as, 'always so patient and uncomplaining, and particularly thoughtful and unselfish.' Frank died of dysentery at the hospital on 3rd September 1917.

The *Record of Service of Old Kelleians in the Great War* quotes Frank's Commanding Officer, 'At times during July and August he was far from well, but he stuck to his work like a man, and did not give in till he could carry on no longer. I have always thought of him as a most plucky and enduring man. He was a sad loss to me, he was always hard working and very popular with his brother officers, and was making a good officer when his life was unfortunately cut short.' The Regiment's Adjutant recalled, 'We all liked him and were awfully sorry when we heard the news. He was so cheery, that we all expected to see him return. He was one of the few officers who understood the native troops. He spoke their language, knew their ways, and took the greatest personal interest in each man, and they loved him and would follow him anywhere.'

The East African campaign was extremely costly, for every man dying in battle, another thirty died from disease, but despite the best efforts of British Empire troops, the *Schutztruppen* remained undefeated in battle. Having retreated into Portuguese East Africa, Paul von Lettow Vorbeck launched raids against Rhodesian forts through 1918 and was busy planning more when a British messenger brought news of the Armistice. On 25th November 1918, von Lettow Vorbeck led his Askari out of the bush and surrendered to the British at Mbaala. He later became a national hero in Germany and a Deputy in the Reichstag where he tried unsuccessfully to establish a conservative opposition to Adolf Hitler. It was his only serious defeat. Paul von Lettow Vorbeck died in 1964 aged 94.

Frank Alcock's body now lies in the Dar Es Salaam War Cemetery in Tanzania. His mother chose the words, 'Dear Son, Dear Brother, I thank my God upon every remembrance of you,' for his headstone.

Private 202817 Alfred Henry DWIGHT
11th Battalion, Essex Regiment

4th September 1917

Alfred Henry Dwight was born at 5 Eddy Street, Gossoms End, during the spring of 1895 and was the youngest of seven children born to William and Mary Dwight. Their eldest child, William Thomas, was born during the summer of 1874, followed at two-year intervals by George and Frank. Their middle child and only daughter, Eliza Ann, called Annie as a child, was born in 1882. Five years later came Fred, then at four-year intervals Arthur, and finally Alfred Henry. Alfred's mother came from Ashridge and William was a labourer from Chartridge, Buckinghamshire. They lived with their family in one or other of the two-up-two-down cottages in Eddy Street for the best part of 40 years.

The two older boys learnt trades; William Thomas was apprenticed to a saddler and George became a basket maker. By the turn of the century they had both left home, with William later becoming a London policeman. Around the time of Alfred's sixth birthday in 1901, his mother died suddenly, aged 50. Alfred's sister, Eliza Ann, took over the running of the household and looked after the remaining children. By this time, Frank was a wood turner's labourer, probably at East's Sawmill, whose main entrance was at the end of Eddy Street, while Fred worked as a gardener's labourer.

Eliza Ann Dwight married Walter Bryant in the summer of 1901, and the following year she gave birth to a baby daughter called Violet. Eliza and her new husband settled in 2 Eddy Street and later her father, William, and younger brother, Alfred, went to live with them. By 1911, Walter Bryant was working as a trapper at a local mill with William Dwight working as a millhand labourer, possibly in the same mill as his son-in-law. Sixteen-year-old Alfred Henry was working as an errand boy, but unlike his brothers, he seemed to have no ambition to learn a practical trade. He later taught at Gossoms End Sunday School.

It is unclear when Alfred enlisted, but on 2nd August 1916, the day he wrote his Will, he was with 1st Battalion, Hertfordshire Regiment and was still with them at the end of the year when territorial soldiers were re-numbered; he became no 266960. However, Alfred and several other Hertshires were soon transferred to 11th Essex Regiment to make up for earlier losses. Alfred was most likely in the draft of 212 former Territorials that joined the Battalion at Annequin, northwest of Lens, on 7th January 1917. From there the new draft went to 6th Division's Training Area at nearby Chocques, before joining the Division, which occupied three miles of front line in the Loos Salient.

January 1917 was extremely cold in northern France, with snow and hard frosts and the troops kept themselves warm as best they could. In consolation, the British trenches were frozen solid and consequently needed little attention. A re-organisation of 6th Division's battalions on 7th February required a period of settling in and training before the Division took over six miles of front by Loos on 1st March. A week later, 11th Essex entered the trenches at Mazingarbe, which were thawing after the recent rains, making progress along them very slow. The Division also began a period of raiding, counter-raiding and artillery duels.

At 19.00 on 24th March, 11th Essex mounted a battalion raid against the German trenches around Posen Crater. All four companies had supplied two officers and 80 men each for the raid, but as they were making ready, German artillery fire hit their assembly trenches and killed and injured a number of men. Quickly reorganised by company officers, the raiding party crossed no-man's-land, passing through gaps in the wire cut by artillery, and entered the German trenches. The raiders stayed behind enemy lines for 90 minutes, penetrating as far as the support line. In that time, they collected nine prisoners, including an officer, numerous documents, a machine gun and a telescopic sight, all of which they brought back to British lines. The raid cost the Essex four officers wounded and 63 men killed or wounded with over half of the casualties coming from the enemy shelling before the attack.

On 9th April, Canadian troops captured the strategic and strongly defended Vimy Ridge, some eight miles to the southeast of the Battalion's position, threatening German troops to the west of Lens, who consequently prepared to withdraw. The Battalion received orders to watch for any significant movement, particularly from the commanding strong points of Bois Hugo and Hill 70 some five miles away.

Having spent twenty-one consecutive days in the trenches in very wintry weather, 11th Essex then raided a German trench called Nash Alley. Although the attack was initially successful, a German artillery barrage forced the Essex to retreat to their lines at the cost of 10 officers and 250 men. The Battalion Commander's report ascribed the attack's failure to the fact that his men already exhausted following three weeks of trench duty, often knee-deep in mud and slush.

By 1st May 1917, the Battalion's strength was just 23 officers and 447 men, compared to 27 officers and 700 men six weeks earlier. The following week, at Les Brebis, a fresh contingent of 50 men joined them, including Private 35581, John Randall, from Northchurch. On 10th May, the Battalion marched from the front line to Hesdigneul-lès-Béthune for several days training and recuperation after their recent ordeals, and leading up to a Regimental athletic sports day.

John Randall's story covers the Battalion's activities up to the end of June, including the raid on Hill 70. Following that raid, in an attempt to recover lost ground, the Germans launched a series of unsuccessful counterattacks on the British lines.

In mid-July, 11th Essex left the front line and entered billets at Mingoval, a few miles south, for ten days' rest and training. They then moved to Allouagne, just outside Béthune, for further rifle and machine gun training and another sports competition. The Battalion's next move, to Estrée-Cauchy on 8th August, brought rifle shooting and boxing tournaments against other battalions and even a gymkhana for the horsemen amongst them. Later, they marched north to Noeux-les-Mines for three days of practice route marches.

On 28th August, two weeks after Canadian forces captured Hill 70, 11th Essex took over some of their trenches, southeast of the hill. Two days later, German artillery bombarded the trenches in a determined effort to dislodge the Essex and Alfred was seriously wounded. Receiving treatment at a nearby Casualty Clearing Station he was sent to 6th British Red Cross Hospital at Étaples. Alfred Dwight, just 22 years old, succumbed to his injuries there on 4th September, and was buried in the nearby Military Cemetery.

Private 76469 George DAVIS
16th Battalion, Sherwood Foresters (Nottinghamshire and Derbyshire Regiment)

20th September 1917

George Davis was born the fourth child of Thomas and Sarah Davis at 1 Eddy Street, Gossoms End, in August 1896. Northchurch-born Thomas Davis, like many of his Gossoms End neighbours, worked at East's Timber Yard, where he operated a band saw. George, however, began his working life on a milkround and was later a storeman in a nearby warehouse, perhaps through his elder brother Arthur's contacts.

As he was barely eighteen when war broke out, George was officially too young to serve overseas. On 18th December 1914 however, he travelled to Watford, aged himself by a year, and enlisted with the Army Ordnance Corps (AOC). Ten days later he was at the Ordnance Depot & Workshops at Woolwich. The Woolwich depot, also called the Ordnance College, was the main training centre for the Army's specialist apprentices and artisans. The AOC preferred to admit men with knowledge of relevant civilian trades and since the AOC was concerned with the procurement, storage and distribution of armaments, ammunition and other warlike materiel, George's experience as a storeman was ideal. AOC depots had been established across France since August. From Boulogne, Le Havre, Calais, Étaples, Abancourt and Rouen, munitions were transported by rail, lorry or cart to the Front. George's medal card indicates that he arrived at one of these AOC depots on 8th March 1915, and thus qualified for the 1914/15 Star. Two months later, George was appointed Acting Lance Corporal.

As the war progressed and casualties increased significantly, the AOC and administrative Corps were forced to give up their 'Class A' men below the rank of sergeant for front line duty in exchange for men of lower medical grades. Clerks and storemen were the easiest trades to replace, so on 5th November 1916, George was among a group transferred to 15th Training Reserve Battalion at Brockton Camp near Stafford, reverting to his substantive rank of Private.

Since the introduction of compulsory military service at the beginning of 1916, the arrangements for training recruits had been overhauled. Previously, every Regular infantry regiment had trained its own recruits at home in its Reserve Battalions, with Territorial Battalions organising their own training. From 1st September 1916, all recruit training became the responsibility of a new Training Reserve, employing fewer, specialist,

Training Battalions organised into Training Brigades. Although these Training Reserve battalions initially kept their County affiliations, the recruits they trained could be posted to any infantry regiment.

In January 1917, George joined 12th Battalion, Notts and Derby Regiment (the Sherwood Foresters), and wrote a Will leaving his possessions to his mother. Three weeks later, on 2nd February, he was posted to 16th Battalion, Notts and Derby Regiment. Nicknamed the Chatsworth Rifles, 16th Sherwood Foresters had been in France with 117th Brigade, 39th Division since April 1916 and had incurred substantial casualties on the Somme later that year.

On the opening day of the Third Battle of Ypres, the Chatsworth Rifles and 17th King's Royal Rifle Corps (KRRC), were the assault battalions for 117th Brigade. At 03.50 on 31st July 1917, in steady rain, they attacked a series of German pillboxes and a strongpoint. Fighting in small teams, they used Stokes mortars and rifle grenades to suppress the German machine guns, allowing parties of men to get close enough to rush the defenders. George helped capture three pillboxes at Regina Cross in this way, together with a German position known as Alberta. Having consolidated its gains, the Battalion spent the following days patrolling into the German lines, sometimes probing quite deeply. After a short break, they were back in the line to take part in the phase of Third Ypres known as the Battle of Menin Road Ridge.

20th September 1917 was forecast to be fine, dry but overcast, and George's Brigade was the only one from his Division to attack that day. At 05.40, 17th Sherwood Foresters led the advance with the Chatsworth Rifles following up in support. Their orders were to advance towards their initial objective, Bulgar Wood, capturing a number of German blockhouses on the way. They managed to make good progress and by 07.00, were ready to press on to their next objective. Despite coming under fire from the northeast, the Sherwood Foresters were able to achieve their final objective some 45 minutes later.

Meanwhile the KRRC, which had been clearing German dugouts and defences by-passed by the first wave, came up to help them secure the new line against German counterattacks. It was late afternoon before the Germans responded, but when they did, they made three attacks at roughly two-hourly intervals. Each time the Sherwood Foresters drove them back using a combination of artillery and infantry fire, but at a cost.

George, who was just 21, was initially posted 'Missing in Action'. His body was never recovered and ten months later, he was formally classified as 'Killed in Action'. Today, George's name is recorded on the Tyne Cot Memorial at Zonnebeke in West Flanders.

Lance Corporal 12930 Richard BEASLEY DCM
4th Battalion, Bedfordshire Regiment

30th October 1917

Richard Beasley was born in West Hagborne, near Didcot in Berkshire in 1893, the third of Vincent and Elizabeth Beasley's six children. The Beasley family originated from the West Berkshire area, but by 1901, they had moved to Dudswell with Vincent Beasley working as a painter and general handyman on a local farm. Ten years later, the family was living in New Road, Northchurch and Richard was working as a butcher, while his father had now become a house painter. Richard's two younger brothers, Vincent and John, were still at school.

At the outbreak of the war, Richard enlisted with the 6th Battalion, Bedfordshire Regiment at Hertford. 6th Battalion was a Service Battalion, raised in August 1914 around a cadre of 200 experienced soldiers from 3rd (Reserve) Battalion. By the following month, it had grown so large that it could transfer 1,000 men to form 7th (Service) Battalion. Initially attached to the 9th (Scottish) Division at Aldershot, 6th Bedfords transferred to 37th Division when it formed at Andover in March 1915, and trained in 112th Brigade on Salisbury Plain.

With specialist training well under way, the division was put on notice to go overseas. On 30th July 1915, 6th Battalion boarded trains at Ludgershall Station to arrive at Southampton later that afternoon. The battalion left Southampton aboard the *Empress Queen* at 18.30, and landed at Le Havre the following morning. Having rested at N°5 Camp just outside Le Havre, the Bedfords entrained at Le Havre on 1st August for the Front. Four days later, they arrived at billets near Hazebrouck.

Lance Corporal Richard Beasley (Source: British Library)

As it was likely the battalion would soon be going into action, the men were advised to make a short Will in their Field Service Pay Book, or AB64. Richard wrote his Will on 6th August, leaving all his possessions to his mother, and signing himself, Private R. Beasley, C Coy. A few days later, a detachment of Bedfords marched towards the Front, not to fight, but to dig reserve trenches north of Kemmel. Nevertheless, 6th Battalion suffered its first casualty there when, on 19th August, a German sniper killed the officer supervising a night-time working party.

Later that month, the Battalion moved by train to Orville, 19 miles southwest of Arras, where they spent eight days in rather poor billets. From there they marched to Fonquevillers where 'A' and 'B' Companies went into the trenches for four days' training, while Richard and the other men of 'C' and 'D' Companies remained in the village until they swapped places. 21st September 1915 saw 6th Battalion holding trenches in their own right for the first time when they relieved a battalion of The Loyal North Lancashire Regiment at Hannescamps. By then the autumn rains had begun and soon the previously good trenches were turned into muddy rivers.

With the onset of winter, and no prospect of either side launching a significant offensive, the battalion settled down to a basic routine of several days manning the trenches alternating with several days in billets and working parties. The first snow fell in mid-December, followed shortly afterwards by heavy rain which turned many of the communication trenches into quagmires. Late January 1916, brought frost, fogs and false gas alarms, and then, in February, the snow returned.

Despite persistent, heavy snow, the Battalion commenced training for the Somme Offensive on 24th March, and this continued into April, interspersed with work on the Corps Line. On May Day, the Battalion moved to Bienvillers-au-Bois and relieved 13th Kings Royal Rifle Corps in trenches nearby two days later. At 03.00 the next morning after an intense bombardment, German raiders attacked the Battalion's sector, causing 66 casualties with another 8 men missing. Throughout May and June, the casualty rate within 6th Battalion slowly began to mount.

6th Bedfords spent the first two weeks of the Somme Offensive in support, but on 15th July the battalion saw its first major action in 112th Brigade's attack on the village of Pozières. Here they suffered over 243 casualties, but new drafts totalling 249 officers and men joined over the following weeks to replace those losses. The Battalion was again in action around Pozières on 8th/9th August, suffering a further 170 casualties. Once again, a draft of 5 officers and 288 men on 17th August brought numbers up to strength. Shortly afterwards the Battalion left the Somme, moving north to the area south of Loos to regroup.

The Battalion spent the following weeks holding trenches in the Loos Salient, alternating with rest in billets. On 15th October, they began the long march south, back towards the River Ancre, while the final engagements of the Somme Offensive took shape. Arriving at the village of Sarton, 6th Bedfords was held ready for suitable weather to support an attack to push the enemy five miles up the Ancre. Mid-November, brought suitable weather, but by then the operation had been scaled back to the capture of Beaucourt village and a two-mile advance.

Early on Tuesday 14th November, 6th Battalion marched via Mailly-Maillet to support 51st Division and 63rd Division, to which 4th Bedfords belonged, that were both already fighting on the Ancre. Beaumont-Hamel had fallen to 51st Division on 13th, but progress was faltering and 4th Bedfords' attack against Frankfurt Trench on Tuesday afternoon failed because nearby Munich Trench had not been captured to plan. 6th Bedfords attacked Munich Trench next day with their Brigade, while at Beaucourt their division was relieving 63rd (Royal Naval) Division, which had recently lost Captain Vere Duncombe Loxley, RMLI. Although 100 men of 6th Bedfords assisted an attack near Frankfurt and Munich Trenches on 23rd November, the first snowfall on 18th November had already marked the official end of the Battle of the Somme, which had left the German defences fatally weakened. At the end of November, 6th Bedfords moved to Rubempré to recover.

The Bedfords returned to the frontline in late December, settling down near Béthune for a third wartime Christmas. Early 1917 saw the battalion in the familiar routine, alternating between trench duties and resting in billets whilst integrating reinforcements at intervals. The Bedfords also trained in new infantry tactics developed during the Somme fighting, that made the infantry platoon the basic tactical unit. French and British plans were agreed for a joint Spring Offensive to break through German defences weakened by the long battles of 1916. The British were to attack first at Arras, drawing German reserves away from the front with General Nivelle's French troops attacking about a week later.

The Bedfords participated in the capture of La Folie Ferme and La Begère during the First Battle of the Scarpe and supported 63rd Brigade in the Second Scarpe Battle. On 28th April, 6th Battalion joined a dawn attack on Greenland Hill, but flanking machine gun fire forced them to dig in just short of their objective. When that part of the Battle of Arleux ended on 29th April, only 58 Bedfords were fit for duty.

Work to re-organise the battalion after this mauling began immediately. Divisional Games, in which the battalion won the Divisional Transport competition by 87 points, followed a weeks' training in May. A week later, the battalion won the Brigade Band Competition, both successes helping to improve the men's morale. On 19th May, the battalion was back in the trenches at Tilloy-lès-Mofflaines, just outside Arras, having relieved 3rd London Regiment.

At midnight on 26th May, Richard was with a strong raiding party sent to capture a German soldier and investigate the string of German-held shell holes opposite their lines. However, the raiders bumped into a screen of German troops protecting a large wiring party working in front of the line of shell holes and a lively fire fight developed. The raiding party was considerably outnumbered and became trapped by a machine gun post, which Richard volunteered to attack. Crossing open ground under heavy fire, he managed to throw grenades into the post, killing its occupants. Finding their Maxim in working order, Richard attempted to machine-gun the surrounding Germans, but he was shot. Richard was brought back for treatment and recommended for the Distinguished Conduct Medal (DCM) for his courage. The citation published in *The London Gazette,* dated 18th July 1917, confirming his award reads:

> '12930 Pte. R. Beasley. Bedf. R.
> For conspicuous gallantry and devotion. He volunteered to attack a machine gun, placed in the open, which was holding up all progress. He crossed the open under heavy fire, bombed the crew, but was wounded while trying to fire the gun on the enemy'.

The War Diary entry for the action ends, 'Several Germans were killed & the whole enemy party appeared considerably frightened & surprised. Fire was opened all along the line & our party withdrew, all men, except three, regaining our trenches. Casualties were 1 Officer & 3 men wounded & 3 men killed. The whole operation was conducted with great determination & was highly successful considering the opposition that was met with'.

Richard's Service Record no longer exists, so the extent of his injuries is uncertain, but the bullet was probably removed at one of the military hospitals at Étaples. Richard's original Will was torn from his Pay Book and filed, probably when he was wounded, so he received a fresh AB64 and re-wrote his Will on 11th June 1917, leaving everything to his mother as before.

Richard was probably held at 17th Infantry Base Depot at Étaples after leaving hospital, together with other soldiers whose wounds had healed together with fresh recruits from England, awaiting postings to front line units. Richard eventually went with one of the drafts sent from Base during August 1917 to 4th Bedfordshire Regiment, just north of Arras. Richard spent his first few days training and practicing trench attacks before dinner and afterwards playing cricket and football. At around this time he was appointed Lance Corporal.

In mid-September 4th Bedfords were again holding trenches in Oppy Wood, which had seen considerable fighting earlier in the year. Two days after being relieved by 7th Royal Fusiliers on 22nd September, the battalion moved to Écoivres, some miles to the rear, to train and prepare to join the battle for Passchendaele. On 7th October, the Bedfords marched to Houtkerque to practise attacking enemy pillboxes.

Two weeks later, in very wet weather, the battle-ready Bedfords were taken by bus to trenches a mile north of Ypres. At dawn on 30th October, 4th Bedfords attacked 600 yards of German line near Poelcappelle, but heavy, boggy ground around the Paddebeek stream, made worse by rain and heavy shelling, made significant progress impossible. The battalion only managed to advance 150 to 200 yards at a cost of two officers and 52 men killed, with a further seven officers and 180 men wounded. A further 23 men were reported 'Missing in Action', among them Richard Beasley DCM, whose body was lost in the Flanders mud.

Richard Beasley's name is now preserved on the Tyne Cot Memorial in Belgium.

Lieutenant John Augustus HARMAN
Royal Flying Corps

17th November 1917

John Augustus 'Jack' Harman was born in South Kensington, London on 15th June 1893. He was baptised the following month at St Mary's, Northchurch, by the Rector, Jack's grandfather, the Reverend Augustus F Birch. Jack was the eldest son of John Eustace Harman, a London barrister, and Mrs Ethel Harman. John and Ethel Harman would have two more boys - Charles, born in 1895 and, five years later, Edward.

Jack Harman was educated first at Edgeborough School near Farnham, Surrey and then at Uppingham School in Northamptonshire, where several Harmans had been pupils, including his father and uncle. Jack's father later became a member of Uppingham's Board of Trustees. Whilst at Uppingham Jack was a keen member of the School's Officer Training Corps. He was also a rugby enthusiast, playing for Rosslyn Park, an amateur sporting club then based at Richmond, southwest London.

On 19th March 1914, Jack Harman boarded the Bibby Line ship *Derbyshire* at Liverpool en route to Colombo in Ceylon to begin a new life as a tea planter, but within months Europe was at war. Jack subsequently enlisted with the Ceylon Planters Rifle Corps at its headquarters in the island's capital, Kandy. Established in 1900 for Imperial deployment or internal emergencies, the Corps was composed exclusively of European volunteers from the tea and rubber plantations in the island's central highlands. Having only just enlisted, Jack missed the Corps departure for Egypt in October 1914 when 8 officers and 229 men were sent to guard the Suez Canal.

Sensing that there was little chance of seeing action whilst in Ceylon, Jack returned to England in the early summer of 1915 and applied for a Commission with the Army Service Corps (ASC). On his application form, Jack's former headmaster, Henry McKenzie, certified that Jack had, 'attained a good standard of education by the time he left Uppingham School in the subjects necessary for an Army exam. He was in our 2nd Army Class'. Harman's Commission as Second Lieutenant duly appeared in *The London Gazette* on 24th August 1915.

The ASC supplied and transported all provisions including food, fuel, horses, clothing, equipment and ammunition, but not heavy equipment and weaponry, which was the responsibility of the Army Ordnance Corps. Harman spent a month at the ASC's Aldershot depot before joining the Mediterranean Expeditionary Force. On 16th September 1915, he left

Portsmouth with an ASC contingent for the Dardanelles aboard HMS *Terrible*, a former cruiser converted to a troopship, arriving at Mudros on 5th October. Harman and his contingent then moved to Sulva Bay, on the Gallipoli peninsula, to form 184 Depot Unit of Supply.

While Jack was en route to Gallipoli, his younger brother, Charles, a Lieutenant with 13th Middlesex Regiment, was fighting in the Battle of Loos. Charles was captured on 27th September and spent the rest of the war in a German Prison Camp at Lambinowice, Poland.

Following the evacuation of Gallipoli, Harman and his unit returned to Egypt and on 19th February, he was transferred to the Divisional Train of 52nd (Lowland) Division. Each British Army division had its own central transport organisation to supply the varied needs of its infantry, artillery and attached elements. Divisional Trains comprised 26 officers and 402 men with responsibility for 378 horses, 17 carts, 125 wagons and 30 bicycles. Harman reported to 52nd Division HQ at El Kantara on 11th March 1916 and was assigned to 218 Supply Company.

El Kantara, some 96 miles northeast of Cairo, was the principal supply centre for N°3 Section of the Suez Canal defences. It was over a year since Turkish forces were last repelled from the Suez Canal Zone, but while Turkey could still threaten Britain's principal supply route to India and Australasia, a garrison of over 35,000 Imperial troops and their 17,000 animals had to be maintained there. This was no easy task.

Supplies were offloaded at Port Said on the Mediterranean, where an officer and his small staff checked the loads either onto barges navigating down the Suez Canal or onto railway trucks, according to a very strict timetable. Facilities at Kantara for unloading, storing and distributing the supplies were extremely poor, with insufficient holding tanks for the enormous volumes of water arriving regularly from Port Said. The Egyptian Labour Corps manned Kantara's wharves, supplemented by gangs provided by local contractors, but there were too few ASC officers and men to regulate transhipment. From Kantara, supplies moved to the front line along narrow-gauge railways or by camel. Huge numbers of camels carrying large 12-gallon copper containers, called fantasses, transported the water to the front-line troops. Motor transport was severely constrained by the local roads, which were mostly rough dirt tracks that wore out vehicles causing frequently breakdowns. Jack's subsequent transfer to Salonika in June 1916 probably came as a relief. He left Kantara on 17th June, and sailed from Alexandria on 21st to join 573 Horsed Transport Company, 3rd Base Depot. He was posted to 362 HT Coy, 34th Reserve Park, three days later.

When Bulgaria declared war on Serbia in mid-October 1915, the Greek Prime Minister allowed a Franco-British force to land at the Aegean port of Salonika, now known as Thessalonica, to help their ally. The Entente forces arrived too late to prevent a Serbian defeat, but despite Greek ambivalence, King Constantine of Greece was pro-German, for example, they were kept at Salonika with the intention of opening an ill-defined Second Front. Troops spent months constructing a defensive perimeter some eight miles north of the port using such enormous quantities of barbed wire that it became known as 'The Birdcage'. By the time Harman arrived, Russians, Italians and surviving Serbian troops had joined the Birdcage, swelling its ration strength to almost 250,000 men plus their animals.

Shortly after Harman arrived at Salonika, Bulgaria launched its expected invasion of Greece. It was repulsed near Lake Doiran on the Macedonian border, where the inevitable trench systems developed. At the beginning of October 1916, Entente troops opened operations on the River Struma, advancing towards the town of Serres, modern Serrai, with Harman and 362 HT Coy in support. The local dirt roads, though dusty, were usable in hot, dry, weather, but the heavy autumn rains quickly turned them into muddy quagmires, adding considerably to the Transport Companies' difficulties.

By late 1916, Harman had tired of logistics and craved a new challenge; he wanted to become a pilot with the Royal Flying Corps (RFC). His transfer came through on 21st January 1917 and he returned to Egypt soon afterwards to join 20th Training Wing of N°3 School of Military Aviation at Aboukir.

The RFC and its Central Flying School at Upavon, Wiltshire, were both established in 1912. By August 1914, the RFC had just 93 pilots and 100 reconnaissance aircraft, but military aviation, and associated casualty lists, expanded so rapidly that the demand for skilled pilots always exceeded their supply. With insufficient space to extend facilities at Upavon, the RFC commandeered civilian flying schools and sought suitable locations for new flying schools abroad. Training at Ismailia began with two Maurice-Farman biplanes in June 1916, and within a month, the embryo flying school was using a new, larger airbase under construction at Aboukir. The first pilot examinations took place in September 1916, and that November, the establishment was renamed N°3 School of Military Aviation.

In March 1917, Harman and 135 other trainee pilots joined 21 Reserve Squadron, RFC at Abbassia for basic training. They were introduced to the theory of flight, aircraft construction, aero engines, wireless, machine guns, bombsights, formation flying, artillery observation and reconnaissance, as well as attending lectures on photography and instruments. In mid-April, Harman and 106 trainees progressed to the next stage with 22 Reserve Squadron at Aboukir, where they would fly their first aeroplane, an American purpose-designed trainer, the Curtiss Jenny. Having completed their initial flying training on the 75mph Jenny, trainee pilots moved on to warplanes like the de Haviland BE2e. Introduced in

1916 and capable of 90mph, the two-seat BE2e fighter was developed from Geoffrey de Havilland's 1912 prototype, which he once landed at Northchurch. Training accidents were commonplace and Harman had his share, crash-landing both a BE2e and a Bristol M1 Monoplane fighter that he managed to turn upside down. He was fortunate to escape with minor injuries each time; many fledgling pilots were killed or seriously injured during training.

Having survived flight training, Harman moved to Suez, where 58 Reserve Squadron was stationed, and graduated as a Flying Officer in May 1917. He immediately applied for an active posting and on 3rd June, Harman left Alexandria bound for Marseilles and England. Harman was posted to 33 Squadron, RFC, which had its headquarters at Gainsborough, Lincolnshire and flew from three nearby airfields, Elsham Wolds, Kirton-in-Lindsey and Brattleby. 33 Squadron was one of the Home Defence Squadrons formed the previous year to counter the growing number of Zeppelin raids on England.

The aluminium framed Zeppelin was the brainchild of retired army officer Count Ferdinand Zeppelin, whose first experimental airship flew in July 1900. The German Army

Lieutenant John Augustus Harman
(Source: Charles Harman)

purchased his third airship, the LZ3, in March 1909, while the German Navy ordered the first of its Zeppelins for maritime reconnaissance patrols in 1912. Zeppelins in army service were joined that year by the first of the technically superior *Schütte-Lanz* airships, although all enemy airships remained 'Zepps' to the British. The Zeppelin threat to Britain was initially more imagined than real, until overnight on 19th/20th January 1915, two Naval Zeppelins bombed along the Norfolk coast from 3,000ft. The Kaiser initially forbade attacks against London, but as soon as it became practical he relented, and on the night of 31st May 1915, LZ38 dropped incendiary bombs and grenades over an arc stretching from Stoke Newington to Stepney, killing seven people and injuring a further thirty-five. Zeppelins carried up to four tonnes of mixed bombs, the largest being 300kg.

The Zeppelin campaign was truly a war of nerves. Early shortcomings in Britain's night-time air defences were offset by the tendency of nervous Zeppelin crewmen to report seeing guns and fighters that did not exist. Zeppelins carried defensive machine guns, although their main defence was height and darkness. Early airships also had significant blind spots. If defending aircraft did manage to approach, Zeppelins climbed rapidly by dropping ballast. Their hydrogen-filled gasbags proved surprisingly difficult to ignite although in June 1915, Lt. R Warneford, RNAS, flying over Belgium, 'shot down' the first Zeppelin by dropping 20lb bombs along its top. Britain's air defences slowly improved and by mid-1916, the RFC had formed dedicated anti-Zeppelin squadrons flying the BE2c from airfields adapted for night flying. Their Lewis guns fired a mixture of newly developed Brock explosive and Pomeroy incendiary bullets intended to tear open the airship's gas cells and ignite the escaping hydrogen.

On 2nd September 1916, the fourteen airship crews targeting London were already dismayed by the number of searchlights and guns that met them, but when Lt. William Leefe-Robinson set *Schütte-Lanz* SL11 ablaze with his third drum of Brock and Pomeroy 12,000ft over Cuffley in Hertfordshire, the largest airship raid of the war dispersed. L-32 was passing over Tring and Berkhamsted Common when her captain saw SL11 fall. Turning away from London, he scattered bombs across Hertford and Ware then, like the others, went home. A BE2c of 39 Home Defence Squadron destroyed L-7 over Essex three weeks later, and another Zeppelin damaged by an anti-aircraft shell at 13,000 feet, crash-landed in Essex the same night. At the beginning of October, cheering crowds in Berkhamsted High Street saw L-31 explode into flames in the distance, set ablaze by Lt. V Tempest.

Germany responded by building Zeppelins that could reach 20,000ft, but with half the bombload, no guns and fewer engines. However, hardly any airships bombed England until mid-1917, when L-48 was shot down on her first raid. By September 1917, 33 Squadron was replacing its BE2s with two-seater FE2s, commonly known as 'Fees'. The FE2 fighter entered service on the Western Front in January 1916, but within the year, it was outclassed by German fighters and withdrawn from daytime operations. Although the FE2's top speed was only 76mph at altitude, with its 47ft 9inch wingspan and powerful 160bhp Beardmore engine, the Fee could be coaxed to 14,000 feet.

Eleven airships came to attack Northern England on 19th October, for their largest raid of 1917. That evening, Harman flew a FE2d from Kirton-in-Lindsey to intercept them, but had to return within 40 minutes following engine failure, a regular problem with the FE2. Two other 33 Squadron machines experienced engine trouble that night and returned without engaging the Zeppelins. Harman went up again later in another FE2, but high altitude winds had already swept the Zeppelins southwards. In fact, L-45 was following the London & North Western Railway mainline directly over Northchurch and Berkhamsted before dropping 300kg bombs on Piccadilly Circus, Camberwell and Hither Green, killing 31 people, and injuring 48. Guns and aircraft brought down five of the raiders over France as they struggled home, another crashed at its base and L-49, having lost her forward cabin, drifted helplessly across the Channel before being forced to land in Eastern France where she was captured by French forces.

The British public demanded that more Zeppelins be shot down, so the FE2 underwent further modifications so it could climb even higher. To reduce weight, the Fees were turned into single-seaters by covering the observer's cockpit with fabric or plywood, allowing them to reach 17,000 feet. On the night of 17th November 1917, Harman took off again in a single-seat FE2, serial B/416. His plane crashed shortly afterwards at Hibaldstowe, about three miles to the northeast of Kirkton-in-Lindsey. 2nd Lieutenant Jack Harman, aged 24, was killed. The Court of Inquiry later heard that B/416 was in a satisfactory state at the time of the crash and concluded that Jack's death was the result of a night flying accident caused by pilot error.

Jack's funeral was held the following Wednesday at Holy Trinity church in Kirkton-in-Lindsey with full military honours. His coffin, draped in a Union Jack, was carried by six RFC officers to the graveside at Gainsborough Cemetery where a firing party from the North Staffordshire Regiment fired three volleys over the coffin and the 'Last Post' was sounded.

John Eustace Harman, Jack Harman's father, later retired to The Hollow at the top of New Road, Northchurch where he died, aged 66, on 27th August 1927. Apart from the Northchurch War Memorial, as his father was a member of Lincolns Inn, Jack Harman's name also appears on the Lincolns Inn War Memorial in London.

Gunner 294266 Alfred CURL
Royal Garrison Artillery

29th December 1917

Alfred Curl was born and bred in Northchurch. His father, George, worked in the local watercress beds fed by the River Bulborne, but later changed occupation and became a platelayer for the London & North Western Railway. Alfred's mother was born Lizzie Davis in Northchurch, and later adopted the name Bignall when her mother, Sarah, married Frederick Bignall in the summer of 1872. Lizzie and George were married at Northchurch on 19th July 1890, aged 19 and 20 years respectively and their first child, Edith, was born soon afterwards. Two years later came Alfred, followed by Emily, George junior, Lizzie junior, Nellie, Dorothy Sarah and finally Phyllis, all of them born in Northchurch.

Alfred was christened at St Mary's, Northchurch, on 3rd July 1892, taking his name from his paternal grandfather. The Curls lived initially in the High Street and then Bell Lane, before moving to Orchard End. After leaving school, Alfred started working as a carter at East's Timber Yard. Around 1913, Alfred left Northchurch and moved to 2 Gladstone Terrace, York, where he started working at one of the city's chocolate manufacturers. Whilst in York, Alfred met and fell for Beatrice Rogers and on 27th October 1915, they were married at York Register Office. Their marital home was a small terraced house in Dale Street, close to York railway station. Not long afterwards, Alfred joined 144th (York) Heavy Battery, Royal Garrison Artillery (RGA) as a gunner.

Raised as part of Kitchener's New Army, 144th Heavy Battery RGA had two sections equipped with a pair of 60-pdr guns, each gun weighing around five tons and requiring a team of eight horses or a caterpillar tractor to move it. The 60-pdr, introduced in 1904/05 as a heavy field gun was the workhorse of the BEF's divisional artillery. It fired a 5-inch shell as far as 10,300 yards, almost 6 miles, which the shell covered in less than 15 seconds. Wartime improvements simplified manufacture and increased the maximum range by another 2,000 yards to reach further into the enemy's rear.

When Alfred's Battery made the ten-hour crossing from Southampton to Le Havre on 18th June 1916, its strength had been increased to six guns divided into three sections. After resting overnight near Le Havre, 144th Heavy Battery entrained for Godewaersvelde, close to the Belgian border, where Alfred wrote his Will. The battery then moved by road to a farm near Poperinghe, where its first gun emplacements in Flanders were being prepared. At that time, guns arriving in new positions were 'registered' by firing a few ranging shots from which their officers could quickly calculate ranges and elevations to hit any other target. Unfortunately, ranging shots also announced the arrival of a new battery to the enemy.

In 1916, 60-pdr and 6-inch howitzer batteries were removed from infantry divisions and organised into Heavy Artillery Groups, or HAGs, under Army Corps control. On arrival in France, 144th HB was placed under 10th HAG. Alfred's battery later participated in the massive barrage preceding the start of the Battle of the Somme and bombardments supporting the follow-up attacks throughout the Offensive.

During prolonged bombardments, the guns were served by small detachments of gunners in rotation. Each battery's ammunition, consisting of shrapnel and high explosive lyddite shells, was always stockpiled well away from the gun emplacements and brought up to them by horse-drawn transport or specially constructed light railways. Heavy guns reached deep into German lines as part of the massed barrages that normally preceded an infantry attack. Their principal role was to destroy enemy gun batteries, which in turn targeted British heavy artillery. Thus, heavy batteries frequently moved between HAGs as they were concentrated in different sectors, then withdrawn to replace casualties and worn-out guns. Reliefs were complex procedures, which could take two or three days for the gun sections to change over. In the first ten months of 1917 alone, Alfred's battery moved between eight different HAGs, although some may have involved changes of management rather than location.

By 9th April, 144th HB was under 15th HAG and participating in the 2,817 gun Easter Monday bombardment that preceded the Battle of Arras, a diversionary attack intended to assist the French Spring Offensive in their sector. The following month, 144th HB was moved to 24th HAG, a month later to 70th HAG and finally, in June 1917, to 13th HAG, which was one of many preparing for the Third Battle of Ypres. In total, the British had 3,091 guns at their disposal, twice the number available to the Germans and the artillery barrage preceding the attack lasted for fifteen days. From Zero Hour, Alfred's battery provided a creeping barrage covering the troops' advance across no-man's-land.

At the beginning of September, the battery's guns were positioned along the ramparts of Ypres, outside the Menin Gate, when German artillery began dropping mustard gas shells around them. Known as *Gelbkreuz*, i.e. Yellow Cross, after the identifying markings on German shells, mustard gas is actually a brownish, oily liquid with a distinctive, pungent smell like garlic or strong English mustard and an insidious, delayed action. Mustard gas vapours so severely affects the eyes that it often causes temporary blindness. Although the British gas mask, called the Small Box Respirator, offered good protection to the eyes and lungs, there was no gas-proof clothing. Mustard liquid on the skin causes redness, followed by severe blistering and contaminated surfaces remain hazardous to touch for days or weeks in cold conditions. The chemical's most dangerous feature is the delay between exposure and the appearance of symptoms, which varies according to the amount of chemical absorbed, but is typically about four hours. The Germans frequently shelled British batteries with Yellow Cross to exhaust their gunners by forcing them to fire the guns wearing gas masks for extended periods and constantly decontaminate weapons and emplacements with bleach solution.

Without modern protective clothing, casualties were unavoidable. Two gunners were gassed by mustard shells on the morning of 5th September and over a dozen more that afternoon. The battery positions were subjected to heavy gas and HE fire every night for over a week, leaving many men and all but two officers poisoned or with mustard gas burns. Eventually, on 15th September, Alfred's battery was withdrawn to a rest camp and placed under 27th HAG. Only five days later 144th HB had to relieve 22nd Heavy Battery, because all of its officers and 80 men were suffering from the effects of gas.

At the beginning of October, 144th HB was moved to III Army Corps, at first with 21st HAG, then on 16th November, to 32nd HAG in preparation for the Battle of Cambrai. Although originally conceived as a substantial raid, this attack across the relatively dry and level ground between the Escaut Canal and the Canal du Nord now offered the potential to relieve the muddy stalemate of Third Ypres.

The plan for the morning of 20th November was to break through the Hindenburg Line, capture Bourlon Wood and the important communication centre of Cambrai, and break out towards Valenciennes with two cavalry divisions. The Hindenburg Line was known to be lightly held there, so absolute secrecy was vital to keep it that way.

Over 1,000 artillery pieces were emplaced to support the

Gunner Alfred Curl
(Source: Peter Addiscott)

attacking troops, but there was to be no preliminary bombardment. Improved ammunition quality, together with the experience of three years' warfare, had made British artillery techniques increasingly sophisticated. Provided with detailed maps prepared from aerial photographs, accurate ballistic tables, up to date meteorological reports and even allowing for the wear and tear of individual guns, battery commanders could hit any target first time by map reference and calculation alone. This technique of 'predictive fire' allowed Alfred's battery to occupy a new position and remain unknown to the enemy until the moment they opened fire at Zero Hour.

Instead of pulverising the German trenches with artillery shells, 410 assault tanks, plus 66 supporting tanks, the greatest number assembled thus far, would accompany the infantry. The Mark IV tanks were driven in secrecy from nearby railheads overnight, while squadrons of the Royal Flying Corps patrolled up and down the German lines to drown out their noise.

At 06.20 on Tuesday 20th November, a massive artillery barrage on their strongpoints and gun emplacements took the Germans totally by surprise. Tanks trailing grappling hooks dragged the German wire apart, while other tanks eased their way across trenches by first dumping a 2-ton bundle of brushwood, called a fascine, into them. All the three trench systems of the Hindenburg line were breached to a depth of three to four miles by British infantry and tanks under cover of a creeping artillery barrage and ground-strafing Royal Flying Corps fighters. About 8,000 German prisoners and 100 guns were captured that day and III Corps reached the St Quentin Canal and forced two crossing places. Unfortunately, the only bridge suitable for tanks was damaged and collapsed under the first tank across.

When news of the victory reached London three days later, church bells rang out in celebration, but as with previous attacks it soon lost momentum with the cavalry being too far back to follow up before the Germans rallied and began their relentless local counterattacks. To keep within range of the fighting, gun batteries like Alfred's had to be hauled across the smashed Hindenburg Line into hastily improvised positions, and without up to date charts they were vulnerable to German counter-battery fire. Finally, Bourlon Wood, which dominated the approaches to Cambrai, proved as difficult to capture as all the Somme Woods had been, and tanks were of little help.

On the last day of November, Alfred's Battery transferred from 34th HAG and took position in front of Villers Guislain with 21st HAG. Suddenly, German artillery fired a hurricane bombardment and shock troops employing infiltration tactics swept over the Battery's position and reached Villers Guislain. Four of its guns were captured. However, one pair of 144th HB's 60-pounders were still left in what became no-mans-land. Over a day or so, the battery prepared two gun limbers, wiring bits of car tyre onto wheel rims and wrapping harness links in string, and double horse teams with sacking on their hooves, to snatch both guns from under the enemy's noses in a daring night-time operation.

Meanwhile, the reinforced Germans regained much of their lost ground until the British withdrew to dominant positions for the winter. The BEF officially went onto the defensive in mid-December, but the dangers of counter-battery fire, burst guns and transport accidents faced by artilleryman continued as hard frosts set in.

On 27th December, 144th HB transferred to 27th HAG and, at around the same time, Alfred Curl was seriously wounded and transferred to 55 Casualty Clearing Station at Tincourt, five miles east of Peronne. He died there of his injuries on 29th December, aged 25. Alfred's body now lies at the Tincourt New British Cemetery with six Royal Garrison Artillerymen who died during the Battle of Cambrai. After the war Beatrice Curl requested, 'Always Remembered', for Alfred's headstone.

Private 48065 Frank Francis (ALLAWAY)
5th Battalion, Bedfordshire Regiment

31st December 1917

Frank Francis is something of an enigma. Frank Francis Allaway, to give his full name, was born in Headington, near Oxford in early 1878. Frank's father, Henry Allaway, was in the building trade and his mother, Sarah Ann, was a dressmaker. Both parents were born in Eynsham, Oxfordshire and Frank was their sixth child and fifth son. When Frank was very small, the family moved to Hemel Hempstead where in 1880, his second sister Clara was born. Within six months the family had moved on to Abbots Langley and another brother, Ronald, was born there a year or two later. By then Henry Allaway was working in Abbots Langley as a bricklayer, alongside his eldest son, Thomas, who was his labourer.

By 1891, the Allaways had returned to the Oxford area, moving to 10 Magdalen Road in Cowley where Sarah Ann's mother, Deborah Buckingham, came to live with them. Henry was now working as a plasterer, although Thomas may no longer have been working with his father, as by then he was living elsewhere. The older children remaining at home were all working; Charles was a baker, daughter, Jesse, was a sewing machinist making shirts, Frederick worked as a publican's porter, and 15-year-old Henry junior was a florist's errand boy. Frank, then just 13 years old, was still at school, along with Clara and Ronald. In spring of 1901, Frank's mother died aged 57, and Clara Allaway took over the running of the household. The 1901 Census shows Henry, Clara, Frederick and Ronald living at 68 Cowley Road in Cowley. Henry Allaway died four years later, aged 65.

Meanwhile, Frank had left home to become a joiner's machinist, moving to Maidenhead, Berkshire. There he met Annie Emily Shail, possibly through her brother George, who was about Frank's age. Annie was a laundress born in Maidenhead a couple of years after Frank. In 1900, Annie and Frank had a summer wedding at Maidenhead and the newlyweds began their married life lodging with Annie's widowed mother, her brother and younger sister at 75 Powney Road. Two years after their marriage Annie and Frank had a daughter, who they named Phillis Norah.

By 1911, Frank was working as a machinist in London, and living at 2 Mozart Street in Paddington with his wife and daughter, and mother-in-law, Emma Shail. What happened over the next few years is unclear, but Frank eventually came to live in Northchurch, where he was known as

Frank Francis and apparently lived alone. Frank found employment as a timber sawyer and gas engine attendant with Henry & James Matthews, a Berkhamsted builder and undertaker in Castle Street. He also became an active member of the Berkhamsted and Northchurch Fire Brigade.

Frank was well into his thirties when war broke out, but still physically fit. He continued to do useful work on government contracts for Henry & James Matthews, although his 'A1' medical grade meant it would only be a matter of time before his call up notice arrived. When it did, his employers appealed to keep him and in June 1917, Frank duly appeared before the Berkhamsted Rural Military Service Tribunal alongside two workmates and a representative of his firm.

His employers told the Tribunal that twenty-six of their men had already enlisted and the firm had an important official contract to fulfil for the General Post Office. Frank was initially granted exemption until the end of 1917, but the Tribunal's Military representative objected, citing Frank's high medical grade and his exemption was withdrawn. Despite his skills, experience and service as a fireman, Frank had no option but to report to the recruiting office at Bedford on 1st September 1917.

Frank was posted to 1/5th Battalion, Bedfordshire Regiment, the Bedfords' Territorial battalion, which mostly drew its recruits from the Luton area. During 1915, 1/5th fought with the Mediterranean Expeditionary Force at Gallipoli and had remained in Egypt after the Peninsula was evacuated. The Battalion had been fighting the Turks in Palestine since the spring of 1917, and consequently required regular reinforcement to replace its losses.

In little more than a month after his enlistment, Frank was crossing the English Channel with a draft of conscripts for 1/5th Battalion. They traversed France by rail to the port of Marseilles, where they boarded the troopship HMT *Aragon* for the voyage across the Mediterranean. *Aragon*, a requisitioned mail packet of 9,588 tons, had previously carried members of the South African Labour Corps to East Africa in the same convoy as Frank Alcock and his comrades of 2nd Rhodesia Regiment. Since the Gallipoli campaign, she had operated in the Mediterranean, mainly sailing between Egypt and either Marseilles or Taranto in Italy.

At the beginning of December 1917 some 2,200 soldiers, including Frank, 150 officers and 160 nursing sisters, boarded the *Aragon* en route to various units in Egypt. Meanwhile all the Christmas mail for Egypt was loaded. *Aragon's* departure was delayed for two weeks however, due to enemy activity. Throughout 1917, increasing numbers of hostile submarines, mostly short range coastal U-boats, sailing from Austrian ports such as Pula in the north Adriatic, were making the Mediterranean so hazardous for shipping that all Allied troopships had to sail in convoys, escorted by British and Japanese warships. On 17th December, *Aragon* finally got under way in the company of another transport, the *Nile*, and the obligatory destroyer escort.

Apart from some cases of seasickness during a period of heavy seas, the first leg of the voyage was uneventful. *Aragon* put in to Malta on 23rd December and stayed there for a few days, allowing everyone aboard to enjoy Christmas in peace and safety. On the fourth day, the little convoy set sail again with a fresh escort consisting of two Japanese destroyers and a British destroyer, HMS *Attack*.

Approaching Egypt at daybreak on Sunday 30th December, the convoy separated; *Nile* and the Japanese destroyers set course for Port Said, while *Aragon* and *Attack* continued towards Alexandria. Shortly before 11.00, *Aragon* and *Attack* were approaching the eight-mile channel leading towards Alexandria's port. The two ships had just passed the marker buoy at the channel's entrance when a minesweeping trawler signalled a warning of mines in the channel. *Attack* immediately instructed *Aragon* to follow her out to sea and turned about. *Attack's* Captain could not have known that Oberleutnant Horst Obermüller, captain of the submarine UC-34 and responsible for the mines, was watching, submerged near the entrance buoy. Launched in May 1916, UC-34 carried eighteen mines and seven torpedoes. Since taking command the previous July, Obermüller had accounted for three of the fifteen Allied ships UC-34 had sunk to date.

At first, *Aragon* was too close for Obermüller to launch a torpedo, but as she slowly manoeuvred to clear the buoy and follow *Attack*, she unwittingly presented a perfect target. One of the duty officers on *Aragon's* bridge later wrote: '[We] saw the periscope of the submarine, and at the next instant the wake of the torpedo, which was coming straight for the ship. An endeavour was made to turn the ship, and avoid the torpedo, but it was of no avail, as the ship was going very slowly. The explosion was a dull crashing blast, and the ship shuddered like a reed.'

Within minutes, all the nurses were in the best lifeboats and had cleared the ship. *Aragon* was listing badly to starboard and had started to sink at her stern, jamming the remaining lifeboats. Eyewitnesses recalled the troops drawn up on deck singing *Keep the Home Fires Burning*. Soon *Attack* came alongside and, by means of ropes, began to transfer soldiers down onto her deck, while *Aragon's* rafts were cut loose and soldiers took to the water. *Aragon* was clearly doomed and about fifteen minutes after the torpedo struck, her Captain ordered, 'every man for himself'. Five minutes later, *Aragon* slid rapidly beneath the water.

Aboard *Attack*, all hands worked to help the survivors and wounded men cramming her decks. Suddenly there was a shout aboard the destroyer and an enormous explosion amidships hurled men into the sea. Another torpedo launched from UC-34 had split *Attack* in two and in barely six minutes both broken halves had sunk.

In all, 18 of *Aragon's* crew, her Captain and 591 soldiers died, many of them having transferred to *Attack* before she too went down. Were it not for the many trawlers that rushed to the scene, the death toll would have been far higher. Of the twenty-five 1/5th Bedfordshire Regiment men who died, only the body of their Quarter Master Sergeant Major was ever recovered for burial.

Within the Alexandria cemetery complex in Egypt stands the Chatby Memorial on which is inscribed the name of Frank Allaway and his comrades among those others who, 'have no other grave but the sea.'

Private 235328 Harold Alfred SHRIMPTON
20th Battalion, Kings (Liverpool Regiment)

13th January 1918

On 10th November 1884, at Great Hasely in Oxfordshire, 24-year-old Blanche Shrimpton gave birth to a son, Harold Alfred. Blanche was born at Great Hasely herself, but when Harold was born, she was working as an Upper Housemaid at Trinity College, Oxford. Harold's baptismal record at St Barnabas church in Oxford shows his father's name as Samuel, a valet.

In the late nineteenth century, the only support a single working mother could hope for would come from her family. Consequently, in 1891 six-year-old Harold was living at 62 Abbey Road, Oxford with one of Blanche's sisters. Another of her sisters was married to a grocer and Harold would later choose to follow the same profession.

In due course, Harold joined the Co-operative Society as a grocer and started work at the Berkhamsted branch. He found accommodation at 181 High Street and whilst there, Harold met a girl a little older than himself called Selina Holloway. Selina, who lived at 63 Shrublands Avenue, was the daughter of a Postal Telegraph Foreman at Berkhamsted, and originally came from Staffordshire. Harold and Selina were married at St Peter's Church on 6th June 1908 in the presence of Hannah Holloway and Harold's uncle, Bertram John Shrimpton. Their marriage certificate names Harold's father as 'John Shrimpton, (dec'd), a farmer'. The newlyweds settled at 71 Gossoms End and about two years later Harold and Selina had a daughter, Lena May Blanche. The family later moved to a nearby house at 57 Gossoms End. Harold worked diligently, becoming a respected member of the Berkhamsted Co-op and he eventually became Manager of the Provident Place branch.

Feeding the Home Front in August 1914 was essential work, so there was no pressure on Harold and his colleagues at the Berkhamsted Co-op to volunteer. However, with the coming of the Military Service Act in 1916, a number of Co-operative Society employees, including Harold, received their call up papers. The Society appealed to keep them and Harold Shrimpton, slaughterman Bert Braley, baker EG Foskett and their General Manager all appeared together before the Berkhamsted Rural Military Service Tribunal that May. On their second appearance in June, Braley and Foskett received exemptions from military service until the end of September, but not Harold Shrimpton. Despite his manager's plea that Harold was 'absolutely indispensable in his department' the Society's appeal was rejected.

On 24th July 1916, Harold reported to the Army Recruiting Centre at Watford before going to a training battalion of the Yorkshire Regiment, probably 3/5th Battalion at Ripon, where he received the Regimental number 242109. Here he was picked for specialist training with a Lewis Gun Section.

Since 1914, the job of British Army Infantryman had become increasingly complex, but the Lewis gunner's role was probably the most physically demanding in an infantry platoon. Lewis light machine guns provided concentrated firepower for the Platoon, both in attack and defence. Although 'light' compared to Vickers Machine Guns, Lewis Guns weighed 38lbs and roughly the same weight of spare parts, boxes of ammunition and other stores, went with them. When Harold completed his training, he was entitled to wear the Lewis gunner's badge of a laurel wreath surrounding the letters 'LG', nicknamed the 'Suicide Badge', because, according to Lewis Gun veteran Harry Patch, 'if you were taken prisoner by the enemy then more than likely you would be shot.'

Towards the end of Harold's time with the Yorkshire Regiment he wrote his Will, leaving everything to Selina. Shortly afterwards, Harold was posted to 5th Kings (Liverpool) Regiment, receiving the number 235328. On 12th June, the battalion marched to the Ypres Prison trenches where they formed working parties in preparation for the attack on the German lines. Each day the working parties came under heavy bombardment from German artillery and they suffered several casualties. The battalion later returned to the St Omer area for training in offensive tactics. Returning to Ypres in late July, the battalion took part in several raids on the German lines and suffering over 100 casualties. They left the front line in early August to spend some weeks training at Zutkerque, southeast of Calais.

In the latter part of 1917, Harold was posted to 20th King's Regiment, most probably after he had recovered from a slight wound he had received in action at Ypres. According to the 20th Battalion's War Diary, 100 men joined at Kemmel, near Ypres, on 28th September and it is likely that Harold was among them, as no more drafts arrived until 1918. The 20th Battalion was originally one of the Liverpool 'Pals' battalions and had fought in the same Brigade as 2nd Bedfordshire Regiment during 1917 where it had lost many men. Harold's new battalion spent most of October training, or assigned to working parties repairing trenches in the waterlogged soil around Ypres, constantly harassed by German artillery. Patrols sent out to reconnoitre the German trenches often had to wade waist-high in water to avoid observation by the enemy.

The Battalion spent most of November 1917 training in various camps south of Ypres. On 3rd December, they moved to the Torr Top Tunnels trench relieving 16th Battalion, Manchester Regiment. Here they spent the next few days salvaging anything serviceable to keep the trenches and tracks in a fit state and repairing the barbed wire defences. After a week, 20th Battalion returned to their billets at Swan Chateau for further training and working party duty. A week later, they moved to the Hedge Street Tunnel near the Zillebeke trenches for yet more repair work.

The Germans had been quiet for several days until they launched a gas attack on 19th December, forcing several members of the battalion to be sent to the rear for treatment. German harassing artillery and machine gun fire continued over the following days and on 23rd December, a German raiding party was successfully repulsed.

The Battalion returned to Swan Chateau on 24th December where they spent Christmas, returning five days later to the Torr Top Tunnels. Here, on the nights of 4th and 5th January, patrols went out to examine some new German trenches identified from aerial photographs. During these patrols, three men were killed and another three wounded. It is likely that Harold was one of those wounded, as the battalion left the front line on 6th January. Harold was evacuated to 2nd Casualty Clearing Station, located south of Ypres and died there on 13th January 1918, aged 31. Harold's body now lies in the Outtersteene Cemetery, near Bailleul.

Harold's mother, Blanche Shrimpton, returned to Great Hasely and it was probably she who ensured that her son's name appeared on the War Memorial there. She died there in 1937. Harold's widow, Selina, and their daughter Lena remained in the Berkhamsted area after the War. Selina never remarried and died at Berkhamsted in 1960, aged 76.

Gunner 68745 William HORN
'Z' Battery, Royal Horse Artillery
2nd February 1918

William Horn was born on 18th May 1893 at Heath and Reach in Bedfordshire, a village two miles north of Leighton Buzzard. It is sometimes nicknamed 'Heathen's Reach', which is the name William's father, entered on the 1911 Census form. William was the third child of Daniel Horn, from the small village of Ivinghoe Aston, and his wife, Mary Ann, from nearby Eaton Bray. Mary and Daniel had a late summer wedding in 1883 and later raised eight children - six sons and two daughters. Their children's birthplaces trace the Horn family's movements as Daniel sought work as a livestock keeper or labourer on the farms around Hertfordshire and West Bedfordshire. Their first child, Frederick, was born at Heath and Reach on 18th January 1887, followed exactly three years later by Alfred who was born at Norcott Hill, Northchurch. In 1893, the Horns were again in Heathen's Reach where William was born, and then two years later Mary Ann was born at Folly Farm in Wigginton.

When William was five years old, his family was back at Norcott Hill, where Frank was born on 17th July 1898. Despite being the youngest child, Frank was the first to receive baptism in September 1898, at St Mary's Church. A month later on 16th October, all the remaining children were baptised there together. Daniel and Mary Ann's next child, John Albert, was born in 1901 at Ivinghoe Aston. Within a few years, however, they were back in Northchurch where their two youngest, Rose and Daniel, were born. The family finally settled in a cottage tied to Hill Farm, on Northchurch Common, where both Daniel senior and William were working in 1911. William was employed at Hill Farm until he joined the Army. His mother worked as a charwoman and one sister, Mary, stayed at home to look after the household and the four younger children.

Around this time, William was courting a Chesham girl named Emily Scott. She was a domestic servant working for the owner of a painting and decorating business and his wife in Charles Street, Berkhamsted. William and Emily were married at St Peter's, Berkhamsted, on 14th April 1912 and they set up home in New Road, Northchurch. Emily gave birth to their daughter, Ruby Gwendoline, the following October.

William enlisted at St Albans in late 1914 or early 1915 and, according to *The Berkhamsted Gazette*, he served with the Mediterranean Expeditionary Force, first in Egypt and then at Gallipoli. William's medal card however states that he first served overseas with the Royal Horse

Artillery (RHA) in France, arriving there on 15th October 1915, as the Gallipoli campaign was nearing its end. The only RHA formation to serve at Gallipoli was XV Brigade, which belonged to 29th Division. Assuming the *Gazette* report to be correct, it would be unlikely that William saw much active service on the Peninsular before 29th Division was evacuated to Egypt on 7th January 1916. That was shortly after William had written a will in his field Pay Book, witnessed by his mate Driver Hughes, leaving his property to Emily.

XV Brigade travelled to the Western Front in late March and took part in the Battle of the Somme. According to the *Gazette*, William received a slight wound in France and came home for a short time to recover. It was probably when William returned to France that he joined 'Z' Battery, V Brigade, RHA, which was attached to 8th Division. At that time, a RHA Battery comprised six 18-pdr field guns, 5 Officers and around 200 NCOs, Gunners, Drivers, Shoesmiths, Farriers, and Saddlers. Introduced in 1904 and drawn behind a limber by a team of six horses, the 18-pdr gun featured in every theatre of the war. The gun had a range of nearly five miles and a well-trained crew could fire up to 30 rounds a minute. V Brigade moved from sector to sector, providing mobile fire support for battalions during offensive operations or providing defensive barrages when under attack.

In January 1917, after a month's rest and training, V Brigade, with William and 'Z' Battery, was at Fresnicourt, due west of Lens, where they were to provide daily harassing fire against local German positions. Unfortunately, German artillery soon identified 'Z' Battery's emplacements from aerial observation and, on 5th February, the Battery was shelled, killing two men and wounding two others. The Brigade later moved to new positions 10 miles southeast of Albert, near the village of Suzanne in the Somme Valley. The front was relatively quiet at the time, allowing a reorganisation of RHA units with V Brigade being transferred to XV Corps, in the Fourth Army. The latter part of February saw the Brigade in action again, firing at the German's barbed wire defences by day and their trenches by night.

At 05.15 on 4th March, 8th Division launched a successful attack on the village of Rancourt, with V Brigade providing supporting fire. The next few days were very quiet and the Batteries returned to their daily routine of harassing fire against the opposing trenches. On 17th and 18th March, 'Z' Battery withdrew its guns from the forward positions soon after began to move north with the Brigade. Ten days later, V Brigade was attached to 1st Canadian Division and established new emplacements near the village of Thelus, north of Arras, to provide extra artillery support for the forthcoming attack on Vimy Ridge.

After the Canadian successful capture of Vimy Ridge, the Brigade continued to support 1st Canadian Division at Thelus, their final attack being on Fresnoy at the beginning of May. The Brigade was reassigned to

3rd Canadian Division on 4th May, moving to new defensive positions at La Folie Farm on Vimy Ridge itself to prevent any German counterattacks. After two uneventful weeks there, V Brigade was sent north to the vicinity of Poperinghe, or 'Pops' in soldier's slang, eight miles west of Ypres, where they were to join the preparatory bombardment for the Third Battle of Ypres.

Between 31st May and 6th June 1917, William's battery fired an average of 900 rounds into the German defences each day. On 11th June, having moved to Zillebeke, closer to Ypres, the Brigade's ammunition wagons came under heavy artillery fire causing several casualties, but work continued preparing new gun pits. However, after a further eleven days of German bombardment had inflicted more damage, the Brigade abandoned their gun pits and relocated to new positions northwest of Ypres.

During the last two weeks of July, 'Z' Battery fired on average 450 rounds per day as part of the artillery bombardment of German defences at Ypres. On 31st July, the first day of the battle, 'Z' Battery joined the creeping barrage supporting the advancing troops by firing a mixture of high explosive and smoke shells. Unfortunately, the High Command had not fully anticipated that the bombardment, combined with the atrocious wet weather, would turn Flanders into the quagmire that became the Battle's lasting image. That night, William and the rest of 'Z' Battery's gunners spent an unconformable time in shell holes close to their guns, getting what shelter they could from the incessant rain. Three days of torrential rain prevented the Brigade building new emplacements, but on 4th August, orders came to occupy fresh positions close to the Ypres Canal, where they continued to provide fire support during the battle. By the end of August, William and the battle-weary Brigade were ready to return to billets for a month of well-earned rest and recovery.

The Brigade's final action of Third Ypres cost its batteries their heaviest losses. Between 1st and 3rd October, the batteries moved into new positions near the village of Poelcapelle, due north of Ypres. The following day they fired a two-hour creeping barrage, while the infantry advanced on the village and consolidated their gains. During this attack, 'Z' Battery alone fired over 1,000 shells and a further 1,000 shells the following day. The deep mud caused problems with the replenishment of ammunition, as the temporary light railways that transported shells from the storage dumps to the batteries could not operate. Instead, the Battery's horses carried the shells in panniers or dragged wagons through the mire.

As V Brigade continued with its daily business of shoots and 'strafes', German aircraft dropped bombs near the batteries on 14th October, causing several casualties, and a few days later German artillery inflicted further losses. The following week, the Brigade supported an infantry advance accompanied by two tanks, but the attack became bogged down in the mud. By the month's end, constant use or enemy counter-battery fire had put most of V Brigade's 18-pdr guns out of action. Consequently, on 28th October the Brigade was withdrawn to Moyenneville, just outside Abbeville, to receive fresh guns and get some well-earned rest.

In mid-November, with its new guns carefully tested and new tactics learnt, the brigade moved to carefully concealed positions by woodlands at Villers-au-Flos. In great secrecy, artillery and 476 tanks assembled for a massive attack against Cambrai. 'Z' Battery camouflaged its guns, but did not fire a single ranging shell. Recently-introduced surveying and mathematical ranging techniques meant that British batteries no longer had to betray new positions to the enemy. Meanwhile all German gun batteries, even hidden ones, were located and mapped using improved sound ranging and flash spotting methods.

Thanks to these innovations, the Germans were surprised when, at 06.10 on 20th November, a hurricane of shells from over 1,000 guns and howitzers fell on their positions, and gun emplacements, along the Hindenburg line. The appearance of massed tanks and infantry completed the enemy's shock. In three days, this new-style, all-arms British offensive achieved hitherto undreamt of success. However, although the methods pioneered at Cambrai would bring the Allies victory in 1918, the attack remained an enormous raid. The forces of 1917 could not expand the deep salient created at Cambrai before the Germans recovered their balance, assembled reinforcements and launched a major counter-stroke on 30th November. All British gains were reversed within a week and the Brigade was obliged to withdraw 13 miles to Ribécourt before continuing to harass the advancing enemy from a safe distance.

Several days later, a deserting German officer revealed details of an imminent German attack close to V Brigade's new positions. With this advanced warning, the Brigade's guns were able to cause mayhem among the German troops the moment they began their attack. The Brigade continued to provide daily harassing fire, but on the night of 19th December, several German chemical shells, probably mustard gas, hit 'Z' Battery's position, killing an officer and wounding three gunners, one of whom was possibly William Horn.

William's obituary in *The Berkhamsted Gazette* states that he was injured on 28th December, but V Brigade had been withdrawn from the front line by then, and the Brigade's War Diary makes no mention of casualties after 19th December. It is certain that William was admitted to the American-run Nº2 Base Hospital in the small seaside town of Étretat, near Le Havre. William struggled hard to recover and, although his situation was bad, his positive attitude made him popular with the staff. The Hospital Chaplain later wrote to William's wife Emily, 'I have visited your husband twice daily, and I have never known a man who had such grit, who was so absolutely unselfish and who fought for his life as he…[William] never murmured, never complained'. Gunner William Horn finally succumbed to his injuries on 2nd February 1918 aged 25 and was buried in an extension to the Étretat village churchyard.

While William was serving in France, his father a labourer all his life, died aged 57, on 23rd June 1916. Daniel's gravestone in New Road Cemetery, Northchurch is in the common local style of a rough stone, plain cross on a base. After William's death, a further dedication was added to the grave: 'Also William Horn, son, Died of Wounds in France Jan 1918 *thy will be done'*. William's mother, Mary Ann Horn, lived out the rest of her life at Northchurch Common. After her death, she was laid to rest alongside her husband in New Road Cemetery.

Drummer 36316 James Arthur GARMENT
6th (Service) Battalion, Royal Berkshire Regiment

11th March 1918

James Arthur Garment was born in June 1885, the third of six brothers born to Lizzie and Edwin Garment. Edwin, a self-employed chimney sweep, came from Aldbury, while his wife, Lizzie, came from Northchurch. In 1891, the family were living in Northchurch High Street, but by 1901, they had moved to 79 Gossoms End with James, now aged 15, working as a coachbuilder's labourer. In later years, James worked for Cooper and Nephews in Raven's Lane, Berkhamsted and later still, like many people living in Gossoms End, for the timber merchants, East and Sons.

In 1903, when he was 18, James enlisted in 2nd (Herts) Volunteer Battalion, Bedfordshire Regiment. He became a keen member of the Volunteers and when the Territorial Force was created in 1908, James took the opportunity to transfer. On 9th April, after 5 years and 79 days' service with the Volunteers, James became Private 5921 Garment of 1st Battalion Hertfordshire Regiment (TF). Every August, James attended the annual training camps including those held at Worthing, Ipswich and Thetford. Soon after his 23rd birthday in 1913, James became a Lance Corporal and in May 1914, a Corporal.

James was attending the annual training camp at Ashridge Park in August 1914 when war broke out. As a corporal, with more than eleven years' part-time soldiering behind him, James was keen to put his experience to good use, but he was to be bitterly disappointed. When James underwent his Embodiment medical examination at Warley Camp, he was declared, 'medically unfit for further military service' owing to the state of his teeth. James returned to civilian life and his work in the blacksmith's shop at East and Sons. A year later, on 14th August 1915, James married his fiancée, 29-year-old Jane Flitney at Tring and they moved into a house at 78 Gossoms End, next door to James' parents. Their son, Donald, was born there on 11th May the following year.

Despite his earlier rejection by the Army, James was keen to re-apply and on 20th November 1915, he successfully re-enlisted in the Hertfordshire Regiment. Perhaps on account of his age and despite his previous military experience, James was accepted not as a fighting soldier, but as a drummer, which meant that he was trained to be a stretcher-bearer.

James arrived in France on 5th July 1916, but he did not stay with the 'Hertshires' for very long. On 5th September, James's fellow villager

Walter Welling, and other men from the Hertfordshire and Cambridgeshire Regiments, were transferred to the 6th Battalion, Royal Berkshire Regiment, which had lost over half of its strength since the opening day of the Battle of the Somme on 1st July.

6th Berkshires saw much action through the Somme Campaign and the following year the battalion took part in the Third Battle of Ypres alongside 7th Bedfordshire Regiment. At the end of December 1917, James was serving as a cook with 6th Battalion's Headquarters Company when it became the Brigade Support and settled into Emile Camp, near Elverdinghe for the New Year. During this time, James began to feel unwell and on 10th January, he reported sick complaining of a cough, hoarseness and pains in his chest.

As his condition worsened, James was admitted to a hospital at Boulogne where he was diagnosed with pulmonary tuberculosis and returned to England. Examined at the City of London Military Hospital, Clapton on 7th February, James was found to be suffering from a shortage of breath with weakness and wasting. The Medical Officer's report certified that James was 100% disabled with tuberculosis, attributable to infection acquired 'On Active Service' with the BEF. The report stated James was medically unfit for further service and recommended his admission to a sanatorium.

James' medical discharge from the Army came into effect on 4th March 1918. Since his illness was directly attributable to his war service, James was eligible to receive a pension, payable from 5th March, and a Silver War Badge to wear on his civilian clothes. Introduced in September 1916, the Silver War Badge was intended to protect ex-soldiers who had been discharged owing to wounds or illness from over-zealous civilians who might otherwise accuse them of shirking.

James Garment died in a hospital in Ware on 11th March 1918 a week after he was discharged from the Army and before he could wear his badge or even return home; he was only 32 years old. His body was brought home to Northchurch for a funeral at St Mary's Church. After the Service, the Reverend Pope and the band of the Inns of Court Officer

Drummer James Garment's Funeral Cortege in New Road, Northchurch
(Source: Bert Hosier)

Training Corps, which was based in Berkhamsted, led his funeral cortege up New Road to the cemetery. At the graveside, the Band played the hymn, *'Jesu Lover of my Soul'* and an honour guard from the Officer Training Corps fired three volleys over the open grave accompanied by a roll of drums. The burial concluded with the 'Last Post'.

A plain cross in New Road Cemetery on the left-hand side, not far from the gate, now marks James's grave. James's name is missing from the Commonwealth War Grave Commission's Register, perhaps because he was officially a civilian when he died. As well as being remembered on the Northchurch War Memorial, James is also commemorated on the Hertfordshire Regiment Memorial at All Saints Church, Hertford, and on the memorial tablet inside St Peter's Church, Berkhamsted, where he is listed as 'James A. Garment 1 Herts R.'.

James's brothers William and Leonard survived the war. William, an older brother, served in Egypt and Gallipoli before transferring to the Western Front where he was wounded in October 1916. After recovering from his injuries in September 1917 William was commissioned into the King's (Liverpool) Regiment. Younger brother Leonard appeared on the Berkhamsted Roll of Honour of 1917, and was also discharged from the army suffering from tuberculosis, but he survived.

James's widow, Jane, lived to be 76. She died in May 1962 and was buried alongside her husband in New Road Cemetery.

Men of the Inns of Court Regiment firing three volleys over Drummer James Garment's grave in the New Road Cemetery watched by local villagers
(Source: Bert Hosier)

Private L/11387 Frank GARNER
7th Battalion, The Queens (Royal West Surrey) Regiment

21st March 1918

Frank Garner was born in Dudswell during the autumn of 1885. Frank's father, David, was a labourer from Hawridge just over the county border in Buckinghamshire, while his mother, Emily, was Northchurch born. David and Emily Garner would have two more children, Arthur, born in 1888, and Esther, born in 1890.

Having left school in 1899, Frank initially worked as a gardener's boy, but later left home for London, obtaining work as a stable hand at a large house near Hanover Square. It was here that Frank met Laura Franks, a self-employed dressmaker from Northampton. Laura was six years older than Frank and the couple married at St George's, Hanover Square in June 1910. Unfortunately, Frank's accommodation was tied to his job and the newlyweds began married life living apart with Laura lodging in a single room at 63, Westbourne Street, on the northern edge of Hyde Park. Meanwhile Frank lived to the east of the Park, by Grosvenor Square, in a stabling and carriage yard which had accommodation for the employees of the adjacent wealthy houses. Frank boarded in the household of William Meacham, and his family at 1 Three Kings Yard, with four other men, who all worked in the stables.

The Meachams had until recently lived in Leigh, near Tonbridge in Kent, where their two small children had been born. It is probably through their influence that the Garners subsequently decided to settle in Leigh. Laura and Frank's son, Frank George, was born there in the early autumn of 1912, and on 27th October, he was christened at St Mary's Church, Leigh.

Two years later, with the coming of war, Frank returned to Berkhamsted and enlisted, perhaps visiting his relatives to say farewell and to wish him luck. In October 1914, Frank joined the Army Service Corps (ASC) and served in the Horse Transport branch in England, where he could put his experience as a stableman to good use.

By 1917, the manpower shortage following the heavy losses on the Somme, and French pleas for more British troops in France, forced the ASC and other support units to release their fittest men for front-line service and Frank was transferred to 7th Battalion, Queen's (Royal West Surrey) Regiment.

7th Queen's belonged to 55th Brigade, 18th Division and had fought on both the first and last days of the Battle of the Somme. On 1st July, it participated in the successful assault on Montauban, and on 18th November, 7th Queen's lay out in wet snow until Zero Hour of the final attack of the offensive, suffering severe losses on both occasions. During the first day at Montauban, a machine gun hidden among old mine craters in no-man's-land enfiladed their flank, and on the final day German light machine gunners infiltrating between the British battalions inflicted heavy casualties on two companies, whilst shellfire wiped out a detachment sent to clear some German dugouts.

Three days after their final attack, the Battalion's survivors were withdrawn from the Somme and marched to the vicinity of Abbeville. On 28th and 29th November 166 reinforcements arrived there and combat training commenced. More reinforcements arrived through December; 30 men on the 6th; 81 men on the 8th; 108 men on the 11th and it is likely that Frank joined the Battalion around this time. Returning to the Somme in mid-January 1917, the Battalion helped to pursue the German Army as it retreated to the Hindenburg Line and fought during the Third Battle of the Scarpe the following May. On 3rd July, Frank and his new comrades in 7th Queen's boarded trains bound for the Salient to join the Third Battle of Ypres.

On 1st August, day two of the Battle, 18th Division relieved some of the units exhausted in the first day's attacks. The Division's first major action was the capture of Westhoek on 10th August. 55th Brigade was to attack with one battalion alongside 54th Brigade following an artillery barrage. Once again, the Battalion suffered misfortune. It was tasked with forming a defensive line along the southern edge of Inverness Copse, to protect the main assault battalion's flank, when it attacked at 04.35. In bright moonlight, 7th Queen's was waiting by the guide tapes when, at 01.10, German troops opened fire and brought down an artillery barrage, causing serious loss. At Zero, the survivors moved off smartly following their own barrage, but struggled over the debris-covered ground and the assault companies lost contact. They found Inverness Copse well garrisoned and hardly touched by the barrage. Other members of the Battalion came under machine gun fire from a blockhouse on the south-western corner of the copse, all of which resulted in the Brigade falling back to form a defensive flank along its old front line.

After its ordeal at Inverness Copse, 7th Queen's left the front line, and at the end of August dispersed around the Eringhem area, twelve miles south of Dunkirk. Here, the men undertook an extensive training programme, alternating with sporting activities and trips to the beaches at Mardyck where they could relax, bathe in the sea and play games. The battalion reached the final of the Division Football Tournament, but lost 9:0 to 12th Middlesex. The Queen's fared better in non-sporting competitions, winning seven events including platoon drill, musketry and driving horse-drawn artillery. Meanwhile, those with farming experience helped local farmers with their harvest.

On 25th September, the Battalion moved from Eringhem to School

Camp, near Poperinghe, for training and more sport, although its unhappy football team lost 3:1 to Brigade Headquarters. Four days later, the quiet behind the lines was disturbed when German planes bombed the Poperinghe area, killing 28 and injuring 75 people.

On 9th October, the battalion, now at full strength with 35 officers and 995 men, transferred to a collection of tents, huts and tarpaulin shelters strung between trees named Dirty Bucket Camp, after a restaurant that formerly stood nearby. Next day, 55th Brigade relieved 33rd Brigade, which had suffered badly during a previous attack in the Ypres Salient, and on Friday 12th, in heavy rain, 55th Brigade attacked Poelcapelle and Meunier House. 7th Queen's, who were in reserve, moved forward an hour after Zero, but the attack failed. After holding the front line for a day, the battalion returned to Dirty Bucket Camp. This action, their first since Inverness Copse, cost 7th Queen's 16 men killed, 89 wounded and 37 missing.

Four days later, the Battalion was sent to hold the line while 53rd Brigade attacked Poelcapelle, but as the Queen's took over 18th Division's trenches, a German artillery bombardment inflicted heavy casualties on 'C' Company. The attack went ahead on 22nd October however, and with the Queen's in support, 53rd Brigade captured all its objectives, including Meunier House, Poelcapelle Brewery and Tracas Farm, and later thanked 7th Queen's for their assistance. By 22.30 that night, Frank and the exhausted battalion were back at Dirty Bucket Camp for two nights' recuperation.

On 1st November, the Queen's moved to Parroy Farm, near Elverdinghe, northwest of Ypres. Here working parties assisted 173rd Tunnelling Coy, RE with road repairs in the forward area, while the remaining men were employed on 'camp improvement'. Moving to nearby Boesinghe Camp on the 5th, the battalion continued working on forward roads and duckboard tracks. It also gave shelter to two companies of 8th Norfolks when they were shelled out of their own camp.

Whilst at Boesinghe, the Battalion's War Diary records that the death sentence passed on Private Thomas Hawkins for desertion had been confirmed by the Commander in Chief. Hawkins was executed by firing squad at 06.53 on the 20th November. Two days later, it was announced that a death sentence passed on Private Parker had been commuted to ten years' penal servitude, suspended. During the Great War, only ten percent of all British soldiers sentenced to death by Courts Martial were actually executed, the remainder being commuted.

The battalion left Boesinghe on 10th December for their final week of trench duty in the Salient before moving to Nordausques, 14 miles from Calais, for more training. The battalion moved again at the month's end, to a new area in Belgium, around Ondank, where their time was split between periods of trench duty and training in Dykes Camp.

Back in London, Prime Minister Lloyd George was horrified by the human cost of the fighting at Ypres and was determined to prevent further substantial losses and force the British C-in-C, Haig on to the defensive. He therefore restricted reinforcements from Britain to a fraction of what the BEF needed to replace its losses, whilst agreeing to take over another 25 miles of French line. Consequently, in February 1918, 18th Division, was sent over 100 miles to extend Fifth Army's front line southwards. The Queen's travelled by train to Noyon, 12 miles south of St Quentin, near the Hindenburg Line and immediately went to work assisting the Royal Engineers in constructing a completely new defence scheme called 'elastic defence' or 'defence in depth'.

Manpower shortages and the dominance of artillery had forced the Allies to copy the Germans by abandoning rigid trench lines packed with men and replacing them with deep zones, dubbed 'Forward', 'Battle' and 'Rear'. The sparsely manned Forward Zone of concealed machine gun posts, strong points, redoubts, mobile artillery emplacements and barbed wire, was designed to slow down and disorganise attackers. The posts were widely spaced to limit the effects of artillery barrages, but close enough to see and support their neighbours with gunfire. Although the guns could fire blind on predetermined co-ordinates, the scheme worked best in good visibility. Next came the Battle Zone, over a mile deep, where the majority of the defenders waited in larger positions, supported by more field artillery. Finally, the Rear Zone, between four and eight miles behind the Battle Zone, held the reserves of men, munitions and the heavy artillery. Unfortunately, the extending of Fifth Army's front by 25 miles had over-stretched its resources and as a result its forward defences were incomplete and much of its Rear Zone was merely a line on the map.

For Erich Ludendorff, Quartermaster General of the German Army, 1917 had been a critical year. His successful withdrawal to the Hindenburg Line had released men and Russia's February Revolution had overthrown the Tsar, while Nivelle's disappointing Spring Offensive had provoked mutinies in the French Army. However, the new Russian government remained committed to the war, French morale was undergoing a painful recovery, Britain still had reserves of manpower which Germany did not, and the United States, with her enormous potential, entered the war against Germany.

That April, Germany successfully smuggled Lenin into Russia and in October 1917, Lenin's anti-war Bolsheviks seized power. Russia stopped fighting, even though Germany demanded the Ukraine as its price for peace, allowing the release of some 400,000 German troops from the Eastern Front. This gave Ludendorff a final, brief opportunity to defeat the Allies with a major offensive in the West before the American Army was strong enough to intervene. Ludendorff planned to split the British and French by attacking the junction between their Armies, but that junction had moved and his assault fell on the British Fifth Army.

At the beginning of March 1918, Frank's battalion was holding new outposts in the Forward Zone near the village of Vendeuil, south of St Quentin. Frank and his comrades had been wiring and establishing supply dumps at their positions in the Battle Zone on 20th March, when, at an hour before midnight they received warning that a German offensive was expected the following morning. To open his offensive, nicknamed the *Kaiserschlacht* or Kaiser's Battle, but officially called Operation MICHAEL, Ludendorff had assembled over 6,600 artillery pieces and some 3,500 heavy trench mortars. At 04.40 on 21st March 1918, they opened fire and during the ensuing hours, they poured more than one million gas and high explosive shells onto the allied lines.

Following closely behind this stunning barrage, through the smoke, gas and thick morning mist, came battalions of aggressive *Stosstruppen*, literally Shock Troops, but commonly called Stormtroopers. Operating in small squads and employing flexible tactics pioneered at Verdun, the *Stosstruppen* were lightly equipped, but well-armed with stick grenades, rifles, flamethrowers, the new MP18 sub-machine guns, Maxim MG08/15 light machine-guns and even light artillery. They were trained to infiltrate quickly through the Forward Zone, dislocating the defence and avoiding resistance when possible or striking hard from flank and rear when not. Having neutralised or isolated their enemy's positions, the *Stosstruppen* pressed on, leaving the ordinary infantry to mop them up.

With visibility between 20 and 30 yards, the Queen's forward outposts could not support one another and many found themselves surrounded before they saw their first German. The *Stosstruppen* broke through in several places, but as the mist cleared, British artillery fire and infantry counterattacks began to exact a heavy toll on them. German prisoners later testified that four divisions had attacked 18th Division's sector alone, but by the first day's end, thanks to the Forward Zone's tenacious resistance, the *Stosstruppen* had not fully achieved their first objectives. At midnight, 18th Division's Battle Zone still held, but the divisions either side had retreated, leaving 18th Division's Commanding Officer no choice but to fall back in line with his neighbours and abandon the battlefield to the Germans.

According to its War Diary, the Battalion's casualties that day were 28 men wounded, 13 reported missing and 10 men killed, including Frank Garner. Frank's body was lost on the battlefield and his name appears on the Pozières Memorial. This memorial records the names of the 14,000 British troops who fell during Fifth Army's retreat during the spring of 1918 and have no known grave.

Laura Garner and her son Frank George remained in Kent, ensuring that, in addition to the Northchurch War Memorial, Frank's name appeared on the War Memorial in Leigh.

Private 75902 Charles Thomas MASHFORD
Royal Fusiliers (City of London Regiment) attached to 2/2nd (City of London) Battalion, The London Regiment

24th April 1918

Charles Thomas Mashford, known as Charlie, was born in Northchurch in early 1899, probably in the family home at 16 New Road. His mother, Alice, came from Aylesbury and his father, John, came from Standbridge in Bedfordshire, and worked as a coachbuilder's labourer at one of the coachworks in Berkhamsted High Street. The Mashfords had one further child, a daughter, Florence, who was four years younger than Charlie. In 1911, the family were living at 3 Eddy Street in Gossoms End, where their neighbours included the Davis and Dwight families.

Charlie's father died suddenly in 1914, within weeks of war breaking out, aged only 42, and Charlie, then aged 15, became the sole means of support for his mother and younger sister. Charlie continued in his civilian occupation until the spring of 1917, when he turned 18 and his call up papers arrived. Although he was his family's sole breadwinner, Charlie had to report to Shoreham for basic training with 21st Training Reserve Battalion. He transferred to the Royal Fusiliers the following May, although he could not be sent overseas until his 19th birthday.

In late March 1918, Charlie was suddenly rushed to France and attached to 2/2nd (City of London) Battalion, The London Regiment (TF). The battalion, which was closely affiliated to The Royal Fusiliers, the Regular Army Regiment of the City of London, had been in France with 173rd Brigade, 58th Division since January 1917. Charlie joined his new battalion on 28th March at Besme, midway between Amiens and Reims, in a draft of 114 men, which included Richard Beasley's 19-year-old brother from Northchurch, Vincent Beasley, who had been called-up around the same time. They immediately entered hell.

Private Charlie Mashford (Source: British Library)

Exactly one week before, the German army had launched Operation MICHAEL, and was steadily reclaiming the territory it had relinquished during the battles of 1916 and the retreat of 1917. Like many other battalions, 2/2nd London Regiment was effectively obliterated on the first day, with losses estimated at 21 officers and 650 men. Only 1 officer, 1 NCO and 40 men had escaped death or capture. The three London battalions in 58th Division had suffered so many casualties during the German offensive that 2/2nd, 2/4th and 3rd London Battalions were withdrawn and reorganised into a single composite Fusilier battalion, to remain a viable fighting unit. Fortunately, the German advance was now beginning to lose momentum as the British troops fell back to their well-prepared defences.

On the night of 28th March, the composite Fusilier Battalion was in the trenches east of the village of Manicamp where the exhausted men held on for the next five days, until relieved by French troops. They withdrew south to Audignicourt, spending the night in nearby caves. Next day, the Fusilier Battalion marched further south to Ambleny and disbanded. On 5th April, Charlie, his surviving mates from his original draft, and the remnants of 2/2nd (City of London) Battalion, moved south to Dommiers and then to Longpont where they boarded a train going northwest to Longueau, just outside Amiens. By now the Battalion consisted of just 10 officers and 250 men. Marching to a copse at Gentelles Wood on the Villers-Bretonneaux front, west of Amiens, the Battalion was immediately put to work digging new trenches astride the old Roman road linking Amiens to Albert. These would be used as new fall back positions in case of another retreat. It was urgent, dangerous work, and German artillery inflicted a number of casualties.

On 17th April, the Battalion relieved 5th Australian Brigade, which had successfully held back the German advance on Villers-Bretonneaux, taking over a section of line to the south of the village near the German-held Hangard Wood. A new defensive line was now formed in conjunction with 3rd and 4th London Regiments, with a continuous belt of barbed wire protecting the trenches. By now, the initial shock effect of the German offensive had worn off and British troops began to patrol aggressively with the intention of discovering the German's strength, while preventing the enemy from identifying the location of the new British defences. The town of Amiens, together with its railway junction, was an important strategic target for the Germans and since Operation MICHAEL had so far failed to deliver a knockout blow, the next attack would probably be their last chance to capture it. All that stood in the German Army's way was Villers-Bretonneaux.

A company from Charlie's battalion shot and captured a German soldier on 23rd April, and brought him back for questioning. The prisoner gave details of a four-division attack planned for the following day, including the time of the preliminary bombardment. All companies were warned and were on the alert when, in the small hours of 24th April, German artillery unleashed a three-hour bombardment of high explosive and gas shells. Unfortunately, the gas combined with an early morning mist and severely limited visibility from the British defenders isolated posts. At 06.00, through the mist, German *Stosstruppen* infiltrated between the London Regiments' positions making determined attacks against neighbouring battalions, but by-passed Charlie's battalion. Although the initial assaults were beaten off, shelling continued and then the noise of powerful petrol engines heralded the approach of new German A7V tanks.

Three days before, the Germans had sent 5 A7Vs into action for the first time at the St Quentin Canal. Of these, three had immediately broken down. For the attack on Villers-Bretonneaux on 24th April 1918, a total of 18 A7Vs were employed. Resembling ungainly blockhouses, A7Vs were armed with a 57mm cannon and six MG08 machine guns, offering reasonable firepower, but their primitive track design and low ground clearance made them prone to bogging down. The A7Vs supporting the attacking *Stosstruppen* soon forced the units either side of Charlie's 2/2nd Battalion to retreat, but three of them suddenly encountered three British Mark IV tanks; a 'male' armed with two 6-pounder guns and three machine guns accompanied by two 'females' with five machine guns each. The 'male' tank knocked out the leading A7V and shot five of its eighteen-man crew. The remaining A7Vs promptly withdrew, ending the first tank versus tank combat in history.

The 2/2nd Londons held on for four hours, but as the mist cleared, they found themselves isolated by German infantry on three sides, giving them no choice but to withdraw immediately or be completely surrounded. Leaving their positions at about 09.30, the Londons, with Vincent Beasley carrying a Lewis Gun, climbed an open slope, under heavy fire and in full view of the Germans, to escape.

Charlie's body was found after the fighting around Hangard Wood subsided. He was buried where he fell. He was just 19 years old and had been at the front for only twenty-eight days. Canadian troops finally recaptured Hangard Wood in August 1918 where they established the Hangard Wood British Cemetery. Several graves from the April fighting, including Charlie Mashford's, were later moved into the new Cemetery.

Although the Germans captured Villers-Bretonneaux on 24th April, it was retaken by Australian troops that night. With Villers-Bretonneaux remaining in Allied hands, the way to Amiens was blocked and Operation MICHAEL finally ended in failure.

Charlie's mate, Vincent Beasley, was awarded the Military Medal for his part in that day's fighting. Vincent survived the war and returned to Northchurch, where in October 1919 he married Kate Welling, the widow of Walter Welling. He died in 1962 at Watford, aged 63.

Private 23096 Thomas Henry TEAGLE
2nd Battalion, Duke of Edinburgh's (Wiltshire Regiment)

6th June 1918

The Teagles originally came from Shenley Church End in Buckinghamshire, some four miles southeast of Stony Stratford, and arrived at Northchurch by a somewhat roundabout route. Thomas's father, Harry Teagle, began his working life as an agricultural labourer whose own father had died while Harry was still in his teens, leaving him the main breadwinner. In 1881, aged 19, Harry was living with his widowed mother and his two sisters, Maud, a lacemaker aged 14, and 8-year-old Annie, in a cottage in Shenley.

It was probably at about this time that Harry's eye was caught by a housemaid of his own age employed at the nearby Rectory. Her name was Fanny Andrews, and she originally came from the Temple district of Bristol. Harry and Fanny were married at Shenley Church in 1885 and soon afterwards started their family, with first daughter, Maude, being born in 1887, followed two years later by Rose.

Around 1890, Harry moved his young family to Cosgrove in Northamptonshire. By then he was employed as a groom and domestic gardener and would expect to be moving from district to district if he wanted to progress. The Teagles lived in four rooms at the Almshouses on Stratford Road, where two more daughters, Annie and Frances, were born. The Teagles later moved the few miles back into Buckinghamshire, this time to 21 High Street, Haversham, a village lying midway between Wolverton and Newport Pagnell. It was at Haversham that Thomas was born in the summer of 1896, followed by Arthur in 1898, Lily in 1900, and Harry James, known as James, in 1902.

By 1911, the Teagles had moved again, this time to Dudswell, where they enjoyed the comparative luxury of living in six rooms with only the three boys and Lily still at home. Arthur was still at school, but 14-year-old Thomas, who had just finished, had yet to start work.

In August 1914, Thomas was about 18 years old and it is not certain where he was living or what his occupation was. Around the middle of November, the following year he enlisted with 3rd (Reserve) Battalion, Wiltshire Regiment at Winchester, so it is likely that he was working in that area. On 25th June 1916, Thomas travelled to 3rd Infantry Base Depot in France and two weeks later he was part of a draft of 109 men from 3rd Battalion sent to replace the casualties suffered by the 6th (Service) Battalion, Wiltshire Regiment, 58th Brigade, 19th Division during a week of heavy fighting on the Somme.

The new draft was inspected on 10th July and the work of training and integration into the Battalion began. Eleven days later, 6th Wiltshires were in Mametz Wood and Thomas had his first experience of German shellfire. Thomas soon learned that an infantryman's principal occupation was digging, not fighting. The Battalion dug and wired new trenches in Mametz Wood, and spent most of August and September repairing and improving trenches, first near Kemmel and then on the River Lys. At least there were opportunities for bathing in the rivers and streams of the Somme during their rest periods, which relieved the inevitable hours spent cleaning equipment and training.

Throughout October, the Battalion took its turn maintaining trenches in the Hebuterne sector, nine miles north of Albert and later around Crucifix Corner, five miles further south at Aveluy. November 1916 represented a typical month for an infantry battalion like 6th Wiltshires. The Battalion spent 12 days in the front line and the remaining time cleaning up, being inspected, training and providing working parties for Aveluy Station. The whole of December 1916, and the 12 days of Christmas, were spent out of the line.

In early 1917, the Battalion moved north and on 30th April went into barracks in Ypres as the Brigade Reserve. Unfortunately, the barracks were within range of German medium artillery so Thomas and his mates had to endure four days of shelling. It was actually a great relief for them to occupy the trenches by Zillebeke for several days, where the shelling was relatively light and mostly from smaller guns. Moreover, from this position the Wiltshires could watch British heavy guns pounding the German lines.

Next month, the Wiltshires participated in the assault against Messines Ridge, capturing five machine guns, three trench mortars and 179 prisoners during their advance and killing about 80 German soldiers. The Battalion then set to work on the partially completed trench lines at Oostterverne Wood, which frequently came under heavy artillery fire. By the time the Wiltshires left the line on 18th June, they had suffered 134 casualties. Training and making up working parties occupied the next few weeks in preparation for the Third Battle of Ypres.

On 31st July, the first day of the battle, the Battalion was in support trenches, which heavy rain soon reduced to an atrocious state. Thomas and his mates endured a week of tension in miserable conditions, constantly put on alert for attacks that never came and denied rest by exposure to German shellfire and the elements. On 4th August, 23 of the Battalion's NCOs and men were evacuated sick, mainly suffering from exhaustion and exposure. Another 30 men were sent back for the same reason when, under heavy shellfire, 6th Wiltshires relieved 9th Cheshires. After the relief had been completed the Battalion was down to just 302 men, roughly half of its full fighting strength.

The Wiltshires were relieved on the night of 7th/8th August, and went into billets at Seninghem, near the extensive British training area around Lumbres, southwest of St Omer, to rebuild their strength. Here they were joined by a new draft of 41 men, mostly returning 6th Wiltshires. A series of sports days were held and the Divisional Commander presented medal ribbons. The Battalion came second to 9th Cheshires in the Brigade cross country race, but they won the 100 yards' sprint, quarter mile and long jump events in the Brigade sports the following day.

Towards the end of August, Thomas and his mates moved to billets near Berthen, close to the Belgian border. Here new reinforcements were integrated into the battalion and a series of training exercises took place. The Battalion then moved to two camps near Ypres where they prepared for the forthcoming attack by Second and Fifth Armies on the Menin Road, in which 6th Wiltshires were to form the right flank of 19th Division. Particular emphasis was placed on practising attacks against defended shell holes.

After midnight on 20th September, 2nd Wiltshires struggled through packed communications trenches and some shelling to their assembly area. Each company then filed through the shell holes, strands of barbed wire and fallen trees of the aptly named Opaque Wood, deploying into an attack formation as soon as they emerged on the German side just before Zero Hour.

At 05.40, the Wiltshires advanced behind a heavy creeping barrage with 9th Welch on their left and 2nd Bedfords, to their right, on the west bank of a canal. On the Wiltshires' left, 'C' Company came under continuous machine gun fire, which appeared to originate from positions beyond the barrage. The dugouts in the wood were cleared and 19 German prisoners taken. On the right, 'D' Company overcame stiff resistance from dugouts to their front after 'C' Company came to their assistance with brisk Lewis machine gun fire.

'C' Company reached its objective and created a defensive flank of posts until 9th Welch arrived 30 minutes later. Meanwhile, the Lewis gunners and Company snipers formed a screen to suppress German snipers on their front and engage enemy troops moving down the railway embankment. The Battalion consolidated its objectives and improved their fields of fire as rapidly as German snipers, shellfire and the particularly wet ground permitted. In places, fire steps had to be constructed from sandbags. Patrols went out, some finding empty German posts, while others came under machine gun fire. The Wiltshires were relieved on the night of 21st/22nd September and marched to a camp near Kemmel, having suffered 152 casualties during the attack and subsequent consolidation.

As the Ypres Salient quietened, 6th Battalion assumed an operational training role. On 14th October, the Battalion sent 250 experienced men to Base, probably to reinforce other battalions, in exchange for a draft of 30 recruits. Thomas and his mates spent more time training and working in camps near Kemmel and Brasserie or firing on the ranges near Lynde and Tilques over the next two months and less time in the line. Spells in the trenches were relatively quiet, but the Battalion diarist still noted handfuls of casualties from shellfire on most days.

By mid-December, the Battalion was back in France, close to the Hindenburg Line, and on 23rd, the Wiltshires went into camp at Havrincourt Wood. The War Diary entry for Christmas Eve reads, 'Resting - Battalion upheld Christmas Day festivals.' The following day, the Wiltshires relieved the 9th Cheshires and they saw in the New Year patrolling no-man's-land.

January 1918 was a very quiet month, spent rotating between trenches by the Hindenburg Line, support positions at Ribecourt and rest at Hawes Camp. The Germans remained quiet into February, when the Wiltshires took their turn manning trenches at Trescault. In mid-February, the Battalion went to a camp near Rocquigny for training and working parties before moving to another camp close to the Hindenburg Line. The first three weeks of March were spent practising assaults and counterattacks and labouring on defensive lines in preparation for an expected German offensive. On 19th March, Field Marshal Haig's Headquarters received definite intelligence that this offensive was imminent.

At 05.23 on 21st March, as Operation MICHAEL began, 58th Brigade instructed the Wiltshires to standby to move at short notice, so they waited under intense German shelling all morning. At 11.30, the Battalion, comprising 21 officers and 478 men, moved to the Assembly Position at Gaika Copse then, as rehearsed earlier in the month, they advanced to the Counter Attack Assembly Position at Doignies and dug in to support 57th Brigade.

In the small hours of the morning, the Wiltshires moved to the Mill crossroads, where they stopped until daylight. At 11.00 on 22nd, they moved again to the 4th Corps Reserve Position in the incomplete third line defences, which stretched along the eastern side of the sunken road from Morchies, to a sugar beet factory on the Bapaume-Cambrai road. The Wiltshires deployed 'D' Coy to the left, 'A' Coy to the centre and 'C' Coy to the right and dug in. An outpost line, about 1,000 yards to the Wiltshires' front, was manned by part of 10th Cheshire Regiment, and a company of about 60 men, the sole survivors of 57th Brigade, was 250 yards in front. Positioned to the Wiltshire's left and slightly back was 9th Royal Welch Fusiliers, with 'D' Coy echeloned back to meet them. On the right, 'C' Coy was in contact with 56th Brigade, which was on the south side of the Bapaume road. 'B' Coy remained in support. What came next was described by the battalion War Diary as, 'a glorious episode in the history of the Wiltshire Regiment.'

At 16.00, German troops advanced from the northeast. The screen of Cheshires along the sunken road began to fall back towards the Wiltshires' positions. The enemy made no attempt to attack the Wiltshires' positions, but continued to move across their front in a south-westerly direction, occupying Morchies. The Wiltshires opened fire on the advancing Germans at a range of 1,200 yards. An hour later, a counterattack with tanks from the Wiltshires' left threw the Germans back, checking their advance for the day. At 20.00, a German raiding party attacked the Wiltshire's post nearest to Morchies, but were repulsed, leaving one of their dead behind. The battalion was unmolested for the remainder of the night. Then units of 56th Brigade pulled back, forcing 'C' Coy to form a defensive flank on the Wiltshire's right. As the last of that brigade withdrew, the Wiltshire's positions, reinforced by the Cheshires, became 4th Corps' main line of resistance to the German onslaught.

By 08.00 on 23rd March, the Germans were advancing from the north and northeast in a general attack towards the Bapaume-Cambrai road. The Wiltshires kept them at arm's length with their steady rifle and Lewis Gun fire. Suddenly large calibre shells, which appeared to be British, began falling among the Wiltshires' positions; then the German artillery joined in. German machine guns swept the slopes between Morchies and Beugny making all movement difficult. At 13.00, the battalion prepared for all round defence by placing a company of Cheshires, reinforced with two 'B' Company platoons, to cover the flanks and rear. German fire increased and at 14.00 a general attack developed against the Battalion's positions.

The order to withdraw arrived from Brigade headquarters at 14.15, but with an exposed slope to retreat up, and pressed by German assaults, the Battalion decided to wait until nightfall before attempting to slip away. By 16.00, the Germans were already working their way around the Battalion's flanks, from the sugar factory on the right and from Morchies on the left. Once again, the Wiltshires' steady, well-directed fire restricted the Germans' movements and inflicted heavy casualties, but after half an hour, the Germans had concentrated enough men along the Bapaume road to begin an enveloping movement.

Thomas and the Battalion had little option but to withdraw immediately and, through a heavy artillery barrage and vicious crossfire from machine guns behind their positions, parties of Wiltshires made a steady retreat to the next line of defence, east of Frémicourt. Captain A Garthwaite, who remained on duty despite his wounds, later described the 25-hour stand at Morchies as, 'a heroic record of self-sacrifice stemming the victorious rush of a superior enemy and a model lesson of a rearguard fight.'

At 16.00 the next day, when the battalion had regrouped at Frémicourt, only 6 officers and 32 men were present. The battalion's transport and support troops moved up to the Bapaume area, sending 81 men to reinforce the surviving Wiltshires holding the front line. That evening, a draft of 64 men arrived from the depot. The Wiltshires had little rest as intermittent artillery and machine gun fire fell on their positions throughout the night.

The tempo of shelling increased markedly towards daylight and continued throughout the day, costing the battalion another officer and several more men.

German pressure forced a rearguard action close to Bapaume and that night the Division withdrew to a line between Grevillers and Thilloy. Here it reformed for defence in depth, with Grevillers on its left, 58th Brigade in the middle and the Bapaume road on the right. The Wiltshires deployed in three lines, each of three, eight-man posts spaced at 100-yard intervals.

At 08.00 on 25th March, strong enemy attacks, supported by machine guns, developed down the Bapaume road, driving a wedge between the brigades and bypassing the Wiltshires, who moved their rear two lines of posts to reinforce their flank along the road. By 11.00, the Battalion was fighting a rearguard guard and flank action, covered by its forward posts and the Machine Gun Corps, as 56th Brigade on their right began to fall back. Throughout this ordeal German rifle grenades, machine gun fire and high explosive and gas shells continuously pounded the Wiltshires' positions. Thirty minutes later, fresh German troops forced the Battalion back, but under such conditions, Captain Garthwaite later noted, 'Organised retirement was difficult.'

By 13.00, Thomas and his Wiltshire mates were in trenches on high ground west of Grevillers, exposed to machine guns and shellfire, while dense cover and hidden ground nearby allowed German troops to assemble unobserved, ready to attack. At 14.00, the Division withdrew to positions north and northwest of Loupaert Wood where, despite running out of small arms ammunition, the Battalion intended to make a stand. The Warwicks, in 57th Brigade, held the Germans for 40 minutes, but the neighbouring division appeared to be in full retreat, leaving 19th Division's right flank exposed.

Inevitably, German soldiers exploited a fold in the terrain to work their way around and assemble for an assault, forcing another fighting withdrawal. Under constant pressure, the Division made another stand in front of Irles, before retreating through Miraumont and briefly forming a line of outposts east of Puisseux. That evening, Thomas and the Wiltshires merged with the other battalions of its brigade to form a single, under-strength, Composite Battalion.

That night, 25th/26th March, the Composite Battalion was relieved and sent back to establish successive lines of outposts about Hebuterne, Fonqvillers and in front of Bayencourt, which became the new British Third Line of defence. The Composite Battalion held that line for two days until a Canadian battalion relieved them and their ordeal ended. The Battalion marched back to Famechon, where the General Commanding 19th Division inspected and congratulated Thomas and the other survivors. Afterwards, they travelled by train and lorry to Locre where they were inspected on 31st March by the Army Commander. Only the wounded

Captain Garthwaite, one sergeant and eighteen men were on parade to represent the Wiltshires, the rest of the battalion having been captured, wounded or killed.

The Wiltshires worked hard rebuilding and absorbing the lessons of its recent ordeal, but their respite was to be brief. Just after nightfall on 7th April, 11 officers and 580 men of the 6th Wiltshires, including Thomas, moved into defences between a small stream called the Wambeke and the Junction Buildings, in the Wytschaete area, south of Ypres.

Although Operation MICHAEL had failed to prise the French and British armies apart, Berlin stuck to its timetable of subsidiary operations. Next came GEORGETTE, otherwise known as the Battle of the Lys, designed to cut the BEF off from the Channel ports. It began with the destruction of the Portuguese Corps, the defeat of 40th British Division and the capture of Estaires on 9th April by the German Sixth Army.

On 10th April, the German Fourth Army launched its attack with four divisions north of Armentiéres. At 03.30, German artillery began shelling communications and gun batteries, first with gas and high explosive shells, then more heavily with high explosive alone, reaching a crescendo on 19th Division's front line at about 06.00. Emerging from the dense morning fog, German *Stosstruppen* burst into the middle positions of 57th Brigade, beyond the Wambeke on the Wiltshires' right. Their neighbours, 10th Warwickshire Regiment, suddenly found enemy troops on their right flank and they swung back towards the Wiltshires.

A long, shallow communications trench ran along the Wiltshires' side of the stream, filled with half of 'B' Company's support platoon and any parties of Warwicks that had struggled across the stream. 'C' Company moved to create a defensive position in a collection of shallow, flooded trenches and 'D' Coy went to stiffen the endangered brigade flank. For several hours, Thomas and his fellow Wiltshires sat tight while their sector was heavily shelled from end to end and much of it raked by machine gun and rifle fire from high ground. At 15.30, German troops assembled about 2,000 yards away for a frontal attack, but as they moved off, the Wiltshires opened fire with Lewis guns and rifles and the attack petered out. An hour later, 56th Brigade ordered the neighbouring battalion to evacuate its front-line posts. Although the Wiltshires received no order from Battalion HQ, they decided to withdraw their forward companies to stronger positions. At 17.30, the Germans advanced, but again the Battalion's deadly rifle and Lewis gunfire held them back. For half an hour, the Germans organised strong attacks on both flanks until the Battalion was told to withdraw to the reserve line. Unfortunately, that order never reached the forward companies, which held their posts until surrounded. Only a very few men escaped the trap.

The Wiltshires' reserve companies, and even Battalion HQ, were heavily engaged on the right flank and had to conduct a fighting retreat to high ground west of Costaverne. The Battalion's CO died of his wounds and Captain Garthwaite, now Second in Command, suffered more injuries. The surviving Wiltshires rallied overnight in the Wytschaete area, while 75 stragglers were gathered and sent to their reformed HQ at Grand Bois. Thomas and his Battalion mates regrouped the next day and on 12th April, went to Rossignol Camp, near Kemmel, where they were joined by 250 reinforcements. On the night of 13th April, the Wiltshires' took over 800 yards of line from the South Africans, including the strategic high ground around the Spanbroekmolen Crater. The crater had been a German strongpoint atop Messines Ridge until, at 03.20 on 7th June 1917, 60 tons of high explosive was detonated beneath it, one of the largest of nineteen mines fired in the opening minutes of the Battle of Messines.

By 06.00 the following day, the Wiltshires were in position between 9th Royal Welch Fusiliers to their left and 12th Royal Irish Rifles (RIR) on their right. It was abnormally quiet, although the Wiltshires' Battalion HQ, located just west of Spanbroekmolen Crater, received such close attention from German artillery that it moved to a safer place. That night, the Battalion moved 'A' and 'D' Companies into the front line, while 'B' Coy supported 'A' Coy on the left and 'C' Coy supported 'D' Coy on the right. The Brigade also placed 'B' Coy, 9th Royal Welch Fusiliers, under the Wiltshires' command to strengthen the crater defences and form a reserve to retake vital high ground if necessary.

Dawn the next day brought a heavy German artillery barrage covering the whole subsector, and then at 05.45 German infantry assaulted the front occupied by 'D' Company and 12th RIR. The enemy stalled before reaching 'D' Company, but managed to get in among 12th RIRs' positions whilst it was attempting to make an orderly withdrawal. The Germans took and occupied two farms, forcing the Wiltshires to deploy half of 'C' Company to cover one of the farms from the north and bend back 'D' Company's right flank to link up with 'C' Company's left. This created a continuous, if thinly held line, although active German machine-gunners and snipers operating from very close range hampered further movement. Two platoons from the borrowed Fusiliers company were filtered up to reinforce and support 'C' and 'D' Companies. The Wiltshires' Lewis gunners and marksmen kept German movements in check on the left, where, despite heavy shelling, the battalion's casualties were light.

That evening, the Battalion was ordered to withdraw from the line south of the Spanbroekmolen Crater. 'A' Company's positions were to be handed over to 62nd Brigade, 9th Division, the rest were to be evacuated altogether. The Battalion withdrew as ordered, but the 120 men defending the crater, consisting of 'A' Company and a platoon of Royal Welch Fusiliers, must have been dismayed to be relieved by only 19 men from 1/7th West Yorkshire Regiment. German troops overran the unfortunate Yorkshiremen and captured the crater next day, resisting all efforts by the

French 22nd Division to recapture it. Meanwhile, the Wiltshires were ordered to support 9th Battalion, Welch Regiment, south of the crater, relieving the Welch and elements of 5th South Wales Borderers overnight on 17th/18th April.

At about 13.30 on 18th April, German artillery opened fire on the support lines and intermittently shelled the front line. Some French troops, who remained in the British line west of Spanbroekmolen Crater after their unsuccessful counterattack, endured four hours of shelling before withdrawing, pursued by small numbers of Germans. The Wiltshires signalled for pre-arranged, defensive artillery support and engaged the enemy with rifles and Lewis guns. For their part, the Germans halted their advance and instead briefly raked the Wiltshire's front and support lines with machine guns from a range of about 300 yards. Everything quickly settled down, prompting the Wiltshire's Commander to comment later that the entire German operation 'seemed more in the nature of a demonstration than anything else.' That night, the French 22nd Division relieved the Wiltshires and, in sleet and snow, they left for new billets near Abeele.

This had been an extremely trying period for Thomas and his comrades. Only five officers and 175 men remained fit for duty on 12th April after leaving the line. Having received reinforcements, the Battalion re-entered the line the following night with 10 officers and 380 men, but on 19th April, near Abeele, just four officers and 250 men answered at roll call.

Having rebuilt once again, the Battalion returned to the front line on May Day. Fortunately, the next ten days were relatively quiet, with the Wiltshires holding the Iron Bridge in the Voormezeele sector as Brigade Support. On 12th May, 58th Brigade moved to the Herzeele area and the battalion went into billets nearby. The following day, 6th Wiltshires paraded at Herzeele alongside 2nd Battalion, Wiltshire Regiment, where the two battalions officially switched places.

2nd Wiltshires had been fighting in France with 21st Brigade for much of the war, most recently in 30th Division. This division had lost so many men during the German Spring offensives that its battalions had now merged to form a single brigade. As a result, 2nd Wiltshires had combined with 2nd Bedfords to form a composite battalion, under command of the Bedfords' Headquarters. Together they resisted the German advance, steadily losing strength, until the surviving Wiltshires re-joined their own battalion HQ on 11th May. A small party of nine Wiltshire men, possibly returning wounded, came up from Base the following day, but there were simply not enough replacements available to bring the Battalion back up to strength. Throughout the British Expeditionary Force too many battalions struggled with too few men and a drastic reorganisation was vital to preserve it as an effective fighting force.

On Monday 13th May, 2nd Wiltshires boarded buses at Le Paradis and travelled to 6th Wiltshires' billets at Herzeele. There, 6th Wiltshires was officially reduced to a training cadre for newly arrived American troops and left 58th Brigade, 19th Division to join 21st Brigade. 20 Officers and 509 men from 6th Wiltshires, including Thomas, were then transferred to 2nd Wiltshires, which took 6th Battalion's place in 58th Brigade.

Following the fighting in Flanders, several British divisions were now being sent to the quiet French sector in Champagne, where they could rebuild and recover. Among them was Thomas's Division, and consequently he and his comrades entrained for Chalons-sur-Marne, southeast of Reims and settled into their new billets at nearby Vesigneul-sur-Marne. 2nd Battalion had been reorganising and training there for just over a week, when suddenly, on 27th May, it was put on one-hours' notice to move. Unknown to Thomas and his comrades, the Germans were launching another offensive, this time along the Chemin des Dames between Soissons and Reims, the very 'quiet' sector where 2nd Battalion were now recuperating.

Seventeen German assault divisions had demolished or pushed aside eight Allied divisions creating a dangerous gap in the front line. With over a thousand heavy gun batteries and another 24 divisions to back them, German *Stosstruppen* reached the River Aisne in under six hours and pushed on to the River Vesle by the evening. 19th Division went to fill the gap in the Ardre Valley, between Brouillet and Serzy and 58th Brigade were rushed forward in buses, with the Brigade artillery following behind.

At 19.30 on 28th May, the Wiltshires received telephone orders to be ready for transfer to an unknown destination. Buses arrived 30 minutes later and drove through the night to drop them at a crossroads between Bligny and Chambrecy, not far from Reims. The Wiltshires were now facing the southern shoulder of the German salient and an uncertain situation. Ordered to take up outpost positions on the heights northwest of Bligny to defend 58th Brigade, the Wiltshires had just settled in when they were sent to join their Brigade in Bligny. Before they could obey however, replacement orders arrived sending them forward to the outskirts of Sarcy and into Brigade Reserve.

The weary Wiltshires moved north that afternoon, taking up positions on high ground beyond Bouleuse and immediately began digging to strengthen their defences. They had to defend a wide front of about 1,500 yards, so three companies had to occupy the trenches with only 'D' company left in reserve. The Wiltshires observed heavy fighting on a northerly ridge, close to Treslon and Germigny. Later, groups from 8th and 25th Divisions began to arrive from the fighting, strengthening the Wiltshire's line. By nightfall on 29th May, their ridge had become the British Front Line.

Early next morning, the Germans attacked again to widen their salient and although the Wiltshires held their own ground, units either side of them came under heavy pressure. At 10.00, 'D' company went forward to strengthen the right, but by midday both flanks had been forced back and soon German machine guns were firing along the Wiltshires' line from the side and into their rear. After about two hours, the Battalion was ordered to withdraw to a ridge running east of Sarcy, a difficult manoeuvre under hostile machine gun fire, but most of the Wiltshires arrived at the ridge and immediately organised new defensive positions.

The Germans followed up quickly, pushing their machine guns forward under cover of smoke screens. Units to the Battalion's right slowly withdrew, dangerously exposing the right flank and the Wiltshires began to suffer heavy casualties. The Battalion had to withdraw once again, taking up a new position southwest of Bligny, with their left flank resting on the River Ardre. 58th Brigade was, in theory, on the right of the Division's front and in touch with the French 154th Division. In practice, the shattered remnants of British and French units were unsure who was where and supported each other as best they could. The Wiltshires were sent to reoccupy their former position by Sarcy that night, but they found it held by French troops and eventually new orders came to return to their fortified line by Bligny.

Having settled in again by dawn on 31st May, the Battalion was put in reserve, but ready to mount counterattacks if required. Fighting was as heavy as the day before and the Germans made some gains, including the capture of nearby Ville-en-Tardennois, but they were not getting it all their own way. Towards evening, the Battalion was ordered to retake the high ground northwest of Chambrecy together with an adjacent farm north of the village. As their commanding officer led his men forward, German artillery and machine guns opened fire on the advancing Wiltshires, but despite suffering losses, the men pressed on to their objective, successfully linking up with French troops on their left.

Still under heavy fire, the Wiltshires quickly consolidated their gains and reorganised. Their casualties had been severe, only five officers and about 120 men, including Thomas, remained fit, barely enough to make up a company, but they had inflicted considerable loss on the enemy. As night approached, French troops arrived to secure the battalion's right flank and the Royal Welsh Fusiliers linked up to create a continuous line. The Wiltshires laboured through the night to strengthen their defences and by dawn on 1st June, 19th Division's line was unbroken, but 58th Brigade was reduced to just 350 men.

That morning, the Germans made strong attacks against French troops on the Battalion's left. At about 14.00, the French informed the Wiltshires that they had orders to withdraw, but having received no orders themselves, the Wiltshires decided to stay put. Two and a half hours later German soldiers crept up on the Battalion's exposed left flank and brought machine guns into action against their rear. After enduring three hours of this enfilading fire, orders finally came for the Battalion to withdraw to a position in front of the Bois d'Eclisse, where they were to link up with the Royal Welsh Fusiliers on one side and 8th Gloucesters on the other. The Wiltshires slipped back in small groups, covered by fire from their comrades, but it was a difficult operation and the Battalion suffered some 30 casualties in the process. The Wiltshires re-assembled at their new position on the Chambrecy to Bligny road, and dug in, carefully camouflaging their posts.

That night and the following day were quiet. The German High Command had abandoned attempts to widen the salient and switched its focus to Paris. The Germans had taken Chateau Thierry on the River Marne and were coming within striking distance of the French capital. For the second time in the war, German troops reached the River Marne, but this time it was fresh divisions from the United States Army, fighting as an entirely American formation under American command, that blocked the way to Paris.

The Third Battle of the Aisne officially ended on 2nd June, and the Wiltshires were undisturbed in their positions near Chambrecy. However, they noticed considerable German activity and informed their artillery. The Wiltshires then watched as the German units, along with a number of known machine gun nests, came under heavy shelling. The Battalion spent the following day digging support and reserve trenches, allowing the front line to be thinned out to reduce casualties from shellfire. That evening, the three battalions comprising 58th Brigade, 2nd Wiltshires, 9th Royal Welsh Fusiliers and 9th Welsh, were each re-organised as single companies to form one, rather under strength, composite battalion of about 14 Officers and 460 men. This temporary 58th Battalion continued to occupy positions astride the Chambrecy, with the Wiltshire Company holding the south side.

Warned of a likely German attack the next morning, the Wiltshires spent the night of 4th June strengthening their positions. They stood ready from 02.00 while Allied artillery fired on German gun positions, roads and likely assembly points. German guns replied in kind, but no *Stosstruppen* came out of the morning mist and as it cleared, the Wiltshires stood down. After a quiet day, only disturbed by the artillery of both sides, they spent the night making further repairs to their defences.

At about 02.15 on 6th June, German artillery began a tremendous bombardment of the entire sector, hitting the Wiltshires' positions with high explosive and dropping large numbers of gas shells into the woods behind. Allied artillery responded with a counter barrage about the same time and fierce shelling continued for two hours, but casualties were few, thanks to the hard digging over previous nights.

Slowly the bombardment lifted and at about 04.30, some 200 German soldiers advanced up the hill south of the Chambrecy road in open formation. Two subalterns assembled a group of 30 or 40 Wiltshires and, under cover of rifle and machine gun fire, they went out to meet the advancing Germans in the half-light. The Wiltshires charged and the enemy turned about and ran, leaving behind many casualties. One officer even captured a German bugle, which was used to signal tactical orders above the noise of battle. Dawn came as the little party of Wiltshires returned to its former positions and the situation became clearer.

The Germans seemed to be trying to widen the neck of their long, narrow salient, or at least to disrupt any Allied plan to pinch the salient shut and trap the leading German divisions fighting on the River Marne. The Germans were making a determined effort to capture the nearby Montagne de Bligny, a key feature from which they could threaten Reims. The Welch and Royal Welsh Fusiliers to the north of the road were still under great pressure and the enemy made some gains, but determined counter attacks drove them back. The Wiltshire Company had to swing its right flank around when the Cheshires withdrew a little, but after some reinforcement, they were back in their old positions by 10.30. The Wiltshires also reinforced the Royal Welsh Fusiliers on the road, but otherwise maintained their positions until nightfall.

At some point on 6th June, 21-year-old Thomas was killed. The same day, American troops counterattacked at Belleau Wood, convincing the Germans to turn their attention elsewhere along the front. Relieved by 150th Brigade the 58th Composite Battalion withdrew into 19th Division's Reserve at Bois de Courton.

Thomas Teagle was buried in one of the many plots scattered around the Champagne region, his name being added to a temporary cross placed above the grave. After the Armistice a new, large cemetery, the Marfaux British Cemetery, was created roughly halfway between Epernay and Reims, to bring these scattered plots together and Thomas's body was re-interred there.

Lance Corporal 4/6982 George CURL
2nd Battalion, Bedfordshire Regiment

1st July 1918

George Curl, the younger brother of Alfred Curl, was born on 19th November 1896 in Bell Lane, Northchurch, the fourth child of George and Lizzie Curl. He was christened at St Mary's on 7th February 1897 and grew up in the village. After leaving school, 14-year-old George started work as a farm labourer.

Within three days of war breaking out, George walked into Berkhamsted and became one of some 250,000 teenage boys from across the country who lied about their age in order to sign up. Unlike many other teenagers, George only knocked three months off his age to enlist with 4th (Extra Reserve) Battalion, Bedfordshire Regiment, stating that he was the minimum enlistment age of 18. At that time, 4th Battalion was based at Bedford, but later moved to Felixstowe to defend the port of Harwich from a possible German attack. The Battalion also trained new recruits destined for other battalions in the Bedfordshire Regiment. George must have made a good impression from the very start, as in February 1915 he was appointed Lance Corporal. In a very upbeat letter Lance Corporal G Curl, wrote to *The Berkhamsted Gazette* not long

Private George Curl in 1914
(Source: Peter Addiscott)

after - 'Just a line to tell you that the boys are faring very well here. We are up here in the morning at 6.30, make the bed up, wash, and are on parade at 7.15 for drill. Breakfast is at 8, when we get jam. We also get splendid meat for dinner and cherry cake for tea. We are having a good time.' The *Gazette* said he was in the Herts Reserve Battalion, training in Thurston, Suffolk, but local men later wrote from that battalion to say, 'that they didn't get cherry cake at Stowlangtoft Hall, Thurston!'

Having completed his training, George was sent to France on 30th September 1915 to join 2nd Battalion, Bedfordshire Regiment. Whilst on the train to catch his ferry George quickly wrote a postcard to his sister, Emily, saying that he was off to the front. At this time, 2nd Bedfords were billeted at le Quesnoy in northern France, recovering from the fighting during the Battle of Loos, in which the Battalion had suffered 355 casualties.

George fought during the Somme Offensive, when fellow Northchurchman, Edwin Morgan, who was serving in the same battalion, was killed. At the beginning of August 1916, following a month of heavy fighting, George's battalion left the front line for just over three weeks' recuperation. After several short periods back in the trenches, the Battalion returned to action at the Battle of Le Transloy, which was one of the closing battles of the Somme Offensive. During the battle, they were one of the few battalions to gain any ground, but at a cost of a further 242 casualties. In March 1917, 2nd Bedfords cautiously occupied the former German trenches, some of which had been booby-trapped, following the enemy's withdrawal to the Hindenburg Line. Next month the Battalion took part in the Battle of Arras, which the Allied commanders optimistically hoped would end the war in two days. Over the four days of bitter fighting the battalion suffered 89 more casualties. During July and August, George took part in the Third Battle of Ypres and for the remainder of the year, the battalion were engaged in numerous raiding parties and patrols and did not take part in any direct assaults on the German lines.

The start of 1918 saw the Battalion holding the front line near the hamlet of Polderhoek near Ypres. On 6th January, they withdrew from the front line for two months of well-earned rest, training and working party duty. By 18th March, the Battalion was ready to return and went to Vaux, west of St Quentin, to hold the Savy dugout. It was here, three days later, that George experienced the full force of Operation MICHAEL. During the next ten days of heavy fighting and retreat, 2nd Bedford's casualties totalled 15 officers and 554 men. By the end of the month George, and the survivors of his Battalion, had been withdrawn and placed in billets in the hamlet of Arrest, west of Abbeville, well behind the front line.

By the beginning of April Operation MICHAEL had lost its impetus, and the British expected a new German offensive further north to threaten the Channel. Consequently, the Battalion's survivors were sent by train to Roesbrugge, near Poperinghe, arriving at Dragon Camp on 5th April. Two days later, they moved to Huddleston Camp and took over two sections of the Battle Zone. On 17th April, as predicted, amid cold, windy weather, *Stosstruppen* attacked British and Belgian forces close to the River Steenbeek, near the town of Langemark, four miles northeast of Ypres.

Despite heavy fighting, the attacking Germans were held.

On 19th April, it became necessary to merge the remnants of 2nd Bedfords with those of 2nd Wiltshire Regiment, in which Thomas Teagle was serving, into a composite battalion under command of the Bedfordshire Regiment's headquarters. The two units fought as one battalion, losing half its strength, until 9th May. The Wiltshires left two days later and, on 25th May, 2nd Bedfords completely absorbed what remained of 7th Battalion, Bedfordshire Regiment.

Throughout most of June 1918, 2nd Bedfords were held in reserve. With the front relatively stable, letters and parcels began to arrive again and whilst sitting in a bivouac, George took the opportunity to reply to the letters that two of his sisters had sent him. In one of these George mentioned that he was looking to return home on leave 'but Lord knows when that will be'. He also mentioned that the Battalion had been given shorts to wear as part of their fitness training, and jokingly suggested 'strolling up Berko' in them with people thinking he was a football player. On 11th June, George replied to a letter from his sister Lizzie, who two months earlier had started work as a secretary in the Women's Army Auxiliary Corps. Once again, he mentioned the shorts that he and his battalion mates were now having to wear and complained that he had fallen over twice and grazed his knees and needed knee caps. He ended his letter with the words 'well I will close now with the best of love from your loving brother, George'. This was probably George's last letter to his family.

On the evening of 29th June, George's battalion relieved 6th Northamptonshire Regiment on the left of the Brigade front, northwest of Albert. At 21.30 the following evening, the Battalion took part in a large attack against German trenches on the Bouzincourt Spur. Under cover of a smokescreen and mortar barrage, 'B' Company attacked alongside 12th Division with 6th Northants on their right. The Bedfords 'D' Company was in reserve in Melbourne Trench and 'C' Company was in support. The attack was a success and the Battalion captured 20 German soldiers and three machine guns. Another raiding party also bombed out several German-occupied dugouts nearby. Casualties were relatively light, but the Germans bombarded and machine gunned the spur, preventing 'C' Company from getting any barbed wire out to strengthen their position.

At 02.00 on 1st July, the Germans launched a powerful counterattack, driving in the Battalion's advanced posts. According to one of George's officers, who later wrote to his family, George was killed having courageously jumped out of the trench he was defending, because some of the soldiers in front of him 'refused to face the Hun bombs'. As a Lance Corporal, George was presumably leading by example and encouraging his fellow soldiers to follow. His officer continued 'it may be some consolation to know that [George] had accounted for several Huns before he lost his life'.

After the fighting subsided, Lance Corporal George Curl's body was recovered from the battlefield. It now lies in the Bouzincourt Ridge Cemetery close to where he died. George was a seasoned veteran, having fought on the Western Front for three years and taken part in all the major battles during that time. He was described as one of the battalion's best NCOs, and yet, like Thomas Teagle, when he died, he was still only 21 years old.

Private T/271032 Thomas FANTHAM
10th (East Kent and West Kent Yeomanry) Battalion, The Buffs (East Kent Regiment)

10th August 1918

Sarah Fantham gave birth to her seventh child, a son named Thomas, in Northchurch late in 1886. Both Thomas' parents had strong links with the nearby Grand Junction Canal; his father, John Fantham, came from Marsworth and his mother from Buckland, both on the canal and just over the county border in Buckinghamshire. John Fantham was a boatman and this is probably how he met his future wife. Thomas's elder brother, George, and elder sisters, Ellen, Minnie, Emma and Sarah were all born at Buckland.

By 1884 the Fanthams had moved to 3 New Road in Northchurch, which was where Thomas's younger brother, Charles, was born. John and Sarah's youngest child, Lizzie, arrived three years after Thomas. All three Fantham brothers subsequently learnt the trade of bricklaying and by 1901, George had married and left home whilst fourteen-year-old Thomas and his brother were working as bricklayer's labourers. Later, Thomas would earn his living from gardening.

Thomas stood 5ft 9½inches tall, was physically fit and had perfect eyesight. He seems to have been a quietly religious man, regularly attending the Baptist chapels, first in Bell Lane and later the new chapel in Northchurch High Street. He was known in the village for his cheerfulness. On Boxing Day 1908, Thomas brought his cheery nature to the stage as reported in *The Berkhamsted Gazette*:

'The capacity of the Girl's Schoolroom was severely taxed on Saturday evening when a highly successful entertainment took place under the capable management of the Rev. E. Wells. The primary object of the entertainment was to provide a counter attraction to the public houses of the village, and judging by the attendance the effort was a successful one in that respect. The entertainment consisted of a play entitled 'The Girl I Left Behind Me', and a number of miscellaneous items, the programme occupying from 7.30 till about 11 o'clock. Those taking part in the entertainment were the Misses E. Aldridge, E. Carter, and N. Hales, Messrs. B. Ashby, G. Carter, J. Delderfield, T. Fantham, J. Freeman, C. Rolfe and A. Winter, Mr E. Winter and others rendering various contributions. Smoking was allowed during the entertainment and tea and coffee were handed round.'

Thomas was also a keen footballer, playing Right Back for Northchurch Football Club, the 'Black and Ambers', and was in the squad that won the West Herts Minor Cup in 1909.

Four years later, in December 1913 and January 1914, banns were read at St Mary's for Thomas Fantham, bachelor of the parish of Northchurch, and Dorothy Caroline Batts, spinster of St Nicholas Parish in Chadlington, Oxfordshire. Dorothy had been working as a housemaid for the well-to-do Pillans family at Fairlight, one of the large houses in Shrublands Road. Thomas and Dorothy were married on 8th January 1914, and made their home at 14 Alma Road in Northchurch. Their first child, Frederick Thomas, was born the following autumn. By then Britain was at war.

Thomas, with a new family to support, did not volunteer straight away, but decided to wait and see how events would turn out. After the bloody battles of 1915, it became clear that compulsory service would soon be introduced so, on 11th December 1915, three weeks before the National Service Act came into force, Thomas volunteered under the 'Derby Scheme'. His enlistment papers describe him as a jobbing gardener, aged 29 years and 1 month, and a member of the Church of England. Thomas was then sent home to await his call-up.

Six months later, with Dorothy expecting their second child, Thomas was instructed to report to the Recruiting Officer at Watford and on 30th May 1916, he officially began his service with the Army. Thomas was sent to Canterbury for training with 3rd (Reserve) Battalion, East Kent Regiment (The Buffs). He would remain with 3rd The Buffs for more than eight months. Meanwhile, on 10th November 1916, Dorothy gave birth to a daughter, Marjorie Brenda.

In February 1917, Thomas was posted to the Egyptian Expeditionary Force (EEF), and embarked at Devonport for the 16-day voyage to Alexandria. On 1st March, the day of his arrival, Thomas wrote his Will. Two weeks later, Thomas joined the 10th Battalion, East Kent Regiment, at nearby Sidi Bishr as part of 'B' Company, which consisted of former Royal East Kent Mounted Rifles troopers.

10th (Royal East Kent and West Kent Yeomanry) Battalion, The Buffs, (East Kent Regiment), to give its full title, had been created on 1st February 1917, out of two Kentish Regiments of Yeomanry, which had been on garrison and outpost duty in Egypt. Both Yeomanry Regiments had fought dismounted as infantry in the cramped confines of the Gallipoli Peninsular during 1915. Following the evacuation, they continued on infantry in Egypt, where lack of water severely restricted the employment of cavalry. Eventually, the dismounted Yeomanry units in Egypt were assembled into a new infantry division, named 74th (Yeomanry) Division. 10th Buffs joined 230th Brigade, 74th Division, and began serious training as a fully-fledged infantry battalion.

When Thomas arrived in Egypt, the Turks had retreated into Palestine and no longer threatened the Suez Canal. The EEF had already established a forward base at El Arish on the Mediterranean coast near Palestine and learning from its earlier mistakes in Mesopotamia, it had set up good supply lines to the town. A wire road, consisting of wire netting secured by pegs, allowed soldiers to march across the soft sand without sinking. A 12-inch wide pipeline pumped water from the Nile Delta into numerous storage tanks, from which it was distributed to the front line by camel. A railway would eventually link El Arish with Kantara, on the Suez Canal, and the town of Belah in Palestine.

Having driven the Turks from Egypt, the British Commander, General Sir Archibald Murray, wanted to push them further into Palestine. In March 1917, the EEF attacked Gaza on the Palestinian coast. Troops surrounded the town, but heavy Turkish counterattacks and lack of water, forced the EEF to withdraw. The First Battle of Gaza thus ended in failure, but there would be another attempt and 230th Brigade was to take part.

On 11th April 1917, Thomas and his comrades boarded a train for Deir el Belah in Palestine on the newly laid Kantara Military Railway. Both track and rolling stock were still rough and ready and the four-day journey jolting in open trucks took its toll on the Buffs. When the Battalion arrived at Deir el Belah on the night of 15th April, Thomas immediately went on the sick list with a bad case of diarrhoea. After five days at the Brigade's Field Ambulance, he was transferred to 24th Stationary Hospital at Kantara for further treatment. As a result, Thomas missed the attempt to take Gaza and would not be fit enough to rejoin his unit until 29th May.

The Second Battle of Gaza was also a failure and both sides settled down for the hot summer months. Thomas re-joined the Buffs at Wadi Ghuzze, which was one of the most important sources of water in Allied hands. There was plenty of water for washing here, which was just as well, because the Buffs were at Wadi Ghuzze to dig. They worked on a strong defensive line to protect the water supply, and prevent Turkish forces cutting through Wadi Ghuzze to Rafa, on the Egyptian border, where they could block all Allied road and rail links into Palestine. Most trench digging had to be carried out at night, however, because with very few Royal Flying Corps aircraft available, the Turkish pilots had the air almost to themselves.

After some weeks, the Battalion faced a lengthy night march to strengthen the defences of Sheikh Abbas and Mansura ridge. The area south of Gaza consisted of deep wadis providing ample shelter for 74th Division to concentrate there. 10th Buffs settled into Wadi Levi and sent out working parties by day and night to improve the forward trenches or construct elaborate redoubts in the second line of defence. It was mostly a quiet area, although the Battalion history noted, 'Sometimes the Turk woke up from his lethargy and shelled a working party, or, as on one occasion, a football match.' At least Thomas got the chance to show what he could do at right back!

Like all heavy construction work however, accidents were the greatest danger. In June, a large piece of wood struck Thomas hard on the shin prompting his second admission to 230th Infantry Brigade Field Ambulance. This blow damaged the outer layer of his shinbone which became inflamed, a condition called periostitis, causing great pain, fever and chills. Thomas' condition was serious enough for his transfer to 31st General Hospital, which occupied a large warehouse on the Port Said waterfront.

Meanwhile, in July, Thomas's brigade was transferred from digging to Divisional Reserve. 10th Buffs commenced three months' training in open warfare, smoke attacks and gas drill at Dorset House, about four miles east of Deir el Belah. It was here that Thomas re-joined 'B' Company after being declared 'Fit for Service'. Unfortunately, Thomas had not been training long before he returned to the sick list. On 9th August, Thomas was admitted to 21st General Hospital in the Egyptian Army Barracks at Ras-el-Tin, Alexandria with a mysterious condition, recorded simply as, 'NYD', or 'Not Yet Diagnosed'.

Thomas finally re-joined the Buffs at Beit Sira on 1st March 1918, but soon afterwards transferred to 74th Division Headquarters, presumably owing to his poor health. The Buffs were then helping 10th (Irish) Division to construct a new supply road to supplement the old Latrun to Jerusalem road. As the rainy season ended, so did the pause in operations, and soon after Thomas' return to active duty he was marching up the new 'Irish Road' with his mates. Their destination was a series of precipitous, trackless, boulder-strewn ridges, between Ramallah and Nablus, which 74th Division would soon be crossing at the centre of a three-division attack.

On 7th March, the Buffs took over an outpost line facing the Turkish trenches at Burje Badawile, which 230th Brigade would be attacking two days later. Thomas and the rest of 'B' Company occupied small positions on the right of the Battalion. Between the outpost line and the Turkish trenches lay the village of Yebrud. Two 'B' Company platoons tried to take Yebrud quietly after dark on 8th March, but they found it heavily defended. 'C' Company followed to help them, but struggling in the blackness and a thick mist, and had only reached the slope opposite Yebrud by dawn. However, after an hour or so, the Buffs entered Yebrud, just as the Suffolk and the Royal Sussex Regiments were advancing to attack the main position. At about 10.00, the Turkish line was captured and the Buffs assembled there to consolidate the trenches, while the rest of the Brigade pressed on. Despite constant heavy machine gun fire and shelling, casualties were relatively light.

The advance continued to the next ridge on 10th March. This time Thomas's Company attacked alongside 'A' Company, with 'C' Company covering their flank. As on the previous day, they faced Turkish trenches, sniper and machine gun posts skilfully constructed of rocks and stones on the forward slope of a precipitous hillside, making them practically invisible. It took Thomas and his comrades three and a half hours of climbing and shooting under Turkish fire before they finally carried the position at 17.30.

The Buffs established their outpost line on a ridge some 3,000 feet up, and settled down for the night. The men were less bothered by the intense cold at that height than by the harassing fire from Turkish machine guns on a neighbouring hill. Then the rain started. Happily, morning brought reports that the next ridge was clear and the Buffs took up the northward advance towards Nablus once more. 74th Division soon pulled well ahead of the divisions either side and orders came to halt. This temporary pause became an extended halt as heavy rains set in, so preparations for a renewed push were made. The Buffs remained in an outpost line established near Turmus Aya and Sinjil, either actually in the line or behind in reserve.

The Battalion's battle casualties were light during the fight for the ridges with just one officer and three men killed and one officer and 23 men wounded, but the physical strain had been enormous. Although Thomas and his comrades had only advanced four miles by the map, they had actually scrambled twice as far over difficult, rocky terrain. The constant climbing and descents had tested their endurance to the limit and sprained ankles alone had caused the evacuation of 16 men.

The Buffs settled back into a familiar routine of alarms, sniping and occasional shelling, which they had come to expect from outpost duty in Palestine. Meanwhile, Germany's Operation MICHAEL on the Western Front was precipitating a crisis so big that 74th and 52nd Divisions received orders to reinforce the sagging British line. The Buffs left Turmus Aya and in the stifling April heat, marched 50 miles down to the olive groves of Sura Fend, near the town of Ludd, the ancient Lydda. A day or so later, they once again boarded the Kantara-Belah Railway, but were pleased to discover that it had improved enormously over the previous year. The journey from Ludd to the Suez Canal now took a mere twelve hours and soon they were camped on the sand at Kantara. The Buffs had been in Palestine for exactly one year, having arrived on 13th April 1917, and departed on 13th April 1918.

On 28th April, the Buffs left Egypt for France. Their voyage across the Mediterranean was peacefully uneventful, but everyone wore life belts all day and slept by them at night, aware of the increased danger from German and Austrian U-boats. The very strict 'no lights' policy aboard ship meant Thomas could not even enjoy his pipe after dark.

The Buffs landed at Marseilles on 7th May, and two nights later 230th Brigade marched to Marseilles Station singing The *Marseillaise*, which 'not only awoke the inhabitants, but brought tears to their eyes.' A three-day rail journey brought them to Noyelles, near Abbeville and by 18th May, the re-united Division was beginning its education in the ways of the Western Front. Gas training was a particular revelation, including the discovery that their anti-gas equipment was mostly defective or obsolete. Billeted in the little village of Foret l'Abbaye, Thomas and his mates trained by day and watched German air raids around Abbeville by night.

A move by rail and foot to Izel-les-Hameau, in the Arras district, followed, where the Battalion remained until the end of June. The Buffs learned to co-operate with tanks and participated in field training, bayonet fighting and, no doubt to Thomas' delight, football competitions. As 74th Division was temporarily attached to the Canadian Corps, Thomas and his mates made full use of the Canadian YMCA at Izel-les-Hameau, as well as visiting cinemas and concert parties, to fill the evenings. Their stay in the French countryside proved so beneficial that the Battalion's historian wrote, '...it is probably true that we were at this time in a finer condition of health and training than at any time since the amalgamation'. Even 74th Division's Commander declared the Buffs' turnout and appearance to be the best in the Division. 74th Division now was considered sufficiently well trained to be placed on standby to reinforce either XI or XIII Corps at four hours' notice. The Division moved to the area around Norrent-Fontes, mid-way between Saint-Omer and Béthune, on 26th June. Thomas' battalion was billeted at Enquin-les-mines, where training, work on rear defences and football continued.

Two weeks later, 74th Division relieved 61st Division's line between the La Bassée Canal and the River Lys, facing the German occupied town of Merville, about 3,000 yards away. The Buffs moved east in two stages and on 11th July, entered billets at La Pierriere by the Aire-La-Bassée Canal. Thomas's Brigade was in the Divisional Reserve, so once again the Buffs worked every night strengthening the line stretching over two miles from Haverskerque to Amusoires facing the small town of St Venant. However, Thomas and his mates still found time to bathe and play football during the day.

A few days later, the German Army launched its next operation intended to pinch out the French salient around Reims, trapping the French divisions there and drawing reserves away from Flanders where the Germans planned to attack next and drive the BEF back to the Channel Ports. One wing of the German pincer move was blocked, but the other drove into the Allied line, tempting the German High Command to replace its original plan with a deep thrust on a narrow front. Ferdinand Foch, the Allied Supreme Commander, kept his nerve and on 18th July, launched four French armies, supported by British, American and Italian divisions, in a massive counter offensive along the Marne that absorbed large numbers of German reserves. By 2nd August French estimates put German losses in the Second Battle of the Marne at around 180,000, marking the beginning of the end for the Imperial German Army.

On 4th August, the Buffs moved into front line trenches midway between St Omer and Lens in the St Floris sector. The terrain there was so low that it was impossible to dig more than a foot or two without reaching water, even in summer. The so-called trenches here were purely a patchy series of breastworks built on the surface and offering doubtful protection, but at least the weather was fine and the men's uniforms were dry. Thomas and 'B' Company were on the right of the Battalion's line, in touch with 229th Brigade, while 'C' Company was on their left, in contact with the Sussex Regiment. Having incurred substantial losses during the recent offensives, the Germans could not meet another attack without weakening their line elsewhere. According to 10th Battalion's history the Germans were 'getting very restive, unsure where they should resist and where they should give ground' and apparently thinning parts of their line around Merville, especially at night. Initial probing by the Buffs attracted heavy machine gun fire, but later there were definite signs of a German withdrawal on their right flank.

Four days later, east of Amiens, British and French infantry and tanks advanced some eight miles behind a creeping artillery barrage across a ten-mile-wide front in a single day, at a cost of about 18,000 casualties. Serious German losses - over 400 field guns, large numbers of machine guns and trench mortars, and 27,700 men, of whom 15,000 had surrendered, provoked Ludendorff to call 8th August, 'The black day of the German Army'.

That night, 230th Brigade was ordered forward to the ruined village of Calonne, on the River Lys. Thomas's company advanced about 1,000 yards, crossing the German trenches alongside 'C' Company, but German posts by St Floris held up the neighbouring Sussex Regiment. The advance on Calonne resumed the next morning with 'A' Company passing through 'B' Company on the right. Despite a stiff counter attack, 'A' Company entered the village alongside 'D' Company and towards evening, the Brigade established a new line in front of the Lys Canal.

On 10th August, 74th Division advanced about 3,000 yards, despite machine gun fire, to the line of the River Lys and a small brook called the Turbeaute. The Germans resisted more strongly there, attacking the Buffs' right flank during the afternoon, which interrupted their advance and caused several casualties. Thomas was mortally wounded during the advance, and his body was quickly buried nearby. A few days later the Buffs were relieved and went into reserve around St. Floris.

The Army returned Thomas' personal effects to his wife, Dorothy, at 14 Alma Road the following February. Among his letters, photographs and foreign coins were his pipe and tobacco pouch, a penknife, two notebooks and three religious books.

Thomas Fantham's body was later moved to the St Venant-Robecq Road British Cemetery, nine miles northwest of Béthune. In addition to the Northchurch War Memorial, Thomas's name is recorded on the Northchurch Baptist Chapel's Memorial Tablet and on the bottom kerbstone of a badly damaged grave in New Road Cemetery whose inscription reads: 'Also of Thomas Fantham. Died of wounds in France, Aug.10th 1918, aged 32 years'; the principal dedication of the grave is missing.

Private 601505 James DELDERFIELD
2nd Battalion, Bedfordshire Regiment transferred to 142nd Company,
Labour Corps, Bedfordshire Regiment
26th August 1918

There have been Delderfields in the northwest part of Hertfordshire since at least the time of the formal registration of Births, Marriages and Deaths in 1838. It remains one of the local 'names', with most of the long-standing families in the Northchurch area having at least one 'Delderfield' in their family tree. James Delderfield was born on 3rd September 1885 in Wigginton, the fourth child of Mary Delderfield and her husband James, a Tring-born gamekeeper and general labourer. James and Mary Delderfield would have four more children and by 1911 they and their family were living in Northchurch High Street with James (jnr) working as a farm labourer. The following summer, James married Elizabeth Fantham in St Mary's Church and early in 1914 Elizabeth gave birth to a daughter named Enid. The family later moved to 13 Middle Road in Berkhamsted.

James Delderfield enlisted with 2nd Battalion, Bedfordshire Regiment at Watford in the Spring of 1915 and landed in France on 30th August. After a few days at the Bedfordshires' base, he joined the Battalion in a draft of 25 men on 11th September at Noyelles, 40 miles northeast of Amiens.

The subsequent details of James' military career is somewhat unclear. The month after his arrival in France his battalion participated in the Battle of Loos and fought during the various stages of the Battle of the Somme in 1916, including the Battle of Albert, the attack on Trônes Wood, the Battle of Delville Wood and the Battle of Le Transloy. In March 1917, James's battalion advanced as the Germans

Private James Delderfield (Source: Linda Pottinger)

retreated to the Hindenburg Line and later that year, they took part in the Third Battle of Ypres. It seems that James was badly wounded at some stage, or became so seriously ill, that he was declared no longer fit for active duty. After medical treatment, James transferred to 142 Labour Company.

The Labour Corps was formed in January 1917 for officers and men deemed medically unfit for combat, but who were still able to perform manual labour, thus releasing fighting troops from some of the work they had to perform while 'resting'. The Labour Corps undertook heavy and hazardous work including the construction and maintenance of roads, railways, bridges and defence works and the loading, unloading and stacking of fuel and other stores. They even undertook battlefield salvage work and cleared battle damage. There were many accidents and the men usually worked within range of German shellfire and mortar bombs. During the German offensives of March and April 1918, Labour Corps men were even employed as emergency infantry. At this time, 142 Company was working at the railhead and ammunition dumps at Puchevillers.

The British Commander in Chief, Douglas Haig, put on record that between May and November 1918, '...the demands upon the Labour Corps were incessant. The British labour companies were composed entirely of men medically unfit for active operations, and more than half of their number owed their incapacity to wounds or sickness incurred while serving with fighting units.'

James died on 26th August 1918, just as the Allies' final advance was gaining momentum, but unfortunately there are no details regarding the circumstances of his death, the only surviving record stating that he died 'In the Field'. The influenza epidemic had just begun, but cases were rarely fatal at this stage. There may have been an accident at the ammunition dump, but it is also possible that he was mortally wounded during an air attack on a nearby Labour Corps camp eight days before he died, which killed 13 men and wounded a further 58. Many of the Labour Corps men killed during this raid are buried in the Puchevillers British Cemetery, twelve miles north of Amiens, and this is where James lies today.

In 1919, the authorities decided that the headstones of men who had died whilst serving with the Labour Corps, and who had previously served with another corps, would only display their original unit. Consequently, James's headstone at Puchevillers British Cemetery bears the badge of the Bedfordshire Regiment.

Private G/89270 Arthur TEAGLE
1st Battalion, Duke of Cambridge's Own (Middlesex Regiment)

20th September 1918

Arthur Teagle, the middle son of Harry and Fanny Teagle, was born on 3rd July 1898 while the family was living at Haversham in Buckinghamshire. The Teagles later moved to Dudswell with their youngest children, Thomas, Arthur, Lily and James, but it was not long before Arthur left home. As he approached his 18th birthday in 1916, Arthur was working as a labourer and living at 181a Gladstone Street in Wood Green, Middlesex with his older sister Annie and her husband Lancelot Goodson, whom she had married in the summer of 1914.

The day after his eighteenth birthday, having received his call up papers, Arthur reported to the Middlesex Regiment depot at Mill Hill Barracks. His Service Record shows that he stood 5ft 5½inches tall with a chest measurement of 33½inches and a chest expansion of 3½inches. Weighing 118lbs and with his physical development only rated 'fair', Arthur left with a medical grade of 'A2'. Arthur was allocated the regimental number G/22510 and posted to 28th Middlesex Regiment, nicknamed 'The Die Hards', a training battalion based at Aldershot.

The British Army had historically been a volunteer force and in mid-1916 it was still coming to grips with the large numbers of 18-year-old conscripts brought in by the Military Service Act. Once trained, these recruits had to be kept occupied at home until their 19th birthday, when they could legally serve overseas. Two months into Arthur's service, all training battalions were re-organised and 28th Middlesex was renamed 102nd Training Reserve Battalion. Arthur, with a new regimental number, TR/10/52907, continued with his training at Aldershot.

Arthur must have shown some leadership potential because on 27th February 1917, after only eight months in the army, he was appointed a Lance Corporal. On 10th October however, Arthur was up before the Commanding Officer, Lt. Col. Parkin, to face a charge that on the 7th October he had been, 'When on active service, absent from Reveille until reporting himself to the Coy. Orderly Sgt. at 9.45p.m. on the 8th inst.' Arthur's conduct sheet records no mitigating circumstances regarding his unauthorised absence, but the Colonel seemed to hand out a minimal punishment. Arthur lost his Lance Corporal's stripe and forfeited two days' pay for the two days he was unavailable for duty.

A fortnight later, the training establishment was again re-organised. 102nd Training Reserve Battalion was redesignated a Young Soldiers

Battalion and, in an apparent change of heart by the authorities, regained its county affiliation, becoming 53rd Battalion, Middlesex Regiment. This gave Arthur yet another regimental number, G/89270.

On 11th December 1917, Arthur was sent to the Depot at Mill Hill to wait his overseas posting. He was sent to the Die Hards' 1st Battalion, which was with 98th Brigade, 33rd Division. When Arthur joined his new comrades in Flanders on 18th December, they were enjoying a quiet period out of the line, although there was plenty of work to keep them occupied. Christmas and the New Year was spent comfortably billeted in the convent at Poperinghe.

Arthur was one of the few replacements that the Prime Minister, Lloyd George, allowed to be sent to France after the bloody fighting of Third Battle of Ypres. Lloyd George was determined to prevent the British Army from conducting further offensive action with the consequent loss of life, by starving the BEF of men. Even while 1st Middlesex was in the front line southwest of the village of Passchendaele in January 1918, it reduced raids and patrols to a minimum in an effort to conserve its strength. Meanwhile the Germans were quietly preparing for their Spring Offensive, and only four men were wounded that month. After it was relieved, the Battalion spent three February weeks training at Meringhem near St Omer.

Come March, the Die Hards were back in the front line, southwest of Passchendaele. On 6th March, and successive days, 1st Middlesex's War Diary noted 'considerable gas shelling in the evening.' The Germans were employing their newest chemical weapon, Mustard Gas, to weaken the British lines. Soon half of the Die Hards's daily casualties were gas cases; half the 28 men lost on the 8th March were gassed, as were 11 of the 21 casualties the following day, and the numbers kept rising. The Battalion's War Diary reported that shelling with mustard gas on 18th March had been 'very heavy', and that three officers and 31 men were suffering after a gas attack the previous night. Overnight on 19th/20th March, German patrols attacked the battalion's posts with hand grenades, and more shelling inflicted another 20 cases of mustard gas poisoning.

Among the latest casualties was Arthur, who developed conjunctivitis and went to N°3 Australian CCS, at Nine Elms, near Poperinghe as a gas case. On the 25th or 26th March, Arthur transferred to 55 General Hospital, (Eastern General Hospital), at Wimereux, north of Boulogne where the doctors considered his symptoms severe enough to send him home. Consequently, on 30th March, Arthur was admitted to the Brook War Hospital, the former Brook General Hospital, at Woolwich. Arthur's admission medical notes simply state that he had 'some conjunctivitis'. Whilst recovering in hospital, Arthur contracted measles, which delayed his discharge until 1st June. He probably had ten days' sick leave before being posted to 5th (Reserve) Battalion, Middlesex Regiment, stationed at Chatham, Kent on home defence duties with the Thames and Medway

Garrison and a handy posting for recovering soldiers.

Arthur re-embarked for France on 30th June and spent his 20th birthday at Étaples waiting to join a reinforcing draft. At last, on 24th July, Arthur re-joined 1st Middlesex on the southern side of the Ypres-Comines Canal, north of Voormezeele. The Battalion had recently taken part in a small, though successful, local operation with 2nd Battalion Durham Light Infantry. At the start of August, 1st Battalion spent a couple of weeks in the line at Brandhoek, some five miles west of Ypres. Elsewhere on the Western Front, Allied armies had begun pushing the German Army inexorably back towards its Homeland and, although nobody knew it at the time, the war had entered its Last Hundred Days.

On 28th August, the Battalion marched to St Omer, and then travelled by rail to Doullens, arriving there at 02.15 the following morning. The Battalion detrained and marched along the Doullens-Arras road to their billets at Pommera, for two weeks' training. Two weeks later, the Battalion was transported to Les Boeufs, five miles due south of Bapaume and prepared to go into the line at Equancourt, another eight miles to the west. The Battalion marched off on 17th September ready to take over the trenches just east of Dessart Wood for a day, before entering positions at Villers-Guislain, ten miles south of Cambrai, in support of 98th Brigade.

The circumstances surrounding Arthur's death on 20th September are unclear. No major attack took place that day, merely 'desultory fighting' over the previous two or three days, which, along with regular bombardment, was now routine for trench warfare. It is likely that Arthur, aged 20, died alongside three of his comrades, Privates Albert Culpin, Maurice Frith and William Lilley as result of an exploding artillery shell or mortar bomb. They were buried near to where they fell, but after the Armistice, the four bodies were moved to the Villers Hill British Cemetery at Villers-Guislain and re-buried, side by side.

Private G/73574 Charles Henry CARTER
17th Battalion, Royal Fusiliers (City of London Regiment)

8th October 1918

Charles Henry Carter was born on 5th January 1900, at 6c Armada Street, North Deptford, Kent, but he already had Northchurch roots. Charles' father, Frederick Charles Dealey, was born in Northchurch and Charles later came to live with his grandparents in New Road, where he stayed until he joined the army. His grandmother, Eliza Ann Hales came from Aldbury from a family of straw plaiters living in Rag Pit, Ivinghoe. In October 1869, Eliza married Walter Dealey, a fellow straw plaiter and six years later, having moved to Northchurch, she bore their only child, Frederick Charles Dealey. Walter Dealey turned out to be a bad father and was constantly in trouble with the police, receiving several convictions for poaching, trespass, drunkenness & disorder, and spent time in prison as a result.

The 1881 Census, shows a 29-year-old Eliza Dealey as the head of household living in Northchurch High Street, although she was actually some four years older. Walter was absent, but one of Eliza's younger brothers, William Hale, was living with her and 5-year-old Frederick. To help make ends meet, Eliza still plaited straw and had taken on a lodger, a 28-year-old agricultural labourer from Northchurch named Charles Carter.

Walter Dealey died in the spring of 1888, aged 39, and that autumn Eliza and Charles Carter were married. They had no children together, but Charles treated Frederick as his own son and Frederick took on his stepfather's surname. By the age of 15, Frederick Charles Carter was working as a general labourer and living with his mother, stepfather and grandfather, Joseph Hale, in Northchurch High Street.

A few years later Frederick left Northchurch and found employment at Deptford as a zinc worker. In time, he met and married Elizabeth Pole, an illiterate Norfolk girl, some eight years older than him, who had come to Deptford by way of Yorkshire and Lancashire. She was also the mother of seven children. Frederick and Elizabeth found a tenement in Deptford, and started their own family.

Fred junior was born in 1898 and Charles Henry Carter followed in January 1900. The following year Frederick senior, who was also known as Charles at this time, his wife and their nine children lived crammed together in just three rooms at 12c Armada Street in North Deptford. By then, Frederick was working as a dock labourer. Three years later, Lily Carter was born, but things were not going well for the Carters and before long, Frederick and Elizabeth separated.

When Charles Henry was about 6 years old, his father married again. Frederick Carter's new wife, Minnie Chapman, came from Deptford and already had a two-year-old daughter. Now working as a bricklayer's labourer, Frederick moved his new family about a mile east to Greenwich. Unfortunately, their accommodation at 2 Clark's Buildings, Eastney Street, was no improvement on Armada Street. The social chronicler Charles Booth described Clark's Buildings as '3 storey tenement houses...One or two room people - labourers, thieves, field hands, etc.'. Nevertheless, Frederick and Minnie started a family there and in 1909, George Thomas Carter was born, followed by Louisa Mary Carter little more than a year later.

Perhaps to make room for their new half-siblings, Charles Henry and his sister Lily moved to their grandparent's home in New Road, Northchurch and started to attend the local school. Maybe to save confusion in the Carter family Charles' grandfather entered his grandson's name on the Census form as Henry Charles, although his birth certificate says Charles Henry.

Charles Henry began attending the Northchurch Baptist Chapel, and remained at New Road until January 1918. His Grandfather, Charles, had died shortly before the outbreak of war and Eliza's health started to deteriorate. She became bedridden with rheumatism and suffered great pain. Minnie's daughter, Emily Beatrice Chapman became her live-in carer, but Eliza died on the evening of 3rd May 1918.

In January 1918, eighteen-year-old Charles was called up and, reporting to the recruiting office in Hertford. He enlisted under the name of Henry Charles Carter. After basic training, he joined 17th (Service) Battalion, Royal Fusiliers, 6th Brigade, 2nd Division. 17th Royal Fusiliers landed in France during November 1915 and in 1916 had fought at The Battles of Delville Wood and The Ancre during the Somme Offensive and had taken part in the Battles of the Scarpe and Cambrai during 1917.

The Fusiliers were still holding trenches southwest of Cambrai at the start of 1918. When the Germans launched Operation MICHAEL on 21st March they forced the Battalion back 25 miles in a week, but although the British line was stretched, it did not break. By the time the German advance faltered at the month's end, 17th Royal Fusiliers was in Aveluy Wood, north of Albert where the Battalion consolidated its new position, constructing defensive lines and laying light railway tracks. To replace the battalion's recent losses, reinforcements arrived at around this time, and it is likely that Charles Carter was among them.

The German spring offensives had made spectacular initial advances, but by concentrating their most highly motivated and aggressive soldiers into elite *Stosstrupp* battalions, which suffered excessive casualties during attacks, the German High Command had turned most of its remaining infantry divisions into poor quality formations. As the German Army struggled to move artillery and ammunition across countryside devastated by the fighting, ordinary German soldiers noticed the well-stocked Allied supply dumps that contrasted painfully with the shortages and starvation back at home cased by the British naval blockade, and their morale began to crack.

The British Army, meanwhile, entered a period of 'active defence' - keeping the Germans occupied with frequent raiding, while building up its own strength, especially in its artillery. It was during this period, on 9th July, that Charles made his final Will in his pay book leaving everything to his mother at 15 Old Woolwich Road, East Greenwich.

Germany's final attempt to deliver a knockout blow had failed in July, leaving its army exhausted as new American divisions were at last taking to the field in strength. Now Marechal Ferdinand Foch, the newly created Generalissimo of the Allied armies, was able to launch a series of strong, co-ordinated offensives with limited objectives up and down the line. It began on 8th August, with the three-day Battle of Amiens.

The second stage of the Allied offensive started on 21st August when the British Third Army, which included Charles' battalion and Canadian troops, advanced along a 33-mile front between Albert and Bapaume. A German counter attack the following day failed to check their advance and two days later, Charles' battalion helped to capture the village of Mory, just north of Bapaume. Troops from the First Army joined the advance on 26th August, extending the front by a further six miles. New Zealand, Australian and American troops then thwarted an attempt by the Germans to form a new defensive line on the Somme and on 29th August, Bapaume fell to the New Zealanders. The Germans continued to fall back, losing Péronne on 1st September, and soon they had lost all the territory recaptured during Operation MICHAEL.

Charles' battalion launched an attack close to the village of Vaux-Vraucourt on 3rd September and by late on the 4th they had driven the Germans back another 9,500 yards to the partially completed Canal du Nord and the Hindenburg Line. On 26th September, French and American forces increased the pressure on the German army by launching a new offensive further south near Verdun.

Charles' battalion was not involved on 27th September during the attack on the Canal du Nord, which forced the Germans further east, and allowed Allied troops to cross the canal. The Fusiliers were resting at Lock 7, which they had previously occupied in 1917, when a German aeroplane attacked the Battalion's position, inflicting 32 casualties. Later, 17th Royal Fusiliers was ordered east to capture the St Quentin Canal northeast of Noyelles. By 08.30 Noyelles village had fallen and troops crossed the River Scheldt, but German resistance on the canal was stiffening. Men of 17th Battalion attempted to navigate a raft down the River Scheldt to a point where the Canal crossed the Scheldt by aqueduct, but passing beneath the aqueduct's low arches proved difficult and most of the men had to cross the canal over nearby locks in single-file and under heavy fire.

A German counter attack in the small hours of 29th September drove a neighbouring battalion backwards into 17th Battalion's positions causing enormous confusion. While Charlie's battalion rallied under their company officers, German machine gun fire was causing carnage among them. Charlie was one of the Fusiliers caught by the gunfire and was transferred for treatment to 56 Casualty Clearing Station, near Bapaume.

Medical staff struggled to save him for over a week, but on 8th October, eighteen-year-old Charles died of his wounds. His body was buried in what is now the Grevillers British Cemetery. Charles Carter is one of the six men commemorated on the memorial plaque in the Baptist Chapel at Northchurch. His name also appears on the Northchurch War Memorial as HC Carter.

Captain Reginald Victor Byron LOXLEY
Royal Air Force

18th October 1918

Reginald Victor Byron Loxley, known in the Loxley family as Roy, was born in Fairford, Gloucestershire on 14th March 1887, the youngest son of the Reverend Arthur Smart Loxley and his wife, Alice. Reginald Loxley, like his father and older brother, Vere Duncombe Loxley, was educated at Radley College in Oxfordshire, leaving there in 1905, aged 18.

Loxley followed two of his older brothers into the armed forces, receiving a Commission in 3rd (Militia) Battalion, Gloucestershire Regiment on 12th March 1906. He completed his basic training at the end of April, although the overall standard of Loxley's year group was apparently lower than the previous one, particularly in shooting. It was unusually cold in May 1906, when Loxley was formally admitted into the Battalion at their annual Tattoo.

Three months later, Loxley was arrested in Cheltenham for riding a motorcycle without the necessary licence, and the following month, at Cheltenham Petty Sessions, he was fined 10 shillings, plus 10 shillings' costs. Later that year, Loxley made another court appearance, this time giving evidence regarding the suicide of his 26-year-old friend, John Baptist Louis Anatole Eugene de Solignac, 3rd Baron Solignac, who had apparently shot himself whilst staying at Fisher's Hotel in Bond Street, London. Loxley, described by the *Gloucester Citizen* as an Army Student, told the inquest that he had spent the previous fortnight teaching de Solignac to drive in London. De Solignac had seemed very well and in good spirits throughout, but he had showed Loxley his revolver the night before he died. Loxley described going to de Solignac's room and receiving no reply had asked for the door to be unlocked. Although de Solignac was conscious when Loxley found him, he was gravely injured. Taken to University Hospital in London, and subsequently transferred to a nursing home in Devonshire Street, de Solignac died of an infection caused by the bullet wound two weeks later. It later transpired that de Solignac feared being sued over certain financial transactions he had made on the Stock Exchange, totalling around £8,000.

Possibly, because of his involvement with this scandal, Loxley resigned his Commission with the Gloucestershire Regiment soon afterwards and emigrated to Australia, setting up in business as a motor engineer in Mount Victoria, New South Wales. By April 1911 however, Loxley was back in England staying at the Rising Sun Inn in Eastgate Street, Gloucester, and described in the Census as being 'of private means'. Two years after that, he was living in Rue d'Armaillé in Paris, not far from the Arc de Triumphe, running another motor dealership selling Daimler cars. On a visit to England in June 1913, Loxley was again arrested for motoring offences, this time for driving at night without a tail light and failing to produce a driving licence when asked to do so. He apparently told the policeman that he possessed a French driving licence, but not an English one. Loxley was back in France when his case came to court and he was fined in his absence – two guineas for not producing his licence, three guineas for not having a rear light, and 19 shillings' costs.

Loxley returned to England soon after the outbreak of war, and on 20th January 1915, three weeks after his eldest brother was lost with HMS *Formidable*, he was commissioned into the Royal Naval Volunteer Reserve. With his mechanical knowledge and buccaneering approach to motoring, Roy was a natural for the Royal Naval Air Service (RNAS) Armoured Car Division.

The first British armoured cars sent to the France with the BEF were mostly standard production models fitted with some armour plate and a machine gun. These open-topped machines were soon found wanting, so in October 1914 the Admiralty formed a small committee to develop a fully armoured car armed with a machine gun in a rotating turret. The Rolls-Royce Silver Ghost chassis formed the basis of the new three-man armoured car, the first vehicles arriving at the newly formed RNAS Armoured Car Division at 48 Dover Street, near Piccadilly, that December. Crew training began immediately, and by March 1915, two squadrons were operating overseas, one in France, and the other in German South West Africa.

The following month, Loxley accompanied several armoured car squadrons to Gallipoli, but the rocky terrain, cleft by gullies and trenches, severely restricted their mobility. RNAS armoured cars did support the attack on Gully Ravine on 28th June, but they were never likely to fulfil their intended purpose of raiding behind enemy lines and within months they were transferred to the army. Loxley, meanwhile, had been evacuated from Gallipoli suffering from dysentery and was admitted to the Haslar Royal Naval Hospital in Gosport, Hampshire on 19th October 1915.

Loxley remained on the convalescent list until the following March, when he reported for duty at the White City, West London. Named after the white marble-clad pavilions built for the 1904 International Exhibition and later used for the 1908 London Olympics, the RNAS had taken over White City at the outbreak of war. Here it established an air gunnery training school, a development centre for armoured cars and armour plate, a central storage depot and a transport depot, which, as a motor engineer, was Roy's natural home.

On 10th July 1916, Loxley transferred to N°3 Wing, RNAS as its Mechanical Transport Officer. N°3 Wing formed part of a joint Anglo-French force based close to German occupied Alsace at Luxeuil-les-Bains and had recently acquired several Sopwith 1½ Strutter aircraft, which could carry up to 130lb of bombs. From its base at Luxeuil the Wing could bomb German factories around the industrial towns of Essen and Dusseldorf. Work on the new airbase had begun in June 1916, but a shortage of Sopwiths delayed the first bombing raid until 30th July, when British and French planes attacked the benzene plant at Mulheim. Loxley's promotion to Lieutenant on 5th October 1916 came as the Wing's 18 pilots and 23 planes were ready to begin regular bombing raids on German industry, but the poor weather at Luxeuil frequently kept them grounded. The French subsequently offered the use of another airfield at Ochey, some 87 miles further north and closer to the German border, which would allow the Sopwiths to attack additional German factories in the Saarland.

Captain Reginald Loxley RNAS (Source: Patrick James Coleridge Sumner)

For some reason, N°3 Wing's headquarters and maintenance elements remained at Luxeuil and consequently, as Mechanical Transport Officer, it was Roy's job to ensure that his mechanics kept the Wing's 4-ton American Peerless Lorries and other vehicles in full running order so that equipment could be easily transported between Luxeuil and Ochey. Loxley was also responsible for logging all incidents involving his vehicles that might incur a cost to the government, no matter how insignificant. For example, he advised his commander on 9th November, that a Peerless lorry towing a field kitchen to Ochey had run over a horse's leg. Having personally interviewed its owner, Loxley was able to report that the horse was unattended at the time of the accident, and consequently the truck's driver was not to blame.

From November 1916 until April 1917, N°3 Wing attacked Germany's iron and steel works, especially the blast furnaces, although the winter fogs often obscured the targets. Ochey's northerly location and unheated hangars brought problems on the ground too. Condensation often prevented the aeroplane's rotary engines from starting and in very cold weather the castor oil lubricant froze.

At the end of January 1917, operational requirements, and rivalry between the RNAS and the Royal Flying Corps, resulted in nine of the Squadron's best pilots transferring to the RFC base at Dunkirk. Two months later, a further nineteen veterans had gone, replaced by less experienced pilots, and the Wing's operational effectiveness fell until, in late March, it was disbanded and its remaining personnel transferred to the RFC. During N°3 Wing's operational life in France, it had made eighteen long- distance raids and dropped 38,617lbs of bombs on German targets. Decommissioning at Luxeuil began that May and when the last truck left on 3rd June, 317 truckloads of stores and equipment had gone to other bases, or been given to the French. The following day Roy departed Luxeuil for the RNAS depot at Wormwood Scrubs, London.

Whilst back in England, Loxley took a few weeks leave to visit his mother at her home at Little Cloisters, by Gloucester Cathedral. Returning to duty on 12th July, Loxley assumed 'T' (Transport Officer) duties for the new RNAS airfield at Vendome, west of Orleans. Chosen for its good weather, Vendome aerodrome had been hurriedly created from ploughed fields to accommodate a RNAS Flying School to train urgently needed pilots. The novices' introduction to take offs and landings was made more hazardous by the partially levelled ground and despatching trucks to recover crashed aircraft became a regular task for Loxley.

On 8th October 1917, Loxley transferred to Executive Officer Duties at Coudekerque, a RNAS bomber station near Dunkirk. Zeppelin raids on London over the past month had provoked mounting public pressure on British air services to retaliate. The RNAS quickly responded by creating 'A' Naval Squadron with ten Handley Page 0/100 bombers to intensify the bombing of German industrial targets. These 100ft wingspan aircraft, powered by two Rolls-Royce engines, flew at 79mph to deliver 2,000lb of bombs with remarkable accuracy. 'A' Naval Squadron's airfield at Coudekerque had most probably inherited much of N°3 Wing's equipment from Luxeuil and within a month the Squadron had also inherited N°3 Wing's former base at Ochey, where it joined 41st Wing to form a strategic night bombing force, later renamed the 'Independent Force'.

The Squadron shared Ochey with another night bombing unit, 100 Squadron, plus a French squadron. The Ochey airfield was laid out on a hillside facing north/ south, with the aircraft hangars, of which 'A' Naval Squadron occupied five, located on the northern and eastern extremities, but it was a depressing station. The squadron's huts were neither rainproof nor warm and obtaining temporary heating stoves required lengthy negotiation with the French. Rain soon turned the ground to mud and the squadron's heavy supply trucks frequently churned the aerodrome's single access road into a quagmire. What most upset the RNAS servicemen, however, was not the weather and the mud, but the infrequent supply of British rations that forced them to eat French food!

At 17.50 on 25th November, nine Handley Page 0/100s took off on 'A' Squadron's first raid, dropping over four tons of bombs on the Burback Works in Saarbrücken. Although the raid was deemed a success, three bombers were lost over Germany.

Thanks to Loxley, the Squadron, recently redesignated 16 Squadron RNAS, avoided another disaster in February 1918. A Handley Page 0/100 was gaining height from Ochey when several German bombers attacked the airfield. Fortunately, they inflicted little damage and the 0/100 continued on its own raid. However, when the Handley Page returned, Ochey's nervous defenders mistook it for another German raider and opened fire. It was only Loxley's intervention, leaping from his trench and shouting for the anti-aircraft gunners to cease-fire, that allowed the pilot of the 0/100 to land safely.

After further German raids, new hangars were built close to nearby woods which offered some protection from the air. The airfield's accommodation huts were also moved, and some personnel were billeted out to local villages. Nightly bombing of German targets continued whenever possible, and on the night of 24th/25th March 1918, 16 Squadron's bombers successfully completed an 8½-hour mission against Cologne's railway station and the adjacent bridge over the Rhine.

When the Royal Air Force was formed on 1st April 1918 following the merger of the RNAS and RFC, 16 Squadron became 216 Squadron RAF and Loxley was promoted to Captain. Soon afterwards, Loxley left 216 Squadron and on 9th July he joined the Department of Aircraft Production as its Adjutant under his former commander. Located in the Paris suburb of Neuilly-sur-Seine, and conveniently close to several aircraft manufacturers, the Department of Aircraft Production procured military aircraft, spare parts and other supplies, and then issued them to the RAF. It also evaluated captured German aircraft, co-ordinated the testing of new aircraft, and even developed camouflage for both aircraft and buildings. Every week, the department produced massive typed spreadsheets, detailing numbers of aircraft on order by manufacturer and aircraft despatched to the squadrons by type. In those days before computers, collating such a large amount of data required the labour of many clerks and administering them was one of Loxley's responsibilities as Adjutant.

When Loxley moved to Paris, a 'three-day fever' had been going around the Western Front for some time. Men suddenly developed the typical flu-like symptoms of chills, fever and fatigue, but could usually return to duty after a few days. However, the disease returned during early autumn of 1918, spreading rapidly in a much more severe form that killed most patients within days as their lungs filled with fluid.

Loxley fell ill in mid-October, and was admitted to the British Red

Cross Society's N°1 Hospital in the Hotel Astoria, Paris. He died of influenza-induced pneumonia on 18th October, aged 31. The Earl of Derby, the British Ambassador to France, attended Loxley's funeral on 21st October and his body was interred in the City of Paris Cemetery, Batignolles, Clichy.

In Loxley's *Times* Obituary, published on 26th October 1918, his Colonel in the RNAS paid him this tribute writing: 'He has been a most admirable officer, setting a very fine example to the other officers, and shown a magnificent spirit of devotion to duty and the welfare of the men, whom he looked after so well and who respected him so much.'

Gunner 101589 George Thomas Keen
Royal Garrison Artillery

9th February 1919

George Thomas Keen was born in January 1879, the first son of Eliza and Joseph Keen, and later christened at St Peter's Church, Berkhamsted. When George was two years old, the family were living in the Crooked Billet at Gossoms End with George described on the census form as a 'scholar'. His father, Joseph, was a farm labourer, but worked his way up to become a dairyman.

After leaving school, George became a gardener and through his horticultural connections, met Sarah Jane Sterne the second daughter of Harry Sterne, another local gardener. They were married on 15th February 1901 at St Mary's, Northchurch. The newlyweds moved to George Street in Berkhamsted, which was then still part of Northchurch Parish. Their first child, George Henry Keen, was born nine months later. George and Sarah went on to raise four further children, including twin girls. George Thomas obtained employment as a gardener at Lagley House in Northchurch, and the family later moved to 9 Swing Gate Lane in Berkhamsted. George became an active member of St Mary's, Northchurch, where alongside John Randall, he was a chorister and a bellringer.

With six children to support, George was prepared to look further afield for new opportunities and so by 1911 the Keens had moved to Cromer, Norfolk, where George probably worked as a gardener at one of the local large houses. Three years later, George moved again, this time to a large, late eighteenth century mansion called Leasam House in Rye, East Sussex, where he became head gardener to the famous soprano, Lady Maud Warrender. George and his family moved into Leasam Lodge and were living there in August 1914 when war broke out. Their youngest child, Kenneth, was born at Leasam Lodge two years later.

George continued working at Leasam House until, aged 37, he was called up under the Military Service Act and enlisted on 3rd July 1916. Passing his medical examination as 'fit for general service', George expressed a preference to serve with the Army Service Corps, but was sent instead to the Royal Garrison Artillery, which was responsible for the very heaviest guns and particularly Britain's coastal defence batteries.

George spent his war at Newhaven Fort, the Headquarters of N°10 Fire Command, which controlled the gun batteries along the Sussex coast, including its own battery of Mark 7 six-inch guns, which had a range of almost eight miles. Newhaven was an important link in the BEF's supply chain and a naval base for destroyers, but life for the Fort's garrison was relatively uneventful. The Royal Navy's command of British waters went unchallenged after the Battle of Jutland, so the younger, fitter gunners were gradually transferred to the Western Front. By 1918, Newhaven Fort was mostly garrisoned by troops of low medical grade or, as in George's case, men near the upper age limit for military service.

Unfortunately, George contracted bronchial tuberculosis near the war's end and, despite receiving treatment at N°2 Eastern General Military Hospital in Brighton he died on 2nd February 1919. George's body was returned to Northchurch for a funeral with full military honours at St Mary's the following Friday. Men of the Inns of Court Officer Training Corps, who were based in Berkhamsted, bore his coffin from the church and up New Road and over the canal bridge to the cemetery. Here, after the committal, they fired a graveside salute.

George is not named on Northchurch's War Memorial - perhaps his family were content with his Imperial War Graves headstone in the New Road cemetery, but he is named on Berkhamsted's memorial cross, albeit incorrectly, as C T Keen.

Lance Corporal James CHANDLER
Military Police Corps

26th February 1919

James Chandler, known as Jim, was born around April 1894 in the small Hampshire brewery town of Alton. Jim's father, George, came from Paddington in London and working as a gardener, he moved from estate to estate around the country. George Chandler had met and married Fanny, a girl from Farnham, Surrey, around 1873. Over their long-married life, Fanny bore George 10 children, although, sadly, one died in infancy. Their first son was born in Battersea, and then they had two daughters while living in Ireland. After returning to England, they produced two more sons and another two daughters in Farnham before moving to Alton. George and Fanny later lived in Bagshot, Surrey, the birthplace of Jim's younger brother, Sam, before finally settling at 166 High Street, Northchurch, a few years later.

At the age of 16, Jim was working locally as a domestic gardener, perhaps alongside his father and brother, George junior. Later, Jim decided on a career with the Police and, being a well-built man standing 6ft 1½inches tall, and possessing perfect eyesight, he had no difficulty in joining the force. Rather than join the Hertfordshire Constabulary however, Jim chose the Luton Borough Police, then an independent force, famous for wearing lightweight summer helmets made locally from plaited straw. Jim Chandler was appointed a Police Constable on 11th September 1914, earning £1 5s 8d per week. At that time, there were 52 officers in the Luton Force, 42 of them Constables. Of these three were Army Reservists and when war broke out, they immediately returned to their regiments. Another 13 constables joined up later, including Jim, although they all remained officers of the Luton Police Force.

Jim was living at 7 Russell Street,

Lance Corporal James Chandler
(Source: Clive Blofield)

Luton when he enlisted on 10th September 1915. After his basic training, Jim was sent to 3/1 Eastern Mounted Brigade Field Ambulance, the training element of a Royal Army Medical Corps (RAMC) Territorial Force unit, which mainly recruited from the Luton area. Jim was then posted to Egypt, arriving on 30th November 1915, just in time to qualify for the 1915 Star. On 5th January 1916, Jim was taken on to the strength of 1/1 Eastern Mounted Brigade Field Ambulance (TF) at Sidi Bishr. He not been there long however, before he developed a high fever, and ten days after his arrival at Sidi Bishr, Jim was admitted to 17 General Hospital at Alexandria.

Jim had all the symptoms of enteric fever, and arrangements were made to invalid him home to recover. The Hospital Ship *Neuralia* took Jim to Naples, where he boarded the *Aquitania* for the voyage home; in fact, he landed in Scotland. Thirteen days after Jim left Egypt, a doctor at the Deaconess Hospital in Edinburgh recorded that he no longer displayed symptoms of Enteric Fever but Jim remained at the hospital for two weeks of further treatment.

Jim remained on 'Home Service' with the Territorial RAMC on 1/6d per day until in late November he was transferred to the New Army RAMC, but retaining his Territorial rate of pay. Three days after New Year 1917, Jim embarked at Southampton to join the BEF, arriving at Rouen two days later. On the 9th January, Jim joined 139th Field Ambulance, one of three mobile front line medical units serving 41st Division, near Ypres.

Each Field Ambulance was responsible for handling the sick and wounded of its Brigade, 139th Field Ambulance being attached to 124th Infantry Brigade. Having received first aid from their battalion's Regimental Aid Post, battlefield casualties were passed to stretcher-bearers at a Bearer Relay Post, where the Field Ambulances took over. Stretcher cases were taken quickly to an Advanced Dressing Station then moved on to the Division's Main Dressing Station. There the responsibility of the Field Ambulances ended, the next link in the evacuation chain being the Casualty Clearing Stations. Each Field Ambulance possessed ten horse-drawn ambulances and seven motor ambulances as well as providing a separate station for walking cases. Field Ambulances had a theoretical capacity of 150 casualties, but they were often overwhelmed, especially during the height of a battle. At each stage, men strong enough to be moved were sent on immediately and only such treatment necessary to allow a man to be moved was given.

As the war progressed, the process of removing wounded soldiers from the front line became very efficient. The report on the effectiveness of 139th Field Ambulance following a set-piece attack by 124th Infantry Brigade on the night of 24th/25th February 1917, when Jim was present, examined the entire process on a minute-by-minute basis. That night, they handled 141 casualties, of whom 63 were 'lying cases'. Of the injuries seen, half were shell wounds, the vast majority of which related to shrapnel. Most of the lightly wounded 'walking cases' would resume front line duties soon afterwards. Out of the line, Field Ambulances dealt with sickness and accident cases and were responsible for sanitary arrangements.

Jim left the RAMC on 2nd May 1917, transferring to the Foot Branch of the Corps of Military Police, becoming a 'Redcap', after the coloured cap cover Military Police wore. Initially attached to Second Army, Jim was soon afterwards appointed acting Lance Corporal and sent to First Army at Armentières.

The Military Police maintained law and order among the troops, arresting deserters, looters, soldiers without passes and those committing offences of any kind. In case of emergency, Redcaps could also demand the assistance of troops in the vicinity to supply guards, sentries or patrols. They patrolled areas deemed out of bounds to soldiers and also had responsibility for collecting battlefield stragglers and anyone retreating without orders, which made them extremely unpopular. However, traffic control was probably their most important role. It was Redcaps who ensured that the complex movements of the whole Army Corps ran smoothly in all weathers, often under fire.

Armentières was an important communications centre and in the build-up to the Third Battle of Ypres in 1917 it attracted a lot of German shellfire. On 29th July, Jim was one of several men injured by gas shells and was initially treated at 54 Casualty Clearing Station. His injuries were severe enough for him to be transferred to a St John's Ambulance Brigade Hospital at Étaples and then invalided home for a second time.

Jim made a full recovery and used his time back in Northchurch well. On three successive November Sundays, banns were read for James Chandler, bachelor of Northchurch Parish, and Elizabeth Sarah Baxter, spinster of Sunnyside Parish, Berkhamsted. Elizabeth was the daughter of a Railway Ticket Inspector and lived in George Street and worked at the clothing factory, known as the Mantle Factory, in Lower Kings Road. Jim and Elizabeth were married at Sunnyside church on 24th November 1917, and the newlyweds made their home at 140 George Street.

Jim returned to France on 6th February 1918, and a couple of weeks later transferred to the Provost Martial, Fifth Army. The Provost Martial directed the work of the Military Police rather like a Chief Superintendent. The following month Fifth Army absorbed the full force of Operation MICHAEL. Three months later, probably exhausted, Jim was placed under the Provost Martial, Fourth Army.

Ludendorff's Peace Offensive, which had stretched, but failed to break, the Allied line, finally ground to a halt on 18th July 1918 and the French immediately counter attacked. With their best men used up and their supplies exhausted, the Imperial German Army reeled back, never to advance again. Meanwhile, with Jim's assistance, Fourth Army prepared to launch a powerful surprise tank attack. On 8th August, Fourth Army broke through the German lines, shattering six divisions and driving the enemy back nine miles in one day. Ludendorff despaired and later told his government that the discipline of the German Army could no longer be guaranteed. Faced with the Allies' relentless, co-ordinated attacks in the West, collapsing morale in the German Army, growing unrest at home provoked by the Allied blockade and fearing a Bolshevik revolution, the Kaiser appointed a more democratic government which, on 4th October, requested negotiations for an armistice based on proposals put forward by the American President, Woodrow Wilson.

Ludendorff was ordered to resign on 27th October after a proclamation he made against the government was leaked. Germany's ally, Turkey, capitulated three days later and was quickly followed by Austria-Hungary. German sailors at the naval ports of Kiel, Wilhelmshaven and Lübeck then mutinied and Bolshevik Soviets began to appear in German towns and cities.

On 8th November 1918, a German delegation arrived at General Foch's headquarters in the Forest of Compiègne, to request terms for the armistice. The following day Kaiser Wilhelm II of Germany abdicated and took refuge in neutral Holland. Representatives of the German Government signed the Armistice Document a few minutes after 05.00 on 11th November, to take effect six hours later. At 11.00 on Monday, 11th November 1918, the guns fell silent; the 'War to end War' was over.

With Germany defeated, concern grew among the Allies that she would quickly follow Russia into anarchy and revolution. In December 1918, Jim transferred to Second Army, which was about to enter the Rhineland with the army of occupation. Under the terms of the Armistice, Allied troops would occupy an area on the left bank of the Rhine, with three large bridgeheads on the right bank opposite Cologne, Koblenz and Mainz. British troops were to occupy the area around Cologne, Aachen and Bonn. Cologne's city government under its mayor and future German statesman, Konrad Adenauer, feared a wave of lawlessness following the departure of German troops and urged the Second Army to enter the city as quickly as possible to maintain order. The first British soldier to cross the Rhine and enter Cologne was actually a Military Police motorcyclist, closely followed by six armoured cars, which took up position before the Town Hall.

After a spell of leave, Jim returned to duty with Second Army on 27th January 1919. Two weeks later, on 13th February, he fell ill with influenza. Admitted to a Casualty Clearing Station in Cologne, his condition worsened, and on 26th February, he died of influenza and bronchopneumonia. Jim is buried with eighteen other Redcaps in the

Cologne Southern Cemetery, three miles south of the city's famous cathedral. More than 2,500 British soldiers are buried there, most of them victims of influenza.

Elizabeth Chandler received Jim's personal effects from the Depot at Aldershot on 10th July 1919. She was awarded a pension of 13s 9d a week, with effect from 8th September 1919, two days before Jim's military service had been due to end. She requested the text, 'Thy Will be done', for Jim's headstone.

Jim's name appears on the Northchurch War Memorial as a member of the RAMC rather than the Military Police Corps, perhaps because Redcaps had an undeservedly bad reputation. The working classes generally disliked the police, frequently carrying that antipathy into military life, which could explain why Jim joined the Luton Constabulary, instead of his local Hertfordshire Force.

The Return of Peace

Cheering villagers gathered in the streets of Northchurch, whilst factory whistles shrieked from East's Timber Yard in Gossoms End and Berkhamsted Waterworks, to celebrate the news that Germany had ceased hostilities at 11 o'clock on the morning of 11th November 1918. Among the congregations that filled St Mary's Church for quickly arranged Services of Thanksgiving, everyone felt great relief tinged with apprehension. An armistice was merely a cease-fire until replaced by a signed Peace Treaty, so Allied Armies had to remain ready to enforce German co-operation. Britain's Imperial commitments were also pressing, trouble was brewing again in Ireland and on India's North-West Frontier, while territories confiscated from the Central Powers in Africa and elsewhere needed administering. The aftermath of war could yet claim the lives of more Northchurch men.

By the time of the Armistice, some Northchurch servicemen had already returned home and been reunited with their families. In February 1915, twenty-year-old Private William Mustill from Cow Roast Lock, serving with 1st Battalion, Northumberland Fusiliers, returned to England. He had lost an eye and suffered a severe wound to his arm during the First Battle of Ypres. Captured by the Germans on 8th November 1914 and sent to a hospital in Germany where his wounds were treated, he was among 150 British Prisoners of War swapped for German POWs the following February. After his arrival in Folkestone William was transferred to a hospital in London to recover. Similarly, Lance Corporal Arthur Hosier was among 49 officers and 367 men that the Red Cross returned to Britain in September 1917. A regular soldier since 1911, Arthur crossed to France with 2nd Bedfordshire Regiment and was also wounded and captured during 1915. After treatment, the Germans sent him to a Prisoner of War camp at Stendahl, about sixty miles west of Berlin. The Red Cross later arranged for a number of British POWs, including Arthur, to be repatriated via Switzerland and discharged from the Army. After undergoing a medical examination in London, Arthur returned home to Northchurch.

Other servicemen had returned home before the war's end having been discharged owing to wounds, sickness or injury. Charles Geary, Walter and Frederick Geary's younger brother, was sent home having developed epilepsy six months after enlisting as an Army Service Corps driver in early May 1915. At about the same time, the Army released Archibald Honor, a butcher from Alma Road, owing to sickness. Both men received the Silver War Badge in public recognition of their service.

Returning soldiers outside the Pheasant Pub in Northchurch
(Source: The Northchurch Society)

During the final year of the war, the number of men in Hertfordshire entitled to wear the Silver War Badge trebled to 3,300, about half of them discharged through sickness or disease. Frank Garner's younger brother, Arthur, enlisted in 1914 and went to Egypt with the Army Service Corps the following year. He was discharged from the Army after contracting malaria in Palestine. Arthur was able to work as a council labourer between bouts of fever, but he died of malaria at his Bell Lane home in June 1919.

Horace Bruton, who enlisted with the ASC at Watford in December 1914, had better fortune. He was serving in France in October 1918, when he fell ill with Spanish flu. Luckily, Horace made a full recovery and was discharged from hospital in England, and the Army, on 16th January 1919. Returning home to Dropshot Cottage, he resumed his employment as a driver and gardener for the Barnett family at Northchurch Hall.

Alfred Jones, a 48-year-old master builder and Territorial from Northchurch High Street, was also discharged in January 1919. He enlisted with the Royal Engineers at Watford in November 1914, and served in France until a German gas attack injured his lungs. Alfred was treated for loss of breath at the Northampton War Hospital, near Duston, before being sent home.

Four years of hostilities officially ended after long and complex negotiations led to the signing of the Treaty of Versailles on 28th June 1919. On Saturday 19th July, all of Britain held Peace Celebrations. At eight o'clock, the bells of St Mary's Church heralded the start of festivities in Northchurch. Some 70 current or former servicemen sat down for a communal meal of beef, pork, mutton, and vegetables, washed down with various drinks provided by members of the parish. A children's sports event began at two o'clock in Durrant's Meadow. Traditional games, with prizes for the winners, and a jazz band made up of local musicians entertained the crowd. A similar event for adults that evening included a tug of war contest and a cricket match between married and single men; the married men won.

Britain's armed forces were now five-and-a-half million men strong and demobilising that many uniformed personnel could not be achieved quickly. Aside from the practicalities of organising pay, clothing, transport, etc., a small army of clerks was required to hand-process their discharge papers. Then there was the issue of employment in a bankrupt economy utterly transformed by the war's demands. The authorities had already developed a schedule for demobilisation that was as fair as possible, albeit with an eye on the national interest. Men still serving under pre-war terms of enlistment and whose discharge was delayed by the war were demobilised immediately, followed by men from key industries such as mining and agriculture. The rest, who had enlisted 'For the Duration', would be released in order of enlistment, early volunteers first and the conscripts of 1918 last.

That was the theory, but some, like Private James Whent, of the Army Service Corps who had attested under the 'Derby Scheme' in December 1915, aged 39, were lucky. He worked as a chauffeur for William Tuke, who leased Norcott Court from the Loxley family, until his call-up papers arrived in mid-1916. James was an ASC driver until being demobilised on 16th January 1919, shortly before Driver Frederick Fenn from Aldbury. Frederick, a thirty-four-year-old horseman, was conscripted into the Royal Horse Artillery in March 1917, and served in France and Italy before returning home to Dudswell Farm in February 1919.

When Frank Alcock's younger brother, John Forster Alcock junior, was commissioned into 6th Bedfordshires in November 1914, he had been reading Mechanical Engineering at Clare College, Cambridge for only a month. Keen to become an aviator, he gained his wings at the Military School, Castle Bromwich in September 1915, flying a Maurice Farman biplane. Having trained as an Observer in Egypt the following year, John became a Flying officer and Assistant Instructor in the Royal Flying Corps. In August 1918, John was briefly again in the Middle East before returning to England that November joining the 'unemployed list' in January 1919. After demobilisation, John returned to Clare College to begin an illustrious engineering career specialising in heat exchangers for internal combustion engines, which would earn him an OBE and numerous British and international patents.

Former gardener Private Frederick Carter of New Road, Northchurch, became a genuine Kitchener volunteer on 20th August 1914, aged 19. Frederick survived the bitter fighting with the 7th Norfolk Regiment at Loos, the Somme, Arras, Cambrai, Amiens and the 'Final Advance' to receive his discharge papers at the end of March 1919. A week or so later, Private Edwin Dell, the stepbrother of Walter and Albert Dell, returned to Northchurch. Although considered too short for the English Regiments, Edwin persisted and on 26th July 1915, he enlisted with the Highland Light Infantry. Serving on the Western Front, Edwin suffered a bullet wound to his leg that left him with a permanent limp. Despite this, Edwin became a postman after the war, and served as a Northchurch Parish Councillor, a governor at the village school, a churchwarden at St Mary's and the valued leader of the Northchurch Scout Troop.

Private Daniel Diplock had to wait until 2nd December 1919 to be demobilised. Daniel was an assistant gardener on Major-General Sir Charles Frederick Hadden's estate and was eager to follow Rossway's Estate Manager and Head Gardener into the Royal Garrison Artillery. In early January 1917, the thirty-three-year-old reported to the Recruiting Officer at Watford, but despite having a reference from his employer, Daniel spent the war in the infantry. He went to Egypt with the Bedfordshire Regiment, before transferring to the Suffolk Regiment in April 1919 and finally the Royal Welsh Fusiliers that August.

The following December, Sergeant Fred Hales of Northchurch High Street returned from Egypt. An artisan labourer from a long-established Northchurch family, Fred attested under the Derby Scheme at Watford in November 1915. He was called up in April 1917 to serve with the Northamptonshire Regiment in Egypt and Palestine where, in November 1917, he received a gunshot wound to the thigh.

The village policeman, PC George Cooling, was one of the last Northchurch men to return. George attested as a married man in December 1915, but was not called-up until the height of Germany's Spring Offensives in April 1918 and served at home with the Grenadier Guards. George transferred to the Reserves in January 1919, and was finally demobilised in March 1920.

Women such as Lizzie Curl, the nineteen-year-old younger sister of Alfred and George Curl, also served their country in uniform. After leaving school aged fourteen, Lizzie spent two years doing secretarial work. After hearing of Alfred's death, Lizzie went to London in April 1918 to join the Women's Army Auxiliary Corps. She was initially posted to Shortlands, near Beckenham, Kent, then extended her initial term of service and transferred to Hazeley Down Camp near Winchester in August 1919. Following her discharge from the Corps in January 1920, Lizzie returned to her parents' home in Orchard End.

Apart from the returning soldiers, many of whom had been injured or traumatised as a result of the war, their families at home were also to suffer for many years. Across the country families experienced the loss of one son, and sadly some like the Dells, Curls, Dyers, Gearys, Loxleys, Morgans and Teagles lost two or more.

Then were the widows who had only been married a matter of weeks, or sometimes days, before their husbands went off to war. A number of wives had children who would grow up never knowing their father. Some, like Walter Welling's wife, Kate, would soon remarry, although as a result of the war the numbers of 'eligible' men were drastically reduced. Others, like Selena Shrimpton, would remain widows for the rest of their lives. Then there were the girls who had got engaged just before their fiancés went off to war, in the hope that they would return safely. Edith Curl, the oldest sister in the Curl family, was one of these and was engaged to George Richard Goodege, a territorial soldier with 1/9th Middlesex Regiment. Known as Dick to his family and friends in Berkhamsted, he was one of 50 soldiers drafted to the Indian Expeditionary Force D in 1915 to fight the Turks in Mesopotamia. Dick Goodege was killed at the Battle of Ctesiphon in November the same year during the ill-fated attempt to capture Bagdad. Following Dick's death Edith remained a spinster for the rest of her life until she died in 1979, aged 89.

Although some ex-servicemen resumed their former jobs in Northchurch, others faced the uncertainty of unemployment. Before the war, John Randall's father, William, had provided recreation facilities for working men in Northchurch by opening up a room in his home in New Road. The Church Room across the road later became a temporary club, accepting soldiers billeted locally as guest members. Demobilisation created the need for a more permanent space where ex-servicemen could meet for recreation and ease themselves back into normal, civilian life. In 1922, thanks largely to William Tuke of Norcott Court, funds were raised for the construction of the Northchurch Working Men's Club in the school grounds. The club's membership later extended to all men from the village, but by the early 1960s, declining membership and pressure to extend the village school forced its eventual closure.

In all previous wars, the bodies of wealthy or celebrated officers were often brought home, whilst ordinary soldiers shared anonymous mass-graves. In 1914, soldiers generally received individual burial in marked graves, but privately purchased headstones soon appeared and influential families sometimes arranged to bring their sons' bodies' home. However, growing public disquiet at this unequal treatment of Britain's citizen soldiers came to a head with the revelation that in April 1915, soldiers had risked their lives under fire to exhume the remains of Lt. WGC Gladstone, an Eton educated Liberal MP, for reburial on his family estate. Noting that repatriating bodies also diverted transport capacity urgently needed by wounded men, the Government decreed that all troops serving overseas must be buried where they died, without exception. The credit for furthering this new principal of equal treatment for the fallen belongs to one man, Fabian Arthur Goulstone Ware.

Fabian Ware, senior educationalist in England and South Africa, Tory Editor of the Morning Post and a director of Rio Tinto Ltd, was rejected by the British Army in 1914 because at the age of 45, he was considered too old. Instead, Ware crossed to France in command of a British Red Cross Society mobile unit. He diligently noted the details of every man that died of wounds, but found official arrangements for recording war graves haphazard and uncoordinated. Ware campaigned for a single organisation to mark and record the graves of all dead soldiers until in 1915, the Army created the Graves Registration Commission, putting Ware in charge with the rank of Major-General. In 1917, Ware's department gained its independence by Royal Charter, to become the Imperial War Graves Commission, later renamed the *Commonwealth* War Graves Commission, with the Prince of Wales as President and Ware serving as Vice-Chairman.

The Commission's guiding principles were that the Empire's war dead should be individually commemorated by name on a permanent memorial or a headstone of uniform design, regardless of rank, race or religion. To preserve the comradeship forged in battle, their bodies should rest together, as far as possible, in dedicated cemeteries. The Commission completed three experimental cemeteries in 1921, deciding that Forceville, near Albert, would become the model for subsequent British war cemeteries. Garden designer Gertrude Jekyll's plan for Forceville, with flowers growing at the foot of each headstone set in uniform rows separated by grass paths and lawns and enclosed by a surrounding wall, achieved a peaceful, English garden feel. Each cemetery would contain both Sir Reginald Blomfield's *Cross of Sacrifice* and the altar-like *Stone of Remembrance*, designed by Sir Edwin Lutyens, which bore text from Ecclesiastes 44:14 selected by Rudyard Kipling, 'Their Name Liveth for Evermore'. Through the 1920s, the Commission established over 2,400 war cemeteries in France and Belgium with others created in Egypt, Palestine, Macedonia, Mesopotamia, and on the Gallipoli Peninsula.

The standard serviceman's rectangular headstone with a rounded top was usually fashioned from white Portland stone and engraved with his name, rank, number, unit, date of death and age if known. Each headstone bore an appropriate religious symbol, and the Service, Corps or Regimental badge or, for Dominion troops, their national military emblem. Early headstones were hand engraved by local masons, taking up to a week to complete, but machines were soon designed to streamline the process. Headstones for men buried in the area around Berkhamsted were ordered from Newman & Harper, 53 Buckingham Street, Aylesbury, who also made the war memorial in Aston Clinton.

There were, in fact, two standard layouts for headstones; one placed the military badge above a slender cross with slightly flared ends, while the second superimposed the badge on a bold, plain cross. All regiments and corps of the Empire were shown the alternative designs and twenty of them, including the Bedfordshire Regiment and the Royal Artillery, opted for the broad cross, which suited the design of their badges. Both Gunner Keen's headstone in New Road cemetery and William Sear's in the Baptist Burial Ground in Bell Lane are the broad cross type. The requisition for William Sear's headstone, addressed to Newman & Harper, is date-stamped July 1930.

Families could choose a personal inscription of up to 66 letters to be engraved at the bottom of their loved one's headstone. They varied widely, Captain Vere Loxley's headstone simply says, 'In Peace', while James Delderfield's family requested, 'Peace Perfect Peace, With Loved Ones Far Away, Loving Wife and Mother'. The Teagle family chose, 'Pilot Me On', for Arthur and, 'Rock of Ages Cleft for Me', for Thomas, but Gunner Keen's headstone in Northchurch reads movingly, 'Still Missed'.

Where possible, soldiers were quickly buried following battles, often side-by-side with linked arms, to be recovered later for individual re-burial, but high explosive shells respected neither the living nor the dead. For the thousands of men with no known grave, the Commission built magnificent 'Memorials to the Missing', beginning with Blomfield's Menin Gate Memorial, unveiled at Ypres in July 1927. Sir Herbert Baker's Tyne Cot Memorial and Sir John Burnet's Helles Memorial on Gallipoli soon followed. Perhaps the most impressive is Sir Edwin Lutyens' Memorial atop Thiepval Ridge, unveiled by the Prince of Wales on 1st August 1932, which symbolises the Anglo-French Alliance throughout the war, but especially on the Somme. Although Northchurch men are commemorated on each of these memorials, some of them may have been found, but not identified, and so rest beneath headstones marked, 'A Soldier of the Great War + Known unto God'.

Sir Edwin Lutyens' Memorial at Thiepval (Source: Richard North)

Northchurch people have always identified more closely with their ecclesiastical parish than with civic boundaries in spite of, or perhaps because of, Berkhamsted Urban District Council's take-over of Gossom's End. Since their parish church was the focal point for villagers' public and private mourning, it was natural during the war to create a 'War Shrine' in St Mary's Church, which villagers regularly decorated with fresh cut flowers. A Roll of Honour attached to the War Shrine celebrated the 220 parishioners serving in the Army or Navy by September 1917, of whom twenty had already died. Private memorials were also installed near the War Shrine, such as the brass plaque, dating from 1916, commemorating Major Hubert Thelwall and his two brothers and another on the same wall dedicated to Captain Nigel Hadden. A marble tablet near the organ remembered Rifleman Charles Ross, while in the South Transept a stone tablet was later installed to commemorate the three Loxley brothers. As the war ended however, thoughts turned to a permanent memorial for the village.

In late 1918, prominent figures in Berkhamsted proposed turning an existing town centre improvement plan for 'the Wilderness' area close to St Peter's Church into a district war memorial that might include a cottage hospital, housing for ex-servicemen and other facilities. The Inns of Court Officer Training Corps, who were based in Berkhamsted, and local parishes including Northchurch, were invited to participate and in January, Mr Edward Greene, the novelist Graham Greene's uncle, publicly offered £4,000 of the estimated £9,000 required to meet the cost. Whilst fulfilling Berkhamsted Urban District Council's desire to recognise the area's substantial contribution to victory, to many people such a grand scheme felt distant and impersonal. For family and friends who could afford neither private memorials, nor visits overseas, a public memorial by their local church represented the best substitute for the graves they could not visit.

The Rector of St Peter's and the Vicar of St Michael's Sunnyside welcomed Berkhamsted's scheme, but still continued with their own memorials, as did the Inns of Court. Northchurch also demurred and on 15th February 1919 a public meeting took place under the chairmanship of Major General Sir Charles Hadden, who had himself lost a son during the war, to discuss its own memorial. After discussing proposals that included a new Village Institute, a memorial cross, a lych-gate for the churchyard, a new pulpit and a stained-glass window for St Mary's, the meeting decided on a memorial cross in the churchyard, with any excess funds going towards a pulpit or a stained-glass window. A 'rather large' committee was appointed to settle the details. Comprehensive official lists of the war dead did not yet exist, so war memorial committees generally started with published Rolls of Honour before inviting families and friends to put names forward for inclusion. Families forwarding names for inclusion on the memorial were apparently asked for a nominal donation towards the costs involved. There were often omissions, but also duplication among men connected to more than one Parish.

The first memorial in the Berkhamsted area to be unveiled was Sunnyside's cross, in St Michael's Churchyard on Saturday 15th November

1919. Over 1,000 people attended the unveiling of the Memorial Tablet inside St. Peter's church, on 30th January 1920, which names many Northchurch men. The Hertshires' Padre, Reverend AE Opham MC who went to war in 1914 with Private Lionel Morgan, delivered the address. Then, at a meeting on Thursday 19th February, it was announced that owing to insufficient funds, 'Mr Greene's scheme' would be abandoned and all subscriptions returned.

Northchurch meanwhile, had raised the necessary funds for its own village memorial. On the wet and wintry afternoon of Saturday 6th March 1920, the service of dedication took place in St Mary's Church for the new War Memorial erected in the churchyard. The large Celtic memorial cross built by Arthur Martin of Frederick Martin and Son, 12 Chapel Street, Berkhamsted stood proudly on a four-sided, sloping base in the churchyard. The dedication read 'To the Glory of God and in memory of Northchurch men who gave their lives for King and Country 1914 – 1919'. The names and regiments of forty-six men from Northchurch who had died appeared on the side panels, the rear panel remaining blank.

The original Northurch War Memorial (Source: Richard North)

For the Unveiling and Dedication Service the front pews of the central aisle in the church were reserved for the relatives of those commemorated on the memorial, many of them holding wreaths to place around it after the unveiling ceremony. Behind sat discharged servicemen from the village and airmen and trumpeters of the Royal Air Force, while the remaining pews were filled with parishioners. The service opened with the hymn *Soldiers Who Are Christ's Below*, followed by prayers and the 23rd Psalm. Reverend GH Siddons, a former Rector of Northchurch, gave the address.

The congregation then went in procession through the churchyard to the War Memorial Cross, covered by the White Ensign that King George V had presented to St Mary's when he was Prince of Wales and its Patron. Before the packed churchyard, and an even larger crowd watching from the High Street, Rear Admiral Sir Lionel Halsey, the Comptroller and Treasurer to the Prince of Wales, unveiled the Cross. The Rector, Reverend RH Pope, read the Prayer of Dedication, then the RAF trumpeters sounded the *Last Post* and the assembled villagers sang the hymn, *On the Resurrection Morning* followed by the sounding of *Reveille* and the National Anthem. As Reverend Pope intoned the blessing, a new, replacement White Ensign, presented by the current Prince of Wales, flew proudly from the church tower. More money than was needed for the Memorial Cross had been raised by the village and so almost exactly a year later, at 15.30 on Sunday 13th March 1921, another Unveiling and Dedication Service was held at St Mary's. Now set towards the back of the North aisle was a newly installed stone plaque, engraved with the names of the 46 men who appeared on the Memorial Cross. Above it, a new stained-glass window depicting St Michael and St George the Martyr gave light. Made by Kempe & Co Ltd, with their golden wheat sheave emblem in one corner, it read: 'To the Glory of God and In Memory of Those Who Gave Their Lives in The Great War 1914 – 1919 This Window is dedicated'.

Northchurch has another, lesser-known war memorial, which can be found in the entrance porch of Northchurch Baptist Church, formerly the Baptist Chapel, in the High Street. In February 1920, the Parish Council had offered the surplus from its Peace Celebration Fund to the Chapel for a memorial tablet. The offer was gladly accepted and an order placed with Martin and Son. The Tablet was unveiled during a simple memorial service on Sunday, 6th June 1920. Beneath a small Cross, a dedication to six men who were associated with the chapel or its Sunday school reads: 'In Loving Memory of the Following Men Who Fell in the Great War 1914-1918', and their names; Charles Carter, Arthur Garner, Albert

The War Memorial Plaque at Northchurch Baptist Church (Source: Richard North)

Rolfe, Thomas Fantham, Walter Purton and William Sear, followed by the words, 'Faithful Unto Death'.

On 9th October 1921, Berkhamsted finally unveiled its War Memorial Cross, designed by Charles Quennell, FRIBA, at the top of Water Lane by the One Bell pub. Arthur Martin fashioned it from Darley Dale Sandstone and engraved 185 names on the octagonal base, including twelve from Northchurch - Joseph Aldridge, George Davis, James Delderfield, Joseph Dyer, Alfred Dwight, James Garment, George Keen (now incorrectly carved *C T Keen*), Charles Mashford, Harold Shrimpton, Charles Talbot, Hubert Thelwall and Walter Welling, (misspelt as *Thelwell* and *Willing*). These errors appeared in 1952 when the Memorial Cross was relocated to its current position by St Peter's church following building works in the town centre with the names being re-engraved onto new panels. The original Calvary was also replaced by a simple Greek cross as a consequence of vandalism.

The dedication of the Berkhamsted War Memorial, October 1921
(Source: Richard North)

Part 2
1939 – 1948

An Imperfect Peace

The men who volunteered for the First World War believed they were fighting the War to end War, but it was not to be. France pointedly held the signing of the Treaty of Versailles in the Hall of Mirrors, where Chancellor Otto von Bismarck had proclaimed the German Empire in 1871, after defeating France in the Franco-Prussian War. Just as Bismarck intended to reduce French dominance in Europe, so France intended to prevent Germany from threatening European peace again. However, even with Allied armies on German soil and threatened with revolution and starvation, the German government was unrepentant, rejecting the Draft Treaty presented on 7th May 1919 and refusing to accept responsibility for attacking Belgium and France. Only when the exasperated Allies threatened to resume hostilities did Germany finally accept the Treaty as written, including the so-called 'War Guilt' clauses, and signed it.

Although the Treaty's draconian restrictions on Germany's armed forces and munitions industries chimed with anti-war sentiments, the substantial reparation payments demanded by France remain controversial. However, considering that during the years between 1914 and 1918, Germany had occupied French mining and industrial districts and employed French resources, including forced civilian labour, to produce armaments that destroyed French homes and killed French citizens, paying back some of that wealth to help France rebuild is not so unreasonable.

Throughout the 1920s and 1930s however, Germany successfully used distorted evidence to persuade international opinion that the Great War had really been a horrible accident that nobody could have prevented. The War Guilt Clauses, territory lost to Poland, reparations to France and the fantasy that the undefeated German Army was stabbed in the back by its own politicians, were exploited by Adolf Hitler and his National Socialist (Nazi) Party in the 1920s and 1930s to gain power and threaten European peace once more.

Tension increased across Europe following the Nazi Party's rise to power in 1933. Its subsequent expansionist and rearmament policies led many to look to appeasement as the way to avoid another damaging war. Others saw no alternative to another war, or at least some form of military action. On 1st September 1939, German forces launched an unprovoked invasion of Poland.

Two days later, at 11.15, the Prime Minister, Neville Chamberlain, announced to the British nation:

'This morning the British Ambassador in Berlin handed the German Government a final Note stating that, unless we heard from them by 11 o'clock that they were prepared at once to withdraw their troops from Poland, a state of war would exist between us.

I have to tell you now that no such undertaking has been received, and that consequently this country is at war with Germany....'

By 11th October, 158,000 men of the Second BEF had been transported to France.

2nd Lieutenant Charles Arthur BLACKWELL
2nd Battalion, Coldstream Guards

1st June 1940

Charles Arthur Blackwell was born in Berkhamsted on 30th April 1917 into a family with strong food industry connections. In 1829, Charles' paternal great-great grandfather, Thomas Blackwell, together with his friend Edmund Crosse, bought out the food processing company of West and Wyatt, renaming it Crosse and Blackwell. The two partners expanded the business by adding additional products to their range and within two years, they had obtained their first Royal Appointment.

In 1861, the Blackwell family were living in Harrow Weald, with Thomas Blackwell and his eldest son, Thomas Francis Blackwell, both described as 'oilmen', presumably associated with the production of cooking oils. Thomas Francis Blackwell had married Emily Stevens two years before and by 1881, they had five children.

Crosse and Blackwell expanded considerably during the mid-Victorian period, buying up numerous firms and opening new warehouses across London and by the 1880s they had become one of the largest companies in Great Britain. Having taken over the company following his father's death two years before, Thomas Francis Blackwell of The Cedars, Harrow on the Hill, is recorded in the Census of 1881 as a 'Preserved Provision Manufacturer Employing 654 Men & Boys & 552 Women'. Thomas's wife, Emily, died suddenly in early 1883, but later the same year Thomas married Louisa Annie Footman. Their first child, Charles's father, Thomas Geoffrey Blackwell, was born in 1885 and a further four children were to follow over the next few years. In 1889, in recognition of the importance of the Blackwell's place in industry, Thomas Francis Blackwell became President of the London Chamber of Commerce and served as High Sheriff of Middlesex in 1894.

Charles's father, Thomas Geoffrey Blackwell, was educated at Harrow School and later joined the family business, taking over the running of the company in the summer of 1907 after his father's death. Through connections within the food industry, he met Shirley Maud Lawson-Johnston, the daughter of an influential Scottish dietician, John Lawson-Johnston.

Born in 1839, Edinburgh-educated John Lawson-Johnston had a keen interest in dietetic research. While working as a butcher's apprentice at his uncle's shop, which he later ran, Lawson-Johnston began to experiment with the large quantities of beef trimmings to make a long-lasting beef stock. Lawson-Johnston moved his family to Canada in 1871 and continuing his research, obtained a contract to supply the French Army with preserved beef products in 1874. He eventually discovered a method of converting his solid beef extracts into a more convenient, semi-liquid form, which was nourishing, stored well and was inexpensive to produce. He named his new concentrate 'Johnston's Fluid Beef' and marketed it under the brand name, 'Bovril'. For this work, Lawson-Johnston later received the Fellowship of the Red Cross Society of France and the Royal Humane Society Gold medal for saving life.

Returning to England in the 1880s, Lawson-Johnston moved to Kingswood House in Dulwich, south London, soon dubbed 'Bovril Castle', where their youngest daughter, Shirley, Charles' mother, was born in 1890. Although he remained Company Chairman until his death, Lawson-Johnston floated the Bovril Company on the London Stock Exchange in 1896, raising two million pounds, some of which he invested in a steam yacht, the *White Ladye*. He died, aged 61, aboard *White Ladye* on 24th November 1900, whilst it was at anchor in Cannes Harbour.

Thomas Geoffrey Blackwell and Shirley Lawson-Johnston were married in 1909, and set up home in fashionable Park Street, in Belgravia, London. Their first son, Thomas Francis, was born there on 31st July 1912, followed by John Geoffrey two years later. During the First World War, Thomas Geoffrey Blackwell served in the Admiralty's Restriction of Enemy Supplies Department, which monitored the naval blockade of Germany, whilst also becoming the Deputy Chairman of Crosse & Blackwell. Early in 1917, Thomas Geoffrey Blackwell and his now pregnant wife, moved to Haresfoot Hall, the former home of General Sir Horace Smith-Dorrien in Berkhamsted, where on 30th April Charles Arthur Blackwell was born. Two daughters were to follow - Shirley in 1919, and Diana in 1922.

The Blackwell family became a well-established part of Berkhamsted and Northchurch life, later moving to Norcott Hall, a large mansion northwest of Northchurch village. Thomas Geoffrey Blackwell was a member of the Conservative Club and elected Chairman of the Northchurch Conservative Association. He was a patron of modern painting, assembling a notable collection of works by contemporary artists and he donated numerous drawings to the British Museum. He was also an active member of Berkhamsted Golf Club and passed his love of golf on to his sons at an early age. Both Thomas and his brother, John, would later serve consecutively as Captains of the Royal & Ancient at St Andrews.

Having spent his formative years at Haresfoot, Charles Blackwell began his formal education at St Peter's Court Proprietary School in Broadstairs on the north Kent coast and later followed his father into Harrow School. When he entered Moretons House at Easter 1930, Charles was the youngest boy at Harrow, but soon became an active member of the school community. Joining Harrow School's Officer Training Corps, he progressed to Cadet Under-Officer and also became a Monitor in 1935, and later a Second Monitor, or deputy Head Prefect.

Charles was a keen sportsman, playing as a forward for the school Rugby XV and captaining Moretons to victory in the 1935 inter-house rugby tournament. He also played for the Harrow Football XI, but Harrow Football had its own, idiosyncratic rules so opponents were limited to Harrovians. The School's first fixture of the 1936 season, as reported by *The Times*, was against Old Boys from Blackwell's own house and resulted in a draw at three 'bases' each. The following week, School beat Old Harrovians from Headmaster's House by four bases to two. School had attacked strongly in the second half and Charles scored with a kick from the ground. The School followed that match with a 5-2 victory against Oxford Old Harrovians, but the high point for Charles must have been School's defeat of Bradby's Old Boys on Saturday 22nd February by six bases to nil. For his contribution to that decisive victory Charles was awarded a 'Flannel', the equivalent of school colours, entitling him to wear a grey waistcoat with his uniform tails.

The boggy pitches that shaped the Harrow Game made traditional rugby football matches arduous and low scoring. Harrow School's home fixture against Rugby School, as reported in *The Times* of 26th November 1935, was typical. The forwards, Charles among them, dominated the game and there was 'keen marking and tackling by both sides with the ball greasy and difficult to hold.' Rugby School scored the only try of the match and won 3:0, but for his hard work, Charles gained a 'Lion' after the match. The following week Charles was a forward against Haileybury, but the visiting team prevailed again, beating Harrow 5:0.

Charles left Harrow School in the summer of 1936 and spent some time travelling in South Africa and Rhodesia. On his return, Charles decided to pursue an Army career and on 13th March 1937, he became a probationary Second Lieutenant with the Coldstream Guards. With his Commission confirmed the following October, Charles joined the Supplementary List of Officers and was formally accepted onto the strength of the Regiment the following August, becoming Signals Platoon Officer for 2nd Battalion, Coldstream Guards.

As Signals Platoon Officer, Blackwell was responsible for maintaining all communication within the battalion and to other units by radio, wire and telephone, with copies of every written order passing through his hands. He had 33 men under his command.

At the start of September 1939, Blackwell and his battalion were based at Aldershot with 1st Guards Brigade and were already preparing for a possible move to France as part of a second BEF should war break out. At 08.45 on 19th September, 1st Guards Brigade travelled by train to Southampton where the battalion boarded SS *Maid of Orleans* for

Cherbourg. Stopping en route at Portsmouth to pick up more men, they arrived at Cherbourg the following morning and disembarkation began at about 11.00. The Coldstreamers shared a train with 3rd Battalion Grenadier Guards, also of 1st Guards Brigade, to arrive at Lille the next day and march to billets in nearby Conlie.

At the month's end, 1st Guards Brigade moved to a concentration area near Arras, in the former Great War battlefields. The day after their arrival, the Brigade's Commanding Officer sent his senior officers to the newly opened Canadian Memorial which dominated the nearby Vimy Ridge and later visited the surviving trenches in the area.

The Coldstreamers returned to the Lille area at the beginning of October, and by 10th had moved twelve miles southeast to Bachy, close to Belgium. The Battalion spent most of the coming weeks digging in, with orders to resist another attack on France through neutral Belgium and to arrest anybody else who tried to cross the Belgian border.

With Christmas approaching and little sign of a German offensive, Blackwell gathered volunteers for a seasonal morale-boosting activity. He produced and directed a pantomime entitled 'Snow White and the Seven Giants', which was performed several times for the brigade's troops, and was acclaimed in the Battalion's War Diary as 'a great success'. Although Christmas Day 1939 was very cold, with a heavy frost, an inter-battalion football competition took place in the morning, followed by an evening concert in the Sergeants' Mess Hall, to which all officers were invited.

On Boxing Day, the Coldstreamers moved to Feuchy, near Arras, where a fresh draft of men joined during a heavy snowfall. The Battalion spent most of its time there training and participating in brigade exercises. On its return to Bachy on 14th January 1940, the Battalion was given four hours' notice to move, but it proved to be a false alarm. After a few days, the Coldstreamers resumed routine training in the biting cold weather of the 'Phoney War'.

The following month, 2nd Coldstream briefly stayed at Lorry Les-Metz, close to the German and Luxembourg borders, in billets 'left perfectly filthy' by the previous British occupants and among somewhat unfriendly local inhabitants. The Battalion soon moved nearer the German border, around Saint-François-Lacroix, but by the month's end, the Coldstreamers were back in their billets at Pont a Marcq and Capelle near Lille, where they continued to train and keep occupied as best they could.

The 'Phoney War' abruptly became a real war at 05.30 on 10th May 1940, when the German *Luftwaffe* bombed strategic points in Belgium, Holland, Luxembourg and across northern France. German paratroops seized key bridges and airfields in Holland, whilst in Belgium they captured the Ebel Emael Fort, which dominated the Albert Canal and River Meuse crossings. *Panzer* Divisions soon advanced across the German border supported by dive-bombers and fighters - the *Blitzkrieg* had begun.

Still believing that the German Army intended to repeat the *Schlieffen Plan* of 1914, the British and French Armies initiated 'Plan D', to advance into Belgium and stop the Germans on the River Dyle. At 20.30 on 11th May, Charles's battalion marched by Sections out of Pont a Marcq, crossing the Belgian border after dark, and at 08.00 arrived at Vert Marais, 21 miles away between Lille and Brussels. 12th May was, noted 2nd Coldstream's War Diary, 'a lovely day,' and the countryside could not have been more peaceful while, 'The inhabitants seemed delighted to see us'. That evening, motor buses transported the Coldstreamers towards Brussels, against the flow of refugees, delaying their arrival at their designated positions on the River Dyle, east of Brussels, until 18.00 on 13th.

The Allies had failed to appreciate that German attacks on Holland and Belgium were diversions. Even as the Coldstream's buses were crawling along refugee-choked roads to the Dyle, German *Panzers* burst from the Ardennes Forest, near Sedan on the Meuse. The British and French were certain that the Ardennes lacked suitable roads for armoured divisions, but German tanks were then small and light and could easily drive down narrow forest tracks.

After heavy fighting around Sedan, the *Panzers* broke through and, with the main British and French strength facing the wrong way in Belgium, the Germans began to drive straight across the Allied rear towards the Channel ports. With its lines of supply threatened, the BEF had to about turn, no easy task for a mechanised army, but 1st Guards Brigade did so and reached the Charleroi Canal on 17th May, blowing up the crossings behind them. Retreating soldiers mingled with fleeing civilians to keep ahead of the Germans, who increased the chaos with indiscriminate air attacks. The Battalion destroyed the main bridge across the River Escaut near Pecq on 19th May, but two days later parties of German soldiers crossed the river elsewhere. A planned counterattack slowed their advance, but at the cost of some casualties and at 02.00 the following morning, the Coldstreamers moved to previously prepared defensive positions about six miles further west.

There was little option now but to evacuate the BEF from France. With Boulogne already in German hands, and with Calais surrounded, the port of Dunkirk was effectively the only way out. Planning for an evacuation began immediately, with British and French commanders meeting the next day to organise a defensive perimeter around Dunkirk, which they viewed very differently. The French saw it as a bridgehead from which to fight back; the British saw it as a means of getting as many British troops back to England as possible.

With arrangements to evacuate the BEF underway, Blackwell's battalion continued to hold their position under considerable pressure. On

27th May, orders came to withdraw to Hondschoote, some twelve miles east of Dunkirk. 1st Guards Brigade, including Blackwell's Battalion, was to form a rear guard whilst the evacuation took place. At this point, Blackwell took command of the Battalion's Transport and at 22.00 the Coldstreamers moved off.

The Belgian Army surrendered the next day, and hordes of Belgian refugees added their carts to the French trucks and horses blocking the roads to the coast. From the sky, German Junker JU87 *Stuka* dive-bombers spread terror all around, while heavy thunderstorms added to the misery of both the refugees and the British troops marching in the open. Later that day, near Poperinghe, the Coldstreamers transferred to 3-ton lorries for the final leg to Hondschoote, but the lorries carrying Blackwell's Signallers and other Coldstreamers became separated. They apparently went directly to Dunkirk and all efforts to trace them failed.

By 29th May, 2nd Coldstream was facing south, emplaced along a 2,200-yard stretch of the Berques–Furnes Canal, which included two bridges. To their right was 126th Brigade, 42nd Division, fresh from England, with 3rd Infantry Brigade to their left. Spare officers, including Blackwell and 120 men were organised into a composite company and instructed to hold the Houthem Bridge across the canal to the south of the Battalion's position. Meanwhile, thousands of British and French troops streamed across the bridges on their way to the evacuation beaches ten miles westwards, while German aircraft circled overhead ready to attack the beaches packed with soldiers and the assembling rescue fleet.

The following day was much quieter. Most of the retreating troops had crossed the canal, leaving their transport, suitably disabled, outside the perimeter as ordered. From their positions, the Coldstreamers could clearly see the BEF's vehicles, burnt out or burning to prevent them falling into German hands. The Battalion's CO advised his troops that their evacuation would take place that night. At 09.00, Blackwell and the improvised company were relieved from the Houthem Bridge and sent to Battalion HQ on Dunkirk beach ready for evacuation. They waited all day, but at 17.00 they returned to the Berques–Furnes Canal, as it was felt that the perimeter defences were too weak. Blackwell joined N°1 Company as the sluices in the dykes were opened to flood the surrounding land and hinder the German advance.

On 31st May, the Germans began to shell the troops defending the perimeter, causing several casualties at Battalion Headquarters which, was forced to retreat. Advised on 1st June of their imminent evacuation, the Coldstreamers began to plan their withdrawal, but the Germans, aware that time was running out for the defenders, intensified their attacks. The battalion on the Coldstream's right was forced back, so N°1 and N°3 Companies formed a defensive flank to protect the Battalion's position. Around 14.00 that day, 23-year-old Charles Blackwell was killed.

Leaving their positions at 21.30 that night the Battalion withdrew to the evacuation beach. Most of their officers were now dead or wounded and a German shell killed more Coldstreamers on Dunkirk beach. All the surviving Guardsmen had returned to England by the end of 2nd June, reassembling at Walton, near Wakefield over the following days.

Charles Blackwell's body now lies in the Warhem Communal Cemetery, some seven miles southeast of Dunkirk. Apart from the Northchurch Memorial, Charles name appears on the Royal Memorial Chapel Roll of Honour at Sandhurst and the Harrow School Roll of Honour.

1257744 Sgt Pilot Stephen H Vavasour DURELL, RAFVR
131 Squadron (County of Kent)

27th July 1941

In 1868, Stephen Harold Vavasour Durell's paternal grandfather, Reverend John Vavasour Durell MA, became the Rector of All Saints with St Vigor's in Fulbourn, Cambridgeshire, which was in the gift of St John's College, Cambridge. Although Reverend Durell was born in Oxford, his career led him to obtain a Fellowship at St John's College and subsequently his appointment as Rector. Reverend Durrell's wife, Ellen, was born in Cape Colony in South Africa and settled into the Rectory to raise their family. Stephen's father, Harold Lancelot Vavasour Durell, both his aunts and all four uncles were born in Fulbourn.

On 3rd May 1915, during the First World War, Stephen's Uncle David travelled from Fulbourn Rectory to enlist with 16th (Public School's) Battalion the Middlesex Regiment at Cockspur Street, London. David Carlyon Vavasour Durell was 34 years of age and gave his occupation as a farmer when he became PS/2094 Private Durell. He landed with 16th Battalion at Boulogne that November, and died on the first day of the Battle of the Somme in July 1916.

Stephen's youngest uncle, Clement Vavasour Durell, was educated at Felsted School and became a well-known mathematician, teacher and author, whose textbooks were widely used in 1930s secondary schools. His 1926 work on Einstein's theory, *Readable Relativity, a Book for Non-Specialists*, which a reviewer described as, 'The best layman's introduction to relativity that has ever been written by anybody', was still in print as late as 2003. Stephen's Aunts, Phyllis and Emily Dorothea Vavasour Durell, on the other hand, were unrepentant members of the Guildford branch of Sir Oswald Mosley's British Union of Fascists. When war broke out in 1939, they went around chalking pro-Nazi slogans on local walls and as a result after the fall of France in 1940, both Phyllis, aged 55, and Emily Dorothea, 57, were arrested and interned.

Stephen's father, Harold, was also educated at Felsted School and later played football for the Old Felstedians. Harold Durell might have wished to forget his performance as the goalkeeper one April Saturday in 1899, playing away at Marlow. To the delight of the home supporters, Marlow put eight goals past Harold, while Old Felstedians only managed to score one.

Stephen Vavasour Durell was born at Johannesburg in 1917, where his father was a mining engineer. His mother, Dorothy Anne Durell, was originally from Croydon and had married Harold in Johannesburg on 6th December 1912. Stephen's elder sister, Jean Dorothy, was born there the following year and his younger sister, Diana, was born in 1919, while the family were living at 13 Cavendish Road in Yeoville, a suburb of Johannesburg.

Harold's work as a mining engineer in South Africa eventually ended in 1920 and the Durells left Johannesburg. They first travelled to Cape Colony to visit family members, before boarding the Mail Steamship *Balmoral* for the 18-day voyage to England, landing at Southampton on 17th May. Stephen's paternal grandparents had retired to Much Hadham, Hertfordshire, the year before, which may explain Harold's decision to settle his family in the county. Harold purchased Whitelea, in Shootersway, Berkhamsted, where Charles Ross had stayed with his grandmother some years previously. This would become Stephen's childhood home.

Stephen was only 12 when his father died suddenly aged 52 on 24th April 1929. Harold Lancelot Vavasour Durell was buried in Northchurch's New Road cemetery. Stephen probably went to boarding school the following year, but his mother remained at Whitelea for several years before moving shortly before the war to 14 Turner's Close in Hampstead, North London.

After he left school, Stephen joined the RAF Volunteer Reserve and volunteered to train as a pilot. When war came, he went to N°22 Elementary Flying Training School, at Cambridge Airfield, just five miles from his father's birthplace. Stephen would have completed about 7 hours flying time in a dual-control Tiger Moth biplane at 22 EFTS when, like many novice British pilots, he was posted to Canada. Here he could become a proficient pilot, safe from interference by hostile aircraft. Stephen completed his training with N°32 Flying Training School, near Moose Jaw, Saskatchewan, and gained his wings on 10th April 1941.

Returning to England as a Sergeant Pilot, Stephen transferred to 131, (County of Kent) Squadron, which had reformed on 30th June as a fighter squadron mainly performing escort duties. Based at Catterick in Yorkshire, 131 Squadron was equipped with the iconic Supermarine Spitfire Mk1a while it worked up to operational status. Stephen had only flown a total of 11 hours in Spitfires before joining 131 Squadron, but under wartime conditions that was ample experience to begin training for operations.

Checking the morning flight schedule on Sunday 27th July 1941, Stephen saw Spitfire 1a, X4662 against his name. He would be practising high altitude aerobatics at 15,000ft that day. Built at Eastleigh in Hampshire, X4662 was flight tested on 1st November 1940 and allocated to

611 Squadron on 20th December. In early 1941, X4662 transferred to 485 Squadron at Driffield, where, on 6th April, it had suffered engine failure during a training flight. The pilot belly landed his Spitfire in a ploughed field north of Hotham, near Market Weighton, and fortunately walked away unhurt, phoning his airbase at Driffield from a nearby farm. Recovered on a 'Queen Mary' trailer, X4662 underwent repairs at Driffield and re-entered service on 25th May before a month later being transferring to N°61 Operational Training Unit, at Heston. On 17th July, X4662 went onto the strength of 131 Squadron and ten days later, at 11.35, Sergeant Pilot Stephen Vavasour Durell took off to fly aerobatics over the area to the east of the airfield.

Stephen climbed to 15,000ft and began to fly the sort of manoeuvres that would have to become second nature to him if he were to survive in combat. After about 12 minutes in the air, Stephen put his Spitfire into a steep dive, but he attempted to pull out of the dive too sharply. Suddenly, the Spitfire's overstressed starboard wing broke away and Stephen's aircraft spun violently out of control into the ground a mile from Northallerton.

Stephen was buried with full military honours in the parish cemetery of Catterick village. His name is also commemorated on his father's gravestone in the New Road cemetery in Northchurch above the motto, 'Dos Est Magna Parentum Virtus' - 'excellence is the great legacy of parents.'

5953382 Private Ronald Reginald Frank HUCKLESBEE MM
Bedfordshire and Hertfordshire Regiment, 1st Battalion, The Hertfordshire Regiment

28th November 1941

The Hucklesbee, or sometimes spelt Hucklesby, family originally came from Boxmoor and maintained roots in the Hemel Hempstead area. Ron Hucklesbee, on the other hand, was Northchurch through and through. Ronald Reginald Frank Hucklesbee was born at Orchard End towards the end of 1916 and was the only son of Annie Hucklesbee, a member of the Dell family, and Reginald Hucklesbee, a 'machine ruler' at Apsley Mills. As a lad, Ron was a boy scout in 1st Northchurch Troop and also joined his father as an active member of both Northchurch Cricket Club and Northchurch Football Club. Ron played well for both teams and was a promising sportsman. On leaving school, Ron followed his father into employment at Apsley Mills, where his Aunt Edith also worked as an Envelope Folder. Ron worked in the Mill's Book Department.

Ron was called up to join the Army on 13th March 1940 and probably went to train with 1st Hertfordshire Regiment, which was then part of 54th (East Anglian) Infantry Division. During this time, Ron, who seems to have used his second name whilst in the Army, received specialist training as a stretcher-bearer. About five weeks into his Army service, on Saturday 20th April, Ron married Daphne Harrison Willis at St Michael and All Angels, Sunnyside. Daphne was the only daughter of Mr and Mrs T Willis of 76 Ellesmere Road, Berkhamsted.

Ron and Daphne Hucklesbee on their Wedding Day
(Source: British Library)

Ron's best man was his uncle, Horace Dell. After their reception at Sunnyside Parish Hall, the newlyweds departed for a short honeymoon in Eastbourne.

Ron left for active duty overseas on 14th August 1941, and travelled to join 1st Bedfordshire and Hertfordshire Regiment, which was then with 14th Infantry Brigade on garrison duty in the Bekaa Valley in Vichy French Lebanon. On 18th September, orders came for a move to an operational theatre. In conditions of great secrecy, 1st Beds and Herts and its Division, renamed 70th Division for this operation, were being prepared to end the longest siege in the history of the British Empire.

Italy had entered the war as a German ally on 10th June 1940. Her most important colony, Libya, was adjacent to the semi-autonomous Protectorate of Egypt, where Britain maintained a strong military presence to defend the Suez Canal. The day after Italy declared war, elderly British Rolls-Royce armoured cars raided Cyrenaica, the old name for eastern Libya, destroying two Italian forts and capturing 70 prisoners. In July, Italy's Fascist dictator, Benito Mussolini, ordered his Libyan forces to invade Egypt and capture Alexandria. After some initial procrastination, on 7th September the Italian commander in Libya attacked. General Wavell's outnumbered British forces recoiled, then counter-attacked, driving the Italians back into Libya. Australian troops then seized the ports of Benghazi and Tobruk during Operation COMPASS in February 1941, capturing significant amounts of Italian motor transport and supplies. Meanwhile, 7th Armoured Division, the famous 'Desert Rats', raced across the desert to Beda Fomm, cutting off and defeating the Italian Army in Cyrenaica.

Forced to rescue his ally, Adolf Hitler reluctantly despatched the *Deutsche Afrika Korps* to Libya, under its commander, *Generalleutnant* Erwin Rommel. Meanwhile, Churchill, perhaps thinking the Italians in Libya were finished, sent experienced British units from Egypt to help Greece fight an Axis invasion, which allowed Rommel to retake Benghazi the following April. The Australian Division firmly held onto Tobruk however, and having resisted Rommel's costly frontal assaults, the Aussies settled down to a siege.

The ports of Tripoli and Benghazi together could handle about 60,000 tons of cargo per month, which then had to be transported by road to the front. By late 1941, the *Afrika Korps* had grown to seven divisions, requiring 70,000 tons of supplies a month to maintain active operations. Adding Tobruk's monthly port capacity of 24,000 tons would considerably ease Rommel's supply difficulties, release precious forces committed to the siege and remove the threat Tobruk's garrison posed to the coast road used by Rommel's supply convoys. This was emphasised in mid-June when Anglo-Indian forces executed Operation BATTLEAXE to relieve Tobruk. Unfortunately, BATTLEAXE cost the 'Desert Rats' most of their tanks and the British had to retreat, opening the way for Rommel's *Panzers* to attack Egypt. However, Rommel's fuel and ammunition were low and Tobruk could threaten his rear, so he stayed put. Rommel understood that he could not invade Egypt without capturing Tobruk, and so began planning a full-scale assault against the port.

The British also understood Tobruk's strategic importance, and worked hard to keep the garrison reinforced and supplied by employing Royal Navy destroyers on the hazardous 12 to 14 hour 'Spud Run'. Convoys sailed from Alexandria on the 'Spud Run', timed to arrive with no lights at Tobruk, during the darkest hour of the night, and never during a full moon. The instant the destroyers slid into their berths, troops swarmed on deck to unload food, ammunition and equipment and carry aboard wounded or sick men, allowing the ships to depart in a matter of minutes. Plans were also being made to replace 9th Australian Division with the British 70th Division, the Polish Carpathian Brigade and some Matilda infantry tanks via the 'Spud Run'.

In the early hours of a late October morning, Ron Hucklesbee and the rest of 1st Beds and Herts were drinking hot mugs of tea in dirty transit billets outside Alexandria. Lorries soon transported them down to the harbourside where Royal Navy destroyers waited to carry them to Tobruk. Destroyers were compact, agile, fighting ships, but on the 'Spud Run', each of them somehow carried about 350 troops with boxes of supplies piled onto the decks.

An advance party with the Battalion Intelligence Officer had already left aboard HMS *Hotspur* with the rest of the Beds and Herts following, divided between two more destroyers. It was not to be a comfortable voyage for Ron and his mates crammed on the deck. The Mediterranean can be extremely rough in October and once the little convoy passed beyond the range of RAF fighters, it could expect attacks by German Ju87 *Stukas* flying from the El Adem Escarpment overlooking Tobruk. Without fighter cover, the destroyers travelled at full speed, shuddering violently with cases of ammunition jumping about the deck and sea spray drenching Ron and his mates. It was not until after sunset that the convoy could resume normal speed.

As their destroyer slipped into Tobruk harbour, Ron and the other Beds and Herts men prepared to disembark. They all wore full equipment, carrying their kitbags, their weapons and their boots securely about them. They wore soft-soled, Army-issue plimsolls on their feet to reduce noise and had just twenty minutes to disembark, it being too dangerous for their destroyer to stay any longer. Gangplanks swung into place fore and aft almost before the destroyer docked. Ron and his mates filed down the narrow forward gangplank, while an equal number of Australians, including their wounded lying on stretchers, climbed the stern gangplank to take their place. All the new arrivals had to carry ashore boxes of tinned food, ammunition and other supplies, which they stacked at dumps outside the docks. Apart from their personal kit, Ron and the stretcher-bearers would have assisted their Medical Officer with tents and medical supplies for the Regimental Aid Post. Within thirty minutes of arriving at the harbour entrance, the destroyers were already heading for the open sea to get beyond the reach of the *Stukas* before daylight. In the event, the Royal Navy completed the entire relief and reinforcement of the garrison without the enemy becoming aware of it.

The Battalion's men went to a staging area some distance from the harbour, where they were met by members of their advance party and Australian guides from 2/17th Battalion AIF. Around 22nd October, the Beds and Herts took over two miles of concrete guard posts and weapon pits, located along the eastern perimeter between the sea and the Bardia Road, running along the coast to the Egyptian border. Constructed by the Italian Army in the 1930s, they were quite deep with barbed wire protection and screened by a 20-foot deep, steep sided, anti-tank ditch. Two miles is a long front for one battalion however, so although some key posts had full garrisons, others were lightly manned, or left empty. There was nothing to see from the guard posts, but a couple of miles of flat desert and a few wrecked vehicles. Behind the Battalion was a field hospital, while the medical officer and stretcher-bearers worked from covered pits.

Water was always short and because it came from low-lying wells near the sea, it was frequently brackish. All work was done at night, with strictly no movement during daylight to prevent the enemy identifying which guard posts were manned, and how strongly. The Australian handover was detailed and comprehensive, down to the constant nightly necessity of sending out patrols to dominate no-man's-land. Up and down the line after dark, dozens of small groups set out in absolute silence on precise, triangular courses designed to prevent friendly patrols from clashing in the featureless dark. Occasionally, platoon-strength patrols would go out a mile or so to penetrate between the Axis posts, sometimes clashing with enemy soldiers when they stumbled upon newly dug positions.

After a couple of weeks becoming familiar with the eastern perimeter, the Beds and Herts withdrew to a reserve area, probably at Fort Pilastrino, where orders came to prepare for the breakout, codenamed Operation POP. Briefings on the breakout used a huge sand model of the eastern sector, constructed using aerial photographs. 2nd Black Watch would be spearheading the Brigade's attack, with the Beds and Herts following a mile or so behind to occupy positions the Black Watch had captured, before leapfrogging past the Black Watch to continue the advance. The night before the attack, Royal Engineers sappers would construct bridges over the anti-tank ditch and clear lanes through the wire. Then the Royal Artillery, which had been hoarding ammunition for some time, would open a bombardment on the Axis positions before the Black Watch moved off. The breakout from Tobruk would begin a few days into a full-scale attack westward by the Eighth Army, codenamed Operation CRUSADER, which would meet 70th Division and lift the siege.

Before dawn on 18th November, a surprise armoured thrust across the Libyan border, opened CRUSADER. Rommel initially ignored Eighth Army's movements towards Tobruk as a feint and continued preparations to capture the port, but the next day, 7th Armoured Division turned north and attacked Sidi Rezegh. This important position encompassed two ridges that were far enough apart to accommodate the settlement of Sidi Rezegh and a large Italian airfield between them. The northern ridge dominated the coast road into Tobruk and led to the detour constructed by the Germans along the El Adem Escarpment to supply the besieging forces and by-pass the town. Rommel belatedly realised that CRUSADER represented a serious attempt to relieve Tobruk, and began to move his *Panzers* to reinforce the Italian armoured division that was already fighting the British. The Desert Rats captured the southern ridge and Sidi Rezegh airfield on 19th November and continued to make good progress the following day. Although, the *Afrika Korp's* 15th and 21st *Panzer* Divisions were beginning to clash with Eighth Army formations, the decision was taken to launch Operation POP the following day. With only 20 miles separating 70th Division's most advanced positions from the Desert Rats, the hope was that they could link-up on the Tobruk by-pass at Ed Duda that same day.

Early on the 21st November, Tobruk's 25-pdr guns, their barrels worn almost smooth after months of continuous action, began a bombardment of the Italian defences that would last several hours. At dawn, 2nd Black Watch, with the Beds & Herts' 'D' Company and its carrier platoon attached, crossed the bridges over the ditch and dispersed themselves widely in the desert. Supported by Matilda tanks of 4th Royal Tank Regiment, their line of advance was east-southeast towards the escarpment and Ed Duda. At the same time 1st King's Royal Rifle Corps, and 6th Royal Tank Regiment began to push towards Ed Duda from Sidi Rezegh. Almost immediately, things began to go wrong. The Universal Carriers carrying troops and many of the Matildas ran onto unsuspected minefields and the remainder lost direction. The Black Watch and 'D' Company also lost direction, missing the strongpoint they were supposed to attack, they found themselves up between two other strongpoints codenamed Jill and Tiger. Deciding to attack them both, they were surprised to find both posts full of Axis troops. However, they took Jill and Tiger at bayonet point, in a costly battle later described as the hardest the Black Watch had fought since the Battle of Loos in 1915.

While the Black Watch and 'D' Company were closing with the Axis strongpoints, the other three Beds and Herts rifle companies were passing through the wire and deploying across the flat desert. At about the same time, Axis observers identified the assault bridges across the ditch and directed their medium artillery to bombard the immediate vicinity. Without cover, the Beds and Herts attempted to dig shell scrapes, but their entrenching tools struck solid rock a couple of inches down so they spent a miserable time lying flat on the surface. Orders then came for the Battalion to occupy the positions gained by The Black Watch, although Brigade Headquarters knew little about the true situation. Increasing shell and mortar fire turned the desert into a dust bowl, lorries raced up and down carrying more and more Black Watch wounded rearwards and casualties among the Beds and Herts began to mount. Amidst all this noise and chaos, the Battalion stretcher-bearers were hard at work. Every one of them risked their life to assist their comrades, but Ron's conduct on 21st November would earn special recognition. A formal report of Ron's actions, signed by his CO, said, 'On this day he remained with a man badly wounded and bleeding from the feet. When he had tended the wound, he carried this man on his back for a distance of 800 yards under Mortar and MG Fire. During the whole of this 24 hrs this man worked unceasingly and without rest collecting and attending the wounded whilst under continuous enemy fire'.

Meanwhile, 1st Kings Royal Rifle Corps and 6th Royal Tank Regiment advanced from Sidi Rezegh and quickly took the northern ridge, from where they could threaten the rear of the Italian division facing Ron's battalion, the *Bologna* Division. However, a serious battle was also developing around Sidi Rezegh itself as both *Panzer* divisions attempted to surround and destroy the Desert Rats and South African Infantry brigades alongside them. The German crews handled their tanks with great skill, often appearing where they were least expected, but the British and South Africans fought hard, inflicting losses that the Germans could ill afford.

70th Division was finding *Bologna* Division's front harder to crack, and by the afternoon it became clear there would be no link-up that day. The Black Watch had penetrated deep into Italian lines, but the Battalion was reduced to less than a quarter of its starting strength with the risk that counterattacks from any of the remaining Axis posts around the wire might isolate and destroy the Jocks. Of particular concern was a strongpoint on the Brigade's right flank that the Australians had named the Tugun emplacement. Consequently, 'B' Company, Beds and Herts and a company of 2nd, The Queens Regiment, were ordered to capture Tugun in a set-piece assault. Attacking at 15.00 alongside a handful of Matilda tanks, they captured more than 200 Italians and several light field guns at a cost to 'B' Company of about 20 casualties. To their dismay, however, they discovered that Tugun was only part of an extensive line of fortifications and they were unlikely to progress any further before sunset.

Over the following days, whilst Rommel attempted to smash the relief force beyond the Escarpment, the Beds and Herts continued to push at the Axis siege lines, but although 'D' Company had returned, progress was slow. When the battalion was pinned down by accurate enemy shellfire on 23rd, Ron again distinguished himself. 'Pte. Hucklesbee left what cover he had to attend a wounded man. He himself was hit but applied his own tourniquet so that other stretcher-bearers might be available. Throughout the operations this man carried out his duties with great devotion, coolness and complete disregard for his own personal safety.' *Afrika Korps* tanks eventually drove in the British at Sidi Rezegh, scattering 7th Armoured Division into the desert, but General Freyberg's 2nd New Zealand Division, supported by 100 tanks, were advancing along an inland track parallel to the coast road straight for Tobruk.

By 24th November, Rommel had only 90 serviceable tanks left, but since a bold drive towards Egypt and the disorganised Eighth Army's rear had caused panic and a British retreat once before, he ordered his *Panzer* divisions eastwards. It was a serious miscalculation. Although they were scattered, the British and Commonwealth formations were by no means disorganised and many units that Rommel believed destroyed had actually regrouped with replacement tanks, guns and equipment. The Commonwealth air forces had also re-asserted air superiority, harassing German columns and driving Axis reconnaissance aircraft from the skies, denying Rommel vital intelligence. The Western Desert contained many large British fuel, water and supply dumps, which might have sustained the *Afrika Korps'* advance into Egypt had they been able to spot them. On at least one occasion, they passed within a couple of hundred metres of large dumps without realising they existed.

Meanwhile, Freyberg's aggressive New Zealanders were close to the rear of the Italian forces besieging Tobruk which 70th Division was attempting to push aside. On 26th November, while Rommel's attention was on Egypt, the New Zealand Corps attacked and captured Belhamed, while 70th Division again attacked the troops barring their way out of Tobruk. The Italian *Trieste* Division resisted fiercely, but 70th Division broke through after heavy fighting, and linked up with the New Zealanders near the Tobruk by-pass. Although Tobruk was technically relieved, the link was fragile and fighting continued as Axis troops, now trapped by the Anglo-New Zealand corridor, attempted to escape and Rommel, belatedly recognising the danger to his rear, rushed his *Panzers* back to close this narrow lifeline.

The leg wound Ron suffered on 23rd November had been serious. The fact that he applied a tourniquet to cut off the blood supply to his leg indicates that he probably risked bleeding to death on the spot. Ron held on, but died of his wounds five days later and was buried on the battlefield amid renewed fighting. At about the time Ron died, Rommel succeeded in prising the British relief force away from Tobruk, but it was a pyrrhic victory. After two weeks of constant driving and fighting the *Afrika Korps* was exhausted giving him no choice but to lift the siege of Tobruk and withdraw his mobile forces from Cyrenaica, at least for the time being. Meanwhile Eighth Army, resupplied and replenished, deemed Operation CRUSADER a success.

Ron Hucklesbee's grave was eventually lost in the battle's chaos and his name now appears on the El Alamein Memorial. The account of his courageous work as a stretcher-bearer during the battle went up the chain of command with the words, 'Recommended for an immediate award of the Military Medal for gallantry and continuous devotion to duty under enemy fire even after being wounded.' Confirmation of Ron's Military Medal duly appeared in *The London Gazette* on 24th February 1942.

Ronald Reginald Hucklesbee is also commemorated on the Sunnyside Memorial in Berkhamsted, but misnamed as 'Hucklesbeer, M.M. R R'.

Driver T/175636 Albert James WELCH
42 Reserve Motor Transport Company, Royal Army Service Corps

15th February 1942

Albert James Welch was born at 43 Twyford Street, Islington on 13th May 1910. His father, Albert Edward Welch, was an insurance agent who grew up in the family home in Highfield Road, Berkhamsted. The 1901 census shows Albert Edward working as a packer at Coopers in Ravens Lane. Albert's mother, Alice Mary Crawley, came from Aldbury, but at the time of his birth, Albert's parents were not married. The 1911 Census form, completed in Albert Edward's own hand, shows that he was sharing three rooms at 43 Twyford Street with two adult boarders, Cicely Collins, a 26-year-old dressmaker from Ireland, and Alice Mary Crawley, whose occupation he gives as a 'domestic', with all three adults recorded as 'single'. Ten-month-old Albert's surname is shown as 'Crawley' on the census form, although his birth certificate says 'Welch'. Under the heading, 'Relationship to the Head of Household' on the Census form however, Albert Edward wrote 'Son'.

Early in 1935, Albert James Welch married Rose Hearn and the following winter he became a father. In 1939, the family were living at 14 New Road, Northchurch with Albert working as a paper bailing machinist, presumably at the Apsley paper mills.

Soon after the outbreak of war, Albert enlisted in the Royal Army Service Corps, and having completed basic infantry training, he progressed to the Driving School RASC, (R Company), at Feltham, Middlesex. The National Service (Armed Forces) Act, 1939 allowed the RASC special priority in selecting men with the technical and mechanical skills the Corps required, especially motor transport drivers. It is therefore quite possible that Albert had done something in the line of motor mechanics or driving in civilian life before becoming a paper bailing machinist.

On completing his specialist driver's training, Albert transferred to 42 Reserve Motor Transport Company, RASC, to drive the tankers and other vehicles at the base petrol depot at the Headquarters, Fortress Singapore. Albert's comrades were a mix of British personnel and Muslim Malays. The RASC's main supply depot was in the Alexandra District close to the marina on the South of Singapore Island and included the island's principal military hospital.

Singapore Island, some 27 miles wide and 13 miles from north to south, lies off the southern tip of the Malay Peninsula, across the Strait of Jahore. In 1941, the island was only accessible from Malaya by a single, 650-yard long causeway across the Strait. The naval base was on the north shore, five miles east of the causeway, while Singapore town, which had a peacetime population of roughly half a million people, was to the south of the island. For decades, the British had built Singapore up to become the most important port and naval base in the Far East. It was also the seat of the Colonial Government for the Straights Settlements, which consisted of Singapore, Penang, Malacca and Labuan Island. The British also had established treaties with the local independent Sultanates, called the Malay States, that made up the rest of the Malay Peninsula.

Malaya then produced 38% of the world's rubber and 58% of its tin and this important strategic material all passed through the port of Singapore. There could be little doubt that resource-hungry Japan coveted Malaya, but Britain's attitude to defending its most valuable possession in the Far East appeared shockingly casual. The Admiralty's supreme over-confidence, aggravated by inter-service rivalry, dogged planning for the defence of Malaya and Singapore. The Commander-in-Chief Far East since October 1940, Air Chief Marshal Brooke-Popham, worked fairly well with the Army Commander, General Percival, but not with the Royal Navy, which reported directly, and in a leisurely fashion, to the Admiralty. The Sea Lords in London were quite content that the Royal Navy could easily intercept and destroy any potential Japanese threat.

Towards the end of 1941, a Royal Naval task force under Admiral Philips, comprising the battleship HMS *Prince of Wales* and the battlecruiser HMS *Repulse,* with an escort of three cruisers and four destroyers, arrived to strengthen the defence of Singapore. A brand-new aircraft carrier, HMS *Indomitable*, should have accompanied them, but she ran aground whilst sailing in the Caribbean. Consequently, *Prince of Wales* and *Repulse* arrived at Singapore on 2nd December 1941 without their own air cover.

By 1938, powerful, modern coastal gun batteries had been constructed to defend Singapore against a surprise naval assault landing. Three 15-inch guns, in fully rotating turrets, covered the eastern end of the straits from the Changi Peninsula, and a battery of two 15-inch guns at Buona Vista guarded the western end, although only one of those had a full traverse of fire. Three 9.2-inch guns were mounted at Keppel Harbour and Blakang Mati Island at the southern tip of Singapore while another three 9.2-inch guns were mounted on an island just off the southern coast. Fourteen 6-inch guns supported these batteries. These new coastal batteries were, however, designed to sink battleships, not engage targets on land. Many of the guns could fire in any direction, but Singapore lacked a central observation and command centre, like Hong Kong's Shin Mung Redoubt, to direct their fire inland. In addition, the big guns' armour-piercing ammunition was unsuitable for land targets because the shells buried themselves deep into the earth before exploding, which smothered their blast. Additionally, there were only 180 shells of high explosive ammunition in total for the 9.2-inch guns.

The Japanese had spent much of the previous 20 years gathering detailed intelligence in Malaya and Singapore. Aside from old-fashioned spying methods, such as passing off Japanese nationals as Chinese servants, they openly purchased tin mines and rubber plantations and established legitimate photographic businesses. Japanese mine owners, rubber planters and photographers worked together to survey every track and path through jungle and swamp, something the British had never bothered to do, and thus produced the only detailed maps of the region.

By 1941, the British army in Malaya and Singapore had 86,700 men under its command, of whom about 15,000 were British soldiers like Albert Welch. Many of the remainder were raw and inexperienced reinforcements recently arrived from India and Australia. These infantrymen had sufficient machine guns, mortars, artillery and effective, though unwieldy, 2-pdr anti-tank guns, but no tanks. There were, however, a couple of hundred armoured cars of mixed quality.

The RAF in Malaya and Singapore possessed 41 Bristol Blenheim medium bombers, 24 Royal Australian Air Force Lockheed Hudson reconnaissance bombers, 24 Vickers Vildebeest torpedo-bombers and about 60 Brewster Buffalo fighters, but the Vildebeest biplanes and Buffalos were outclassed by Japan's modern *Zero* and *Oscar* fighters. Some Hawker Hurricane fighters did eventually arrive, but they were too few and too late.

With the war against Germany and Italy stretching Britain's resources to the limit, it would be hard to fight Japan as well. Although Germany's Atlantic U-boat campaign had pushed neutral America into supporting Britain against Hitler, it was not certain that the USA would intervene in Asia unless Japan threatened America directly. Since it was clear to everyone, apart from Japan's military leadership, that attacking America would be suicide for Imperial Japan, Britain was very careful not to take any action that Japan could portray to neutral public opinion as Imperialist aggression.

At the beginning of December 1941, convoys of Japanese warships and transports were fleetingly seen sailing south in the Gulf of Siam, their destination uncertain. Japan had made no declaration of war, so until there was undeniable proof of hostile intent, nothing could be done except watch.

Shortly before 01.00 on 8th December 1941, Indian troops guarding the east coast of Malaya suddenly found themselves under heavy shellfire from ships of the Imperial Japanese Navy. Japanese troops landed near Kota Bharu, forcing the outnumbered defenders to withdraw. Although

Australian Hudsons from Kota Bharu airfield and Vildebeests attacked the invasion fleet, sinking a troop transport and damaging some landing craft, it made little difference. In fact, the main Japanese landings were at Singora in Siam, now modern Thailand. The Siamese military regime was aligning with Japan and had agreed to allow the passage of Japanese troops to attack Malaya from the north. Although a pre-war plan to intercept a Japanese invasion force on Siamese soil existed, Brooke-Popham hesitated to attack the Singora landings and Singapore town remained brightly lit until 17 Japanese bombers attacked the island's airfields at 04.00, scattering bombs on civilian areas.

Seventy minutes after the Malayan landings, at 07.55 Honolulu time, 7th December 1941, the first wave of Japanese naval aircraft struck the US Pacific Fleet anchored in Pearl Harbor, Hawaii. Later that day, as much of the US Pacific fleet lay in ruins, the United States declared war on Japan.

Meanwhile, personnel at the Alor Setar airfield, the most northerly in Malaya, knew nothing of the opening of hostilities until they were attacked by Japanese aircraft operating from airfields in south Siam. Elsewhere, with uncanny timing, Japanese bombers caught RAF aircraft refuelling after abortive sorties against the invasion fleets. Systematic Japanese raids destroyed aircraft on the ground or as they landed and quickly rendered the mainland airfields unusable. The few surviving fighters flew to Singapore. Following these attacks, the Japanese Army and Navy now had effective command of the air over Malaya.

Admiral Phillips had already left Singapore aboard *Prince of Wales,* together with *Repulse* and four destroyers, ready to attack the Japanese ships supporting the landings in Siam. He had requested fighters to meet him on 10th December, but having adopted radio silence, he was unaware that the RAF fighters could no longer reach him. While Phillips investigated false reports of new landings on 10th December, Japanese reconnaissance aircraft confirmed his position south of Kota Bharu. At 11.00 torpedo and dive-bombers attacked his two capital ships and, despite evading dozens of torpedoes and bombs, both ships were overwhelmed. *Repulse* sank with 513 hands lost at 12.33, while *Prince of Wales*, limping at 8 knots, received two more torpedo hits and capsized with 377 of her crew. By 13.20, the Royal Navy in the Far East had been defeated and the Japanese could land troops behind British lines at will.

The Japanese Army commander, General Yamashita, had decided to attack Malaya with only three divisions, believing this to be the largest force he could keep supplied over a three-month campaign. Japanese infantry in Malaya were lightly armed shock troops, experienced and battle-hardened after years of campaigning in China. Using bicycles, they could transport light mortars, machine guns, ammunition and food very quickly down the narrowest tracks. They also employed 150 light tanks as very effective mobile guns platforms, and used front line engineers to perform quick repairs to bridges and roads damaged by British demolitions. General Yamashita constantly forced his commanders to push on without pausing to consolidate or encumber themselves with prisoners of war, which led to the routine killing of most of the surrendering Allied soldiers, together with the wounded.

Hurried, ill-planned British withdrawals allowed tons of stores, guns and vehicles to fall into Japanese hands, which they called 'Churchill Supplies'. After four weeks of retreat and constant air attack, lightly armed and exhausted British troops were attempting to hold a defensive line astride the main north-south road before the Slim River in west Malaya. At 04.00 on 7th January, in bright moonlight, Japanese infantry, leading some two dozen tanks, guns blazing, burst through the forward positions. First Indian troops, then Scottish soldiers, fought the tanks at close quarters with small arms, grenades and petrol bombs, knocking out and disabling several, but men inevitably gave way to machines. No word of the battle reached the rear echelons before Japanese tanks drove into Slim River village, 15 miles from their start line, and seized the road bridge intact at 08.30. The Japanese also captured large quantities of 'Churchill Supplies', 23 heavy artillery pieces and 600 motor vehicles, including 50 armoured cars. The British strategy of defending Singapore by fighting on the Malay Peninsula was collapsing under the weight of the Japanese *Blitzkrieg*.

General Percival, however, believed that Singapore Island could hold out for three months as more reinforcements arrived, but many units were under strength, short of equipment, barely trained, and those that had been fighting on the mainland desperately needed rest and re-equipment. The unfortunate reinforcements included 5th Battalion, Bedfordshire and Hertfordshire Regiment, which landed on the 29th January without its transport or heavy equipment and was rushed eastwards to defend Changi. Two days later, the last British troops evacuated the Malay Peninsula, and the siege of Singapore began.

The Japanese had also been reinforcing, and could land troops anywhere on the island. Percival expected the main Japanese attack to come from the mainland across the causeway, but in case of possible amphibious landings elsewhere, he spread his forces around Singapore Island, making concentrated counter attacks almost impossible. The last reinforcements arrived on Singapore under heavy air attack on the night of 4th/5th February, but there was little time to organise them.

Over the first week of February, Japanese artillery had been routinely bombarding the causeway, where the British were expecting their attack, together with other parts of the north coast. On 8th February, 22nd Australian Brigade bore the brunt of the Japanese artillery fire on the northwest corner of the island, losing most of its telephone lines by nightfall. During a brief lull, the Australians expected the fire to move towards the causeway as usual, but, instead, the Japanese bombardment of their sector resumed with increased ferocity.

Either because communications were severed, or through a misreading of Japanese intentions, the likely enemy assembly areas on the mainland were not shelled. When Japanese landing craft approached shortly before midnight, the landing beaches were not immediately bombarded either. The Australians fought the first wave of Japanese troops, but were forced back as more landed and by the morning, units of the Imperial Guards Division came across the causeway. Japanese engineers quickly bridged the gap created by British Sappers, and before long, tanks and reinforcements were pouring across. By evening on 9th February, the Japanese had established a firm bridgehead on Singapore Island, which the Army appeared incapable of counter attacking. In fact, the Australian Division, with a few exceptions, was not far off collective insubordination.

As the situation deteriorated, some RASC men were withdrawn from their normal duties and ordered to fight as infantry, while many infantry units were without transport around the coast, far from the battle. Percival withdrew to a last stand position around Singapore City and the last airfield. By the morning of 12th February, despite a gallant stand by 2/9th Gurkhas and Australian anti-tank gunners, Japanese tanks captured large stocks of British ammunition, rations and fuel at Bukit Timah, only five miles from Singapore City.

Japanese troops occupied the military hospital at Alexandra on 14th, bayoneting or beheading all but a handful of the wounded and medical staff. Percival realised that further resistance would soon be impossible. His reserve ammunition stores were either ablaze or captured, the Australians had all but given up, and his water supplies could last no more than 48 hours. Meanwhile, fires raged out of control in Singapore City and hospital staff were unable to care for the mounting civilian and military casualties. On the morning of 15th February, as the Japanese made further gains, Percival sent a deputation to Yamashita, under a white flag, to seek terms. That evening Percival signed the instrument of unconditional surrender.

When Japanese soldiers occupied Singapore City they indulged in an orgy of rape and murder. Nobody really knowing how many Chinese and Malay civilians died at their hands. Albert Welch was among the Allied personnel listed as killed on the day of surrender. His body now lies in the Kranji War Cemetery, known locally as Kranji Memorial Cemetery, on the north of Singapore Island.

Albert's parents, having lived together for over thirty years, were finally married at Pitstone Parish church exactly eleven months after Albert's death.

The destruction of the Far East Fleet and the loss of Singapore, involving the greatest surrender of British troops in history, were enormous blows to British prestige in the East. Japanese determination, skill and efficiency, and particularly the superior performance of their aircraft, was a tremendous shock. Recent figures suggest that 145,000 or more Japanese troops fought in the Malayan campaign against 108,700 British Empire troops, including the 22,000 reinforcements that arrived after the mainland was lost, and many non-combatants. British Empire forces lost well over thirteen thousand dead and missing, but the Japanese themselves dedicated two war memorials to the 35,000 dead and missing in Malaya and 25,000 men lost on Singapore. Both memorials, built by the forced labour of British prisoners of war, were destroyed in 1946.

Thousands of prisoners of war were taken from Singapore and worked to death constructing the Burma-Siam Railway for the Japanese. Among them was Private Leonard Geary of the Bedfordshire and Hertfordshire Regiment. Leonard lived at 13 Gossoms End with his wife, Nellie whilst his parents lived in Granville Road, Northchurch. Before the war, Leonard worked at Cooper's in Berkhamsted and joined the Army in June 1940, leaving for Singapore with 5th Battalion in October 1942. POWs from 5th Battalion began arriving at Chungkai Camp, near Kanchanaburi Station, to work on the railway in the spring of 1943. Leonard died on 30th August 1943, aged 29, in Chungkai's hospital, built by the prisoners themselves from bamboo and thatch. His body now lies in Chungkai Cemetery, Thailand and his name appears on the Berkhamsted War Memorial.

2nd Lieutenant Geoffrey Albert DELDERFIELD
12th Coast Regiment, Royal Artillery

2nd October 1942

Geoffrey Albert Delderfield, the only child of Alice and Albert Delderfield, was born in Central London on 13th February 1917. Although Geoffrey's father, Albert was born in Bushey, his family originated from the Aldbury area before moving to Northchurch, where Albert grew up. He was a general labourer until, on 18th March 1901, Albert moved to London and joined the Metropolitan Police. At that time, aspiring police constables were required to be at least 5ft 9inches tall and aged between 21 and 27, able to read well and write legibly, have a fair knowledge of spelling, be generally intelligent and free from any bodily complaint including flat feet, stiff joints, a narrow chest and facial deformities. By April 1901, Police Constable 87209 Albert Delderfield was on duty at Vine Street Police Court in Central London.

Albert served in 'C Division', covering Mayfair and Soho, throughout the First World War. Whilst lodging in Charing Cross Road, Albert met and started to court Alice Featherstone. They were married on 17th April 1915, at St Jude's Church, Kensington, and moved into rented accommodation at 278 Newport Dwellings, just off Shaftsbury Avenue in Soho. Geoffrey Albert Delderfield was born two years later and christened the following month at St Anne's, Westminster. In March 1926, Albert left the Metropolitan Police and brought his family to Northchurch, where in time Geoffrey attended Berkhamsted School.

The 1939 Electoral Role shows Geoffrey, aged 22, living at the Bloomsbury House Club in the then fashionable area of Cartwright Gardens, south of Kings Cross Station. On the outbreak of war, Geoffrey enlisted with the Royal Artillery and quickly became a Bombardier. Identified as having officer potential, Geoffrey completed his training with 123 Officer Training Unit at Catterick Camp in North Yorkshire on 25th May 1940, and was duly commissioned as a Second Lieutenant, RA. Geoffrey's first posting was to 12 Coast Regiment, Royal Artillery, protecting the British Colony of Hong Kong.

By 1941, Japan's decade-long aggression against China had swollen Hong Kong's population to around 1,750,000 including some 750,000 refugees. In 1938, Japanese landings in Canton had effectively isolated the colony from China and although some 12,000 British and Dominion troops were garrisoned in Hong Kong, the British authorities were aware that they could not defend it should the Japanese invade. Nevertheless, in November

1941, the garrison was reinforced with 2,000 inexperienced Canadian troops, while Chinese volunteers and trained specialists from Britain, including Geoffrey Delderfield, strengthened the coastal artillery.

Geoffrey's new unit, 12th Coast Regiment, consisted of a 'Defence Battery', dispersed in small detachments, and two Coast Batteries. 24th Coast Battery had three 9.2-inch guns at Mount Davies, on the most western promontory of Hong Kong Island. 26th Coast Battery had three 6-inch guns, covering Jubilee Bay, south of Mount Davies, plus three 6-inch guns and a pair of Great War vintage 60-pdrs on Stonecutters Island, off the western shore of Kowloon. Also under command of 12th Coast Regiment were 965th Defence Battery, which had one 6-inch gun and two 4.7-inch guns at Belcher Point, just east of Mount Davies and three pairs of old 18-pdrs emplaced at Repulse Bay, Stanley Bay and Tai Tam Bay on the Island's south coast. The Defence Battery also manned four 2-pdrs distributed singly in smaller bays.

In theory, this was a substantial amount of firepower, but the thinly-spread guns had widely differing capabilities. The 9.2-inch guns on Mount Davies were excellent anti-shipping weapons, which could also bombard the mainland, as could the 6-inch battery on Stonecutters, but they were large, immobile and in emplacements that were easy to locate and attack from the air. The 60-pdrs and 18-pdrs were effective, mobile field guns, but they were elderly. Two of 965th Defence Battery's 18-pdrs were obsolete Mark 1s kept for ceremonial 21-gun salutes! The modern 2-pdrs could knock out any Japanese tank, but they only fired solid anti-tank shot, which was useless against infantry.

The frontier with China was considered too long to defend, so in November 1941 work began on a shorter, 11-mile defensive line. Dubbed the Gin Drinkers Line, it ran across the mainland from Gin Drinkers Bay westwards to Port Shelter, with a redoubt south of Shing Mun Reservoir dominating the centre. Unfortunately, Kowloon was only three miles further south so, with neither space nor resources for a reserve line, the Gin Drinkers Line would have to be defended until the Royal Navy had destroyed or removed what it could before evacuating Kowloon Dockyard. There were insufficient men and guns available to hold the Line even that long, but reports of Japanese troops massing across the frontier in mid-November prompted work.

By dawn on 8th December, as Japanese surprise attacks erupted against Pearl Harbor and Malaya, four divisions of the Japanese 23rd Army were approaching Hong Kong's border. At 07.30, the Hong Kong Volunteer Defence Corps destroyed all bridges across the Sham Chun River. Thirty minutes later, 12 Japanese bombers and 36 fighters pounced on Kai Tak Airfield, destroying Hong Kong's five obsolete military aircraft and eight civilian planes, while Japanese troops crossed the frontier and methodically pushed forward in two columns. On 9th December, Japanese troops came within range of the 60-pdrs on Stonecutters Island. They opened fire, directed by the Observation Post in Shing Mun Redoubt, but were quickly attacked by enemy aircraft. At sunset, Japanese troops were probing the Gin Drinkers Line and at 22.00, a Japanese regiment surprised the platoon holding Shing Mun Redoubt. The tiny garrison soon fell, but not before their observation post brought artillery fire down onto the redoubt itself, causing many Japanese casualties. Afterwards, the 6-inch and 9.2-inch guns continued shelling the approaches to Shing Mun Reservoir.

At noon the next day, the Stonecutters Island 60-pdrs put down a concentrated barrage on the Japanese holding Shing Mun Redoubt, and causing Japanese aircraft to retaliate, while the 9.2-inch guns on Mount Davis engaged targets on the mainland. That night, Japanese 5.9-inch howitzers shelled both Stonecutters and Mount Davis. Although the Japanese made little further effort to force the Gin Drinkers Line, it was clearly no longer defendable and the planned retreat from the mainland and destruction of Kowloon Docks began. After a fierce infantry and artillery assault on the 11th December, the Royal Scots on the mainland fell back, support by direct fire the Stonecutters Island battery, despite coming under artillery and aerial bombardment itself. However, casualties from around 40 direct hits on Stonecutters Island forced the gunners to begin evacuation at 15.00. The artillerymen destroyed their guns and anything they could not take before withdrawing to Kowloon's Naval Dockyard. British artillery and rear-guard actions covering the destruction of installations were so effective that all British forces withdrew to Hong Kong Island without interference and the final Japanese assault fell on empty positions.

On 13th and 14th December, 24th Coast Battery on Mount Davis, which had been shelling Japanese troops on the mainland, came under fire itself and lost a 6-inch gun. The battery command post also suffered a direct hit on 14th, but fortunately the shell was a dud. Two days later, 965th Defence Battery received six 12-pdr guns from the Royal Naval Dockyard to defend the southern shore of Hong Kong Island, freeing the 18-pdrs and 2-pdrs for the defence of the north shore. While British troops drove off Japanese probing attacks against the island, a Japanese naval task force cruised off Hong Kong Island's south coast, leaving the British Brigades uncertain where the main assault would come. At 20.30 on 18th December, the Japanese 38th Division made assault landings on the north shore.

British gunners fired constantly over the next six days, often at point blank range, until destroyed or overwhelmed. Surviving gunners reinforced other batteries, or joined the fight as infantry. Uncoordinated movements between the British East and West Brigades eventually opened a gap and the Japanese quickly forced their way down the island to South Bay. With the defence split, further resistance was impossible, so the remaining 6,500 defenders, including Geoffrey Delderfield, blew up their guns and surrendered on Christmas Evening.

Initially, the Japanese distributed their new captives, both military and civilian, among the numerous barracks on Hong Kong Island and the mainland. After a few days being moved about, Geoffrey and most of the British troops were ferried to the mainland and interned in the Sham Shui Po Barracks on the west side of Kowloon. Built on reclaimed land, Sham Shui Po originally housed several thousand men, but many of its wooden accommodation blocks had been gutted by fire during the fighting and then looted. The POWs thus found themselves sleeping on the floors of the concrete administration buildings with glassless windows, doors and electrical cabling removed by looters, and no working toilets, the only water source being a single tap.

A typical Prisoner of War's day started with reveille, followed by a muster parade in all weathers, a meagre breakfast and a medical examination. Dinner at 12.30 comprised a small bowl of rice and either some soup or lentils. An identical meal came in the early evening, then another muster parade and 'lights out' at around 21.30 or 22.00. With morale falling, self-preservation often overcame discipline and, despite lectures from their officers, pilfering from the POWs' few possessions became widespread. Without electricity or fuel, prisoners burned whatever wood they could find to keep warm, often removing every other roof beam from the huts. Confinement, malnutrition and vermin bred disease, but without a proper hospital at Sham Shui Po, the POWs could only improvise. Japan had signed the Geneva Convention governing the treatment of POWs in 1929, but never ratified it. In the immediate aftermath of Hong Kong's surrender, Japanese soldiers pillaged, raped and murdered civilians and killed wounded prisoners. Little brutality was shown to the prisoners in Sham Shui Po however, unless they attempted escape.

In April 1942, about 500 British officers, including Geoffrey, moved from Sham Shui Po to the nearby Argyle Street Camp where they spent the next five months in conditions little better than before. Then on 25th September, nine months after their capture, 1,816 POWs were paraded at Sham Shui Po and Argyle Street Camps and told that they were being transferred to Japan where they could be well cared for, although they were actually to be used as slave labour. After a medical examination, the men boarded lighters at the dockside and transferred to the 7,000-ton, armed Japanese freighter *Lisbon Maru* anchored in Kowloon Harbour.

The men were crammed deep into the freighter's holds, Royal Navy prisoners in N°1 Hold, POWs from 2nd Royal Scots, 1st Middlesex Regiment and other units in N°2 Hold, while Geoffrey and the other Royal Artillery POWs went into N°3 Hold. They were so crowded, that the men could not all lie down at once. Although meals were the usual small bowls of rice, more vegetables and bully beef were included than in the camps.

However, drinking water was tightly rationed with none for washing. The toilets were simply wooden hutches hanging over the ship's side. Within hours of boarding, with outside temperatures around 30°C, the stench in the holds became unbearable and the Japanese agreed to allow small groups of POWs to take turns on deck.

At daybreak on 27th September 1942, Captain Kyoda Shigaru gave orders to set course for Japan. For three days, the voyage north was relatively uneventful and the weather good, but below decks, medical officers struggled to cope with epidemics of diphtheria and dysentery using the limited anti-diphtheria serum available. Laden with 1,676 tons of freight, 25 guards and 778 Japanese soldiers occupying the upper part of the holds and most of the deck space, *Lisbon Maru* displayed no sign that she also carried POWs. On the night of 30th September, 120 miles south of Shanghai was she sighted by the American submarine, USS *Grouper*. Since leaving Pearl Harbor a month before, *Grouper* had sunk the freighter, *Tone Maru*, and to Lt. Cmdr. Rob Roy McGregor, *Lisbon Maru* appeared to be another fair target. Deciding the night was too bright for a surface attack, McGregor shadowed the freighter to ascertain her speed and course and then positioned *Grouper* to attack as the sun rose behind her.

At about 07.00 on 1st October, *Lisbon Maru* suddenly changed course. Fearing *Grouper* had been seen, McGregor ordered an emergency dive and released a pattern of three torpedoes. They all missed, but *Grouper's* fourth torpedo launched from periscope depth at 07.10 brought *Lisbon Maru* to a dead stop. A fifth torpedo then hit her bow. The prisoners had no idea whether the two explosions reverberating through the hull signified mechanical failure or an attack, but the Japanese soldiers who pushed any POWs on deck back into the holds were extremely agitated. Finally sighting *Grouper*, *Lisbon Maru's* gunners opened fire, although she was out of range. *Grouper* then launched two more torpedoes, hitting the freighter once more, before Japanese aircraft appeared forcing her to dive beneath the surface.

Despite suffering three torpedo strikes the freighter remained afloat, but the POWs were kept below decks and refused food, water or toilet visits. Later, the commander of the Japanese troops aboard ordered the hatches battened down and covered with tarpaulins, leaving the prisoners without light or air. Several hours after the attack, the Japanese destroyer *Kure* and the freighter *Toyokuni Maru* arrived to take off the Japanese troops. All the POWs and 25 guards remained aboard as *Lisbon Maru's* crew prepared for her to be towed into shallow waters. After nearly 24 hours in the hot, airless holds without food, water or relief, the prisoners were increasingly desperate. The men in N°2 and N°3 Holds could talk through a small vent while Morse code tapped on the bulkhead kept N°1 and N°2 Holds in contact. Seawater now began seeping into N°3 Hold and Geoffrey and the

Royal Artillerymen attempted to work the bilge pumps in the stifling heat. Most collapsed exhausted after only a few strokes.

By dawn on 2nd October, it was evident that *Lisbon Maru* was slowly sinking and with conditions below deck now beyond description, prisoners in N°2 Hold attempted to break out. They cut through the tarpaulin and ropes with a knife they had kept hidden, and managed to help some gunners climb from N°3 Hold. Approaching the ship's bridge, they pleaded for the other prisoners' release, but were met with gunfire. The guards then began firing into the open hold, killing more POWs. Suddenly, *Lisbon Maru* lurched, seawater flooded into the open hatch and she settled onto a sandbank with her stern above water. With nothing to lose, the senior British Officer, Colonel Stewart, ordered the prisoners to abandon ship. POWs were shot at as they clambered from the holds and those who reached nearby ships were pushed back into the sea by their Japanese crews. Fortunately, others were carried to nearby islands on the strong current, or were rescued by Chinese fishing boats. The Japanese, realising that they could not hide what they were doing, began to retrieve the rescue POWs from the water.

By 5th October, most of the surviving POWs had been rounded up by the Japanese and taken to Shanghai Docks for a roll call. Only 970 of the POWs who left Hong Kong on 27th September answered to their name leaving 846 men missing, presumed dead, from disease aboard ship, shootings by their guards, or being allowed to drown by the Japanese. Among them was Lieutenant Geoffrey Delderfield. Of the surviving POWs, the most serious dysentery cases remained in Shanghai, while the remainder boarded the cargo ship, *Shinsei Maru*, for Japan, where many would later die of diphtheria, diarrhoea, pneumonia or malnutrition.

Geoffrey Delderfield's name now appears on the Northchurch War Memorial, the memorial at Sai Wan in Hong Kong and the Roll of Honour in Sandhurst's Royal Memorial Chapel.

200636 Lieutenant Ronald Charles Boyd-Smith
Royal Wiltshire Yeomanry

2nd November 1942

Ronald Charles Boyd Smith, commonly known as 'Smithy', was born in Middlesex during 1913 to Charles Smith, a railway official and his wife, Daisy. Smithy attended Watford Grammar School for Boys and after leaving school went to work in the stationery department of John Dickinson & Co Ltd at Apsley Mills. He became interested in social and welfare work and ran a 'house magazine', writing many humorous articles himself. He also wrote his own material when he compèred the Dickinson Apsley Guild of Sport (Dramatic Section) concerts held at the Guild House. For the Revue *Let's Sing a Song* he wrote and performed an entertaining monologue in the Lancashire dialect style of *The Lion and Albert*, made famous by the comic actor Stanley Holloway. Smithy's version had Mr and Mrs Ramsbottom, take their accident-prone son Albert on an excursion to visit Dickinson's paper mill at Croxley. Naturally, the lad falls into the paper machinery and Smithy's witty monologue describes young Albert's passage through the entire paper making process. His monologue was such a success that Smithy wrote another for the John Dickinson News in 1938, celebrating the official opening of Apsley Station on 22nd September, with the Ramsbottom family in attendance, and Albert's scrapes with the factory operations at Apsley Mill. Smithy was also a principal in Berkhamsted's Amateur Operatic and Dramatic Society and an accomplished batsman for the town's Cricket Club.

Lieutenant Ronald Charles Boyd-Smith (Source: British Library)

It may have been through amateur dramatics that Smithy met Maisie Plaice. Maisie's father, Henry Plaice, was the butler at Hurstdale, Northchurch, and had previously been valet to the businessman, Sir George Cooper. Henry had often travelled with his master to New York, where Lady Cooper had wealthy relatives. When Lady Cooper inherited her fortune, the Coopers bought the Hursley estate, near Winchester, which included the village of Hursley. Henry Plaice married in 1910 and Sir George apparently made him the licensee of Hursley's village pub, *The Kings Arms*. In 1911, Henry was the publican, assisted in the business by his wife and sister-in-law. Maisie was born there towards the end of 1911.

When, or why, Smithy added 'Boyd' to his name is unknown, but it was under the name of Ronald Charles Boyd Smith that he married Maisie Plaice at St Peter's, Berkhamsted on 27th April 1940. Prior to his marriage, Smithy was living at his parent's home at Ingleside, 35 High Street, Berkhamsted, but soon he was at Sandhurst. Smithy passed out from 101 Royal Armoured Corps Officer Cadet Training Unit a Second Lieutenant in the Royal Tank Regiment on 2nd August 1941 and shortly afterwards joined the Royal Wiltshire Yeomanry to begin his training in tank warfare.

The Wiltshires had gone to Palestine as an old-style cavalry unit with 4th Cavalry Brigade in early 1940. Two Wiltshire squadrons fought as lorry-borne infantry in 1941 to quell the pro-Axis rising in Iraq and then to prevent the *Luftwaffe* operating from Vichy Syria. Meanwhile in January 1941, 'B' Squadron converted into a searchlight unit and went to Tobruk where it supported the besieged garrison for much of the year. 4th Cavalry Brigade eventually became 9th Armoured Brigade and in December, the Wiltshires permanently exchanged their horses for American Stuart light tanks, which British crews nicknamed 'Honeys' for their reliability.

After Operation CRUSADER, Rommel had regrouped his defeated Italian armoured divisions and the *Afrika Korps* into *Panzerarmee Afrika*, and regained much of the territory he had lost. By May 1942, he was before the British Gazala line, poised within striking distance of Tobruk, and with sufficient supplies and fresh equipment ready to launch a strong offensive codenamed Operation THESEUS. Although decrypts from codebreakers at Bletchley Park warned of THESEUS, they could not provide enough detail to prevent the subsequent Battle of Gazala, which resulted in the loss of Tobruk and a pell-mell Allied retreat across the Egyptian border to Alam el Halfa. Rommel's advance finally stopped following the First Battle of El Alamein in July, which left both sides exhausted along a static 40-mile front, stretching from the Sea to the almost impassable Qattara Depression. Behind it lay the obscure railway halt of El Alamein, a mere 50 miles from Alexandria.

The Wiltshires arrived in Egypt in May 1942, with 9th Armoured Brigade under the operational control of 2nd New Zealand Division. Smithy, now a fully-fledged tank commander, joined the Wiltshires at their base at Qassasin Al Azhar on 31st July. The Wiltshires had only nine Crusader Mark II tanks, one Honey and two scout cars still operational, with many armoured vehicles still under repair. The Crusader, hurriedly developed from a pre-war design, was fast, but its 2-pdr guns fired only armour-piercing shot that was inadequate against the heavier armoured German *Panzer* III tanks and almost useless against dug-in anti-tank guns.

However, eight days after Smithy's arrival, Winston Churchill inspected 9th Armoured Brigade, watched the Wiltshires' armoured cars in training at Qassasin Al Azhar and announced that they would shortly be receiving 94 of the latest American M4 Sherman tanks and Mark III Crusaders armed with the formidable 6-pdr gun. Churchill wanted Tobruk retaken and, believing a new General was required to do it, he appointed Lt. Gen. Bernard Law Montgomery to command Eighth Army. Montgomery took over on 13th August and immediately set to work reorganizing his forces, rebuilding morale and improving El Alamein's defences.

Meanwhile, Rommel launched an offensive against the southern sector of the El Alamein front that lasted from 30th August to 5th September. The Wiltshires' role in the battle was to guard against landings by German airborne troops southeast of Alexandria, but thanks to Bletchley Park, Montgomery knew exactly where the real attack would land. Leaving a tempting gap there, he dug in most of his tanks further back on the Alam el Halfa ridge to pick off the *Panzers* as they advanced. The resulting defeat of *Panzerarmee Afrika* at the Battle of Alam el Halfa turned Rommel's last major offensive in North Africa into a retreat.

By the late summer of 1942, British Commonwealth forces had strong and mostly secure supply lines. New aircraft and spares entered Egypt from America via Accra in the Gold Coast, ammunition, vehicles and reinforcements travelled from South Africa, and troops and supplies arrived from India through the Suez Canal. All of these routes were immune from Axis interference. Supplies only had to come a relatively short distance from the Egyptian ports to the forward dumps and specially constructed pipelines carrying fresh water and petrol reduced the need for road transport. Rommel's supplies, by contrast, were mostly shipped across the Mediterranean, under frequent attack from Malta-based Allied aircraft and submarines guided by Bletchley Park's decrypts of shipping movements. Although Rommel captured hundreds of tons of Allied fuel and stores at Tobruk, its battered port no longer had the capacity to supply all of his needs. Some fuel and vital spares were flown directly to *Luftwaffe* airfields from German occupied Crete, but the Russian Front had priority over use of transport aircraft. The bulk of Rommel's supplies also required transporting hundreds of miles by truck along the single, metalled coast road from Benghazi.

Aware of Rommel's limited fuel, Montgomery attacked up and down his line in sequence, first to the south, then the north along the coast road, and then at Mitteiriya Ridge in the centre, in an attempt to keep *Panzerarmee Afrika* moving. Realising he was wearing out his vehicles and burning up valuable fuel and uncertain where the main attack would fall, Rommel distributed his mobile units along the whole line.

The Wiltshires had been receiving Sherman tanks and some new Crusader IIIs since early September, together with several M3 Grant tanks, from which the Sherman had been developed. In mid-October, Smithy and the Wiltshires held a three-day regimental exercise in their new tanks for tank commanders to practise tactical manoeuvres, including co-operation with engineers and infantry. With training completed by the third week of October and the regiment's tanks receiving a fresh coat of sand and green camouflage paint, perhaps Smithy recalled his old school's motto, *pugnam sperate parati*: 'look forward to the battle, being prepared'. The Wiltshires were now ready for Montgomery's set-piece offensive at El Alamein that would remove the Axis threat to Egypt in three operations, BERTRAM, LIGHTFOOT and SUPERCHARGE.

Operation BERTRAM was a deception plan intended to mislead Rommel into diverting his limited resources southwards, away from the main assault. Dummy fuel pipelines and fake supply dumps were constructed, while large numbers of cleverly designed dummy tanks, convincing from a distance or from the air, were massed in the south. In the North, meanwhile, real tanks disguised as lorries assembled for the wearing out phase, Operation LIGHTFOOT, which would culminate in the capture of Miteiriya Ridge and prepare for the breakout phase, Operation SUPERCHARGE.

LIGHTFOOT opened on 23rd October, with an 800-gun barrage and infantry advancing on foot across the German minefields, safe from anti-tank *Teller* mines, but carefully avoiding anti-personnel *S-mines*. Engineers followed to clear the anti-tank mines and create safe lanes for the tanks, which moved off at 22.00. However, it took longer than anticipated to lift each *Teller* mine and soon the Wiltshire's tanks were caught together in a bottleneck, presenting a perfect target. German anti-tank guns quickly destroyed six Shermans and three Grants and damaged several others, forcing the Wiltshires to withdraw from LIGHTFOOT having lost ten men killed and 32 wounded. Put into reserve, the Wiltshires quickly received replacement vehicles ready for SUPERCHARGE, although the majority of them were battle-damaged tanks, hastily repaired and rushed from the field workshops with unchecked guns or faulty radios.

Rommel's defence at El Alamein was anchored along the Rahman Track, running in a straight line from the coast, parallel to the front line. Positioned alongside this track was a strong line of anti-tank guns, including many of the dreaded 88mm guns that could destroy allied tanks at 2,000 yards' range. They provided a secure screen, behind which Rommel's *Panzers* could concentrate to meet a British armoured thrust. Any British tanks crossing the minefields and passing through the infantry strong points would then be picked off and destroyed by the gun-line along the Rahman Track.

SUPERCHARGE began with a night assault by New Zealand, Durham and Highland infantry supported by massed artillery and night bombers, followed by a tank attack timed to overrun the German gun-line at first light. At 01.00 on 2nd November, the infantry attacked behind a creeping barrage towards Tell Aqqaqir on the Rahman Track and quickly achieved their objectives on schedule.

Meanwhile, 9th Armoured Brigade's tanks were passing carefully down cleared lanes through the Axis minefields under heavy shellfire. Since leaving their concentration area at 19.30, some of the hastily repaired tanks broke down or had problems with their guns and radios. Of the Wiltshires' 44 Shermans, Grants, and Crusaders, 13 failed to reach the start line while 3rd Hussars lost ten tanks from their 35 starters. Diehard German gunners held up the Warwicks, but 9th Brigade's commander waited for their arrival before he attacked with only 30 minutes left until dawn. The 90 remaining tanks had no infantry support, so Smithy and the other tank commanders had extra hand grenades to throw from their turrets. Fortunately, the Durhams and New Zealanders had left the enemy infantry too shocked and demoralised to interfere, although German artillery remained troublesome, while dust and the darkness forced the tanks to move in single line.

The Wiltshires were still approaching Rahman Track in the centre of the brigade when the sun rose behind, making them perfectly silhouetted targets. The Wiltshires were in the open and face-to-face with a battery of deadly 88mm anti-tank guns which knocked out all three squadron commanders' tanks in minutes. With radio control gone, each tank commander fought his own battle, but with the same thought - to stay put or retreat up the slope would be suicidal, so their only hope was to charge their tormenters.

The Wiltshires' remaining tanks drove straight at the German gun-line, machine guns blazing. The 9th Armoured Brigade destroyed some 35 anti-tank guns along the Rahman Track, allowing armoured cars of the Royal Dragoons to pass through and create havoc in the German rear. Unfortunately, 2nd Armoured Division arrived too late to exploit the breakthrough before tanks of 15th and 21st *Panzer* Divisions reached Tel Aqqaqir and the biggest tank action of the battle developed along the track, with the surviving Wiltshires in the thick of it. Although the Wiltshires' tanks were practically wiped out for a second time, Rommel's losses in *Panzers* and 88mm guns were more serious and his fuel was almost gone. Rommel had no choice but to disengage his armoured and motorised divisions, leaving 90th Light Division astride the coast road as a rear-guard. On 4th November, the Second Battle of El Alamein became a pursuit as *Panzerarmee Afrika* retreated to its prepared line at Fuka, some 50 miles to the west.

When the Wiltshires regrouped after SUPERCHARGE, Smithy and his crew were among those reported missing. A year later the International Committee of the Red Cross confirmed that a shell, probably fired by an

88mm anti-tank gun on the Rahman Track, penetrated Smithy's tank, killing the crew instantly.

In February 1944, Smithy's widow, Maisie, was one of ten local women who answered a call for Women Auxiliaries to assist the Berkhamsted Home Guard Company with Signals in the build-up to D-Day. The women also took their share in maintaining the cables, including one running through Northchurch railway tunnel that was often nibbled by rats. In November 1944, Maisie was serving at 7th Hertfordshire Battalion Home Guard HQ at Chipperfield.

Alongside the Northchurch War Memorial, Smithy's name also appears on the Berkhamsted Memorial, as RC Boyd Smith, the Bovington Tank Museum Roll of Honour and the Royal Memorial Chapel, Sandhurst, Roll of Honour.

1151718 Sergeant Observer Michael Philip SATOW
Ferry Command RAFVR

26th November 1942

Michael Philip Satow was directly descended from a general merchant of north European ancestry named Hans David Christoph Satow, who came to London in 1825. Born on 18th February 1801 in Wismar, a Hanseatic port on the Baltic then belonging to Sweden, Hans was the son of a merchant sea captain. When Wismar later came under Napoleon's Continental System, intended to smother maritime trade with Britain, the Satows moved to Riga, a German-speaking port belonging to Imperial Russia, and thus became Russian subjects. Five years later, Napoleon invaded Russia and so, to escape this turmoil, Hans's father secured him a berth aboard a ship embarking on a round-the-world trading voyage. In 1814, 13-year-old Hans returned to Riga and eventually joined a large trading firm owned by a man named Schnakenburg, who became his friend and mentor.

Herr Schnakenburg later gave Hans a substantial loan to start a business in London and in 1825 Hans set up as a general merchant at 3 Love Lane, just off Eastcheap in the City. When he married Margaret Mason, the daughter of a London law stationer, Hans was a well-established businessman and in 1846 he became a naturalised British subject. The Satows settled in Hackney to bring up their children, including the future author, Japanologist and illustrious diplomat, Sir Ernest Mason Satow, born in 1843, and Michael's grandfather, Samuel Augustus Mason Satow, born in 1847, who in time became Master of the Supreme Court.

Following their marriage at St Anne's Church, Tottenham in 1875, Samuel Augustus Mason Satow, and his new wife, Katharine Jarvis Dakins, also settled in Hackney, alongside Clapton Common. While Samuel pursued his legal career, Katharine gave birth to four sons in four years, Michael's father, Philip Alexander, born in 1880, being the fourth. A fifth son and their only daughter, Norah, were born in Hackney before Samuel moved his family to 36 Kitsbury Road, Berkhamsted, which he renamed Northcote. Their youngest son, Christopher, was born there in August 1891.

Philip Alexander Satow, studied at the Royal School of Mines in South Kensington and qualified as a mining engineer. On 6th August 1902, he sailed from London to Singapore to begin a successful Colonial Civil Service career in the Straights Settlements, which comprised Singapore, Penang, Malacca and Labuan Island. Philip was appointed Inspector, and later Warden, of Mines for the province of Perak, which was extremely rich in tin. Philip's role was to ensure that mining companies carried out their operations, 'in an orderly, skilful and workmanlike manner,' and that they took, 'all due and proper precautions necessary to ensure the safety of all miners and workmen employed on the land.' It was Philip's duty to initiate a prosecution against any mining company failing in its responsibilities. In his off-duty hours, Philip Satow was an active member of the Kinta Golf Club, competing on the Batu Gajah links.

Back in Northchurch, in the autumn of 1909, one of Philip's elder brothers, Hugh Satow, married Gynnedd Thelwall, the daughter of Lt. Col. Eubule Thelwall and sister of Hubert Wallace Thelwall. Philip himself became engaged to Beatrice Barnett, second daughter of Mr and Mrs Herbert Barnett of Northchurch Hall, during a period of home leave. Philip and Beatrice arranged to hold their wedding in Colombo, Ceylon, modern Sri Lanka, and announced their forthcoming marriage in *The Times* on 24th February 1915. Shortly before Easter, the young bride-to-be started the long sea voyage to Ceylon, arriving on the eve of her wedding day. They had a simple wedding ceremony at St Peter's Church, Colombo, on 25th April 1915. Mr JW Boyd Walker, a planter in Malaya, gave the bride away and Philip's best man was Mr ES Stewart, a banker in Colombo. The newly-weds spent a short honeymoon on the island before beginning married life in Perak. The birth of their first child, Michael Philip Satow, was announced in the *Singapore Free Press and Mercantile Advertiser's* 'Domestic Occurrences' section on 20th March 1918, as follows: 'SATOW - on the 17th inst. at the European Hospital, Kuala Lumpur to Mr. and Mrs. PHILIP SATOW, a son'.

When Michael was one year old, Beatrice brought her infant son home from Singapore aboard the Japanese mail steamer *Kitano Maru*. They disembarked at London on 6th April 1919 and came to stay with Beatrice's parents at Northchurch Hall. The following May, Philip boarded the SS *Rhesus* to leave Singapore for good and join his young family in Northchurch. The Satows settled in Rosemary Cottage in Northchurch High Street, and later became one of the few village households to have a telephone installed, their telephone number being simply '6'. On 16th April 1923, exactly four years after Michael first set eyes on England, his sister Rosemary was born at Northchurch. Two years later, Michael's grandfather, Samuel Augustus Mason Satow died, leaving a substantial estate worth £15,505 for Philip's brother, Hugh, to administer.

Michael Satow attended Furzie Close Preparatory School in the seaside village of Barton-on-Sea, Hampshire, where the Headmaster, Philip Stubbs, and his wife strongly promoted the beneficial effects of fresh air on small boys. A contemporary of Michael's recalled that they played football all year round in only shorts and boots, no shirts, even in the snow. Another boy wrote, 'We were up by 6.30 and had to have a cold bath before we changed into singlet and shorts, even in winter. Then quite a long run whatever the weather was like. Back at school a hot mug of cocoa, changed, and an hour's class before breakfast'. Michael apparently received part of his education at Berkhamsted until, shortly before his 14th birthday in January 1932, he entered Marlborough College, Wiltshire. The College Houses had simple alphanumeric names; Michael was in B3 House until he left Marlborough in December 1935.

Michael entered the Royal Air Force through the RAF Volunteer Reserve in January 1940. His training as an Air Observer included reconnaissance duties, aircraft recognition, gunnery and assisting the specialist aircrew aboard larger aircraft. Michael completed his aircrew training in Canada on Avro Ansons, the first aircraft in RAF service with a retractable undercarriage. Nicknamed the 'flying greenhouse', because of the many large windows along its fuselage, or simply 'Faithful Annie', the Anson's main role was in maritime reconnaissance, communications and training.

Meanwhile, Michael's parents were active on the home front. Philip Satow sat on the Dacorum Guardian Committee, which administered relief for the poor and infirm locally, and was Treasurer for the Northchurch Parochial Church Council. Beatrice Satow organised several flag days in Northchurch for the British Sailor's Society, raising £6 14s in June 1941 and £5 17s 2½d the following year.

After his aircrew training, Michael was posted to Ferry Command, which played a pivotal role in the North African campaign by delivering aircraft straight to the front line. Formed on 20th July 1941, it brought together a number of established routes operated by Overseas Aircraft Delivery Units. The 'West African Reinforcement Route', or 'Takoradi Route', was created to allow shipments of British-built aircraft bound for Egypt to bypass the narrow, spy infested Straits of Gibraltar and avoid the long voyage around Africa. Crates of Hurricanes and Blenheim bombers were unloaded at Takoradi, on the Gold Coast, today's Ghana. Once reassembled and tested, the planes flew in groups along Imperial Airways' 1930s commercial airmail route via Nigeria, French Equatorial Africa and Sudan, before finally arriving at Cairo.

American crews later flew US-built aircraft, such as Lockheed Hudsons, along the 'South Atlantic Route' southwards from America's East Coast, across the Caribbean to British Guyana and Natal in Brazil, before crossing the South Atlantic via Ascension Island and to the Gold Coast. After servicing at Accra airport, Ferry Command aircrews flew them to Cairo by the Takoradi Route. In this way, Desert Air Force squadrons in North Africa received thousands of aircraft, including 700 before the Battle of El Alamein alone.

By November 1942, the war in North Africa was entering its final phase. Montgomery's Eighth Army had driven Rommel out of Libya into

Tunisia, while Operation TORCH on 8th November, put Anglo-American forces ashore in French North Africa to squeeze the Axis armies in a giant vice. As Eighth Army's lines of communication from Egypt lengthened, its need for transport aircraft increased.

Sergeant Michael Satow was with an Overseas Aircraft Delivery Unit operating from the Gold Coast's capital, Accra. Checking the operations board as dawn broke on 26th November 1942, he saw he was with Sgt George Henry Wheway's crew flying FK-643, a Lend-Lease Hudson Mk VI general-purpose transport aircraft, to the Middle East. Two Wireless Operator/Gunners from County Durham, Sgt. John Faill Christopher and Sgt. Robert Henry Clark, were also on the crew. There was no navigator since the smaller aircraft types normally flew in formation with a leader who knew the route. Michael's role was to keep an eye on the other aircraft, watch for landmarks and scan the horizon for bad weather.

The four sergeants were probably quite relaxed as they walked out to their Hudson an hour after sunrise. The first leg of their route was straightforward, following the coastline eastwards to the Bight of Benin, and then turning inland to the first staging post at Ikeja, a short distance north of Lagos in Nigeria. Accra is at its hottest between November and January, so they would have been keen to get away before the sun rose much higher.

At 07.05, Sgt. Wheway lined up on the runway and opened the throttles of the Hudson's two Twin Wasp radial engines. In a cloud of red dust, FK-643 picked up speed and lifted from the runway. What happened next is unclear, perhaps an engine lost power, but the fully-fuelled Hudson stalled, crashed back to earth and exploded into flames, killing Michael Satow and the rest of her crew instantly. They were buried alongside each other in Christiansborg War Cemetery, two miles east of Accra, Ghana.

Michael's parents remained in Northchurch for the rest of their lives. Philip Satow died in 1959, and Beatrice died in 1983, aged 97. In St Mary's churchyard, beneath a large yew tree between the church and the school, stands the modern Celtic cross they dedicated to Michael's memory with the inscription: 'Underneath are the Everlasting Arms'. Below Michael's cross lies a memorial tablet marking his parents' grave.

92188 Sergeant James Reginald BAMFORD
97th General Transport Company, Royal Army Service Corps

4th April 1943

James Reginald Bamford, named after his grandfather, Reginald J Bamford, was born in Kensal Green, northwest London, on 15th February 1913. James' father, Jesse John Bamford, was born in the London parish of St George, Hanover Square and worked for the Post Office as a postman. He was still living with his parents in Wandsworth when, in October 1911 he married Frances Annie Dean at her home parish of Chorlton in Lancashire. Two years later, just before James was born, they moved to 30, Buchanan Gardens, Kensal Green.

On 3rd November 1915, shortly before the introduction of conscription, Jesse travelled from Kensal Green to Whitehall and enlisted in the Army Service Corps. He went to the Mechanical Transport Depot at Osterley Park for training, and served during the war in Mesopotamia, progressing to the rank of Sergeant before his discharge in 1919.

Meanwhile, James completed his schooling and remained in London where he met Winifred Nellie Sudwell. They married in Chelsea in late autumn of 1934 when James was 21, and while living in London they had two children. At some point before the war, James and his family moved from London to Northchurch, where he became the chauffeur to Thomas Geoffrey Blackwell of Norcott Hill, the Deputy Chairman of Crosse and Blackwell and father of Second Lieutenant Charles Blackwell, who was killed at Dunkirk.

On 15th September 1939, James enlisted as a driver in his father's old corps, now called the Royal Army Service Corps, or RASC, at Edgware. James' service papers describe him as 5ft 7inches tall, weighing 137lbs, with hazel eyes and brown hair. Posted to 83 Station Transport Company in Kensington, James became an Acting Corporal in March 1940. Three months later, James was promoted to Corporal and a qualified Driver Mechanic. On 28th July 1941, James transferred to the RAF, but the following November he was returned to army duties. James' Service Record gives no explanation of this.

James, now with 2 Supply and Transport Company RASC, was made an acting Sergeant on 14th March 1942, and the following month he was posted to 72 General Transport Company (GTC). He was there only four days before he moved yet again, to 132 Infantry Brigade Company and on 29th May, James embarked for Egypt ready to help the Eighth Army fighting Rommel's *Afrika Korps*.

When James arrived in Egypt, Gazala had just fallen to the Axis forces and in June Tobruk fell. Rommel's pursuit of the British forces into Egypt ended, however, at the First Battle of El Alamein. In August 1942, James joined 97 General Transport Company, which was in the process of absorbing men, trucks and equipment from the remnants of other companies. Another arrival that month was Lt. Gen. Bernard Law Montgomery, the new Commander of the Eighth Army.

With a holding line established, 97 GTC continued with the varying tasks of transporting troops, delivering fuel and rations as well as mines. To prevent any further eastward advance of the *Afrika Korps* new minefields were laid and 97 GTC transported them from the base depot to the front line. Unfortunately, on one occasion, having unloaded its cargo of mines, one lorry drove over two mines and was destroyed, killing the driver and injuring his co-driver. Around this time, several members of 97 GTC started to suffer from desert sores. The passage of trucks and armoured vehicles through the Western Desert created an all pervading, fine dust contaminated with *staphylococcus streptococcus* bacteria that infected any cuts, abrasions, and insect bites. Being very fine, it easily penetrated field dressings, reinfected existing wounds and chafed skin under tight clothing. In an attempt to combat this problem, 97 GTC installed hot baths at its base camp, which gave some relief when used daily, but were of little use during mobile warfare.

Even if the war on the ground had eased somewhat whilst both sides regrouped, the war in the air continued. During August 1942, 97 GTC, as well as its neighbouring transport companies, came under attack on several occasions from German fighter-bombers, but the damage inflicted was relatively small. On another occasion, the company witnessed the shooting down of a British airplane by a German fighter. September saw the start of the build-up in preparation for the Allied attack at El Alamein and at the end of the month, 97 GTC received 130 new Bedford OY 3-ton 4x4 trucks to replace some of their aging transport.

After their defeat at the Second Battle of El Alamein, the Axis forces retreated westwards and although Rommel assured Hitler that he was only falling back to Fuka, he continued across the whole of Libya. As the Allied troops pursued Rommel, transport companies followed, their drivers spending long hours behind their steering wheels in a constant struggle to supply the advance. Frequently driving in the dark, along congested roads, the drivers faced the constant threat of mines laid by the retreating Germans. Mines were not the only danger however, fierce winds, rain and sandstorms were common and later, as they reached the swampy areas near to the coast, mosquitoes became a problem. It was only after the marsh scrub was set alight by the Allies that the mosquito problem abated.

On 8th November 1942, Anglo-American troops landed in the French colonies of Morocco and Algeria under the codename, Operation TORCH.

Having overcome initial resistance from the Vichy French forces in Casablanca, Oran and Algiers, the Anglo-American Army advanced eastwards, becoming the anvil for the Eighth Army's hammer. Benghazi fell to Eighth Army on 20th November and 97 GTC received orders to maintain the daily supply of stores to the port, a return journey of six days. Keeping their trucks running in these difficult desert conditions consequently put considerable pressure on 97 GTC's maintenance unit. Meanwhile, the discovery of a well close to the Company's new base, allowed the construction of a hot water shower using a 44-gallon drum, two 4-gallon petrol cans, a pump and a length of hosing. This 'desert innovation', as the Company's War Diary described it, offered some relief to men suffering from desert sores and the general dusty conditions.

Towards the end of December 1942, 97 GTC relocated to Benghazi, where James' 'B' Platoon, alongside 'A' Platoon, had the job of helping to clear up the docks. The *Luftwaffe* and the Italian *Regia Aeronautica* bombed Benghazi several times soon after 97 Company's arrival, causing minimal harm ashore, but inflicted sufficient damage on a fully loaded NAAFI ship to sink it. James and his platoon spent Christmas Day morning loading trucks in fine, warm weather before enjoying their Christmas lunch together. That afternoon, they set off in their supply column, but the next day brought torrential rain and winds. Dreadful road conditions, and lax traffic control, caused frequent delays to the convoys, putting extra strain on 97 GTC's vehicles and their overworked maintenance units began to run out of tyres and spare parts.

As Monty pushed Rommel out of Libya, Eighth Army's advance averaged 39 miles per day until by January 1943, the *Afrika Korps* had taken up defensive positions along the Mareth Line, a natural defensive position on the Tunisian side of the border. James's company was able to move into Tripoli within days of the port's capture by New Zealand troops on 24th January and soon 97 GTC convoys were carrying stores and ammunition some 130 miles west for the troops preparing to attack the Mareth Line.

German messages decoded at Bletchley Park warned Montgomery of a counterattack at Medenine on the 6th March, which he was able to defeat. This was Erwin Rommel's last action in North Africa and three days later he returned to Germany on sick leave, suffering from jaundice and general exhaustion. The Allied offensive against the Mareth Line commenced on 20th March, with XXX Corps attacking directly, while New Zealand and Free French troops attacked to the south, around the German right flank. After six days of heavy fighting, Rommel's replacement, General Hans-Jurgen von Arnim, was forced to fall back onto the next Axis defensive line along Wadi Akarit.

Constantly short of spare parts, 97 GTC continued running supply convoys along the coastal road by day and night, getting ever closer to the fighting in Tunisia. The drivers began to hear the noise of the battle not far away, while overhead, German FW190 fighter-bombers strafed and bombed the transport columns at every opportunity. On 4th April, German aircraft attacked a convoy of 97 Company trucks, destroying two Bedford 3-tonners, one of which was being driven by James Bamford. Both James and the driver of the other Bedford died of their injuries.

Two days later, on 6th April 1943, Akarit fell to troops of the Eighth Army and four days after that, the linkup between Eighth Army and the Anglo-American armies advancing from the west took place near the port of Sfax. The remaining Axis forces retreated up the coast towards the port of Tunis. On 7th May, Allied troops captured Tunis and six days later, some 275,000 weary and defeated Axis troops surrendered. The war in North Africa was over.

In a special Order of the Day, following the fall of Tunis, Montgomery himself paid tribute to James and his comrades of the RASC saying, 'these men drive long distances by day and night for long periods; they always deliver the goods.'

Initially buried close to where he died, James' body was later reinterred in the War Cemetery in the south of Sfax.

39528 Squadron Leader Raymond Thomas HUNN
Royal Air Force

20th July 1943

Raymond Thomas Hunn was born on 9th April 1914, in East Ham, London. His father, Harry, was a clerk at John Lenanton & Son, one of the largest timber merchants in London, while his mother, Florrie was a housewife. The Hunn family originated in East Anglia, with both Raymond's great-grandfather, George Hunn, and grandfather, Frederick, being natives of Great Yarmouth. Frederick was a rope maker who settled in Wortham, Suffolk, where he met and married his future wife, and where Raymond's father, Harry, was born. By 1890, the Hunn family had moved to Newcastle-upon-Tyne, with two of Raymond's uncles, Reginald and Percy being born there. Another uncle, Frank, was born after the family had returned to Wortham. In due course Harry Hunn left home and was lodging in Poplar, East London when, in the spring of 1911, he married Florrie Hart. Their first son, Donald, was born in 1912, with Raymond following two years later.

In 1917, John Lenanton & Son purchased the timber merchants, East and Son in Berkhamsted and Harry Hunn relocated his family there. It was here that Florrie gave birth to two more boys, Percival in 1919, who sadly died the following year, and Bernard, born in 1923. Harry Hunn became the Manager of East and Son, and lived in Gossoms Lodge, the former home of the company's founder, Cornelius East, close to the timber yard in Gossoms End.

Raymond went to Berkhamsted School in 1923 and later played for his House First XV and became a Private in the School's Officer Training Corps. He was a talented violinist and in 1930, Raymond entered the Royal College of Music in London to study violin and piano, and played the violin in a number of local concerts. Although awarded a Licentiate of the Royal Academy of Music (LRAM) Raymond decided that a career in music was not for him. Instead, in 1936 he decided that he wanted to become a pilot, and just before Christmas he entered the Air Service Training Ltd's school at Hamble near Southampton.

Established five years earlier by the founder of Armstrong-Siddeley Ltd, JD Siddeley, Air Service Training Ltd aimed to meet the needs of both the RAF and civilian airlines for aircrew and engineers trained on advanced types of aircraft, including flying boats. Instruction was to RAF standards by experienced RAF instructors from the Training Reserve, so it was natural that trainee pilots hoping for short service commissions should go there.

On 8th March 1937, Raymond joined the RAF as an Acting Pilot Officer on a four-year short service commission. He spent seven months undergoing officer training at N°5 Officer Training School before transferring to N°206 General Reconnaissance Squadron based at Bircham Newton near Kings Lynn, Norfolk. Two months after arriving at Bircham Newton Raymond became a fully-fledged Pilot Officer flying Avro Ansons.

The airbase at Bircham Newton was somewhat isolated, with a very poor bus service linking it to Kings Lynn, so many of the servicemen decided that a better alternative for a night out was to walk across the fields to the pub at nearby Docking. Officers from the airbase led a somewhat privileged life, taking part in frequent shooting parties on the nearby estates and accepting dining invitations with the local farmers and landowners. It was probably through one of these events that Raymond started dating a local girl called Eileen Thompson.

As war with Nazi Germany became increasingly likely, in August 1938 Bircham Newton and other stations in the area commenced a series of exercises to familiarise ground staff and airmen with air defence and also test their efficiency. Twenty-three fighter and 14 bomber squadrons were to participate, including the Ansons of 206 Squadron. Blackouts were organised across large parts of East Anglia and the Midlands, but unseasonal thick fog and low cloud grounded the Bircham Newton squadrons and consequently the exercise was only partially successful.

At the start of 1939, Raymond went to train with N°1 Air Observation School at North Coates, Lincolnshire. Whilst there, Raymond extended his short service commission to six years and that June he became a Flying Officer. He also made regular trips to Bircham Newton to see Eileen and they were married at nearby Fakenham in early 1940. In May, before returning to 206 Squadron, Raymond was sent to N°1 (Coast) Operational Training Unit (OTU) stationed at RAF Silloth in Cumbria. Here he gained operational experience flying actual patrols in Bristol Beauforts, Blackburn Bothas, and Avro Ansons and, especially, the new American Lockheed Hudson Mk1s. 206 Squadron had already converted to the Hudson, which offered a greater range than the Anson and were capable of carrying bombs large enough to damage a U-boat.

Raymond returned to 206 Squadron as a fully qualified pilot on Hudsons. The Squadron history records that on 18th June 1940, he was on reconnaissance patrol off the Dutch coast in Hudson P5162, when anti-aircraft fire over Ijmuiden hit his aircraft in several places. Although his Hudson had a hole shot in one of the fuel tanks, Raymond skilfully brought P5162 safely home.

Raymond became a Flight Lieutenant exactly a year after Britain declared war on Germany. Now an experienced, operational pilot, he transferred to N°2 Service Flying Training School (SFTS) at RAF Brize Norton, Oxfordshire in October, to begin a flying instructor's course. On 23rd November, he transferred again to N°7 SFTS, which specialised in naval aviation and, being based at Peterborough, was much closer to his Bircham Newton home. Unfortunately, he would not be there for long.

Early recognition of the UK's unsuitability as a location for aircrew training led Britain, Canada, Australia and New Zealand to create the joint British Commonwealth Air Training Plan (BCATP) in December 1939. Canada, with its wide-open spaces, varied, but predictable climate, access to plentiful fuel supplies and the capacity to build its own training aircraft, was the ideal location for the Plan and construction of training facilities began. Following France's defeat in June 1940, German aircraft were now within easy range of British airfields, so the RAF began to move its existing training units to Canada, beginning in late August.

When Raymond arrived at Peterborough in late 1940, the third of four contingents had just left for N°7 SFTS's new station at Kingston Aerodrome, near Ontario, where the school was renamed N°31 SFTS. The move to Canada proved fully justified as nuisance raids by individual German aircraft became a daily occurrence around Peterborough. Raymond left with the last contingent of RAF training personnel on 7th January 1941, arriving at Kingston in the middle of a snowstorm on 25th.

Kingston in mid-winter could hardly have presented a greater contrast to the RAF stations in Great Britain. Off-duty servicemen could no longer leave the base to enjoy the countryside and local social life, and married officers, like Raymond, had to endure separation with no prospect of their wives joining them. The officers and men of 31 SFTS therefore had to create their own social life centred on the base. They started a unit magazine called *The Pioneer,* containing news, stories, jokes and cartoons, and set up a cinema screening the latest films. A homemade ice rink and sporting tournaments, including boxing, were especially popular with the men, but not so popular was the food. The Training School's War Diary preserves a catalogue of complaints against the Station Cookhouse, particularly the lack of such staples as liver, kidney, mustard and tinned fruit. Replacing them on the menu were rice, macaroni and prunes, which were all deeply unpopular with the British, but favourites such as boiled mutton with onion sauce were dismissed as 'strange British food', by Canadian pupils.

By January 1941, the BCATP was well underway at Kingston, although frequent blizzards and lack of serviceable aircraft made courses fall behind. However, the first intake of Fleet Air Arm pilots graduated from 31 SFTS in April, despite training on Fairey Battles, which lacked spares, had inefficient brakes and air intakes that tended to ice up. Eventually, in July 1941, North American AT-6 advanced training aircraft, named the Harvard in RAF service, and fitted with British instruments and radios, replaced the unsuitable Battles.

The Fleet Air Arm pilot training course with 31 SFTS lasted 16 weeks, much of it hard work at ground school learning navigation, armaments, signals, aero engines, aircraft and ship recognition. Hours were also spent in the Link Trainer, an early flight simulator. Meanwhile, the distinctive, penetrating drone of bright yellow Harvards echoed day and night, as novice pilots clocked up their minimum of 100 hours flying time, half of which had to be solo.

In April 1942, Raymond transferred some 900 miles due east to N°31 Operational Training Unit at Debert, in the Province of Nova Scotia, another airfield constructed for the BCATP, along with an adjacent Canadian Army camp. Raymond was reunited with Hudson reconnaissance bombers and Avro Ansons at 31 OTU, and some single-engined Lysander spotter planes arrived later. Debert's weather was as bad as Kingston's, with heavy winter snows presenting particular difficulties, but the OTU offered programmes of day and night flying, including genuine armed patrols, to bring replacement pilots, navigators and wireless operators/air gunners, known as 'WAGs', up to operational standard.

Three weeks after arriving, Raymond flew a fully armed Hudson on Debert's first operational flight. Two Hudsons investigated reports of an unidentified submarine off the coast, but after a fruitless search, both planes returned to base with bomb loads intact and novice aircrew disappointed not to have seen their first action.

Since 31 OTU was expected to make an active contribution to the Battle of the Atlantic in all weathers, incidents causing damage to aircraft occurred almost daily. Inexperienced pilots accounted for most, but aircraft often slid off icy runways during winter landings. Damage was generally superficial and repaired quickly in Debert's own workshops, but accidents causing serious damage or destruction of an aircraft triggered a formal Inquiry and Raymond was appointed one of the Station's investigating officers. In late April 1942, Raymond investigated the circumstances surrounding the destruction of a Hudson that ran off the runway during take-off, broke its undercarriage, and burst into flames. Another of his investigations concerned a Hudson whose wing tip hit the water whilst the trainee pilot was attempting a low-level turn during a training exercise. Fortunately, on both occasions, the aircrew escaped unhurt, but when airmen were killed at Debert, Raymond was responsible for formalising their estates after a Committee of Adjustment had reviewed the airmen's financial affairs such as his debts and assets, together with any pay due.

During the winter months at Debert, the airmen's main form of entertainment took the form of dances to which local girls were invited, together with concerts. There was also a station cinema showing films such as the *Maltese Falcon*, *The Roaring Twenties* and *They Died with their Boots On*. A unit magazine called *Pukka Gen*, airmen's slang for 'accurate information', was also very popular. Flying time increased considerably when spring arrived and airmen were encouraged to cultivate plants outside their huts to brighten up the airbase. The warmer weather also brought the opportunity to arrange sporting events against the adjacent Army Camp cultivating a friendly rivalry. An ice hockey rink opened on the airbase in early 1943, and soon had enough teams for three leagues to form. An amateur dramatic society also started putting on productions.

Raymond became a Squadron Leader that June and continued to fly occasional operational anti-submarine patrols, particularly during the last three months of the year. Although Raymond's short service commission ended on 21st December 1942, he remained on the Active List and continued as a senior instructor at Debert. Charlie Matthews and Walter Geoffrey Macauly (Geoff) Papworth were on the same trainee pilot's course at Debert in 1943. Charlie recalls that Squadron Leader Hunn was not part of the teaching staff, but would fly with students to assess their progress.

During the early hours of Tuesday 20th July 1943, Raymond climbed into the cockpit of BW777, a Lockheed Hudson Mark III, with 19-year-old Pilot Officer Geoff Papworth, to undertake some night-time circuit and landing practice. After completing the normal checks, the Hudson sped down the runway and took off, but failed to gain height. At about 04.45 hrs, BW777 struck the treetops about a mile from the end of the runway and crashed into the woods. Soldiers from Debert Camp rushed to the crash site, but both occupants were already dead. A formal Inquiry was unable to establish the precise cause of the accident.

On 22nd July, a Memorial Service was held for Squadron Leader Raymond Hunn at St John's Church in nearby Truro. Debert's Commanding Officer and many off-duty senior officers joined his friends from the local community in attending the service. The following day, Raymond's body was escorted with full military honours to St John's, New Brunswick for cremation. His ashes were flown home and interred with his infant brother in the New Road Cemetery, Northchurch.

On 14th December 1946, a Service of Commemoration took place in the Chapel of Berkhamsted School for the 125 Old Boys, including Raymond, who made the supreme sacrifice during the Second World War and whose names were added to the Berkhamsted School War Memorial. Raymond's name is also recorded on the Royal College of Music's Roll of Honour Memorial Plaque at its headquarters in Prince Consort Road, London.

14379260 Private Harold WEEDON
8th Durham Light Infantry

9th August 1944

On the first three Sundays of July 1906, the congregations in St Mary's, Northchurch heard marriage banns read for 20-year-old Nellie Meager of Northchurch, and 23-year-old William John Weedon, a bricklayer from the Parish of St Peter's, Berkhamsted. William and Nellie were married soon afterwards in St Mary's, and set up their own household in Northchurch High Street. The Meagers were a long-established Northchurch family and Nellie had relatives living all along the High Street. Nellie's father and brothers were bricklayers and quite probably, workmates of William, whilst Nellie and her sister worked in the Mantle Factory in Lower King's Road, Berkhamsted.

Nellie and William lost their first child, Frederick, soon after his birth in the spring of 1907, but in March 1909, Nellie gave birth to another boy, Harold Wilfred. Harold grew up in the family home with his sister, Elsie, born in the spring of 1913, and younger brother Stanley, who was born two years later. After Harold left school, he followed his father's example and became a bricklayer.

In time, Harold met and became engaged to Gwendoline Lily Collier, an Aldbury girl two years his junior. Gwendoline's father, Ernest Collier, was the Verger at Aldbury Parish Church, and they were married there on 27th June 1931. Harold's father and Gwendoline's older sister, Ivy, were the witnesses and their marriage certificate shows their address as Station Road, Aldbury. The newlyweds soon moved to Hendon, Middlesex, where their four children were born.

It is unlikely that 30-year-old Harold immediately volunteered for the forces when Britain declared war in September 1939. He had a very young family to support and he was near the upper age limit for regular enlistment, but the National Service Act obliged him to register with his age group for service, which he duly did at Berkhamsted, one Saturday in early July 1940. He was eventually called up in 1942, and posted to 8th Battalion, Durham Light Infantry.

8th DLI had a proud record of service with 50th (Northumbrian) Division through both world wars. It had joined the British Expeditionary Force with 151st Brigade, 50th Division in January 1940 and during the Battle of France, the Durhams participated in the most effective counterblow against General Erwin Rommel's 7th *Panzer* Division at

Arras. After the Dunkirk evacuation, 151st Brigade was reformed and sent to North Africa where 8th DLI was once again a thorn in Rommel's side at the Gazala breakthrough, during the Battle of El Alamein and the battles that followed.

In January 1943, with victory in North Africa imminent, British Prime Minister, Winston Churchill and US President Franklin D Roosevelt met at Casablanca to plan the next phase of the campaign against the Axis powers. Landings in Western Europe would have to wait, but Allied superiority in the Mediterranean could be exploited to attack Europe's 'soft underbelly' through Italy, knocking her out of the war and perhaps invading Germany through Austria.

Sicily, with its large airfield complexes, was an obvious base from which to attack the Italian mainland. The Germans appreciated that an Allied invasion of Italy or Italian-occupied territory in the Mediterranean could happen anywhere from Sardinia to Greece. An elaborate campaign of deception by British Intelligence, including Operation MINCEMEAT, made famous in the film *The Man Who Never Was*, led German Intelligence to convince itself that Greece, not Sicily, was the next Allied target, and German divisions were moved from Italy to strengthen the Greek defences.

In Tunisia, 8th DLI was being rebuilt after losing many men and almost all of their officers during the fighting to break the German Mareth Line. On 20th April 1943, Harold and his battalion heard that their division was to leave Tunisia, travelling by road back to Tobruk then rail to Egypt. Including sightseeing breaks in Sfax and Tripoli, the Battalion took exactly three weeks to cover the 1,300 miles to Sidi Bishr. After spending a day cleaning up following their journey, the troops were given four days' leave to spend in either Cairo or nearby Alexandria.

On 22nd May, the battalion travelled by rail and road to the Combined Training Centre at Kabrit, at the southern end of the Great Bitter Lake, to receive intensive training in beach landings from LCAs, (Landing Craft Assault). In the first exercise, Operation DREDGER, held on 28th, the battalion 'attacked' the west coast of the Sinai Peninsula in full battle order, followed by Operation DUCHESS, involving the whole Brigade. On 6th June, the Durhams moved south via Port Suez to the Gulf of Aqaba for a full-scale invasion exercise, Operation BROMYARD, in which 5th and 50th Divisions 'captured' Aqaba itself. Returning to Suez on 16th June, the battalion spent their final days and nights in Egypt embarking in LCIs, (Landing Craft Infantry) and live firing on the ranges. The Durhams also fired their brand-new platoon anti-tank weapon, the PIAT, (Projector Infantry Anti-Tank). At last, in great secrecy, the battalion boarded MV *Ruys* and sailed up the Suez Canal to drop anchor at Port Said. More ships joined 5th and 50th Divisions' convoy until, on 5th July, the invasion force set sail. Only then did the Durhams find out that they were going to invade Sicily.

Operation HUSKY's landings were concentrated around the southeast corner of Sicily. Eighth Army's sector stretched south from Syracuse around the Pachino peninsula, which contained several airfields, to join the Americans at Ragusa. Low-quality Italian regiments defended the beaches, but crack German and high-quality Italian armoured divisions were known to be waiting inland to counter attack. Eighth Army was to capture Syracuse, then press up the east coast towards the narrow straights between Sicily and Italy. Meanwhile, US Seventh Army would be crossing the island to capture Palermo, before turning east to rejoin Eighth Army and surround any Axis forces still on the island.

The day before the landings, the ships in Harold's Port Suez convoy were joined by other vessels from Malta, North Africa and the UK. An unseasonal Force 7 gale was blowing at 03.00 on 10th July when 8th Durhams, seasick in their landing craft, began their run onto the beaches. The 6th and 9th DLI were ashore first and had already achieved their objectives when 8th Battalion landed. Apart from one stubborn gun and a lone machine gun, which were soon silenced, the defenders quickly gave up and the Battalion was able to secure the villages of Avola and Noto that covered the landing beaches. Anglo-Canadian troops, supported by fighter-bombers and heavy fire from offshore warships, initially encountered little Italian resistance, but the US Seventh Army was counter-attacked at Gela by an Italian armoured division and *Fallschirmjäger* paratroops of the elite *Hermann Göring Panzer Division*, which was driven back by US Navy destroyers firing at almost point-blank range.

Eighth Army took the undamaged port of Syracuse that night, having already captured airfields inland for Allied squadrons to use. Now XIII Corps, to which 50th Division and Harold's battalion belonged, received orders to advance up the coast to Catania. At 05.00 on the 12th, the Battalion moved 15 miles northwards, crammed onto the few vehicles that had been brought ashore, plus a couple of 'liberated' civilian saloon cars. However, they had to relinquish their limited transport to 524 Coy RASC that night, so on 13th July, the Durhams marched the ten miles to Sortino, arriving there after dark.

While the Battalion was taking up defensive positions at Sortino, 1st Parachute Brigade's seized Primasole Bridge, 25 miles up the road to Catania, and disarmed demolition charges set by Axis engineers. Whoever held this 400ft long bridge, with its boxy superstructure of iron girders spanning the River Simeto, held the key to the plain of Catania. The Paratroops' mission was to hold the bridge until 50th Division reached them, but their drop had gone badly, and they were too widely dispersed to resist successive counter attacks by their *Fallschirmjäger* counterparts for long.

The Paratroops had to be reinforced quickly and, as the Durham Brigade was nearest, its battalions immediately set off on foot, 9th DLI leading, followed by 8th, then 6th Battalions. Understanding the Para's predicament, the Durhams pushed themselves through fierce midday heat to march the 25 miles to Primosole. By dusk on the 15th, 9th Battalion and an armoured brigade were within a mile of the bridge, but they found that the surviving paratroops, exhausted and short of ammunition, had been forced away from the river only two hours earlier, although they still prevented the Germans from interfering with the bridge itself. 8th Battalion arrived a mile or two behind the 9th at about 02.00 and, tired out, Harold and his mates flopped onto the hard ground to snatch some sleep. Two hours later, they were woken by firing and explosions as 9th Battalion was raided by Italian Marine armoured cars, which they quickly knocked out.

At 07.30, 9th Battalion advanced in open formation towards the bridge supported by self-propelled artillery, while 8th Battalion took over 9th Battalion's old position. The far bank was held by *3rd Fallschirmjäger Regiment*, hardened veterans of Crete and the Russian Front, concealed among thick vineyards, two farms and a hidden, sunken road. Advancing across flat, open ground, 9th DLI were easy targets and they failed to reach the bridge, while an 88mm antitank gun firing straight down the Catania road kept tanks at bay. The 9th Battalion lay out all day, unable to move, but still protecting the bridge from demolition. Harold's battalion stood by, but their attack was postponed until after dark.

At 01.00 the next morning, an artillery and heavy machine-gun barrage began to keep the *Fallschirmjägers'* attention on the bridge, while the paratroops' CO guided two companies of 8th Battalion 300 yards upstream. They waded across the river Simeto at two points, formed up in full moonlight and moved eastwards through the vines towards the bridge. Surprise was total, the 90-minute barrage had persuaded the Germans to withdraw from the bridge and any remaining enemy personnel were subsequently dealt with. After a delay, 'B' and 'C' Companies crossed the bridge to form a perimeter 500 yards beyond. Advancing down the Catania road in the dark and the shadows of the poplars, 'B' had gone 300 yards when they stumbled onto German MG42 machine guns, commonly known as *Spandaus*, that cut down the lead platoons at point-blank range. As 'B' Coy retreated, *Fallschirmjäger* counter attacked from the sunken road and a deadly game of hide and seek began in the vineyards.

Gradually the Mortar and Carrier Platoons crossed the bridge and there was fire support from 105mm *Priest* self-propelled guns, but the Sherman tanks were knocked out or driven back by the 88mm gun. Harold's battalion held on through a day of close-quarter fighting. The 3-inch mortars did especially good work, breaking up at least three counter attacks, and *Priests* finally destroyed the eighty-eight. At 01.00, 6th and 9th Battalions crossed by the same fords 8th Battalion had used, and joined the bridgehead. The *Fallschirmjäger* were ready this time and resisted fiercely, but the weight of a two-battalion attack shook them and when

Shermans joined the bridgehead six hours later, the Germans began to surrender. After the dead had been buried and the battlefield cleared, men who had endured the worst of the North African campaign testified that the slaughter at Primosole Bridge was the worst fighting they had ever experienced.

The capture of Primasole Bridge opened Eighth Army's way across the plain of Catania, but the Germans were not ready to give up the town, so 50th Division was put on the defensive while Montgomery worked round the landward flank. The Allies took Catania and its port on 5th August. Meanwhile, the Americans made fast progress along the north coast from Palermo, forcing the Germans to begin to abandon Sicily. Harold's battalion slogged up the east coast, harassed by German rear guards at every town and village, until on 11th August, the Durhams took the town of Giarre, at some cost, in their last battle on Sicily. The last Germans slipped across the Straits of Messina overnight on 15th/16th August and next day the Americans occupied Messina.

Still recovering from the fighting in Sicily, Harold's battalion spent some weeks training by day and being entertained by Gracie Fields and George Formby after dark. On 23rd October 1943, the battalion left Augusta Harbour aboard the Dutch freighter HT *Sibajak*, joining a convoy bound for Scotland via Algiers and Gibraltar. Two weeks later, the Durhams entrained at Gourock for Haverhill in Suffolk, which would be their base for the next few months. Harold and his comrades were given a period of leave before they began to prepare for their next big operation: OVERLORD.

The Germans had long expected the Allies to invade Occupied Europe, and the Pas de Calais was the obvious place to land from Britain. Easily reached by sea and air from Kent, the Pas de Calais had several large ports, which an Allied invasion force would need to import food, equipment, ammunition, reinforcements, and especially fuel. Since 1942, the Germans had been constructing extensive coastal defences in the west called the *Atlantic Wall*, concentrating on seaports, especially the Channel ports, because it was an unbreakable rule of military logic that the Allies must quickly capture working ports to survive.

Which was why the Allies decided to break the rules and make their own by constructing two artificial harbours, codenamed MULBERRY, from floating, prefabricated concrete sections, and pumping fuel directly to the beachhead through PLUTO (Pipe Line Under The Ocean). Meanwhile, a wide-reaching deception operation, including the creation of an entire, fake American Army in East Anglia, kept German attention firmly on the Pas de Calais and away from the proposed landings in Normandy. Five invasion beaches were designated between the Cotentin Peninsular and the mouth of the River Orne, UTAH and OMAHA, both American beaches, the Anglo-Canadian JUNO Beach, and the British SWORD and GOLD

Beaches. Employing hard-earned lessons from the disastrous operation against the port of Dieppe in 1942, together with the successful landings in North Africa, Sicily and Italy, detailed planning for Operation OVERLORD began under US General Eisenhower, the Supreme Allied Commander. Montgomery would be in command of the British and Canadian forces.

Montgomery wanted men experienced in amphibious landings, such as Harold, to spearhead OVERLORD. After three months' recuperation and reorganisation at Haverhill, Harold and his comrades moved to Southwold in mid-March 1944, for intensive training. They studied detailed scale models of the German defences, conducted field exercises at Thetford and Colchester, and were introduced to the 'Funnies', the specialist armoured vehicles that would be supporting their assault. Moving to Romsey, near Southampton, in April 1944 the Battalion was reacquainted with the LCIs it had used in Sicily and practised landings on the Dorset coast, finishing with a full-scale dress rehearsal of D-Day.

The Durham Brigade was in the second wave of 50th Division's landings on GOLD Beach, which lay between La Riviére and Arromanches. 6th and 9th DLI were the Durham Brigade's assault battalions and Harold's battalion was the brigade reserve. Leaving Romsey on Saturday 3rd June, Harold and his comrades boarded their troopship in Southampton Water. However, gale force winds and bad flying conditions had been forecast for the next few days so Eisenhower decided on a 24-hour postponement. Meanwhile, the troops whiled away the time as best they could aboard their transports surrounded by the greatest ever invasion fleet. Then meteorologists identified a possible break in the weather on 6th June and Eisenhower, taking an enormous gamble, ordered the armada to sail. The Battalion's troopship left Southampton at 20.30 on 5th June and as it passed the Isle of Wight, detailed maps of the Normandy coast were distributed to the troops along with their orders. At 08.00 on D-Day, the French coast came into view and the spectacular scale of the Allied air and naval bombardment could be witnessed. Two hours later, the Durhams were in landing craft, heading for KING Sector of GOLD Beach.

As the last battalion landing on their sector, 8th DLI encountered little German opposition. The Americans began pushing west across the Cotentin Peninsular, to take Cherbourg from behind, while the British made for the canal port of Caen, but progress through the Normandy Bocage was slow. The 8th Battalion moved inland on foot, with 'D' Coy riding bicycles towards the road centre of Villers-Bocage, to help isolate Caen.

On 9th June, the Battalion rode over undulating cornfields on Sherman tanks of 24th Lancers, while 'D' Coy, pushing their bicycles, by-passed German-held Audrieu, to reach Point 103, overlooking St Pierre, where the Shermans halted. That village was strongly held and was to be attacked by

Harold's battalion at 17.45. After a 15-minute bombardment, 'C' Coy moved off followed by 'D' Coy. The Germans waited until the last moment before firing their machine guns and mortars. Ignoring heavy casualties, the Durhams quickly closed with the enemy and a short, but vicious, battle ensued with Brens and Sten guns used at close range. The village was cleared, but the enemy had not given up. German *Spandaus* and mortars made movement difficult and inflicted more casualties, while the Shermans were hit by long-range anti-tank fire.

Early next morning, accurate salvos of artillery and mortar fire straddled the battalion's positions in St Pierre and a strong German counter attack developed forcing 'C' Coy back. Concentrated fire from 'D' Coy stalled German infantry and tanks approaching from Fontenay-le-Pesnel, but they came on again. The Lancers were called to help, but the first Sherman to enter St Pierre was knocked out, blocking the way. More tanks were hit as they tried to disperse around the village. The noise of battle was deafening; wounded were coming into the Regimental Aid Post faster than they could be treated, while batmen, cooks, and clerks helped beat off an assault on Battalion HQ. At one point, three German tanks came down a narrow street in single file, driving cows before them. An NCO grabbed a PIAT and fired three shots in quick succession between the startled cows' legs, stopping the tanks' advance.

By midday on 11th, the battle had died down and the enemy withdrew, allowing the Durhams to secure their position and take stock, while the Sherwood Rangers relieved the depleted Lancers. At 19.00, a heavy German bombardment heralded a powerful attack by German tanks approaching the village from the east and southeast. They picked off the Shermans and then moved into St Pierre, blasting and machine-gunning the Durhams at close range. The Durhams stubbornly hit back, using anti-tank guns and every other weapon they had, until darkness fell and the enemy *Panzers* withdrew. Later, the battalion discovered that they had fought off the elite *Panzer Lehr Division* and fanatical *Waffen SS* troops.

Meanwhile, a failed attempt by 7th Armoured Division to capture nearby Tilly-sur-Seules had left St Pierre in a dangerous salient so 8th DLI, reduced to half strength after three days of fighting, was withdrawn. Arriving at a rest area at dawn on 13th June, Harold and the utterly exhausted Durhams got off the troop carriers, ate a hot meal and collapsed asleep. The Battalion then had two days to re-equip and receive 11 officers and 190 men as reinforcement.

The other Durham battalions had meanwhile taken and held on to Lingèvres on the Tilly-Balleroy road. By midday on 15th June, Harold's battalion had relieved another battalion in the Lingèvres area. Once again, they were facing troops of *Panzer Lehr*. The following day, 6th Battalion attempted to capture Tilly, supported by 8th Battalion's mortars, but enemy resistance was too strong.

On 18th June, Harold's battalion advanced by silent infiltration to occupy the heavily wooded Parc de la Mare area between Hottot and Tilly. Unfortunately, the leading sections surprised some Germans, most of whom were quickly shot, but others escaped to the Chateau Cordillon, raising the alarm. The Durham's advance, occupation and digging in had to continue as mortar bombs, exploding in the branches overhead, inflicted many casualties. The following day, in heavy rain, 8th Battalion were on the receiving end of a British barrage that was supposed to be supporting an attack by 1st Hampshires and 2nd Dorsets against Hottot to the south. The Durhams then endured the German retaliation from mortars, artillery, tanks and large *Nebelwerfer* rockets.

The Normandy Bocage landscape of sunken lanes and small fields divided by earth banks topped with thick hedges reduced visibility, hindered movement and provided plentiful cover for the defending Germans. For the remainder of June, Harold's battalion patrolled constantly to assess the enemy's strength and positions, and the mortar platoon perfected the art of shooting 'off the map' at targets they could not see. Elsewhere, the Allied breakout had turned into a slugging match as the Germans clung tenaciously to Caen, preventing further progress eastwards.

After a brief rest in reserve, the Battalion returned to the Tilly-sur-Seulles area at the beginning of July. By now, the veterans of *Panzer Lehr* had been relieved by the German *276th Infanterie Division*, which had taken a month to come up from the South of France having been hindered by the French Resistance and constant Allied air attacks. The Durhams patrolled regularly and constantly harassed these troops with all available weapons until 'bomb happy' deserters started to give themselves up.

On July 13th, the Durhams received their first issue of fresh bread since D-Day. Five days later, they heard that the enemy was beginning to give way. On Monday afternoon, 7th August, Harold and his battalion advanced south through the villages of Feuguerolles-sur-Seulles and Villers-Bocage to Aunay-sur-Odon, which had been levelled by Bomber Command Lancasters in attempt to impede the movement of German vehicles. Montgomery's constant pressure had held and worn down the Germans and the Allies were now breaking out of their beachheads. The American First and Third Armies swept south past Avranches and into Brittany, then eastwards towards La Havre and the River Seine, capturing Le Mans and Alençon in the process. Other US Corps pushed northwards towards Argentan, aiming to meet up with Canadian and British troops advancing from the North. The intention was to trap the remains of the German Seventh Army in an area around Falaise, the so-called 'Falaise Pocket'. 50th Division's task was to take Condé-sur-Noireau, closing off a possible escape route from the 'Pocket'.

On 9th August, the Durham Brigade was to attack at midday from le Plessis-Grimault - 6th Durhams on the right and 8th Durhams on the left -

with the intention of capturing an important junction, just over four miles south on the Condé road. Another brigade would then pass through to continue the advance. However, the road to le Plessis-Grimault led the Durhams over the crest of Mount Pinçon in full view of enemy artillery, which immediately pounded Mount Pinçon and the village. The two battalions only just managed to form up ready to start when the British barrage began. The Durhams moved off just behind the shells, closely supported by tanks that raked the near and far field hedges with their machine guns. The Durhams quickly found pockets of dazed Germans from *276th Division,* and soon around 120 of them had willingly surrendered.

As the advance continued, the Durhams began to lose men from artillery and mortar fire, including most of 'C' Company's officers, but they were in aggressive mood. Firing Bren guns from the hip and using grenades and Sten guns at close range, the Durhams overcame stiffening German resistance to take their objective right on time. At 16.00, 69th Brigade passed through them and went on to secure its own objectives by nightfall. At the day's end, the Battalion was securely dug-in, but many Durhams, including Harold Weedon, lay dead on the battlefield. Comrades recovered and buried Harold's body in a marked grave the next morning, before clearing the battlefield of debris. After the war, a new Commonwealth War Cemetery was created at Hottot-les-Bagues, close to Tilly-sur-Seulles, where the bodies of many who were killed fighting south of Bayeux, including Harold, were reinterred.

Harold's widow, Gwendoline, brought up their children in Aldbury and lived to see her grandchildren before she passed away on 24th September 1990. Gwendoline Lily Weedon's grave is in Aldbury churchyard, beside the main footpath. Frank Weedon, Harold's brother, also served in the Army and survived the war. After his demobilisation, he returned to his wife, Mary and their children in Bovingdon. Mary Weedon was the daughter of John Randall, the former Sexton of St Mary's Northchurch, who died in France serving with the Essex Regiment in 1917.

5783822 Private Donald Ernest SAUNDERS
1ˢᵗ Dorset Regiment

13ᵗʰ August 1944

Donald Ernest Saunders was born in the spring of 1923, the only son of William Henry Saunders and Florence Martha Tabor. Donald's parents, who had a winter wedding in 1910 at Chesterton, Cambridgeshire, came from families with extensive, deep roots in the villages of Cherry Hinton, Chesterton and Great Shelford that ring the outskirts of Cambridge. Donald's grandfather, Frederick, was born in Great Shelford, but as a gardener with ambition, he frequently moved his family to obtain better jobs. William Saunders was born in the London suburb of Camberwell in 1880, and four years on the family moved to Hoddesdon and later to Cobden Hill, near Radlett, Hertfordshire.

In time, William Saunders became a postman and then a telegraphist at Berkhamsted. William and Florence lived initially at 17 Cross Oak Road before moving to 46 Billet Lane, where

Private Donald Saunders
(Source: British Library)

Donald grew up. As a boy, Donald was a member of Sunnyside Parish Church choir and continued his singing with the Northchurch Baptist Church choir. After leaving school, Donald went to work for JH Durrant & Sons, Cabinet Makers, in Gossoms End.

Donald was only 16 when the Second World War broke out, but he was called up when he reached 18 years and 6 months. On 29ᵗʰ January, Donald joined the Royal Norfolk Regiment for basic infantry training and remained in Britain with the forces preparing for the invasion of Western Europe. In the spring of 1943, 20-year-old Donald returned to Northchurch on leave to marry his sweetheart, Grace Louise Briscoe. Known as Louisa, she was a Northchurch-born munitions worker, two years Donald's senior. After their wedding on 22ⁿᵈ April 1943 at St Mary's Church, the newlyweds made their home at 1 Home Farm on Northchurch Common where, in February 1944, Grace gave birth to a son.

During the D-Day landings on 6th June, Donald was in East Anglia with the Royal Norfolk Regiment. Four days later, whilst in Kings Lynn, he completed his Will on Army Form B2089, bequeathing everything to Louisa. Soon afterwards, he was transferred to 1st Battalion Dorsetshire Regiment, 50th Division and embarked for Normandy with a party of Battalion reinforcements.

Since D-Day, 1st Dorsets, alongside 1st Hampshires and 2nd Devons, had steadily fought their way inland against elite German *Panzer* Divisions, but there were not yet enough British divisions in Normandy to allow for rest and reorganisation. Over the first weeks of July, the Dorsets had been pushing slowly towards Hottot, about 12 miles south of Bayeux. At last, overnight on 19th/20th July, the exhausted Dorsets left for their first proper rest after six weeks of heavy fighting. The battalion spent two days in the Les-le-Gallois concentration area, before, on the 22nd, marching to the rest area at Les Fietées, between Bayeux and La Belle Épine. Officially, their brigade was in Divisional Reserve, but the Dorsets were able to spend time training in the difficult Bocage terrain of Normandy around Les Fietées. This is probably when Donald joined the battalion.

Meanwhile, the battles to break out of the Normandy bridgehead were beginning. The Americans started their push on 25th July, and Donald's 50th Division had the task of cutting off the Germans' line of retreat from the Americans. The 50th was to advance towards the village of Villers-Bocage, eliminating the German positions stretching from Caumont southwards and eastwards, astride the River Seulles. As a first step, Donald's Brigade took over positions in the sector La Croix des Landes to Le Lion Vert on 27th July and the Dorsets began patrolling to identify the German dispositions at Les Landes in preparation for the Brigade advance a few days later.

At 06.00 on 30th July, 'D' and 'A' Companies of 1st Dorsets, each supported by a troop of Sherman tanks, and with the Hampshires on their right, moved off in a south-easterly direction, through thick Bocage. Between them and Villers-Bocage lay a succession of ridges, each one lined with German machine gun and observation posts and behind them, concealed mortar and artillery positions. Moreover, on the Dorsets' left, 151st Durham Brigade was making a limited diversionary attack, so that flank would be open.

The Dorsets' 'D' Company had a relatively easy start, but on the left, mortars and machine guns covering the approaches to Les Landes pinned down 'A' Company until its captain and eight men bayonet-charged the nearest machine gun post, at a cost of six casualties. Both 'A' and 'D' companies then came under fire from nearby concealed mortar positions and from mortars and artillery directed from observation posts on a ridge near Launay. Heavy machine gun fire then held up 'D' Company at a place called La Pignerie, inevitably nicknamed 'The Piggery', while German infantry armed with armour-piercing *Panzerschrecks* prevented the Shermans advancing. Once again, junior leaders led small parties of men to attack and silence the most troublesome machine gun posts, allowing the advance on the right to resume.

The forward companies now had to move down an exposed slope into the valley, cross the stream at the bottom and climb up the other side. By about 11.00, 'D' Company reached some farm buildings 500 yards south of 'The Piggery' and captured a mortar position. On the left, 'A' Company reached the stream, but it had lost many men and its left flank, facing Orbois, was completely open. With the forward companies of the Dorsets and the Hampshires suffering heavy casualties, the Brigade commander decided to halt them and pass 2nd Devons through to attack the ridge near Launay.

At midday, the Dorsets sought to clear their left flank as they consolidated their gains. $N^{o}13$ Platoon of 'C' Company set off, supported by flame-thrower-armed Churchill tanks, called 'Crocodiles', to clear the southwest corner of 'Thick Wood', where they found the terrain thickly sown with German anti-tank and anti-personnel mines. Meanwhile, the enraged inmates of a wasp's nest blown up by a German mortar round, tormented 'D' Company. That evening, at about 19.30, the rest of 'C' Company accompanied by Sherman tanks fitted with heavy, motorised flails to detonate the mines, skirted the northern edge of 'Thick Wood' to outflank the German troops at Orbois Chateau and the nearby crossroads who had been holding up 9th DLI. 'C' Company duly overran the Germans, taking four prisoners.

Meanwhile, German infantry were infiltrating around the left flank of 'A' Company through thick undergrowth alongside the stream. Half an hour after 'C' Company's attack, and before the Devons had begun to pass through towards Lictot, the Germans counterattacked. They partly overran 'A' Company, but 'B' and 'D' Companies supported by Bren Guns and 2-inch mortars from the anti-tank detachment, managed to hold them off, and as the leading Devons came to help, the counterattack failed. By midnight, the battalion was considerably weakened and without its reserve company, 'C' Company, which was still at Orbois Chateau. The Brigade commander therefore ordered 2nd Devons to relieve 'D' Company and the remains of 'A' Company, who were withdrawn into reserve positions that also blocked German troops from infiltrating through 'Thick Wood'.

During the heavy fighting on 30th July, 4 officers and 11 men of Donald's battalion were killed, with a further 4 officers and 78 men wounded or missing. The following day, it was decided that the Dorsets' left flank had to be cleared before 2nd Devons could make any further progress towards the Launay ridge. 'B' Company patrols, accompanied by pioneers, pushed down tracks in the northern half of 'Thick Wood', where they found and removed large numbers of German anti-personnel *S-Mines*. An 'A' Company patrol found Orbois village clear and the rest of the Company moved in. Using Orbois as a base, 'C' Company was able to send a patrol to check the southern portion of 'Thick Wood'.

Later, 'A' and 'C' Companies were relieved from Orbois and 'Thick Wood' by 151st Brigade. 'C' Company received orders to occupy an orchard threatening the Dorsets' left flank, south of the wood. Although patrols reported that the orchard was empty, they were mistaken and 'C' Company had to mount a set piece attack. Supported by a heavy concentration of 3-inch mortar fire, 'C' Company passed through 'B' Company and entered the orchard, but encountering mines and fire from mortars and at least four machine gun posts, 'C' Company was obliged to withdraw into 'B' Company's position for the night. Early next morning, 'D' Company rushed the orchard with tanks, but found no Germans, only mines and booby traps. At 07.00 the Devons and Hampshires occupied the Launay ridge practically unopposed.

Early on 2nd August, Dorset patrols probing from the northeast reported the final ridge overlooking Villers Bocage as all clear. By midday, the battalion occupied positions on the ridge and began to patrol forward. 'A' and 'B' Companies patrolled overnight and the next day reached as far as the River Seulles, but with orders not to cross the river, because 59th Division was advancing along the far bank to take Villers Bocage.

Although there were clear indications that the Germans were preparing to withdraw from Villers Bocage, the Battalion still came under heavy artillery fire on and off during 3rd August and suffered more shelling that evening. Their Corps Artillery responded by bombarding roads out of Villers Bocage. The Germans covered their retreat next morning with several artillery bombardments on the battalion's positions. German stragglers surrendered to patrols from 'C' and 'D' Companies, while a patrol from 1st Dorsets' 'C' Company, accompanied by a war reporter, became the first Allied force to enter the village itself.

With the front narrowing, 50th Division was withdrawn on 5th August, the first time the whole division had left the fighting since D-Day. The division enjoyed two or three days' rest with light training, and the opportunity to reorganise and absorb replacements. Afterwards, Donald and his fellow Dorsets advanced through the ruins of Villers Bocage and Aunay, reaching the northern slopes of Mount Pinçon where 69th Brigade paused while the Durham Brigade attacked. Moving forward through Le Plessis Grimault, the Dorsets saw for the first time a wrecked Tiger II tank, with its improved, longer 88mm gun.

Leapfrogging the Durhams, 69th Brigade took Crapouville and La Buotière on 9th August, but it could not overcome the German resistance beyond. On 11th August, 231st Brigade took up the advance behind a barrage from the division's 25-pdrs and Army Group Artillery. The Hampshires and the Devons had to capture Point 229, St Pierre-la-Vieille, Rousseville and the ridges to the south beyond Les Forges, helped by Shermans from 4th/ 7th Dragoon Guards. Meanwhile the Dorsets followed up to occupy a succession of secure bases in support, but the Brigade was going into an uncertain situation with little knowledge of the enemy's dispositions and as its forward battalions advanced, their narrowing front would be creating a long, thin salient with exposed flanks.

The day was particularly hot, and although Donald and his battalion wore shirtsleeves, moving along the hot, dusty tracks was very trying. By 11.00, the Devons were successfully dealing with the few Germans in Rousseville, but the Hampshires were having a hard fight on the right. German troops holding Point 229 and St Pierre-la-Vieille refused to give in and the Hampshires were struggling to maintain their positions on the eastern slope of Point 229. The Dorsets were ordered to capture Point 229, but conferring with the Hampshires's CO, their own commanding officer discovered the difficulties that 5th East Yorkshires and the Hampshires had already experienced in attempting to seize this feature. The Dorsets' CO then briefed his brigade commander, who wisely decided to reinforce success and redirected the Dorsets to attack alongside the Devons on the left, while the Hampshires contained the enemy on Point 229 and St Pierre-la-Vieille.

Faulty information, hostile German action, a couple of blown bridges and the heat hampered the Dorsets' movements, but at last they assembled south of Rousseville and, despite German shellfire, as planned, they formed up on the Devons' right. At 18.45, the Royal Artillery laid down a heavy barrage and the leading companies, 'B' on the right and 'C' on the left, moved off, each supported by three Dragoon Guards Sherman tanks. Meanwhile, 'A' and 'D' Companies created a firm base in the assembly area, although they suffered continuous shelling.

Advancing into the claustrophobic Bocage, 'B' Company almost immediately came under fire from German positions around the east and southeast of St Pierre-la-Vieille. The Company mopped up some posts in a small copse, but encountered stiff opposition from a strong point at a road junction southeast of St Pierre. The company commander was killed leading a bayonet charge against this post. 'B' Company suffered many more casualties, but also inflicted losses on the enemy, capturing a number of prisoners and a field gun. 'C' Company, with both flanks secure, could concentrate on its front and moved ahead of 'B' Company and the Devons, destroying four enemy posts, killing several Germans and taking 45 prisoners that evening. As darkness fell, the Dorsets' CO came up to assess 'B', and 'C' Companies' situation. He instructed the forward companies to consolidate the ground they had gained and ordered four anti-tank guns to join them by first light. Meanwhile, 'A' and 'D' Companies closed up, ready to send out patrols or leapfrog ahead as necessary. The supporting Shermans had done well, but a number had been lost and their crews had suffered casualties. That night, 'D' Company captured a German battalion commander searching for his own companies in his staff car

At 06.00 on 12th August, the Dorsets and Devons advanced down valleys thick with mist and smoke to attack a commanding ridge south of Les Forges. They had artillery support and the Hampshires covered their advance by containing St Pierre. Passing to the west of Les Forges, 'C' Company patrolled ahead before 'D' and 'A' Companies passed through it to take the battalion's final objective.

A company of Devons had already climbed the ridge, but was encountering some opposition when 'D' and 'A' Companies emerged from the misty valley on the Les Forges side, persuading the Germans to give way. Having taken the ridge south of Les Forges, the Companies began to secure it. 'D' Company, with the survivors of 'B' under its command, formed the right flank protection on a reverse slope. 'A' Company was positioned slightly ahead of 'D', just below the crest of the ridge. Battalion headquarters was in the valley from which the Dorsets had attacked, holding 'C' Company to its right rear in reserve. Unfortunately, the ridge was very large there and unknown to the Dorsets, who were at the tip of a long salient, there was an exposed gap between them and the Devons' left flank.

German infantry and artillery remained south of St Pierre La Vieille and although a patrol from the Dorsets captured some Germans, including one with a heavy machine gun, more organized German patrols attempted to infiltrate through the gap between the Dorsets and the Devons. A Universal Carrier dealt with one enemy patrol, and Germans entering an orchard and buildings to the west of 'B' and 'D' Companies suffered at the hands of the Battalion's 3-inch mortars.

Just before last light on 12th, an entire battalion from the German *276th Division* attacked 'D' and 'B' Companies from the west and south. 'A' Company enfiladed part of this attack, killing or capturing several Germans, while 'D' and 'B' Companies stood their ground, beating off the enemy. Another party of Germans, accompanied by a tank, pushed through the gap between the Devons and the Dorsets. Advancing up the road to Les Forges, they headed straight for Battalion Headquarters. The Germans overran the HQ's defensive screen, setting a Universal Carrier ablaze, but in the main headquarters position, signallers, regimental police, batmen, drivers, intelligence section, and some of the Support Company, resisted. Silhouetted against the burning Carrier, the Germans fell to rapid, accurate rifle, Bren, PIAT and 2-inch mortar fire, while HQ called 90th Field Regiment RA to bring down defensive fire on the attackers' rear elements.

Between 11th and 13th August, 231st Brigade engaged large, but disorganised remnants of the German *276th* and *326th Divisions*. 1st Dorsets advanced as far as the German gun area, capturing 4 officers, including the battalion commander, 158 men, a 105mm gun, an 88mm anti-tank gun and 18 machine guns.

The Battalion had lost fewer than 70 men, but one of them was Donald Saunders. He was killed on 13th August, which turned out to be the very last day of fighting 1st Dorsets would see in Normandy. Donald was probably buried on the battlefield, but his grave was subsequently lost. His name now appears on the Bayeux Memorial.

5961214 Private Edmund Albert BARBER
1st Loyal (North Lancashire) Regiment

25th August 1944

Edmund Albert Barber, known as Eddie, was born in Northchurch during the spring of 1922 to Dorothy and Albert Frederick Barber. Dorothy, who came from Potten End, and Albert, from Berkhamsted, were married two years before Eddie was born. Albert worked as a boot and shoe repairer in a workshop next to the family home at 32 Gossoms End. Eddie was educated at the council school and later apprenticed to Coopers at the firm's printing works, the Clunbury Press, in Manor Street, Berkhamsted.

Eddie joined 2nd Battalion, Bedfordshire and Hertfordshire Regiment, in January 1942 when he was 19 and spent the next year in training at Carronbridge in Scotland, qualifying as a Bren gunner. Developed from a Czech design, the Bren gun had replaced the Lewis gun in British Army's light machine gun during the 1930s. Weighing some 22.5lbs the magazine-fed Bren gun could fire 500 rounds per minute.

On 1st March 1943, orders came for 2nd Battalion to leave Carronbridge and proceed by train to Glasgow docks. The Battalion sailed for North Africa on 11th March and arrived at Algiers on 23rd, to be greeted by weather warm enough to bathe in the Mediterranean. However, incessant rain arrived within days, flooding some of the roads to a depth of four feet. At the beginning of April, the Battalion moved inland to join the front line. By then the *Afrika Korps* was conducting a fighting retreat, keeping the Allied troops at arm's length with booby traps, mortar and sniper fire. Eddie would have belonged to the crew of a Universal Carrier, commonly known as 'Bren Gun Carriers', which were open-topped, fast, tracked light armoured vehicles crewed by four to five men. Eddie's company commander was Lieutenant Jim Harrowell, a well-known Berkhamsted solicitor and sportsman.

There was heavy fighting towards the end of April, as the net closed around the *Afrika Korps*. During the final battle for Tunis on 6th May, Eddie's company came under heavy mortar fire and Lieutenant Harrowell was wounded. By 10th May, the fighting in North Africa was all but over and two days later over 250,000 Axis troops formally surrendered to the Allies, although mopping up activities continued for some weeks.

With North Africa secured, the way was open to invade Italy and knock her out of the war. Sicily was chosen as the first target for invasion, but Sicily was protected by Mussolini's answer to Malta, the fortress island of Pantelleria. With its naval base and airfields only 53 miles east of Tunisia and 63 miles from Sicily, rocky Pantelleria dominated the narrow waters that convoys to Malta, and the invasion fleet, had to navigate. If Pantelleria could be captured the route to Sicily would open.

21 gun batteries of various calibres and a string of pillboxes protected the island, all garrisoned by around 12,000 men. Added to this was the fact that Pantelleria had no suitable landing beaches. Consequently, to minimise casualties during the assault on the island, Desert Airforce bombers spent four days dropping thousands of tons of high explosive on the island's gun batteries, ammunition stores and communications centres, particularly concentrating on the port area, so that the assault landing craft could land troops of 1st Division on a beach of rubble at the shoreline.

Eddie was among many soldiers transferred to 1st Battalion, the Loyal (North Lancashire) Regiment, for the assault on Pantelleria. During the afternoon of 10th June 1943, Eddie and the Loyals left Tunisia on a calm sea. Next day at dawn, the naval fleet opened fire whilst the air bombardment resumed with increased fury, and an hour later the first landing craft arrived off Pantelleria. Closely supported by American long-range fighters, the first wave of the main force began landing at midday to be greeted with white flags. Although almost half of Pantelleria's guns were still usable, the garrison had already had enough and by late afternoon, the Italian admiral commanding the island had surrendered, having sabotaged the freshwater supply. Apart from some hit-and-run bombing raids from Sicily, the Germans made no effort to counterattack and Pantelleria quickly came under Allied control.

Within days, most of 1st Division had returned to North Africa and were given five days' rest and recreation in camps along the Tunisian coast. Inter-regimental and other sporting events were common, as were trips to the Mediterranean coast to bathe. Meanwhile, thousands of German POWs needed to be kept occupied until their transfer to newly established prisoner of war camps was arranged. During this time, musical bands formed of German prisoners provided regular entertainment, their concerts proving extremely popular with the British troops.

On 10th July, the Allies landed on Sicily. Although Eddie's regiment was not involved, the men saw and heard the Allied bombers streaming overhead en route to their targets. With the invasion underway, training soon resumed, as did the rainy season, making the roads impassable at times and training extremely arduous. Following the loss of Sicily's three large airfields, Foggia's extensive airfield complex protecting southern Italy could be neutralised and the mainland invaded. Italy's dictator Benito Mussolini was soon overthrown and imprisoned, and a new government opened negotiations with the Allies, leading to the Italian surrender on 3rd September, supposedly without the Germans' knowledge.

Montgomery immediately began preliminary landings on the mainland, but just before the main landings at Salerno and Taranto on 9th September, the Italian government made its capitulation public. Unsurprised by their erstwhile ally, the German forces in Italy immediately carried out a well-prepared operation to disarm their former allies, sometimes by force. The battle for the Italian peninsular, with its narrow coastal strip, intersected by rivers, coves and ridges, winding roads and mountainous interior, was going to be much like the recent fighting up the Tunisian coast; an infantryman's battle, a tough slog from defended line to defended line.

Eddie's battalion began a period of concentrated training in preparation, starting with Operation ALMA, a joint exercise pitting the Loyals, North Staffordshire Regiment and the Gordon Highlanders against the Grenadier and Scots Guards. ALMA ended on 30th September and while its lessons were being absorbed, the troops continued training and competing in sporting events despite the constant, heavy rain. On 5th October, the popular Tyneside comedian, Wee Georgie Wood, entertained the troops.

The following week, the Battalion moved to a tented camp in the Atlas Mountains previously occupied by the Kings Shropshire Light Infantry. However, before their mountain warfare training could begin, the Battalion tidied up the clutter of war debris, including a knocked-out German Tiger tank, and dug new drainage trenches to prevent heavy rain flooding the camp. Eddie then learnt about rock climbing, map reading, the use of mules to carry equipment, hill walking with heavy packs, as well as the usual mortar, rifle and Bren gun practice. At the month's end, the Loyals participated in a four-day exercise to test their battle-readiness for the mountainous conditions they would experience in Italy, followed by two more one-day exercises.

On 1st December, the Loyals's first contingent loaded the Battalion's lorries, tracked vehicles and anti-tank guns onto an LST (Landing Ship Tank) at Bizerta docks and sailed the following day. On 4th December, the rest of the Battalion was transported by LST to a LSI (Landing Ship Infantry), the LSI *Cuba*, anchored offshore. Two soldiers became casualties as they clambered up ladders and scrambling nets onto the larger vessel, but by noon on 5th, the convoy and its destroyer and corvette escort sailed for the foot of Italy. Two days later, the battalion disembarked at Taranto to join the advance party at a staging camp five miles' march inland. Having rested, the Loyals entrained for another staging area at Spinazzola, some 80 miles northwest, where they stayed until the end of 1943.

As expected, the German Army had created a series of strong defensive lines across Italy that could only be broken by costly frontal assaults. The Allies were stuck at the *Gustav* Line, which was dominated by the large monastery on Monte Cassino. In an effort to outflank the Germans and drive towards Rome, a plan was prepared to land two Divisions, under the American General Lucas, to the north of the *Gustav* Line, codenamed Operation SHINGLE. Experience had taught the Allies that air superiority was essential for successful assault landings and the furthest north that could be covered from existing Allied airfields was the area around the town of Anzio

At Salerno on 1st January 1944, Eddie's battalion began two weeks of practice landings using American General Motors DUKW amphibious lorries, which the British called 'ducks'. Based on the proven 2½ ton Deuce and a Half truck, the incredibly seaworthy DUKW could transport infantry and supplies from ships moored offshore onto the beach and directly inland.

On 22nd January, the Loyals landed virtually unopposed, with 1st Division six miles north of Anzio, while the American 3rd Division landed six miles the other side. The beachhead was secured the following day, but General Lucas decided not to advance inland until both divisions had all of their vehicles, artillery and equipment ashore and organised, even though the way to Rome appeared open. After a week, Lucas felt ready to move, but it was already too late. German units had moved in and throughout February repeatedly tried to crush the Anglo-American bridgehead. A particularly strong attack on 19th February, inflicted heavy casualties, but the bridgehead held and by early March, the exhausted Germans went onto the defensive. The Anzio bridgeheads then took on some characteristics of trench warfare. Weeks of painful attrition, frequent mortar and artillery fire and aggressive, active patrolling were needed to probe and uncover camouflaged enemy strongpoints. Allied patrols were in constant danger from German booby traps, such as a bamboo cane laid across a track from two thin wires that detonated an explosive charge buried by the trackside when the cane was touched.

With no immediate prospect of a breakout from Anzio, the *Gustav* Line, dominated by Monte Cassino, remained a formidable obstacle. It took the Allies four months of bitter fighting before Monte Cassino finally fell on 18th May, enabling the US 5th Army to drive north towards Rome. A week after the fall of Monte Cassino Allied forces finally broke out of the Anzio bridgehead and linked up with 5th Army two days later. The Germans slowly fell back northwards, mining the roads as they went and putting up strong defensive fire whenever possible. On 4th June, 5th Army entered Rome, which had been declared an open city. Eddie's battalion arrived at its outskirts two days later. With the fighting temporarily over, the Loyals established a shuttle service allowing its men to spend two hours each in the city.

Eddie and his battalion settled down for a period of well-earned rest and light training. As well as day visits to Rome, other recreations such as a mobile cinema and trips to the Ostia Lido began. Training restarted in early July, with exercises taking place day and night. King George VI inspected the Battalion on 30th July and the next day it left Rome and moved north.

After losing Rome, the Germans had withdrawn to the *Gothic* Line, which stretched from the Mediterranean across the Apennines to the Adriatic and passed just north of Florence. The Loyals arrived on 16th August, taking up defensive positions south of Florence in co-operation with local partisan groups. The partisans were left to fight any Germans and Fascists remaining in the city itself, while the Loyals protected Florence from any German retaliation.

The Battalion also conducted regular combat patrols to locate German positions, frequently coming under fire from concealed machine guns and mortars. On 25th August, Eddie was with a patrol sent to reconnoitre Fiesole Ridge, northeast of Florence, and investigate reports that the Germans positions there were empty. The reports were inaccurate and several powerful *Spandau* machine guns and mortars opened fire from concealed enemy positions. Eddie and seven of his comrades were killed, whilst 39 officers and men were wounded in the crossfire. Eddie was 22 when he died.

Exactly one month after Eddie's death, Eighth Army attacked up the Adriatic coast and the US Fifth Army advanced through the Apennines and breached the *Gothic* Line. Unfortunately, the Allies were unable to break out onto the Lombardy Plain before winter closed in. All further progress had to wait until the Allied Spring Offensive the following April, which ultimately led to the capitulation of German forces in Italy on 2nd May 1945.

Today, Eddie's body lies alongside the River Arno in the Florence War Cemetery, east of the city.

Peter Noel LOXLEY
Foreign Office & Diplomatic Service

1st February 1945

Peter Noel Loxley was the only son of Commander Arthur Noel Loxley RN and his wife, Gladys Maud Loxley. Born in Kensington on 27th March 1905, Peter was christened five weeks later at All Saints, Knightsbridge. At the time of Peter's birth, his father was enjoying a home posting and saw a good deal of his son during his early years, but it was not to last. When Peter was seven, his father, now a Captain, was posted to a new command at Malta. Soon afterwards, Gladys and Peter travelled to Malta aboard the *Borneo* to stay for just over a year.

Peter was privately educated at home until 1914 when, having reached the age of nine, he went to board at West Downs Preparatory School. Standing on a hill west of Winchester, West Downs School was founded in 1897 by a former House of Commons Clerk called Lionel Helbert, whose first six pupils were from the families of MPs and others he knew from the House. Helbert liked to get to know his pupils' parents and wrote them letters at least once a day to update them on their sons' health and progress. A mark of the school's success was the frequent repetition of the same surnames on the rosters of new boys. Peter Loxley was one of twenty-five pupils joining the school in the late summer of 1914, something that Peter's father alluded to in one of his last letters home. Peter would have been enjoying the Christmas holidays at home when his father went down with HMS *Formidable* on 1st January 1915, his Airedale Terrier, Bruce, at his side. Peter had bought Bruce three months earlier as a gift to keep his father company aboard his new command.

In 1918, Peter left West Downs School and entered Eton College as a King's Scholar, or 'Colleger', the following April. Peter excelled in history, earning the 1st History Prize in the 1922 July examinations, the 1st Headmaster's History Prize a year later, and the top history prize, the Rosebery, in December 1923, as well as two other prizes. The following year, Peter gained an open scholarship to Trinity College, Oxford where, not surprisingly, he chose to read Modern History. Whilst at Trinity, Peter played an active part in college life, joining a debating and reading society, called the Gryphon Club, as well as the Claret Club, and represented Trinity College at golf.

Peter left Trinity in 1927 with a First in Modern History and received a Laming Travelling Fellowship at Queen's College. Established by a bequest of Henry Laming, a former member of Queen's, these fellowships allowed linguists to travel and study in Europe and were specifically aimed at future businessmen and diplomats, not academics. Peter had planned a career in the Diplomatic Service, for which French and German were compulsory languages, and the fellowship allowed him to spend two years travelling in France, Germany and Austria. During his time in Weimar Germany, Loxley probably witnessed the 1928 elections for the Reichstag. Although the Social Democratic Party remained the largest party with 153 of the 491 seats, Adolph Hitler's Nazi Party won 12 seats, despite polling fewer than 3% of the vote.

Returning to England in the summer of 1929, Loxley joined the Foreign Office & Diplomatic Service as a Third Secretary and was given a four-year posting to the British Embassy in Warsaw. In 1933, he transferred to the British Embassy in Tehran and was promoted to Second Secretary the following year. Whitehall quickly identified Loxley as a high-flyer and on his return from Iran in 1937, he became secretary to Richard (Rab) Butler, the Conservative MP and a junior Foreign Office minister. On 11th March 1938, Loxley and Butler's Parliamentary Private Secretary called at Rab Butler's flat in Little College Street, to brief him as Nazi Germany's annexation of Austria unfolded.

Loxley's engagement to Elizabeth Lavender Dawnay appeared in the national Press on 25th May 1938. Lavender's father, Major General Guy Payan Dawnay, had served with distinction during the First World War in France, Gallipoli and Palestine, where he nominally commanded Lawrence of Arabia during the Arab revolt against Turkey. Peter Loxley and Lavender Dawnay were married on 26th July 1938, at the Dawnays' parish church of St Nicholas, Longparish, Hampshire, the Curate of St Paul's, Knightsbridge taking the service.

Peter and Lavender Loxley on their Wedding Day (Source: British Library)

The newlyweds set up home at 18 St Leonards Terrace in Chelsea, where they employed a cook/housekeeper. Their first child arrived during Autumn the following year with a second child born in 1942.

On 1st December 1939, Loxley became an Acting First Secretary at the Ministry of Economic Warfare, which the Prime Minister, Neville Chamberlain had established the previous year, 'to so disorganise the enemy's economy as to prevent him from carrying on the war' and 'deprive the enemy of the material means of resistance and war making'. Ministry staff identified parts of the German economy that were not self-sufficient and consequently vulnerable to disruption. Economic pressure, in the form of 'incentives', would be applied to neutral countries exporting vital raw materials and so entice them away from Germany. The Ministry also identified the locations of Germany's main industries, particularly armaments, chemicals, and iron and steel works, which would become targets for early bombing raids.

Over half of Germany's imports were sea-borne, making a repeat of Britain's 1914-1918 naval blockade an obvious measure, but success then had depended on virtual immunity from air attack, assistance from the French and Japanese navies, and Germany's relatively limited conquests. By June 1940, Germany had occupied Czechoslovakia, Denmark, Norway, the Low Countries and France, absorbing their resources and industries into her war effort and extending the reach of the *Luftwaffe* to cover the whole of the North Sea and the English Channel. This made a repeat of the naval blockade impossible.

The new Prime Minister, Winston Churchill, responded in July 1940 by directing the Ministry of Economic Warfare to create a Special Operations Executive (SOE), to conduct espionage, sabotage and propaganda, and assist resistance movements against German occupation and 'Set Europe ablaze!' SOE replaced and absorbed existing bodies responsible for sabotage, subversion and propaganda, including Section D of MI6, the Secret Intelligence Service, or SIS. No doubt Loxley encountered spies during his embassy postings, but his involvement in the SOE's formation would have introduced him to leading figures in the security services.

Loxley returned to the Foreign Office in late June 1941, as Principle Private Secretary to Sir Alexander Cadogan, who was by then the most senior civil servant in the Foreign Office. Cadogan had been a prominent critic of appeasement towards Nazi Germany, but also realised that war with Germany would risk exposing Britain's Asian Empire to Japanese aggression. Loxley's main role as Cadogan's effective deputy was to be the Foreign Office's Intelligence Liaison Officer, making him the focus of relations between MI6, which answered to the Foreign Office, MI5, domestic counter-intelligence under the Home Office, and Churchill's SOE. Loxley was well aware that Britain also imported vital commodities from neutral countries, so he had to ensure that British espionage would not damage relations with them.

The week before Loxley joined Cadogan's staff, Germany had invaded the Soviet Union, but another surprise event was about to hit his desk. At 17.45 on Saturday 10th May 1941, an unarmed Messerschmitt Bf110 fighter with long-range fuel tanks, left an airfield near Augsburg in Bavaria and headed towards Glasgow. British radar plotted the

Messerschmitt and a fighter was scrambled. Before the raider could be intercepted however, its pilot bailed out and his aircraft crashed onto a farm near Eaglesham. The pilot, who had broken his ankle on landing, told his captors he was 'Alfred Horn' on a special mission to see the prominent British opposition leader, the Duke of Hamilton. The Duke, who was then a Wing Commander stationed near Edinburgh, was brought over to meet 'Horn' in private. When they were alone, 'Horn' announced to the Duke that he was actually Deputy Führer, Rudolf Hess.

Born in Egypt to German parents in 1894, Rudolf Hess had served in the Bavarian infantry during the First World War and trained as a fighter pilot. Following Germany's defeat, Hess joined the right-wing *Freikorps* that violently opposed the Communist uprisings in Germany during 1918 and 1919. Hess later joined the *Nazi* Party and was arrested for his part in Hitler's failed 1923 *Putsch* to seize power. Hitler dictated *Mein Kampf* to Hess in Landsberg prison and he became Hitler's personal secretary for several years, receiving political appointments in the *SS* and the *Nazi* Party for his loyal service. On 21st April 1933, Hess became Deputy *Führer* of Germany, a largely ceremonial role that mostly involved introducing Hitler at *Nazi* Party rallies and whipping up the adoring crowds to fever pitch.

The Duke had only met Hess once, five years before at the Berlin Olympics, but several minutes' conversation convinced him that this was indeed Hess and Hamilton immediately flew to London to brief Churchill and Cadogan, who's office took charge of the case. A few days later, with an experienced interrogator already checking the prisoner's story, Loxley was put in charge of all Hess-related matters.

Hess was given the codename *Jonathan* and moved to Camp Z, which was actually a safe house equipped with secret microphones called Mytchett Place in Aldershot. When questioned, *Jonathan's* answers were vague and often confused, especially regarding his reasons for flying to Scotland, but Hess consistently maintained that he had planned and rehearsed the flight for some time without Hitler's knowledge. From the start, interrogators questioned his mental state: Hess showed signs of paranoia, insisting his food was being poisoned and on one occasion actually attempted suicide by jumping down the stairs at Mytchett Place, but only succeeded in breaking his leg. It soon became apparent that any information Hess provided was extremely unreliable.

Huge amounts of paperwork generated by the Hess affair swept across Loxley's desk. There were medical and psychological reports, transcripts of interrogations and copies of Top Secret memoranda from the legendary Head of SIS, Colonel Stewart Graham Menzies, better known as 'C'. On 11th July 1941, 'C' wrote a memorandum to Churchill reporting signs of improvement in Hess's mental condition, but that he professed ignorance of any atrocities carried out in German concentration camps and demanded to see proof. The following day, Loxley, acting on behalf of 'C', requested the relevant documents with which to confront Hess.

By August 1941, three options for *Jonathan's* long-term future were being considered: transfer Hess to a Prisoner of War camp or hospital, relocate him to a house similar to Mytchett Place, or leave him in 'Camp Z'. The War Office asked Loxley to decide the most appropriate option, but Loxley was absent from work recovering from an illness at the time. In his absence Cadogan decided that 'Camp Z' was the best place for Hess, subject to a number of alterations being made designed to keep him secure and alive, including reglazing the windows with armoured glass, replacing his toilet chain with a lever, changing the direction doors opened and creating an exercise area in the garden secured with wire fences.

After ten months, Hess was assessed to have no further useful intelligence left to offer and that he should be transferred in secret to Maindiff Court Military Hospital and POW Reception Centre near Abergavenny, Wales. Unfortunately, Hess's transfer proved to be anything but secret when the staff of Maindiff Court lined up to greet him on his arrival. Loxley still had to deal with the mounds of paperwork concerning Hess, much of it insignificant, such as a Conservative MP's query whether Hess received better food than other German officer POWs, or mundane, such as organising the Swiss Ambassador's frequent visits and gifts of cigars to Hess. *Jonathan* himself remained troublesome, frequently complaining about his new accommodation and that noise from the nearby railway disturbed his sleep.

Hess was to remain at Maindiff Court until the war's end. Convicted of crimes against peace at Nuremburg in 1946, Hess received a sentence of life imprisonment in West Berlin's Spandau Prison. He eventually became Spandau's only inmate, still guarded by soldiers from the four Occupying Powers, until his suicide there in August 1987 aged 93. The circumstances surrounding Hess's suicide and his flight to Scotland remain controversial to this day.

If managing the Hess affair was not troublesome enough, Loxley had a particularly sensitive issue to handle from the moment he became Intelligence Liaison Officer, namely Soviet Russia. Ever since October 1917, the Soviet Union had worked to spread Communist revolution across the world, either through the overt political actions of the Communist International, or Comintern, or through the sometimes-aggressive espionage of the NKVD, the forerunner of the KGB. In 1925, the SIS formed 'Section V', under Valentine Vivian, with specific responsibility for anti-communist counter-intelligence. However, Section V's tiny pre-war staff of three officers failed to realise that the NKVD had been recruiting the undergraduate sons of the British establishment throughout the 1930s.

Germany had invaded western Poland in September 1939, and for that, Britain and France declared war on her. Two weeks later, Soviet Russia occupied eastern Poland thanks to the non-aggression pact concluded with Germany the previous month. Since Russia was siding with the enemy, Section V expanded under Vivian, who was also appointed head of military activities at the codebreaking facility at 'Station X', better known as Bletchley Park. Germany's invasion of Russia on 22nd June 1941, now made her Britain's ally and British intelligence suddenly had to tread carefully. In spring 1943, 'C' asked Vivian to create 'Section IX' specifically to monitor illegal Communist and Soviet activity in other countries and investigate suspected cases of penetration and espionage. Loxley told Vivian that he had no objection to this work, provided that Section IX did not upset the Soviets and kept its activities outside Russia itself. However, Loxley thought it likely that the Soviets were already operating in Britain noting, 'The Russians will simply take us for fools if we do not exploit these opportunities, all the more since it is quite evident that they have an extensive network of agents in England'.

Loxley would have been shocked at the degree of Russian penetration within the SIS and Foreign Office, and that some of his contacts were actually Soviet spies. In September 1941, for example, Loxley was preparing a report for Churchill on Japanese contacts in Britain using information from MI5 compiled by Anthony Blunt. In September 1944, Loxley received documents from the newly appointed Head of 'Section IX', 'Kim' Philby, which included a detailed report of Soviet Intelligence operations in the UK. Philby was a long-term Soviet agent who was unmasked as the 'Third Man' of the 'Cambridge Five' spy ring within SIS and fled to Russia in 1963. Anthony Blunt would be exposed as a Soviet agent and the 'Fourth Man' of that spy ring in the 1970s.

Loxley's wartime liaison with the SIS became so successful that official Foreign Office memoranda occasionally described the SIS as 'Mr Loxley's friends'. From its inception in April 1943, Loxley also sat alongside intelligence chiefs on the Secret Service Co-ordinating Committee. Working at such a high level, Loxley had access to, or was aware of, all the key plans regarding the conduct of the war, including the existence of coded German and Japanese messages decrypted by Bletchley Park. By decoding German *Enigma* and *Lorentz* military communications, Bletchley Park was winning the war in the Mediterranean and greatly assisting the battle against German U-boats in the Atlantic.

By the spring of 1943, with the threat of a German invasion receding, Whitehall began planning for the long-term future. Drawing on the insights gained from his close association with the Security Services, Loxley wrote to 'C' highlighting a number of weaknesses he saw within SIS that included its recruitment policy favouring private wealth over ability, the lack of a professional career structure, or even pension rights, and, incredibly, no deputy nominated to take charge should 'C' become indisposed.

On 8th October, Cadogan appointed Loxley as the Secretary to a committee chaired by Sir Neville Bland and created specifically to examine the future of the SIS. Victor Cavendish-Bentinck, the Joint Intelligence Sub-Committee Chairman, completed the committee, but Loxley, who liaised closely with 'C' throughout proceedings, acted as its driving force. A year and four days later, the committee's top secret 38-page report entitled, 'Future Organisation of the SIS', was given strictly limited circulation within the Security Services and Whitehall.

Unsurprisingly, its recommendations for the post-war SIS largely reflected Loxley's ideas, especially that it should remain under Foreign Office control. The Bland Report also recommended that trade organisations should be established as 'fronts' to provide 'cover' for SIS officers abroad and that genuine British businessmen should be recruited as intelligence gatherers. The SIS should particularly watch Soviet Russia and her activities worldwide; Germany, especially any move towards re-armament; communist infiltration in France and, specifically, any re-establishment of links between the French and German chemical industries. Important recommendations included a review into operational overlaps between the SIS and its home security counterpart, MI5, and significantly to disband Churchill's pet, the SOE, and return its remit for covert action and sabotage to the SIS. Although the Bland Report naturally received a mixed reception, it eventually formed the cornerstone of the Security Services' post-war reorganisation and was arguably Peter Loxley's greatest achievement. The report remained classified until 2013.

On 15th April 1944, as plans for the Normandy landings neared completion, Loxley received a letter from the British Political Officer at Supreme Headquarters Allied Expeditionary Force, (SHAEF), headed 'Assassination Priorities for OVERLORD'. The letter asked him to approach 'C' informally for his views and advice on the question of eliminating key German personnel, including senior commanders in France, such as von Rundstedt and Rommel, as well as prominent French collaborators, immediately before the planned invasion, with the objective of causing chaos within the German High Command. Forwarding the letter to 'C' for urgent consideration, Loxley commented that the intentions were vague, but he considered the matter 'relatively plain sailing' if the French resistance agreed to undertake the task. However, he doubted whether assassinating Rommel was realistic and to kill him after capture could be seen as murdering a prisoner of war. 'C' replied that if the 'removal' of senior commanders might assist OVERLORD, then SHAEF should identify the relevant officers. The SIS could only contribute the names of key Army and *SS* intelligence officers, but 'C' was reluctant to pursue the matter without clarification from SHAEF. What SHAEF actually had in mind, Loxley discovered three days later, was not the assassination of the Field Marshals, but to have the French resistance kill Gestapo officers and other key Nazi officials. 'C' had already cautioned Loxley about the likely scale of German reprisals and when Cavendish-Bentinck expressed his deep concerns to 'C' that assassinations would do little to assist the invasion and that British POWs would probably be killed in retaliation, SHAEF quietly dropped the scheme.

Three months later, with the Allies starting to close on Germany from both east and west, Loxley accompanied Cadogan to Dumbarton Oaks, a large, private mansion in Washington DC, for a business-like international summit conference. From 21st August, high-ranking delegations from Great Britain, the USA, China and the USSR thrashed out proposals for a new international body to replace the League of Nations and safeguard peace after the war had ended. The resulting document, submitted to all Allied and neutral governments on 7th October, was essentially the blueprint for the United Nations Organisation as it exists today.

The next summit between Churchill, Roosevelt and Stalin, codenamed MAGNETO, to be held in the Crimean resort of Yalta in February 1945, would discuss the inclusion of France as an Occupying Power in Germany, the bringing Russia into the war against Japan, the Dumbarton Oaks proposals, and the new United Nation's Security Council's voting procedure. Cadogan and Antony Eden, the Foreign Secretary, left early for preliminary talks between Churchill and Roosevelt in Malta, while Loxley assembled the 'Top Secret' papers he would be carrying to the former imperial palace at Livadiya in Yalta for use by the British MAGNETO delegation.

In the early hours of 1st February, Loxley carrying his secret documents, was driven to RAF Northolt, where two C-87 Liberator Express transport aircraft had been standing by for the MAGNETO personnel. The first leg was to the Pomigliano d'Arco airbase near Naples, where they would stop overnight before flying on to Yalta. Loxley, accompanied by Cadogan's private detective, various Foreign Office civil servants and military officers, boarded their Liberator Express. Delayed some hours by fog, the first Liberator Express eventually took off, but Loxley's plane developed an untraceable electrical fault before take-off and, with no spare aircraft available at Northolt, his party was rushed by coach to RAF Lyneham, Wiltshire, where an aircraft was hastily put at their disposal.

At Lyneham, 27-year-old Flight-Lieutenant Alfred Eaton-Clarke of 511 Squadron waited, while Loxley's party of VIPs ate a late breakfast. Eaton-Clarke's Avro York, serial MW116, had been commandeered from its scheduled flight to Colombo for this special flight via Naples and he went over his new flight plan again. They were to traverse France, avoiding the German's western *Flak* belt, cross the Mediterranean coast at Sète heading towards Corsica, then locate the Italian coast and turn south for Naples. The estimated flying time was six and a half hours, which would mean landing in darkness. Although Eaton-Clarke's six-man crew had not flown together before, they were experienced airmen, so even a night landing at an unfamiliar airfield should not be a problem.

With breakfast over, the thirteen VIPs were seated aboard MW116 by the steward, Corporal Burge, while Loxley had his papers stowed in a special compartment in the York's cabin. The Avro York had been adapted by Roy Chadwick from his successful Lancaster bomber design by mounting its wings high up on a capacious, box-like fuselage. The York also inherited the Lancaster's engines and tail assembly as well as its range and reliability. Eaton-Clarke's Squadron was the first to be fully equipped with the unarmed Yorks, although on this flight an Air Gunner, Flying Officer Appleby, was on the crew. At 10.15, MW116 lifted off Lynham's runway and turned for France.

The flight to the Mediterranean was uneventful and they reached Corsica earlier than anticipated, giving an estimated landing time of 16.00 at Pomigliano d'Arco, but then the weather closed in and heavy cloud obscured everything below. Eaton-Clarke called a nearby Italian airfield for a weather report, but its reply contradicted the conditions through which the aircraft was flying. Eaton-Clarke descended from 8,000 to 5,000 feet to catch a glimpse of the coast, but the few gaps in the cloud quickly disappeared and because flying lower than 5,000 feet near Naples risked a collision with Mount Vesuvius, Eaton-Clarke decided to turn out to sea and hope for a break in the cloud. As the York turned, he saw a dark thundercloud extending down to sea level and static interference swamped the wireless, preventing his navigator from obtaining a radio fix. Easing the York down to 500 feet, two small islands appeared below, but the navigator considered them too small to identify and with mainland Italy still nowhere in sight, Eaton-Clarke abandoned his approach and passed a message to Loxley and the other passengers that the York was diverting to Malta owing to bad weather.

Over Sicily at 8,000 feet, radio interference diminished enough for the navigator to tune briefly into the Malta Beacon for a bearing before losing reception again. In darkness and without radio navigation aids, Eaton-Clarke followed that last bearing on instruments, but he was running out of options. Suddenly, two inhabited islands appeared below and the pilot circled above them while the radio operator attempted to contact Malta, but after nearly an hour, they were unable to confirm their position or establish contact with Malta. When only twenty minutes of fuel remained, Eaton-Clarke judged his safest option was to ditch the York close enough to the larger island for his passengers and crew to reach land by inflatable dinghies. Corporal Burge advised his passengers they should remove their collars and ties and put on lifejackets. Everybody aboard remained calm as the crewmembers opened the York's hatches and readied the dinghies for the passengers' escape. Meanwhile, the radio operator broadcast a Mayday and the crew removed their battledress and shoes ready to evacuate the aircraft.

The sea was calm as Eaton-Clarke lined up on the island's harbour, checked for floating obstacles and eased his plane down to sea level. The York was travelling at around 135mph as it broke the waters' surface, but hoping to get closer to the harbour Eaton-Clarke opened the throttle and with water already gushing through the open hatches the straining fuselage suddenly split in two. Eaton-Clarke and his injured co-pilot dragged themselves from their shattered cockpit and were quickly picked up by a man and young children in a rowing boat. Searching about the wrecked aircraft by the light of a hurricane lamp, they found an unconscious passenger, a senior RAF officer, still strapped in his seat. Releasing the man, they hauled him aboard, but when they recovered a dead body, they almost swamped the overloaded boat and their lamp went out. Shouting for help, the pilot received an answer from his Navigator who had swum to a nearby rock on the edge of the island. Soon more boats arrived on the scene and gradually the survivors and the dead were brought ashore.

The survivors discovered they had been circling the island of Lampedusa, some 100 miles west of Malta and about 70 miles east of Tunisia. The islanders tended the survivors' wounds and gave them food. The following day, an American naval vessel arrived in Lampedusa's small port to take the survivors, together with the bodies of the dead, to the 90th General Hospital in Malta. All told, four of the aircrew died during the ditching, the others escaping with various injuries but only one passenger had survived. Post mortem examinations later established that Loxley and the majority of the passengers had suffered fractures to the base of their skulls, caused when the aircraft struck the water and broke up.

When news of the crash reached the Foreign Office, the immediate concern was to recover Loxley's Top Secret papers. A 16-strong RAF Regiment taskforce was despatched from Malta to guard the York, which rested tail up in around 15 feet of water, some 30 yards off the shore of Lampedusa. Senior military officials from Malta began a detailed search of the wreckage employing a 'water-glass' to look beneath the surface. The passenger cabin, at the centre of the aircraft, was clearly visible, but inaccessible until Royal Navy divers arrived. They discovered that some of Loxley's papers had already washed ashore, but islanders had handed them in the previous day. Divers and salvage experts arrived the next morning and successfully dragged the wreckage closer inshore. Following the retrieval of further documents from the wreck, all the recovered papers were flown to Malta.

Cadogan and the rest of the British delegation were shocked when news of the crash reached Malta on 2nd February. Cadogan felt Loxley's death particularly deeply, considering him a very valued friend and helper. There was, however, no time to mourn; Cadogan, Eden and Churchill continued to Yalta where they met with Roosevelt and Stalin as planned.

A Board of Inquiry convened in Malta on 10th February 1945, and heard statements from 34 witnesses, including the surviving aircrew, ground based radio operators from Italy and Malta, and staff from RAF Lyneham and Hendon. Having considered the evidence, the Inquiry delivered its findings on 3rd March.

While they found that no individual was to blame for the crash, the Inquiry identified several shortcomings. The navigator was criticised for dismissing the small islands observed off the Italian coast without consulting his charts properly and for failing to verify that the bearings he took actually came from the beacon on Malta. The pilot was flying too fast when his York struck the water, which, combined with the application of increased power, led directly to the break-up of his aircraft. The Board made allowances for the fact that Eaton-Clarke had received an inaccurate weather report, and that he had to ditch in darkness. Remarkably, the Inquiry heard that no drills took place at RAF Lyneham for ditching a York on water. The Inquiry therefore concluded that no significant changes were required to existing procedures and considered that Eaton-Clarke was put in an unfair position having to manage a change of flight plan at very short notice with a crew he did not know and who were unused to working together.

Referring to the crash in Parliament during the adjournment debate on 15th February 1945, Quintin Hogg, the MP for Oxford, described Loxley as an 'urbane brilliant servant of this country'. A Memorial Service for the six Foreign Office members of the Yalta delegation who died, took place at St Margaret's, Westminster on 11th April 1945.

After the war, the Loxley family home of Norcott Court was finally sold, although it had been a long time since a Loxley had lived there. Loxley's widow, Lavender, later moved to Boswick House in Dudswell and became a member of Northchurch Parish Council and St Mary's Parochial Church Council. Lavender commissioned a stained-glass window from Hugh Easton, who designed the Battle of Britain window in Westminster Abbey, in her late husband's memory. Easton's window was installed in the south transept of St Mary's church, close to the plaque commemorating Loxley's father and his two uncles who died during the First World War. The window's dedication reads, 'He maketh me lie down in green pastures. He leadeth me beside still waters. In memory of my beloved husband Peter Noel Loxley who died 1st February 1945 aged 39 years'.

Loxley's body now rests in the Imtarfa Cemetery in Malta, in a grave administered by the Commonwealth War Graves Commission. His name is also recorded on the memorial at West Downs School and the Civilian War Dead Roll of Honour, located near St George's Chapel in Westminster Abbey.

The Coming of Peace?

The defeat of *Nazi* Germany was officially celebrated on Tuesday 8th May 1945 - Victory in Europe Day. Church bells pealed throughout Northchurch and Berkhamsted, commercial buildings were floodlit and houses decked with flags of the Allied Nations, although one householder in Gossoms End preferred to hang an effigy of Hitler by a noose instead. With rather more dignity, at 8pm that evening, the Reverend Guy Beech celebrated a Special Service of Thanksgiving for Peace in Europe at St Mary's Church. There must have been mixed feelings among the congregation; there was relief that Britain was truly safe from German bombs and that the war in Europe was over, but many villagers were still serving overseas and the prospect of a long and bloody campaign to defeat Japan remained in people's minds.

When the end finally came, it came suddenly. The destruction of Hiroshima and Nagasaki by atomic bombs was not public knowledge and when Emperor Hirohito, against the wishes of many Imperial Army officers, broadcast Japan's capitulation on Tuesday 14th August, it took the Allies by surprise.

Many Northchurch people arrived for work on the Wednesday morning unaware that it was Victory over Japan Day and a two-day holiday had been declared. Shops and off-licences opened for two hours, but although retailers had kept back some stock after VE Day, supplies were even shorter on VJ Day and Berkhamsted quickly ran out of beer! Gradually flags and bunting came out again and later street bonfires were lit as it dawned on everybody that the Second World War really was over.

At 11am the following Sunday, Reverend Beech held a Special Form of Service at St Mary's, giving thanks for the surrender of Japan and final Victory. The theme was renewal and the collections from each service that Sunday, £13 5shillings in total, were for Christian Reconstruction in Europe and Aid to China.

The build-up of forces for a Far East campaign could now be reversed and demobilisation began in earnest. Word began to arrive of Northchurch men who had been prisoners of the Japanese. Some of it was good, such as the news that Lance Bombardier Ronald Dell, Royal Artillery, of 10 Tring Road, was safe in Australian hands, some bad.

Unfortunately, no war really has a neat and tidy end. British Forces had many remaining commitments overseas and the aftermath of both wars was still exacting its human toll on Northchurch.

42596 Flight Lieutenant Charles Robert DWIGHT DFC
RAFVR

5th June 1946

Charles Robert Dwight was born at Moore Cottage, Berkhamsted in the spring of 1912 into a well-known local sporting family. Charles, or 'Bob' as he was known, was the second son of William Henry Dwight, and the grandson of the noted local pheasant breeder, William Dwight. Bob Dwight was educated at Berkhamsted School, where he played rugby and hockey, before progressing to Trent College, Derbyshire. There he proved to be an excellent rifle shot and represented the college in a team competing for the Ashburton Shield during a public schools' match at Bisley. Bob specialised in engineering and in 1938, at the age of 26, he decided to join the Royal Air Force.

The day before war broke out, Bob Dwight gained a short service commission as Acting Pilot Officer. After flight training, he transferred to 98 Squadron, Bomber Command, a reserve squadron that spent the 'Phoney War' in northern England familiarising new aircrew with the Fairey Battle day-bomber. Underpowered, ungainly and lightly armed, the single-engined Battles were already obsolete by the time 98 Squadron joined the Advanced Air Striking Force in France on 16th April 1940. The Squadron's role was to accustom fresh aircrews to operational conditions in France, before sending them to operational squadrons with replacement aircraft.

When the Germans launched their *Blitzkrieg* in May 1940, the Battles proved no match for the *Luftwaffe's* Messerschmitt fighters and suffered grievous losses from ground fire. At the beginning of June, with the Battle for France lost, 98 Squadron returned to England and Bob flew home with its surviving aircraft. The Squadron's 244 remaining personnel were to follow in the SS *Lancastria*, but 98 Squadron was to suffer a terrible tragedy. Shortly after *Lancastria* left St Nazaire on 17th June, Junkers Ju88 bombers attacked, hitting her with several bombs. *Lancastria* sank in just 25 minutes, taking with her half of the 5,000 military personnel aboard and at least 75 airmen from Bob's squadron. The remnants of 98 Squadron made their way first to RAF Lossiemouth, and then to the RAF station at Gatwick, to face an uncertain future.

After such a devastating blow, there was a real possibility that 98 Squadron would be disbanded, but in July, Bob learned that it would be transferred to Iceland under Coastal Command. Later that month, an advanced party from the squadron arrived at an unpromising, boggy field by the river Ölfus at Kaldaðarnes, on the southwest coast of Iceland, which was to be Bob's home for the next eighteen months. While airmen struggled to create a usable airfield there, 98 Squadron's Battles flew to Scotland by stages, where they waited for suitable weather to make the long, hazardous sea crossing to Iceland. At the end of August, the first group of Battles set off, shepherded by two Sunderland flying boats, and it was with great relief that they all landed safely at Kaldaðarnes.

The remaining Battles arrived during September and immediately a number flew to an outlying airfield at Mergerdi, in northern Iceland. It was the first of many such deployments around Iceland's long coastline. Iceland's interior is almost entirely high mountains or bleak glaciers and flying conditions are harsh, especially in the winter. The Squadron lost a Battle during a ferry flight on 13th Sept 1940, when its pilot made a forced landing on boulder-strewn terrain. The three-man crew and their passenger reached safety, but the Battle was abandoned until it was recovered and restored by the RAF long after the war and is now displayed at the RAF Museum, Hendon, in 98 Squadron markings. The following year, a Battle crashed on a high glacier in fog, minutes after leaving Mergerdi, killing all those aboard.

On 24th March 1941, Bob was promoted to Flying Officer and with the arrival of spring, 98 Squadron could actively undertake shipping reconnaissance, anti-U-boat patrols, and defend Iceland from attack. A few days later, one of the Squadron's Battles found and bombed a German U-boat; the first time 98 Squadron had engaged the enemy during the war.

As well as flying routine shipping reconnaissance sorties, Bob participated in the hunt for the pocket battleship *Bismarck* during late May 1941. Commissioned in August 1940, *Bismarck's* role was to attack British convoys in the North Atlantic. On 22nd May, Bletchley Park warned that *Bismarck* and the cruiser, *Prinz Eugen* had left Norway, apparently heading towards the shipping lanes and the Admiralty despatched HMS *Hood* and HMS *Prince of Wales* from Scapa Flow to intercept them. Reconnaissance sorties by Bob's squadron, helped track down *Bismarck* and *Prinz Eugen* in the Denmark Strait between Greenland and Iceland. They observed from the air as *Hood* and *Prince of Wales* opened fire, but within minutes, a German shell exploded in one of *Hood's* magazines, tearing her in half and killing some 1,400 sailors. Unable to take on both German vessels alone, *Prince of Wales* broke off the fight.

Bismarck had also suffered damage during the exchange of shells and headed for St Nazaire, on the French Atlantic coast, at reduced speed and leaking fuel. 98 Squadron's Battles tracked *Bismarck* on her journey south, until she was beyond their range, but contact was maintained and on 26th May, Swordfish torpedo bombers from HMS *Ark Royal* attacked, jamming

Bismarck's rudder. Unable to manoeuvre, *Bismarck* steamed in a slow circle while the British battleships HMS *King George V* and HMS *Rodney*, with two heavy cruisers, closed for the kill. The British battleships quickly put *Bismarck's* guns out of action, killing most of her senior officers and *Bismarck's* crew scuttled their ship to prevent her capture.

The ageing Fairey Battles had proved adequate in the hunt for the *Bismarck*, but Iceland needed fighters and larger, long-range aircraft. In June 1941, 98 Squadron received a flight of Hawker Hurricane fighters at Kaldaðarnes. Then 98 Squadron's Battles were crated up and shipped to British Commonwealth Air Training Plan units in Canada, while the Hurricanes were moved to Reykjavik and renumbered 1423 Flight. Finally, on 15th July 1941, 98 Squadron was disbanded and 1423 Flight was transferred to Fighter Command.

Bob Dwight remained in Iceland flying 1423 Flight Hurricanes on operations, including shipping escort duties, until his return to Northchurch on leave in late September 1941, where he was surprised to receive a summons to Buckingham Palace. For services during the operations to find the Bismarck, Bob had been awarded the Distinguished Flying Cross. A few days later, Bob's proud mother and thrilled 16-year-old sister accompanied him to the investiture at Buckingham Palace and watched as King George VI pinned the DFC medal on his uniform.

Returning to operations in Iceland, Bob found that the Americans were gradually taking over responsibility for the island's defence. 1423 Flight ceased operations on 3rd December 1941, and shortly before Christmas, Bob and the Flight arrived at RAF Ouston in Northumberland, for decommissioning.

On 21st February 1942, Bob was given command of 611 Squadron's 'B' Flight, flying Spitfires from RAF Drem, East Lothian and a month later, he was promoted to Flight Lieutenant. Bob's new Squadron belonged to the Auxiliary Air Force, the RAF's equivalent of the Army's Yeomanry regiments, with which they shared similarities in social profile and a fondness for foxhunting. 611 Squadron had fought in the Battle of Britain and spent 1941 flying offensive sweeps over occupied France before moving north to rest, recuperate and retrain for shipping reconnaissance and escort duties. Although Bob did not fly on operations with 'B' Flight, he applied his extensive experience hunting the *Bismarck* and flying fighters in Iceland to train his pilots in their new role. That March, 611 Squadron flew nearly 370 hours of daylight training and some 20 hours of night training, compared with only 79 hours on daylight operations and around eight operational hours in darkness.

At the end of March 1942, Bob's name appeared on a list of 15 pilots on notice to deliver Spitfires to Malta, but he was not on the final list three weeks later and there is no further mention of Bob's name in the squadron records. It is possible that he transferred to another Squadron around this time, but according to *The Berkhamsted Gazette's* obituary, Bob was grounded for a time owing to an ear complaint caused by continuous flying, which may explain this gap in his record.

Placed on the Reserve List, Bob later returned to active duty on ferry and test flying. He was probably the Flight Lieutenant Dwight who delivered Spitfire F21, serial LA193, to N°29 Maintenance Unit (MU) in Shropshire on 5th January 1946. Maintenance Units employed service personnel and civilian engineers and fitters to hold new and repaired aircraft ready for issue to squadrons as required. The MUs also had facilities for major overhauls or repairs that the squadrons were unable to perform themselves. Bob was with N°10 MU at RAF Hullavington, Wiltshire, when he was listed to fly KA-265, a Canadian-built De Havilland Mosquito FB26 powered by two American-made Packard Merlin engines.

On the afternoon of 5th June 1946, Bob took KA-265 on a flight test with Mr J Trimble, one of the civilian fitters, as his passenger. As Bob put the Mosquito through its paces, the aircraft's port engine failed. Despite Bob's best efforts it would not restart so Bob 'feathered' the port propeller to reduce air resistance and prevent further damage. Bob was bringing KA-265 round on one engine to land when a short distance from the runway the port wing suddenly dropped and the Mosquito went out of control, diving into the ground. Mr Trimble survived the crash, but Bob Dwight was killed.

Bob's funeral took place at St Michael and All Angels Church in Sunnyside, Berkhamsted on Monday 10th June 1946. Among the family mourners were many friends including Flight Lieutenant Benny, Bob's commanding officer representing N°10 Maintenance Unit. Many members of staff from The Pheasantries also attended. Bob now lies in the Sunnyside churchyard under a Commonwealth War Graves Commission headstone.

1464909 Leading Aircraftman Donald George BEDFORD
Royal Air Force

4th August 1946

George Bedford of Dudswell made his living as a coal dealer and later as a market gardener. He married Rose Howlett in late summer 1917, and their son Donald George Bedford was born in the late summer of 1921. Growing up in Dudswell, Donald developed an interest in mechanical and technical matters, owning motorcycles from the age of 16 and learning to maintain them himself. With the coming of war, Donald joined the RAF Volunteer Reserve and when Donald was called up, his technical aptitude was recognised and the RAF trained him as a Radio and Radar mechanic. After qualifying, he became a Leading Aircraftsman in RAF Technical Command.

At the time of Germany's defeat in May 1945, there were some five million men and women serving in uniform. The servicemen alone represented a quarter of Britain's working-age population and their reintegration into a post-war economy required careful planning. Ernest Bevin, the Minister of Labour in the wartime government, had published a demobilisation scheme in September 1944, placing service personnel into two classes. Class 'B' men had experience in essential occupations such as coal mining, building and civil engineering, teaching or the police service, which would be demobilised first. However, most service personnel belonged to Class 'A', which was to be demobilised in 75 batches according to their date of birth and the month in which their war service began, as laid out in a forces guidebook entitled *Release and Resettlement*. The first batch began their demobilisation a month after VE Day.

Personnel Dispersal Centres were established across Great Britain to process returning men and women, but 'demob' soon ran into problems and many people faced months of inactivity, frustration and boredom in these camps. Some were fortunate enough to resume pre-war occupations or educational studies, others struggled to find work, but officialdom catered for them with Employment Exchanges. Less well catered for were the psychological scars left by the horrors of combat or the abuse suffered by Far East POWs. Prolonged separation and bereavement altered personal relationships with family and friends on a scale unimaginable today.

Donald's 'demob' finally arrived at the start of July 1946. Reporting to

N°101 Personnel Dispersal Centre, at RAF Kirkham, near Blackpool, he handed over his kit in exchange for a three-piece demob suit, leaving pay and a rail travel warrant to Berkhamsted. After a brief talk on 'Civvy Street' practicalities - ration books, clothing coupons and employment exchanges, Donald boarded a southbound train at Preston and returned home to Dudswell.

Donald's overjoyed father bought him a motorcycle to celebrate his safe return. Donald was proud of his new machine, riding it every day and making adjustments on it to his own satisfaction. Almost five weeks after his demobilisation, on Sunday 4th August, Donald took his motorcycle out for a run. It was a particularly warm day and it seems he was not wearing a crash helmet or heavy clothing. About six miles from home, on a straight section of road near the picturesque village of Ivinghoe, Donald's motorcycle suddenly began to oscillate violently. Struggling to regain control at between forty and fifty miles per hour, Donald overtook another motorcyclist, a Mr Alfred Wayman. As Donald passed, Mr Wayman noticed that his machine was 'wobbling', but then he watched, horrified, as it suddenly turned over a few yards in front of him and rolled two or three times along 30 yards of road.

Donald was admitted to hospital unconscious and in shock. Apart from multiple lacerations on his arms, legs and both sides of his forehead, Donald showed signs of a severe head injury. In fact, his skull was fractured and two hours after admission Donald died of a brain haemorrhage.

A subsequent examination of Donald's motorcycle showed the steering to be functioning normally, although the shock absorbers appeared rather stiff. At the inquest, Mr Wayman agreed that Donald's machine had probably gone into a 'speed wobble'. The Coroner returned a verdict of accidental death.

Donald's body now lies beneath a plain cross in the New Road cemetery in Northchurch.

3030341 Sergeant Herbert Frederick Wallis OLLIFFE
2702 Squadron RAF Regiment

17th November 1946

Olliffe, or Oliffe, is an old, local surname in the south Buckinghamshire and west Hertfordshire areas. Herbert Frederick Wallis Olliffe, known as Fred, was named after his father, Herbert and either Grandfather Frederick or Uncle Frederick, who all belonged to an established branch of the family from George Street, Berkhamsted, which had until 1909 formed part of the Parish of Northchurch.

Fred's great-grandfather, Eli, was a chimney sweep from Aylesbury who lived next door to the Rising Sun pub in George Street with his Wigginton-born wife, Mary and their children. During the 1870s, the Rising Sun fell vacant, so Eli became a licensed victualler and moved his family, including Fred's grandfather, Frederick, next door. Unfortunately, the pub trade did not suit Eli so he resumed his business as a chimney sweep and coal seller, although other members of his family continued running the Rising Sun as a beer house.

Grandfather Frederick joined his brothers as a coal merchant. In 1892, he married Eliza and the following year Fred's father, Herbert senior, was born. Grandfather Frederick kept his young family close to the Rising Sun in a four-room house at 25 George Street. He and Eliza later lived at 70 George Street, where they raised twelve children.

After Herbert senior left school, he worked for his father as a coal hawker, selling coal door-to-door. He was also a pre-war Territorial Gunner in 2nd Herts Battery, (TF), RFA. When the Battery was embodied in August 1914, it went to guard the Essex coast where Herbert quickly gained promotion to Bombardier. In April 1915, 2nd Herts Battery joined 1st/4th East Anglian Brigade, East Anglian Division and went to Gadebridge Camp, Hemel Hempstead. Crossing to France in November 1915, the battery sailed for Egypt in February 1916. It fought through both Battles of Gaza in 1917, and the following year, 2nd Herts Battery advanced into Palestine, where it saw out the war.

The ancient names, Palestine, Syria, Mesopotamia, and the Hijaz, described the diverse, ill-defined, lands between Egypt, the Mediterranean, Anatolia and Persia where the Arab, Kurdish, Christian and Jewish populations had been ruled by Ottoman Turkey for almost 400 years. The victorious Allies formally broke up Turkey's empire in 1920 and a stew of pre-war national interests, wartime promises, post-war negotiations, force and idealism began to shape its borders. The 1916 Sykes-Picot Agreement, which envisaged Arab states ruled by Arab governments under the guardianships of France in the north and Britain in the south, laid the foundations. Britain wanted the leaders of the Arab Revolt, Prince Faisal and his brothers, who were Hashemite descendants of the Prophet Mohammad's family, to govern the lands in Britain's sphere. Assisted by TE Lawrence, better known as Lawrence of Arabia, they had attacked Turkish supply lines, captured Aqaba and finally taken Damascus. However, political figures, who had served on the Ottoman side, such as the *Mufti* of Jerusalem, Amin al Husayni, would oppose them.

Sykes-Picot originally envisaged the Holy Land around Jerusalem, called Palestine, as an international protectorate, but there was a complication. The 19th century movements of European unification had inspired Jewish communities around the world to campaign for their own nation state in Palestine, to be called the land of Israel. Called Zionism, their movement was given urgency by a series of violent, anti-Jewish riots, or *pogroms* that from 1882 onwards drove Jews from the Russian Empire to Palestine. They were joined by idealistic Jews from America and Europe, inspired by Zionism and socialism, who established collective farms on land purchased from the Turkish authorities.

In November 1917, the British Cabinet demonstrated its support for Zionism by authorising the Foreign Secretary, Arthur Balfour, to write a famous letter to the leading Zionist international banker and founder of the Tring Natural History Museum, Lord Walter Rothschild. Known as the 'Balfour Declaration' it stated that, 'His Majesty's Government view with favour the establishment in Palestine of a national home for the Jewish people', and would help to achieve it, on condition that the civil and religious rights of non-Jewish communities in Palestine would not be harmed. At the Paris Peace Conference three years later, Prince Faisal, who had ambitions to rule Syria and Palestine, declared his support for Jewish immigration into Palestine to Lord Rothschild of Tring, and the Zionist delegates championed Britain as the preferred guardian of Palestine.

After the Peace Conferences, the newly created League of Nations granted Britain and France 'Mandates' over the newly-created Arab states, which obliged them to help the indigenous government maintain civil order, defend them from attack and preserve their independence. Because a British company had negotiated Mesopotamian oil concessions from the Turkish government in 1912, and Britain had confiscated Egypt from Turkey in 1914, the Council of the League of Nations gave Britain the Mandates for Mesopotamia to Palestine, which bordered Egypt. Meanwhile France, which had the Syrian Mandate, expelled Prince Faisal from Damascus. The following year, he was crowned Faisal I, King of Iraq.

In 1922, King Faisal replaced the Mandate with an Anglo-Iraqi Treaty that preserved existing oil agreements and confirmed Britain's responsibility for Iraqi security. The RAF had been policing Iraq since 1920, but a Kurdish rebellion had shown the limitations of airpower alone. Consequently, in 1922 the RAF formed two Independent Companies of Rolls-Royce armoured cars with about 100 Officers and airmen in each with bases in Iraq and Jordan, plus a depot at Sarafand in Palestine. In time, Fred Olliffe would later come to know N°2 Armoured Car Company very well.

Herbert Olliffe senior returned to Berkhamsted early in 1919, found employment with the Grand Junction Canal Company and married his sweetheart Florence Wallis. For a time, Herbert and Florence lived in Hemel Hempstead where Fred, their only child, was born in 1926. When the Canal Company gave Herbert the tenancy of the Lock Cottage at Cow Roast, the Olliffes relocated to Northchurch, where Fred grew up and attended the village school. Herbert became a well-known personality in the parish and an active member of the British Legion.

Meanwhile in Palestine, the Mandate, which included the 'Balfour Declaration' in full, obliged Britain to assist Jewish immigration, but *pogroms* In Eastern Europe made it hard to regulate with 67,000 Polish Jews fleeing to Palestine in 1924 alone. Palestinian Arab leaders orchestrated increasingly violent anti-Jewish riots, ostensibly to protest against excessive immigration, but actually intended to drive all Jews out. In response, Palestinian Jews organised an illegal self-defence force, the *Haganah*. Palestinian Arab opposition unified around the *Mufti* and mounted a series of uprisings between 1936 and 1939. Britain worked with regional Arab allies to mediate an end to the revolt, but the *Mufti* refused to grant Jews citizenship or guarantee their safety in a future Arab Palestine. Britain had to choose between imposing partition or handing back the Mandate and permitting civil war. Instead, she improvised, cracking down on the Arab opposition and expelling the *Mufti*, who went to Nazi Germany. Arab militants began attacking British forces with landmines with the result that in 1939, N°2 Armoured Car Company reinforced their cars' armour and remounted the hulls on stronger Fordson lorry chassis. Britain unofficially allowed British officers to arm and train the *Haganah* and shortly before the outbreak of the Second World War, the disturbances subsided.

Fred Olliffe was about 13 when the revolt in Palestine ended. On Tuesday 16th January 1940, his father died suddenly aged 47 and Herbert's well-attended funeral was held at St Mary's Church the following Friday. Two years later, Fred joined 1113 (Berkhamsted) Squadron Air Training Corps. Although boys aged 15 years and 6 months could join the Corps, cadets had to wait until they were 16 before they received their uniform and become full members. The first recruits for 1113 Squadron had been sworn in on 19th March 1941, at a ceremony in Berkhamsted Town Hall.

Parades were held on Mondays and Fridays at Berkhamsted School, which also donated workshops to accommodate various aero engines and other training equipment. Cadets were introduced to the skills required by aircrew, flight mechanics, electricians, instrument repairers, motor mechanics and other trades.

Herbert was possibly among the many ATC Cadets who worked at RAF stations in their free time. During a particularly busy period in 1943, hundreds of Cadets made up and distributed ammunition belts, unloaded lorry-loads of bombs and helped to service, wash down and refuel aircraft. One Station Commander told the *West Herts and Watford Observer*, 'It was difficult to get the cadets to stop working, they were so keen'. In mid-1944, aged 18, Fred left the Air Cadets to enlist in the Royal Air Force. He spent the rest of the war with flying squadrons, rising to the rank of Sergeant. Following VJ-Day, many RAF squadrons were disbanded and surplus airmen, both aircrew and ground crew, were redeployed. Fred was remustered to N°2 Armoured Car Company, which, at the war's end, was the only ground unit in Palestine available to protect airfields.

The RAF Armoured Car Companies kept their own identity throughout the war, although when Italy invaded Egypt in 1940, N°2 Company was attached to the Army and, as 'D' squadron, 11th Hussars, participated in the British victory at Beda Fomm and the subsequent capture of Tobruk. Returning to the RAF, it defended airfields in Iraq against a pro-Axis insurgency. Although airfield defence troops were re-organised as the RAF Regiment in 1942, the Armoured Car Companies somehow stayed within the RAF's Air Branch. Airmen despised the RAF Regiment as being little better than the Army, but since the Armoured Car Companies were independent, former aircrew were content to be posted to them. Soon Fred found himself stationed in Palestine, where his father had ended his war thirty years before.

With Nazi Germany defeated, British-trained Jewish saboteurs, fresh from the underground campaign in occupied Europe, returned to Palestine and joined offshoots of *Haganah*, such as *Irgun Zvai Leumi* and the 'Stern Gang'. They planned to end the British Mandate with a campaign of terrorism, and in January 1946 systematic Jewish attacks on RAF facilities began. That February, three RAF airfields came under simultaneous attack with the loss of twenty aircraft, although one Spitfire was saved when a section commander from N°2 Armoured Car Company personally removed an explosive device from its radiator. Jewish terrorists were shooting anyone in British uniform, so RAF personnel only left the base in groups of four or more, and wore guns at all times, even in bed.

Eventually, on 3rd October 1946, N°2 Armoured Car Company was transferred to the RAF Regiment and renamed 2702 Squadron. In addition to protecting RAF establishments and equipment, 2702 Squadron cars escorted road convoys and Squadron personnel participated in joint patrols with Police Officers of the Palestine Police Mobile Force (PMF). The *Irgun*, led by future Prime Minister of Israel, Menachem Begin, increased its attacks during 1946, concentrating on destroying road and rail infrastructure. The less popular, and more radical, 'Stern Gang' robbed banks to raise funds, kidnapped and murdered military personnel and left suitcase bombs in railway stations to harm civilians. They also placed remotely detonated roadside bombs in pairs either side of a road or concealed them under bits of glass, loose stones, sand or soil with the intention of inflicting casualties and often aimed at PMF patrols.

On Sunday 17th November 1946, Fred, two fellow airmen, and four PMF constables were returning from 1st Parachute Regiment's Camp at Sarona in a 15cwt truck. At about 22.45, as they drove through the Montefiore district of Tel Aviv, Jewish terrorists exploded a twin charge mine as Fred's truck passed and then opened fire on the burning vehicle. The other airmen were slightly injured, but Fred died in the blast, alongside three police officers. Two days later, Fred Olliffe was buried at the Ramleh War Cemetery, as were the Palestine Police Constables.

Fred's widowed mother, by then living at 46 Granville Road, Northchurch, later arranged for Fred's name to appear on the Northchurch War Memorial.

For Them's Sake

Fred Ollife is currently the last serviceman from Northchurch to die serving his country. By the time of his death in 1946, thoughts had once again turned to remembrance and the decision was made to commemorate those men lost since 1939 on the blank side of the War Memorial's base. For a second time, the community raised sufficient funds and a list of 13 Northchurch soldiers and airmen who had served between 1939 and 1946 was compiled to join their forbears from the First World War.

On a fine spring day, Sunday, 4th April 1948, a special ceremony was held at St Mary's Church after Matins. At midday, the inscription on the Memorial Cross recording the men lost between 1939 and 1946 was unveiled and dedicated by the Rector, the Reverend Guy Beech. It was the first Sunday after Easter, a time to celebrate renewed life and hopes of peace. It would be a shaky peace, however; the Cold War was just beginning with the Soviet blockade of West Berlin and within weeks Britain would take part in the Berlin Airlift. Then again, later that year, the National Health Service would be founded and the Olympic Games would take place in London, both ushering in a new era after two terrible world wars.

At the end of the ceremony marking the war memorial's rededication, the villagers drifted away from the churchyard. One way or another, those Northchurch people would play a part in rebuilding their community - for the sake of them that gave so much.

The restored Northchurch War Memorial
(Source: Richard North)

Appendix 1: First World War Roll of Honour

Name	Regiment / Service	Died	Memorials / Cemetery
Walter F **DELL**	Grenadier Guards	02/10/14	Northchurch War Memorial
			City of Paris Cemetery, France
Charles **TALBOT**	Bedfordshire Regiment	16/11/14	Northchurch War Memorial
			Ypres (Menin Gate) Memorial, Belgium
A Noel **LOXLEY**	Royal Navy	01/01/15	Northchurch (memorial plaque)
			Chatham Naval Memorial
			Lamport War Memorial
			HMS Formidable War Grave
Frederick **GEARY**	Border Regiment	02/05/15	Northchurch War Memorial
			Helles Memorial, Turkey
Walter **GEARY**	Border Regiment	29/06/15	Northchurch War Memorial
			Helles Memorial, Turkey

Nigel C C **HADDEN**	Royal Field Artillery	09/04/16	Northchurch War Memorial
			Basra Memorial, Iraq
Hubert W **THELWALL**	West India Regiment attached Nottinghamshire & Derbyshire Regiment	23/04/16	Northchurch (memorial plaque)
			Berkhamsted War Memorial
			Le Touret Military Cemetery, Richebourg-l'Avoué, France
George H **SHORLAND**	Royal Navy	31/05/16	Northchurch War Memorial
			Portsmouth War Memorial
			Guys Hospital War Memorial
			Lancing College War Memorial
			Bloxham School War Memorial
			Mill Hill War Memorial
			HMS Invincible War Grave
Lionel **MORGAN**	Hertfordshire Regiment	12/06/16	Northchurch War Memorial
			Béthune Town Cemetery, France

Arthur J **FROST**	Royal Warwickshire Regiment	01/07/16	Northchurch War Memorial
			Serre Road Cemetery No.2, France
Walter **HOWLETT**	Bedfordshire Regiment	01/07/16	Northchurch War Memorial
			Thiepval Memorial, France
Charles W **ROSS**	Queens Westminster Rifles	01/07/16	Northchurch War Memorial,
			Northchurch (memorial plaque)
			Thiepval Memorial, France
Philip C **FEIST**	Duke of Cambridge's Own (Middlesex Regiment)	02/07/16	Northchurch War Memorial
			Thiepval Memorial, France
Edwin **MORGAN**	Bedfordshire Regiment	01/08/16	Northchurch War Memorial
			Corbie Communal Cemetery Extension, France
George **BIGNELL**	Bedfordshire Regiment	04/08/16	Northchurch War Memorial
			Heilly Station Cemetery, Mericourt-L'abbe, France

Thomas E **HENDERSON**	South Staffordshire Regiment	31/08/16	Northchurch War Memorial
			Delville Wood Cemetery, Longueval, France
Joseph W **ALDRIDGE**	Northumberland Fusiliers	24/09/16	Northchurch War Memorial
			Thiepval Memorial, France
William J **SIBLEY**	Northamptonshire Regiment	26/09/16	Northchurch War Memorial
			Thiepval Memorial, France
Walter **WELLING**	Princess Charlotte of Wales's (Royal Berkshire Regiment)	29/09/16	Northchurch War Memorial
			Warloy-Baillon Communal Cemetery Extension, France
Walter **PURTON**	Bedfordshire Regiment	24/10/16	Northchurch War Memorial
			Regina Trench Cemetery, Grandcourt, France
Albert E **PICKTHORN**	Australian Infantry Force	03/11/16	Northchurch War Memorial
			Villers-Bretonneux Memorial, France

Vere D **LOXLEY**	Royal Marine Light Infantry	13/11/16	Northchurch (memorial plaque)
			Knightsbridge Cemetery, Mesnil-Martinsart, France
Royden S B **PORTER**	Honourable Artillery Company	06/02/17	Northchurch War Memorial, Northchurch (memorial plaque)
			Étaples Military Cemetery, France
J Ambrose **BROWN**	Queen's (Royal West Surrey Regiment)	02/04/17	Northchurch War Memorial
			Croisilles British Cemetery, France
William **SEAR**	Bedfordshire Regiment	08/04/17	Northchurch War Memorial
			Northchurch Baptist Chapel Burial Ground
Albert J **DELL**	Manchester Regiment	23/04/17	Northchurch War Memorial
			Arras Memorial, France
Joseph **DYER**	Royal Field Artillery	14/06/17	Northchurch War Memorial
			Point-du-Jour Military Cemetery, Athies, France

John **RANDALL**	Essex Regiment	02/07/17	Northchurch War Memorial
			Loos Memorial, France
William **WAITE**	Machine Gun Corps (Infantry)	11/07/17	Northchurch War Memorial
			Nieuport Memorial, Belgium
Arthur **WELLING**	Machine Gun Corps (Infantry)	08/08/17	Northchurch War Memorial
			Ypres (Menin Gate) Memorial, Belgium
Charlie **SUTTON**	Australian Infantry Force	26/08/17	La Plus Douve Farm Cemetery, France
Frank D **ALCOCK**	2nd King's African Rifles	03/09/17	Northchurch War Memorial
			Dar es Salaam War Cemetery, Kenya
Alfred H **DWIGHT**	Essex Regiment	04/09/17	Northchurch War Memorial
			Étaples Military Cemetery, France
George **DAVIS**	Sherwood Foresters (Nottinghamshire and Derbyshire Regiment)	20/09/17	Northchurch War Memorial
			Tyne Cot Memorial, France

Richard **BEASLEY**	Bedfordshire Regiment	30/10/17	Northchurch War Memorial
			Tyne Cot Memorial, France
John A **HARMAN**	Royal Flying Corps	17/11/17	Northchurch War Memorial
			Gainsborough General Cemetery
			Lincolns Inn War Memorial
Alfred **CURL**	Royal Garrison Artillery	29/12/17	Northchurch War Memorial
			Tincourt New British Cemetery, France
Frank F **ALLAWAY**	Bedfordshire Regiment	31/12/17	Northchurch War Memorial
			Chatby Memorial, Egypt
Harold A **SHRIMPTON**	Kings (Liverpool Regiment)	13/01/18	Northchurch War Memorial
			Outtersteene Communal Cemetery Extension, Bailleul, France
William **HORN**	Royal Horse Artillery	02/02/18	Northchurch War Memorial
			Étretat Churchyard Extension, France

James A **GARMENT**	Royal Berkshire Regiment	11/03/18	Northchurch War Memorial
			Northchurch Cemetery
			Hertfordshire Regiment Memorial, Hertford
			St Peter's Church, Berkhamsted
Frank **GARNER**	The Queens (Royal West Surrey Regiment)	21/03/18	Northchurch War Memorial
			Leigh War Memorial
			Pozières Memorial, France
Charles T **MASHFORD**	The London Regiment	24/04/18	Northchurch War Memorial
			Hangard Wood British Cemetery, France
Thomas H **TEAGLE**	Duke of Edinburgh's (Wiltshire Regiment)	06/06/18	Northchurch War Memorial
			Marfaux British Cemetery, France
George **CURL**	Bedfordshire Regiment	01/07/18	Northchurch War Memorial
			Bouzincourt Ridge Cemetery, Albert, France

Albert **ROLFE**	Bedfordshire Regiment	01/08/16	Northchurch Baptist Church
			Dernancourt Communal Cemetery, France
Thomas **FANTHAM**	The Buffs (East Kent Regiment)	10/08/18	Northchurch War Memorial
			Northchurch Baptist Church
			St. Venant-Robecq Road British Cemetery, Robecq, France
James **DELDERFIELD**	Bedfordshire Regiment	26/08/18	Northchurch War Memorial
			Wigginton War Memorial
			Puchevillers British Cemetery, France
Arthur **TEAGLE**	Duke of Cambridge's Own (Middlesex Regiment)	20/09/18	Northchurch War Memorial
			Villers Hill British Cemetery, Villers-Guislain, France

Charles H **CARTER**	Royal Fusiliers (City of London Regiment)	08/10/18	Northchurch War Memorial
			Northchurch Baptist Church
			Grevillers British Cemetery, France [1]
Reginald V B **LOXLEY**	Royal Air Force	18/10/18	Northchurch (memorial plaque)
			City of Paris Cemetery, Batignolles, Clichy, France
George **KEEN**	Royal Garrison Artillery	09/02/19	Northchurch New Road Cemetery
			Berkhamsted War Memorial[2]
James **CHANDLER**	Military Police Corps	26/02/19	Northchurch War Memorial
			Cologne Southern Cemetery, Germany

---

[1] As H C Carter
[2] As C T Keen

Appendix 2: Second World War Roll of Honour

Name	Regiment / Service	Died	Memorials / Cemetery
Charles A **BLACKWELL**	Coldstream Guards	01/06/40	Northchurch War Memorial Warhem Communal Cemetery, France
Stephen H Vavasour **DURELL**	131 Squadron (County of Kent)	27/07/41	Northchurch War Memorial Catterick Cemetery, C. of E.
Ronald Reginald Frank **HUCKLESBEE**	Bedfordshire and Hertfordshire Regiment, 1st Battalion, The Hertfordshire Regiment	28/11/41	Northchurch War Memorial Alamein Memorial, Egypt St Michael Sunnyside
Albert J **WELCH**	Royal Army Service Corps	15/02/42	Northchurch War Memorial Kranji War Cemetery, Singapore
Geoffrey A **DELDERFIELD**	Royal Artillery	02/10/42	Northchurch War Memorial Saiwan Memorial, Hong Kong

Ronald C **BOYD-SMITH**	Royal Wiltshire Yeomanry	02/11/42	Northchurch War Memorial
			El Alamein War Cemetery, Libya
Michael P **SATOW**	Royal Air Force	26/11/42	Northchurch War Memorial
			Christiansborg War Cemetery, Accra, Ghana
James R **BAMFORD**	Royal Army Service Corps	04/04/43	Northchurch War Memorial
			Sfax War Cemetery, Tunisia
Raymond T **HUNN**	Royal Air Force	20/07/43	Northchurch War Memorial
			Northchurch New Road Cemetery
			Berkhamsted School War Memorial
Harold W **WEEDON**	Durham Light Infantry	09/08/44	Northchurch War Memorial
			Hottot-les-Bagues War Cemetery, France
Donald E **SAUNDERS**	Dorsetshire Regiment	13/08/44	Northchurch War Memorial
			Bayeux Memorial, France
Edmund A **BARBER**	The Loyal Regiment	25/08/44	Northchurch War Memorial

	(North Lancashire)		Florence War Cemetery, Italy
Peter N **LOXLEY**	Foreign Office & Diplomatic Services	01/02/45	Imtarfa Cemetery, Malta.
			Memorial window, St Mary's Northchurch
			Civilian War Dead Roll of Honour, Westminster Abbey, London.
Charles R **DWIGHT**	Royal Air Force	05/06/46	Northchurch War Memorial
			St Michael Sunnyside, Berkhamsted Churchyard
Donald G **BEDFORD**	Royal Air Force	04/08/46	Northchurch War Memorial
			Northchurch New Road Cemetery
Herbert F W **OLLIFFE**	Royal Air Force	17/11/46	Northchurch War Memorial
			Ramleh War Cemetery, Israel

Acknowledgements

We would like to thank the following people for giving us access to family photographs and / or letters or by simply leading us in the right direction during our research:

Peter Addiscott, Kevin J. Baker, Elizabeth Bingham, Clive Blofield, Rondo Blue, Peter Bradshaw, Stephen Cooper, Robert Cruttenden, Alan Fantham, Karen Gunnell, Charles Harman, Bert Hosier, David Loxley, Charlie Matthews, Linda Pottinger, Ken Scudder, Valda Shrimpton, Janet Stupples, Andrew Sumner, Patrick James Coleridge Sumner, Simon Thelwall and Kay Weedon.

Additionally, we are indebted to the following organisations for allowing us full access to their archives and their helpful advice during the preparation of this book:

The Rector and Churchwardens of St Mary's Northchurch, Berkhamsted School, British Museum Newspaper Library, Camden Library, Canadian National Archive, Commonwealth War Graves Commission, East Sussex Record Office, Eton College, Fleet Air Arm Museum, General Register Office, Gloucestershire Regiment Museum, Grenadier Guards Archives, Guys Hospital, Harrow School, Hertfordshire Record Office, Honourable Artillery Company, Kelly College, Museum of the Mercian Regiment, National Archives, National Archives of Australia, Northchurch Baptist Church, The Northchurch Society, RAF Museum Hendon, Royal Artillery Library, Royal College of Music, St John's and the Queen's Colleges, Oxford, The Rifles (Berkshire & Wiltshire) Museum.